Negro Leaguers
and the Hall of Fame

Negro Leaguers and the Hall of Fame

The Case for Inducting 24 Overlooked Ballplayers

STEVEN R. GREENES

McFarland & Company, Inc., Publishers
Jefferson, North Carolina

This book has undergone peer review.

LIBRARY OF CONGRESS CATALOGUING-IN-PUBLICATION DATA

Names: Greenes, Steven R., 1949– author.
Title: Negro leaguers and the Hall of Fame : the case for inducting 24
overlooked ballplayers / Steven R. Greenes.
Description: Jefferson, North Carolina : McFarland & Company, Inc.,
Publishers, 2020. | Includes bibliographical references and index.
Identifiers: LCCN 2020033217 | ISBN 9781476672687 (paperback : acid free paper) ∞
ISBN 9781476641119 (ebook)
Subjects: LCSH: Negro leagues—History. | African American baseball
players—Biography. | National Baseball Hall of Fame and Museum.
Classification: LCC GV875.N35 G74 2020 | DDC 796.357/6408996073—dc23
LC record available at https://lccn.loc.gov/2020033217

BRITISH LIBRARY CATALOGUING DATA ARE AVAILABLE

ISBN (print) 978-1-4766-7268-7
ISBN (ebook) 978-1-4766-4111-9

Front cover illustration of Oliver Marcelle by Sanjay Verma (Courtesy of Helmar Brewing)

Printed in the United States of America

*McFarland & Company, Inc., Publishers
Box 611, Jefferson, North Carolina 28640
www.mcfarlandpub.com*

For my Dad,
Robert Greenes,
who took me to my first game.

For my children,
Sam and Max,
who played the game, both real and fantasy.

For my grandchildren
Jetson, Preston and Aaron,
in the hope that they will carry on the tradition.

"The Hall of Fame meant even more to those great Negro League players who never got their chance to play in the Major Leagues. Buck [O'Neil] said to them the Hall of Fame meant redemption. A Hall of Fame induction was their chance to hear at last after all the years that they were great. They belonged in the gallery with Babe Ruth and Stan Musial, Sandy Koufax and Walter Johnson. To those few Negro Leagues players elected to the Hall of Fame, it was bigger than immortality. It was an apology."—Joe Posnanski, *The Soul of Baseball: A Trip Through Buck O'Neil's America* (2007).

"You start thinking about it all. You wonder about your life, all your good years behind you, up and down the highways. You think about all the talent in Negro baseball.... We played in all the big parks, got pretty good write-ups in the New York *Daily News*. We had more white fans at exhibition games than colored. Why couldn't we have been in the major leagues? I'd like to be remembered just like Joe DiMaggio, Babe Ruth, all those guys."—"Wild Bill" Wright, interview with Todd Bolton and John B. Holway, *Black Giants* (2010).

"The Hall of Fame is an established institution, and sometimes institutions are slow to accept any change, especially from outsider influences. But if there are still many deserving [Negro League] players not yet recognized within its walls, the Hall of Fame is technically not a Hall of Fame, but only a partial one, and falls short of what it could ultimately be—a place where all great players are honored."—Kevin Johnson, "The 'technically … not' Hall of Fame," *Seamheads* (2019).

Table of Contents

Preface

The first baseball game my father took me to was Don Larson's perfect game in 1956. I was seven years old and my father was an ardent Yankee fan. I figured all games ended with the catcher jumping into the pitcher's arms. In any event, I was hooked. When a neighbor's dad brought me to a New York Giants game at the Polo Grounds, I broke with family tradition and adopted the Giants as my team and Willie Mays as my favorite player. I can still recall the elation I felt when, listening on a transistor radio in my buddy Andy's driveway, I heard Bill Mazeroski hit the winning home run to beat the Yankees in the 1961 World Series. On the other hand, I will never forget the sick feeling I got when the Giants' Willie McCovey (my second favorite player) lined out to the Yankees' Bobby Richardson to end the 1962 World Series. If McCovey had hit the ball just one foot higher, I suspect I might be a more optimistic person.

My interest in the game evolved into studying the accumulated statistics of the players. Each year, I biked to town to buy Street & Smith's annual guide in order to see where players stood on the all-time career charts of home runs, RBIs, and wins. I would then follow the Hall of Fame voting and compare it to my own analysis. It was clear to me then, and it I believe is even truer today, that becoming a Hall of Famer is the holy grail for players and is treated as such by fans. It would not be an overstatement to say that the work of Bill James in the early 1980s, as he published his annual *Baseball Abstracts*, sparked my interest as never before. Bill James analyzed players and potential Hall of Famers in new ways by using his unique analytical methods.

A parallel interest of mine was studying the game's outliers—those players who were denied full careers through accident, scandal, or otherwise. Ballplayers such as Pete Reiser, Joe Jackson, and Ray Chapman always fascinated me. Imagine my surprise when I discovered, through Robert Peterson's 1970 book *Only the Ball Was White,* an entire league of elite players who were outsiders and played in the Negro Leagues. A wormhole had opened up to a parallel universe. I began reading and studying all I could on the Negro Leagues.

It was only a matter of time until my dual interests coincided as Negro League players began to be admitted to the National Baseball Hall of Fame, in Cooperstown, New York. What particularly drew my attention was the seemingly ad hoc manner in which Negro Leaguers were voted on for the Hall of Fame. The more I looked into the matter, the stranger the story became. As I compared statistics of Negro League greats, and studied the Hall of Fame voting process, it became apparent that the selection procedures were political and filled with intrigue. Once I uncovered that story, I understood why not all of the best Negro League candidates have been inducted yet. The 35 Negro Leaguers elected to the Hall of Fame to date have received much attention and acclaim. However, there seemed to be little evaluation of those passed over.

My evaluation of the Negro Leagues led me from Negro League histories, to Negro League statistical databases, to oral testimonies of the Negro League veterans, to polls of the players and historians, and then to modern statistical analytics, which have only recently become available for the Negro Leagues. I felt the time had come to apply all of these resources in a comprehensive manner to the Negro Leagues in the context of the Hall of Fame selection process.

This book tells that story of the Hall of Fame voting for the Negro Leagues. It examines how well it has worked and why it may have failed to achieve an optimal result. To reach a proper conclusion, this book is divided into four sections.

The first presents a critical history of the actual Hall of Fame voting for the Negro Leagues. The second section attempts to determine correct standards for Negro League voting, which have never been properly provided to the voters in a manner which recognizes the individuality of the Negro Leagues. Thirdly, I combine modern statistical analysis with polls of Negro League veterans and historians, to provide a position by position evaluation of how well the voting for each position succeeded in securing the proper result. I conclude therein, based mostly upon modern analytical criteria which have rarely been applied to the Negro Leagues, that there are at least 24 additional Negro League players who have clearly earned Hall of Fame selection. In the fourth section, I propose a framework for carrying the Hall of Fame voting process to a fair and proper conclusion.

Introduction

It was October 14, 1926, in Chicago. The 1926 Negro League World Series was down to its final, winner-take-all game. Following a post-season playoff series with the Kansas City Monarchs, the Chicago American Giants had won the Negro National League title and were facing the Eastern Colored League champion, the Atlantic City Bacharach Giants. The 1926 Negro League World Series had been scheduled as a best-of-nine game format. However, as a result of two tie games, the teams had four wins apiece and it was now the 11th game.

Future Hall of Fame pitcher Willie Foster of the Chicago nine had surrendered 10 hits but was somehow holding Atlantic City scoreless in his duel with Atlantic City's journeyman Hubert Lockhart. The score was tied at 0–0 through eight and a half innings. In the bottom of the ninth, Jelly Gardner, a Chicago outfielder, led off with a single. Dave Malarcher, the player-manager for the American Giants, regarded by many as one of the greatest clutch hitters in Negro League history, approached the plate. He proceeded to lay down a perfect sacrifice to move Gardner to second base. With the season hanging in the balance, Sam Thompson laced a line drive to center field that was bobbled by Chaney White. Jelly Gardner rounded third and raced to home plate with the winning run. A mere 1,089 fans had witnessed one of the most thrilling games in Negro League history.

They were here, they were glorious, and they played electrifying ball in what seems in retrospect to be a vacuum. Now they are gone. Once they were the pride of black America, and they invented a fast-moving brand of baseball that would not be seen by the wider public until Jackie Robinson's appearance for the Dodgers in 1947. Starting in 1933, the Negro League had its own all-star game each year, which became a focal point and social celebration for much of black America. With crowds up to forty or fifty thousand people, the East-West Classic All-Star Game, usually held in Chicago's Comiskey Park, sometimes outdrew the Major League All-Star Game. Yet most of the time their games were played before sparser crowds and with smaller gates. When their youngsters entered Major League baseball in the early 1950s, they would reinvigorate the game of baseball with their speed and power. After the National League seized the initiative by signing more African Americans than the stodgy American League, it would win 30 of the next 36 All-Star Games. Between 1950 and 1959, African Americans, limited to a few per team by an informal quota, would still win 8 of the 9 National League MVP awards.

In a world before the public discovered professional basketball or football, baseball reigned as the national game for all Americans. Think of the Negro Leaguers' performance as analogous to urban basketball in the 1960s and 1970s, before the street style entered and dominated the NBA. It is no wonder that Commissioner Landis of the Major Leagues did all he could in the pre-integration era to prevent exhibition games between Major League players and the Negro Leaguers—games in which Negro Leaguers either won or held their own. As is now well documented, African Americans, barred from the Major Leagues until 1947, had their own leagues and their own stars. Author Donn Rogosin called them Invisible Men. Film documentarian Ken Burns called their game Shadow Ball. Both terms are perfect.

Black ball was larger and more vibrant than is widely known. African American baseball clubs emerged as social clubs shortly after the Civil War. Other teams arose in the early 1880s as American hotels that employed African Americans, often as waiters, started teams to entertain their guests. With their players excluded from major league ball (except for limited periods between 1879 and 1884), many of these teams morphed into traveling squads who competed against all comers, sometimes even against teams including major leaguers. As early as 1887, the Cuban Giants played 165 games in a single season.[1] These African American teams also vied annually for regional and even national supremacy. Author Todd Peterson has located well over 100 of these black ball championship contests occurring between 1866 and 1923.[2] From 1920, African Americans formed and operated their own leagues starting with the Negro National League which ran from 1920 to 1931. Other formal leagues followed including the Eastern Colored League (1923–28), American Negro League (1929), Negro Southern League (1932), East-West League (1932), a second Negro National League (1933–48) and a Negro American League (1937–54).

Yet African American teams also operated independent of these leagues during this entire time period and league teams even played a majority of their games during the season by barnstorming in non-league games against each other and local nines. In the 1931 season, the Homestead Grays, the best team in black ball, played as an independent team entirely outside the framework of any league. That year, Homestead played 174 games in 65 cities.[3] Even more intriguing is the fact that many Negro League stars played high level ball year round. They played winter ball in the Caribbean, Mexico and South American venues, for Florida hotels, and even in the California Winter League which integrated as early as the winter of 1909–10. Based upon the complex world in which they lived and played, the job of ascertaining which Negro Leaguers belong in the Hall of Fame is difficult at best.

So why is it so significant that we assess the Hall of Fame voting procedures for the Negro Leagues and whether that process has achieved the right result? It is important because the Negro Leaguers were denied the right and the opportunity to test their abilities in the Major Leagues. All we have left to properly remember them is to fairly assess their skills as best we can in order to respect those players, managers, and executives who truly belong in the National Baseball Hall of Fame. We also need to strive to achieve the correct outcome to truly honor the game of baseball in its shrine—the Hall of Fame. There is no remaining course available to secure this result other than to assess the available evidence of the black ballgame and to use our best efforts to draw the correct conclusions. It has always been a given that many of the world's heroes were neither duly honored nor fully respected during their lifetimes. History and the passage of time, however, have a way of correcting the misconceptions of the past and bringing us around to the truth. That process has begun with respect to the Negro Leagues and the Hall of Fame. To assess the extent to which it has succeeded is the purpose of this volume.

This book is not a work of original research and is it not intended to present a new and unique statistical measure of value. It is an attempt to collate and compile the hard work done by others in order to search out valid conclusions. It is the thesis of this book that sufficient scholarship and statistics have now been compiled by leading researchers so that their work, when viewed as a whole together with opinion polls of Negro League veterans and historians, has created an objective consensus as to which Negro Leaguers should be in the Hall of Fame. Of course, my own opinions will have slipped into my writing, as would be the case for any author.

It is important to note that much of the research cited in this volume did not even exist at the time of the last Hall of Fame special election for the Negro Leagues, held in 2006. Because Negro League teams filled their weeks playing against any independent team willing to take them on for a share of the gate, many of those statistics are lost or are not particularly valuable. It is also a fact that Negro League statistics were not always reliable, and many teams neglected even to send them in to the central office or local newspaper.

With respect to the late 19th century and the early 20th century in the pre–Negro League era, little statistical evidence exists and therefore we will need to rely more heavily on such data as can be found, as well as the oral testimony of Negro League veterans and the opinions of Negro League researchers and historians. But we must look at all of the available evidence because not to do so denigrates the true contribution of the African American ballplayers in an era when they were often judged by their reputation and performance—rather than recorded statistics. In many cases, that reputation was well earned and is confirmed by multiple contemporaries who were in a position to judge. For who knew the players better than their peers? When Casey Stengel or John McGraw expressed an opinion about a player, it should not be ignored. Does one need to have fought in World War II to write a book about it? Or can one rely on recorded history? I never saw the Negro Leagues in action, and I doubt that many of those reading this book have either. That does not prevent any of us from surveying the historical record and drawing what we believe to be fair conclusions.

We have now entered the second stage of Negro League research. Prior to 1970, when Robert Peterson opened the door to Negro League history with his book *Only the Ball Was White*, virtually nothing was recorded in any comprehensive form concerning the Negro League players or their statistics. However, much study has been undertaken on Negro League regular season games and player performance since that time, so that a sufficient statistical basis finally exists to determine the relative performance of players. Many of the games uncovered relate not only to the competition in the Negro Leagues themselves, but also to direct competition between the Negro Leaguers and their white Major League counterparts in off-season exhibition games. When added to the mix of recorded opinions and oral histories of Negro League players and historians, there is enough data, when assessed as a whole, that a certain collective consensus can be objectively drawn.

Of course, every Hall of Fame ballot contains some degree of subjectivity. It also turns out that the Hall of Fame voting process for the Negro Leagues, always well intentioned, has also been political in nature and fraught with other issues at every turn. Did it achieve its goal with respect to the Negro Leaguers or does the Hall of Fame have more work to do? This book presents my conclusions and is therefore ultimately a work of opinion. Others may disagree with the conclusions drawn and I encourage them to join the discussion. Not even Babe Ruth received a unanimous vote of the electorate in a Hall of Fame election because unanimous opinions are rare (in 2019, Mariano Rivera was the first ever unanimous pick).

By now, every knowledgeable baseball fan knows about the existence of the Negro Leagues, as well as some background concerning Satchel Paige and Josh Gibson. But it is time that baseball aficionados learned about the other superstars of black ball who were the Willie McCoveys and Rod Carews of their time. This book visits with the memory of extraordinary but largely forgotten players who remain Hall of Fame candidates and presents evidence that at least 24 more of them should be admitted into the Hall of Fame. I hope this work brings the stories of these great players to a wider public and encourages more fans to appreciate their careers. This book is my tribute to the Negro League veterans still on the outside whom I strongly believe that credible evidence demonstrates should be in the Hall. It is also intended as an homage to those researchers who have done the necessary investigation that enables the rest of us to figure it all out. Using all of these criteria, I believe that there is now sufficient information to determine which remaining Negro Leaguers truly belong in the Hall of Fame, and which have been passed over for various reasons but are worthy of further discussion. Like every baseball fan with an opinion, I believe it is possible to get it right. It is at least important to try.

Any consideration of the Negro League Hall of Fame admissions to date must begin with the Hall of Fame voting process itself. The Hall of Fame has twice appointed special Negro Leagues voting committees (1971–1977 and 2001–2006) with the stated purpose of reviewing and admitting all qualified Negro Leaguers to the Hall of Fame. How well have they succeeded?

PART ONE

History of the Hall of Fame Voting for the Negro Leagues

CHAPTER 1

Phase 1: The Committee on Negro League Baseball Leagues (1971–1977)

> Baseball gives every American boy a chance to excel. Not just to be as good as anybody else, but to be better. This is the nature of man and the name of the game. I hope that someday Satchel Paige and Josh Gibson will be voted into the Hall of Fame as symbols of the great Negro Players who are not here only because they were not given the chance.—Ted Williams, Hall of Fame Induction Speech, July 26, 1966[1]

The Negro League Hall of Fame admissions process has been conducted in four distinct phases over a 40-year period and can be characterized as idiosyncratic at best. A review of the at-times haphazard selection process will offer a better understanding as to how so many top-quality players may have been overlooked.

Many factors came together in opening of the Hall of Fame to the Negro Leagues. The actual spark that seemed to motivate the Hall of Fame came from an unlikely source, Ted Williams. Perhaps it was his memory of 1931 when, as a 12-year-old, he had seen Satchel Paige throw a one hitter against a local team in San Diego, the single hit being a single which Williams perceived Paige had intentionally given up to the team's weakest hitter. Perhaps it was his recollection of his 1939 rookie year when the other players would point to where Josh Gibson had hit towering home runs in each American league park. Perhaps it was when Williams himself faced Paige in 1952 and noticed Paige turning his wrist at the top of his windup for a curve ball, only to watch a strike three fastball fly by him. The next day, Satchel walked over to Williams and whispered: "You ought to know better than to guess with Ol' Satch."[2] Most likely it was that Ted Williams, too, regarded himself as an outsider as a result of his largely unknown Mexican heritage and the unfair treatment he believed he had received from the press and the Boston fans.

In any event, Ted Williams used his 1966 Hall of Fame induction speech as a call to action seeking the admission of Negro League players who were not given the chance to play in the Major Leagues. The Williams speech led to growing press coverage urging Major League Baseball to take action on behalf of the excluded Negro Leaguers.[3] The leading spokesman for the cause became Dick Young, of *The Daily News*, who was then one of the country's leading sportswriters.[4] Young apparently had a conversation with Roy Campanella in which Campanella, a star in both the Negro and the Major Leagues, told Young that there were at least eight or nine players with Hall of Fame credentials. Campanella actually believed that the numbers were much higher but felt he had to lowball the number so whites would not discount his opinion.[5] Young used the information anyway to campaign for the Negro Leaguers' admission to the Hall of Fame.

In the late 1960s, following a period of social unrest and riots in the inner cities, Major League Baseball responded by securing a coaching job for Larry Doby with the Montreal Expos and appointing Monte Irvin to a job in the commissioner's office. Irvin was thus placed fortuitously in a role where he would soon be positioned to take charge of the Negro League induction process.[6] Shortly after he became commissioner in 1969, Bowie Kuhn (who claimed he had seen Josh Gibson play when he operated a scoreboard in Griffith Stadium during his youth)[7] reacted to growing criticism from the sportswriters by calling a meeting in his office that included Paul Kerr, president of the Hall of Fame, Ford Frick, Dick Young, Monte Irvin, and others from Kuhn's staff. Apparently, the meeting turned acrimonious, with the acerbic Dick Young attacking the traditionalists led by Ford Frick. At that meeting, the Kuhn/Young group failed to convince the Frick/Kerr faction to recommend that the Hall of Fame board open the doors of the Hall to the Negro Leagues. The Frick/Kerr group argued that admitting Negro Leaguers would lessen Hall of Fame standards, that Negro Leaguers were ineligible under the rule requiring 10 years of play in the Major Leagues, and that there were no statistics to support their entry.[8] Because of what he perceived as Young's rudeness to Ford Frick, who was regarded as the father of the Hall of Fame, Kuhn got into a heated exchange with Young even though they were on the same side of the issue. Monte Irvin's take on the meeting is that the traditionalists were motivated more by fear that the public would perceive that Hall of Fame standards would be lowered by admitting Negro Leaguers to the Hall of Fame than by outright bias.[9] Realizing that he did not have the support of the Hall of Fame members at the meeting, Kuhn delayed any action.

In 1969, pressure mounted as the Baseball Writers' Association formed its own committee with the avowed purpose of admitting Negro Leaguers to the Hall of Fame.[10] By the early 1970s, Bowie Kuhn worked around the Hall of Fame Board by privately convincing Paul Kerr to authorize a Hall of Fame "display" of Negro Leaguers. He assured Kerr that the display plaque would be placed in a separate wing and no Negro Leaguers would be given the individual plaque that regular Hall of Famers received. Kuhn based his argument on the premise that, because Negro Leaguers were not permitted to play in the Major Leagues, the admission of Negro Leaguers was democratic and that a separate "display" would not be deemed a diminution of standards by players already admitted to the Hall of Fame.[11] Kuhn's solution was inherently flawed from the outset because it basically created a second class of admission to the Hall of Fame, the same type of discrimination to which the Negro Leagues had been subjected.

In January 1971, in accordance with his understanding with Paul Kerr, Kuhn convened a Special Committee on the Negro Leagues in the commissioner's office to select candidates for the "display." Monte Irvin was named to chair the Committee. Added to the Committee were nine other surviving individuals who had personal knowledge of the Negro Leagues in its final years: Judy Johnson and Roy Campanella, Negro League veteran players; Bill Yancey,[12] a Negro League veteran player and manager; Frank Forbes, a Negro League veteran and former promoter for the Negro National League; Ed Gottlieb and Alex Pompez, former Negro League owners; Wendell Smith and Sam Lacy, two leading Negro League sportswriters who covered the Negro Leagues for the African American press and had been instrumental in the campaign for the integration of baseball; and Everett Barnes, who had managed a semi-pro team that played against the Negro Leagues.

Jackie Robinson, who played only one year in the Negro Leagues, was invited to serve on the Committee but declined membership because he felt he did not have sufficient experience.[13] Aside from the public relations value, it was probably for the best that Jackie Robinson declined the honor because he had never been a strong supporter of the Negro Leagues, which he regarded as mobbed-up.[14] Sportswriter Dick Young and Joe Reichler, a special assistant to Bowie Kuhn, were added to the Committee as non-voting members. Reichler afterwards claimed that, as Kuhn's representative, he was the true, de facto leader of the Committee.[15]

The composition of the committee seems to have been particularly haphazard, and it contained a number of individuals who had minimal qualifications. Bill Yancey, Frank Forbes, and Everett Barnes were hardly Negro League luminaries. It was almost as though the structure of the committee was a quickly patched-together afterthought by Kuhn who had won the larger battle of opening up the Hall of Fame to Negro Leaguers.

The Hall of Fame prepared a set of rules for the committee to govern their selections:

1. Selection would be based on the basis of playing ability, integrity, sportsmanship, character and their contribution to the team on which they played and to baseball in general.
2. Only one man will be selected yearly at one annual election to be held the first week in February.
3. The player must have played prior to 1946.
4. The player must have played in the Negro Leagues for at least 10 years.
5. Those selected must receive 75 percent of the committee's votes.[16]

Dick Young, who had caused such acrimony in the prior meeting, opened the substance of the meeting by thanking Paul Kerr and Ford Frick for their "friendly and cooperative manner."[17] By choosing those words, it was almost as though the acerbic Young knew of the trap Kuhn was about to spring. Frick and Kerr, representing the old guard, immediately responded by reminding the group that the Negro Leaguers plaque would be placed in a different location in the Hall and be of a "different design" than those of the other Hall of Famers. Kerr also seemed to feel it necessary to add that the selection committee's vote would be subject to the right of review by the Hall.[18]

The formation of the Committee was announced to the world on February 3, 1971, in a press release referencing that the tablets honoring the Negro Leaguers would be "part of a new exhibit."[19] Apparently, even this limited press release set off a firestorm with the existing Veterans Committee because on the very next day, Paul Kerr sent the Veterans Committee a memorandum disdaining the distortion of certain New York newspapers that had reported the impending "election" of Negro Leaguers. Kerr pointed out to the Veterans Committee that "The Commissioner stressed the fact that these Negroes were being honored *but they were not being elected* to the Hall of Fame [emphasis added]."[20]

The Committee created a list of 25 Negro League greats, each of whom had the requisite 10 years of service in the Negro Leagues and all of whom the Committee believed were Hall of Fame worthy.[21] The 1971 ballot (see Appendix B), was, however, heavily slanted with names of players from the latter years of the Negro Leagues with whom the Committee members were familiar. The Committee's first job was to elect the first Negro League designee for a "plaque." The Committee made the popular Satchel Paige its first Negro League selection. Whether or not Satchel Paige was the greatest Negro Leaguer, it was a crafty selection. Paige was the Negro Leaguer most widely known to the white public at the time, was still alive, and had a popular following. There was really no better choice to get the ball rolling.

On February 9, 1971, Bowie Kuhn's office announced the selection of Paige and informed the public that he would receive a bronze plaque as part of a new exhibit.[22] Those who were allied with Kuhn's strategy, such as Dick Young and Monte Irvin, publicly supported the concept of a separate plaque because they knew how tough it had been to accomplish even that feat. The statement of sportswriter Wendell Smith, who served on the Committee, was typical: "Naming Satch to the Hall is a token, of course. In a way it's baseball's acknowledgment of past sins. But none of us on the committee feels that any form of segregation is involved in setting up a separate section for the black leagues."[23]

Outsiders were not all as supportive. Buck O'Neil asserted: "The only change is that baseball has turned Paige from a second-class citizen into a second-class immortal."[24] Jackie Robinson was particularly outspoken: "If it's a special kind of thing, it's not worth a hill of beans [probably a cleaning up of his real words]. It's the same goddamned thing all over again. If it were me under those conditions, I'd prefer not to be in it."[25] Publications such as *Newsday* and *Ebony* jumped all over the Hall for its proposed action, *Ebony* noting that "Satchel and other black stars do not belong in any anteroom."[26] Wells Trombly, of *The Sporting News,* jumped in: "Jim Crow still lives.... So they will be set aside in a separate wing. Just as they were when they played. It's an outright farce."[27]

A.S. Doc Young, one of the country's leading African American sportswriters, wrote a blistering letter to Monte Irvin bemoaning the Eastern slant of the nominees and noting how ridiculous it was that Rube Foster, the father of Negro League baseball, was not the first inductee. He went on:

> I also disagree with this business of putting in one Negro each year. Especially since the "special section thing" is tainted, and little positive publicity or goodwill is gained from it, I think there should have been one mass election, taking care of this matter once and for all.... I don't mean to sound like a grouch; but I feel I have strong points.[28]

Doc Young may have been correct on all of his points, but he either was not aware of, or did not really care about, the hard politics involved in moving the matter forward at all. Spurred by the newspaper and magazine uproar, the public began sending letters to the Hall of Fame that were overwhelmingly critical of treating Paige as a different class of inductee. A sampling of these letters is retained in the archives of the Hall of Fame:

> I have been a life long supporter of baseball.... But your latest decision to admit the great black players into the Hall on a "nigger only," "back-of-the-bus" only, token basis is a slur on baseball and on the integrity of the Hall.... This is 1971 not the ante-bellum south. These black players should be admitted to the Hall of Fame with full standing.... It was not their fault that their major league skills were stultified by a racist society ... you should ... accept them for who they were, major leaguers who were excluded from the major leagues.—Letter to Paul Kerr, February 15, 1971 (BL-175.2003, National Baseball Hall of Fame Library Archives).

> Count me as a white, middle-class, ex-baseball fan ... until you have the guts to put Satchel Paige where he belongs I've crossed baseball out of my entertainment schedule. Why don't you put the damn thing [Hall of Fame] in Mississippi—that's where it and you obviously belong.—Letter from Betty Geismar to Paul Kerr, February 16, 1971 (BL-175.2003, National Baseball Hall of Fame Library Archives).

Howard Talbot, the Hall's treasurer, monitored the public letter-writing response and reported to Paul Kerr that the public overwhelmingly wanted Paige admitted as a full member. Paul Kerr then presumably weighed whether the public outcry was of more concern than pacifying the Hall of Fame veterans. The public reaction that ensued ultimately

Satchel Paige, the first player admitted to the Hall of Fame as a Negro Leaguer, visits with members of the Hall of Fame Negro Leagues Committee in 1971. Top: Wendell Smith, Judy Johnson, Satchel Paige, Sam Lacy, Monte Irvin. Bottom: Joe Reichler, Frank Forbes, Eddie Gottlieb, Roy Campanella. (National Baseball Hall of Fame, Cooperstown, New York.)

compelled Kerr and the Hall of Fame Board to reverse the concept of a separate "display" and award full Hall of Fame membership to Paige right before his induction.[29]

What followed was strange and a bit awkward—hardly the reception that Satchel Paige deserved. When Paige's flight left for New York and his Hall of Fame press conference, he was still unaware that full Hall of Fame membership awaited him.[30] Author Bob Luke reports that Paige was uncomfortable at the press conference being badgered with questions about whether he was bitter at baseball, questions he deflected with stories about his age and adventures.[31] At his induction that summer, Paige was better prepared and told the press "There were many Satchels, there were many Joshes." But how Paige truly felt may have been more reflected in the fact that Paige never returned to Cooperstown again.[32]

History is not clear as to whether Kerr and Frick, who together controlled the Hall of Fame board, had been outmaneuvered by Kuhn or if happenstance had dictated the result once the process was begun.[33] In any event, Kuhn should be given substantial credit as a motivating impetus guiding Paige's election.

Following Paige's selection, the Committee's rules were modified in the second year to permit election of as many players in any given year who received the requisite 75 percent vote. In its second year, the Committee was reduced to nine members after the death of Bill Yancey the previous summer. As a result, it would now take seven votes to elect a new member. In February 1972, the Committee unanimously elected Josh Gibson and also cast seven ballots to include Buck Leonard as that year's second selection.[34] Gibson and Leonard,

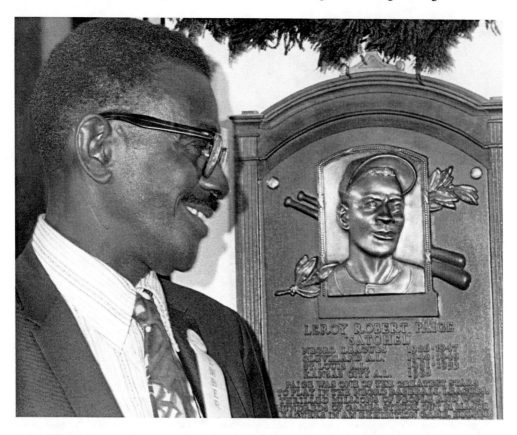

Satchel Paige admires his plaque at his Hall of Fame Induction Ceremony on August 9, 1971. Paige's selection was the culmination of a lengthy and tortuous political process spearheaded by Bowie Kuhn. (National Baseball Hall of Fame, Cooperstown, New York.)

then and now, are generally regarded as the greatest catcher and first baseman in Negro League history. The only others receiving votes that year were Pop Lloyd and Willie Foster, who received one vote each.[35]

Josh Gibson, the greatest slugger in Negro League history and the greatest box office draw other than Satchel Paige, was an obvious second choice. What is less clear is why Buck Leonard was chosen third while pivotal and more towering figures such as Rube Foster and Oscar Charleston were not inducted. The answer may lie in an extraordinary letter that non-voting Committee member Joe Reichler wrote to future Negro League Hall of Famer Effa Manley, the former co-owner of the Newark Eagles, in August 1972, which said, "It is important, in my opinion, to honor the men who are still living so that they can make personal appearances, meet the press and public, and spread the Gospel of Negro Baseball. Except for a Josh Gibson, a great player who passed away makes very little impact upon the voters as well as upon the public and the press."[36] Thus, Buck Leonard, as well as Monte Irvin, Cool Papa Bell, and Judy Johnson, who directly followed him into the Hall of Fame, may have owed their early selections to the fact that they were lucky enough to still be alive. The Reichler letter also constitutes an implied acknowledgment that the Committee was not attempting to elect players solely on their accomplishments and merit.

Another interesting portion of the correspondence between Effa Manley and Joe Reichler is Manley's stated concern that certain players who, in her opinion, were clearly

Hall of Famers—to wit, Willie Wells, Ray Dandridge, Biz Mackey, Dick Lundy, Mule Suttles, and Leon Day—would not be given fair consideration by the Special Committee of the Negro Leagues because "a couple of members of the committee picking them had a real hatred for [her husband and business partner] Abe Manley and I am afraid his team The Eagles."[37] Although Effa Manley does not name the members of the Committee about whom she was concerned, she certainly had in mind Eddie Gottlieb. Gottlieb was a white booking agent with whom the Manleys had fought head to head in the past over what Effa Manley regarded as his excessive booking fees and overcontrol of venues, which adversely affected Negro League ball.[38] Certainly her concern seems fully justified, since none of the players she cited were elected by the Special Committee, while all of them (except Dick Lundy) were subsequently admitted to the Hall of Fame after the Special Committee disbanded. Politics appears to have been at play even at this early stage of the voting.

Between 1971 and 1977, the Committee elected a total of nine players, one at each position, as follows:

P	Satchel Paige	1971	3b	Judy Johnson	1975
C	Josh Gibson	1972	Of	Oscar Charleston	1976
1b	Buck Leonard	1972	2b	Martin Dihigo	1977
Of	Monte Irvin	1973	SS	Pop Lloyd	1977
Of	Cool Papa Bell	1974			

As Paul Kerr had threatened, the Committee's work was not simply rubberstamped by the Hall of Fame's board. When the Committee first elected Martin Dihigo in 1975, the board initially found that "The record is insufficient to establish a career of at least 10 years in the Negro Baseball Leagues of the United States."[39] That objection seems to have either been satisfied or dropped since Dihigo was subsequently admitted together with Pop Lloyd in 1977.

At that point, the Committee disbanded. Monte Irvin publicly announced that its work was done and that no eligible players remained. Despite his public pronouncements to the contrary, Irvin well knew that more players warranted Hall of Fame election but was responding to pressure from the Hall of Fame in order, as Irvin stated privately in an interview with author Bob Luke, "to back off a little bit."[40] Irvin also suggested that the decision to dissolve the Committee "was hinted at by the powers that be at Cooperstown." He stated that "No one wanted to embarrass anybody and we all wanted to keep up the spirit of cooperation."[41] Joe Reichler conceded that the commissioner of baseball was under pressure to end the admission of Negro Leaguers.[42]

As one unidentified Committee member acknowledged to writer Joseph Durso: "The politics of this thing were important. When we started, we drew up a list of 25 stars of the Negro Leagues who looked like sure things for the Hall of Fame. At first they wanted a separate wing, then they felt we were going too fast in electing people. We got up to nine. Then, rather than hassle it every year, we decided to disband."[43] By taking a public step back, as if he had any real choice, Committee chair Irvin was putting the best face on the decision and clearly hoped that public pressure would eventually force a reopening of the process.

Any analysis of the first phase of the Hall of Fame admission process indicates that the Committee was not truly constructed for a full and fair review of the eligible candidates. The Committee was made up exclusively of representatives of the Eastern Negro Leagues.

Monte Irvin, who served as chair of the first Special Committee on the Negro Leagues from 1971 to 1977, receives his own Hall of Fame plaque as a Negro Leaguer from Bowie Kuhn in 1973. Irvin spent 10 years in the Negro Leagues as a prelude to 8 years in the Major Leagues. (National Baseball Hall of Fame, Cooperstown, New York.)

It elected six members who played exclusively in the Eastern League and three members who played both in the Eastern and Western leagues. Western League greats such as Rube Foster, Smokey Joe Williams, Willie Foster, Willie Wells, and Turkey Stearnes were not selected. The Committee also focused entirely on players who played in the 1930s and 1940s they were familiar with.

As indicated earlier, some members of the Committee appear not to have been the best available choices and were hardly well qualified for their roles. Joe Reichler also conceded that the Committee worked without benefit of any statistics and was therefore relying upon the word of mouth of the Committee members.[44]

It is also apparent that the Committee took care of its own. The selection of Monte Irvin as the first outfielder elected, and the election of Judy Johnson before Oscar Charleston or Rube Foster, demonstrated that the Committee followed the time-honored tradition of the Veterans Committee by focusing first on themselves, their teammates, and their confederates. It is not that Irvin and Johnson were not worthy, it is simply the fact that neither were in the top echelon of Negro League stars with men such as Rube Foster or Smokey Joe Williams, who were passed over by the 1971 Committee. As historian John B. Holway noted: "Irvin and Johnson were only being human…. Many of us had criticized the whites on the Hall's (separate) veterans' committee for overlooking black super-stars in order to elect their own white friends. Now here were blacks seemingly doing the same thing, although Irvin strongly denied it."[45] Eventually six of the ten members of the 1971 Committee were themselves selected to the Hall of Fame, including two to its Writers Wing.

What is particularly intriguing is that the 1971 Committee, initially instructed to select a nine-man Negro Leagues All-Star team to be honored by a separate plaque, seems to have followed the original outline on its own once the Hall of Fame bowed to public pressure to admit Negro Leaguers to full membership. The Committee selected one player for each position and then adjourned permanently. The fact that votes were cast for only four players in the 1972 election, and that the Committee was never permitted to elect more than two players in any one year, is fairly strong evidence that the Committee was treading lightly. That said, the nine players elected by the 1971 Committee were all true Negro League stars and all worthy of admission. Of course, it would have been hard to miss too badly when selecting only nine Negro League players. Given the processes in place, it is understandable why they were also not the best selections available.

In fairness, one must always keep in mind that the Committee was chaired by Monte Irvin, an employee of the same commissioner's office that had worked so hard to convince the Hall of Fame to widen its door to the Negro Leagues. Irvin appears to have been politically astute by using the open door provided by Kuhn in order to commence the process and to then back off, trusting in future history to complete the Committee's work.

CHAPTER 2

Phase 2: The Veterans Committee (1978–1994)

Following the "voluntary" disbanding of the Committee on Negro Baseball Leagues, outside sources applied pressure to extend the process of considering further Negro Leaguers. Sportswriters and Negro League veterans and historians continued to challenge and to chastise the Hall for its inaction. One example was former executive Richard Powell, of the Negro League's Baltimore Elite Giants, who wrote a column stating that the nine admitted players fell far short of the "thirty or forty" who deserved the honor.[1] Sportswriter Doc Young was extremely critical of the abortive induction process: "I must say it is time to end this project, to relegate it to the attic where baseball keeps its other embarrassing mistakes. At best, this thing was no more than a left-handed compliment ... to Negro League baseball. At worst, it is an insult to the 10 times more great Negro League players than it honors."[2] Future Hall of Fame umpire Jocko Conlon publicly questioned how any equitable process could have selected Monte Irvin before Oscar Charleston, Rube Foster, or Bullet Rogan.[3]

Petitions were filed with the Hall of Fame by Negro League veterans asking that the admissions process be carried forward. Researcher John B. Holway attempted to have Negro League veteran Wester McDonald address a meeting of the Hall of Fame's board of directors on an induction weekend, but the two of them ended up sitting uninvited outside the meeting.[4] The ACLU sent three attorneys to meet with counsel from Bowie Kuhn's office to threaten a claim for violation of the Civil Rights Act of 1964.[5]

For whatever reason, beginning in 1978, the Hall of Fame determined to open up the door and to relegate the job of naming any additional Negro League players to its regular Veterans Committee.[6] The Veterans Committee was an existing group of former major leaguers who were empowered to review players who had been passed over and should have been admitted to the Hall of Fame. Two Negro Leaguers, Monte Irvin and Roy Campanella, were named to the 18-member Veterans Committee. Of course, Irvin and Campanella had both been members of the prior Committee, which had declared its work complete.

The Veterans Committee was instructed to name no more than two candidates per year from three categories: former Major Leaguers, non-playing personnel, and black old-timers. Over the course of the next 17 years, the Committee usually elected two new entrants every year, although twice it elected no one and once it elected only one man. Despite the many new members it added to the Hall of Fame over that period, it became readily apparent that the Veterans Committee had little interest in selecting Negro Leaguers, as it chose only two of them over the same 17-year period.

In 1981, it picked Rube Foster, a great pitcher and founder of the Negro National

League, arguably the single most important figure in Negro League history. The day before the 1982 Hall of Fame election, a petition was filed with the Hall of Fame by 742 signatories asking that the regulations be revised so that more Negro Leaguers could be admitted.[7] But it was not until 1987 that the Veterans Committee selected another Negro Leaguer, third baseman Ray Dandridge. Ray Dandridge was another odd choice. He was an excellent player, but not in the class of others such as Pop Lloyd, Biz Mackey, or Dick Lundy. What he did have in common with some earlier choices is that he played on the Newark Eagles with Monte Irvin and he was still alive.

However, it is important to consider that, at this time, there were no comprehensive Negro League statistics available to the Committee and Irvin and Campanella had to rely on their personal knowledge and persuasiveness to convince the 16 white members to accept their choices. Campanella acknowledged that the lack of statistics was a major stumbling block in securing votes of Committee Members for Negro Leaguers.[8] This inequity in voting may also be the best rationale for why the Veterans Committee never selected Biz Mackey, Roy Campanella's mentor, and now generally acknowledged as one of the two greatest catchers in Negro League history. Or perhaps Campanella was not as vigorous a participant in the proceedings as anticipated. After Roy Campanella died in 1993, Buck O'Neil was named to and joined Monte Irvin on the Veterans Committee. (Monte Irvin would retire from the Veterans Committee in 1997, thereafter leaving Buck O'Neil as the sole Negro League representative.)

During this entire time period, public consciousness of Negro League baseball was on the rise. Starting with the seminal publication of *Only the Ball Was White*, by Robert Peterson in 1970,[9] the following 40 years saw an unprecedented explosion of research and writing focusing on the Negro Leagues and its players. Historians John B. Holway, James A. Riley, Dick Clark, Donn Rogosin, Leslie Heaphy, William F. McNeil, Phil S. Dixon, Brent Kelley, Larry Lester, Paul Debono, Thom Lovero, and Neil Lanctot were among those who published significant Negro League research where none had existed before. The Society for American Baseball Research (SABR) established a working group dedicated to the Negro Leagues, and the Negro Leagues Baseball Museum was founded in 1990. It is an inescapable conclusion that this scholarship and the increased public awareness it created helped foster a growing consensus for the inclusion of additional Negro Leaguers in the Hall of Fame.[10] For example, Bowie Kuhn acknowledged that his original approach to the Hall of Fame on behalf of Negro Leaguers was inspired by his awareness of Robert Peterson's 1970 book and his belief that it provided a factual basis for, and focused greater attention on, the accomplishments of, Negro League players.[11] Because no statistical data for the Negro Leagues was readily available, the Negro League researchers and historians would one day play the critical role in filling this gap.

CHAPTER 3

Phase 3: A Quota System
Is Implemented (1995–2001)

By 1995, there was open resistance on the Veterans Committee to the admission of more players who had not played in the Major Leagues. Hall of Fame chairman Ed Stack acknowledged at that point additional Negro League members would not be selected by that Committee without additional prodding.[1] Committee member Buck O'Neil also came to the conclusion that the Veterans Committee, the supermajority of which were former Major Leaguers, was unlikely to cast 75 percent of its votes for players of whom they had never heard. At O'Neil's urging,[2] the Hall of Fame formed an advisory group under Hall Vice President Bill Guilfoyle to select additional Negro League nominees.

The advisory group prepared a separate Negro League short ballot containing eight names. The Veterans Committee was then expressly instructed to vote on the separate ballot for Negro Leaguers from 1995 to 2001 with an absolute requirement that they select one player per year.[3] The Veterans Committee, with its mandate and quota so clearly prescribed, selected the following seven members to the Hall of Fame over the next seven years, beginning with yet another Monte Irvin teammate, Leon Day:

Leon Day	1995	Joe Williams	1999
Willie Foster	1996	Turkey Stearnes	2000
Willie Wells	1997	Hilton Smith	2001
Bullet Joe Rogan	1998		

As had occurred with the now defunct 1971–77 Committee on Negro League Baseball Leagues, all of the players elected by the Veterans Committee were acknowledged stars of the Negro Leagues and all were richly deserving of the honor based upon any fair metric. (Willard Brown, the only one of the eight players listed on the ballot given to the Veterans Committee who was not elected by it, would subsequently be elected to the Hall of Fame in 2006.)

If there were two players elected during this period who seem slightly less deserving than the others, one might be Leon Day, Monte Irvin's old teammate from the late Negro League era whose career WAR of 22.5 was not comparable to some of the others. For example, fellow pitchers "Bullet Joe" Rogan's career WAR was 62.2, and Smokey Joe Williams had a WAR of 55.2. However, the early selection of Leon Day was attributed by Buck O'Neil to the fact that Leon Day was one of the best potential candidates who was still alive.[4] Unfortunately, Day did not survive until the induction ceremony and his plaque was accepted by his widow.

Leon Day was the first pick of the Veterans Committee in 1995 after it was instructed by the Hall of Fame to elect one Negro League player for each of the next seven years. Day died six days after being informed of his selection for the Hall of Fame. His plaque was accepted by his widow Geraldine from Hall of Fame president Don Marr (left) and HOF chairman Ed Stack. (National Baseball Hall of Fame, Cooperstown, New York.)

The other anomaly was the selection of Hilton Smith, a former teammate of Buck O'Neil. Hilton, with a career WAR of 26.1, was a solid choice, but again not at the level of players such as Cristóbal Torriente (WAR 61.6) or Ray Brown (WAR 44.5), who were not on the ballot. Hilton was actually the first and only Negro League relief pitcher admitted to the Hall of Fame, as his role often consisted of finishing games Satchel Paige had started. Paige was almost always the primary draw and the crowds expected to see him start the game and pitch a few innings. The other players elected by the Veterans Committee were among the best choices available and, of course, they were among the only names available on the short ballot (other than Willard Brown). Even if one suspects that many of the veterans did not know who they were voting for, and they acknowledged that they were simply following Buck O'Neil's recommendations,[5] they elected worthy candidates. This is, of course, easier to do when you are basically told who to vote for.

CHAPTER 4

Phase 4: The Historians Take Over (2001–2006)

By 2001, a backlash against the admission of additional Negro Leaguers was again increasing on the Veterans Committee and the eight-name short ballot was ended. Most of the veterans had little interest in the Negro Leaguers and were voting for players they did not know and for whom few written records existed.[1] At the same time, as we have seen, Negro League history was being written by a new generation of scholars, and statistics were being compiled at an increasing rate. It was also of great significance that a more modern generation had assumed leadership of the Hall of Fame in the persons of Dale Petroskey as president and Jane Forbes Clark as chairman of the board, leadership which was no longer opposed to change for its own sake.

In February 2001, the directors of the Hall of Fame sought to remedy this problem of Veterans Committee resistance by commissioning a new statistical study. The Hall secured a $250,000 grant from Major League Baseball to conduct an 18-month study (later extended to 20 months) designed to secure as much statistical data as verifiable for the Negro Leagues commencing in 1920. (There was plenty of black ball but no formal Negro Leagues before 1920.) The study was conducted by three leading Negro League historians, Dr. Larry Hogan, Dick Clark, and Larry Lester. They compiled a database using box scores provided by over 30 researchers, who provided 3,000 day-to-day records from sanctioned Negro League games from 1920 to 1954. It is hard to overemphasize the import of the work compiled and sacrifices made by the Negro League historians and researchers. Many of them had spent years and thousands of their own dollars carefully culling old newspapers of the African American community compiling statistics from box scores. The MLB grant money was the first time they had been officially reimbursed for their toil.

Since there were no official Negro League statistics, the group decided to limit its study to only published box scores and credible scorebooks. Upon completion of the study in 2005, the Hall of Fame had compiled a statistical database using box scores from 345 different newspapers that published official Negro League games from 1929 through 1948, with 1948 decided on as the last year of the study because it was the final year a Negro League World Series was held. It is likely that the 1948 cutoff was chosen because that was also the year there was a serious falloff in the quality of the Negro Leagues after the integration of the Major Leagues.

The final study covered 9,500 pages of information containing hitting and pitching statistics for over 6,000 players culled from 3,000 day-to-day records. The dataset collected encompassed information from all of the substantial American-based Negro Leagues: Negro National League (NNL), Negro American League (NAL), East-West League (EWL), Negro

Southern League (NSL), and the Eastern Colored League (ECL). Included were all official league games, all-star games, and playoff and World Series games. The resulting study, according to the Hall, reflected close to 100 percent of games in the 1920s, over 90 percent of the games from the 1930s, and 50 to 70 percent of the games from the 1940s.[2]

While other games outside the official Negro League games were certainly an important part of the black ball world, they were not included in the database, which the historians decided to keep as authoritative as possible. Obviously, this approach resulted in glaring gaps in the study and in the lack of many statistics. It did not include the vibrant pre–1920 period or any of the independent games that were the principal economic staple of the Negro Leagues. Historian John B. Holway has argued forcefully that all games played by the Negro Leagues should be included in any full analysis, succinctly summing up his philosophy as "If Josh [Gibson] could hit it, I can count it."[3]

The Hall of Fame then fully recognized the essential role played by Negro League historians by turning to those researchers and historians to select new Negro League members—the first time in Hall of Fame history it had looked beyond the sportswriters and veterans to select its members. In July 2005, the Hall of Fame commissioned a five-person blue ribbon screening panel of leading Negro League historians, under the non-voting chairmanship of former Major League Commissioner Fay Vincent, to meet and select a ballot to determine new Negro League members for the Hall of Fame. The screening panel was composed of Adrian Burgos (Latin America), Dick Clark (Negro Leagues), Dr. Larry Hogan (overall history), Larry Lester (Negro Leagues), and Jim Overmyer (Eastern teams and 19th century).

In the first stage of the work, the Hall of Fame sought recommendations from fans and non-committee members. Among those proposing candidates to the Hall of Fame's initial list were Monte Irvin and Buck O'Neil.[4] The screening panel was presented with a pre-ballot of 94 Negro Leaguers who were recommended by the Hall of Fame for further consideration. The 94 name list had been pared down from recommendations submitted from fans, historians and Hall of Fame members, but it was not announced who had done the paring.[5] For the first time, the 94-name preliminary ballot included pre–Negro League players from the period prior to the creation of the Negro Leagues in 1920 and the names of managers and executives from the Negro Leagues. The screening panel was instructed by Jeff Idelson of the Hall of Fame to consider the names on the pre-ballot only and not to add any further candidates.[6]

The five-person screening group met for two days at Dodgertown, in Vero Beach, Florida, and discussed and voted on the 94-name pre-ballot. It required three out of five votes from the screening committee for a candidate to make the final ballot.[7] Through this process, the screening committee winnowed down its preliminary list to a final ballot of 39 names, which was published on November 21, 2005. (The pre-ballot and final ballot are set forth in Appendix B.) The Hall of Fame then added seven more voting members, who had participated in their statistical gathering study, to consider the final 39-name ballot. The seven additional voting members were Todd Bolton (Latin America), Greg Bond (19th century), Ray Doswell (overall history), Leslie Heaphy (women's history, Negro Leagues), Rob Ruck (Negro Leagues Eastern teams), Sammy J. Miller (Eastern and Western teams), and Robert W. Peterson (overall history). Rob Ruck was appointed to replace Neil Lanctot, who had authored two books on Negro League history. Excluded from the voting panel were certain leading Negro League historians who had either offended the Hall or not participated in the study. The omission of leading researchers John B. Holway, James A. Riley, and William F. McNeil surprised some on the committee.[8]

The 2006 Special Committee on the Negro Leagues, composed of historians and researchers, elected 17 new Negro Leaguers to the Hall of Fame. Standing left to right: Dale Petroskey (Pres. HOF), Sammy Miller, Jim Overmyer, Larry Lester, Jane Clark (Chair, HOF), Ray Doswell, Todd Bolton, Rob Ruck. Sitting left to right: Greg Bond, Leslie Heaphy, Dick Clark, Fay Vincent (Chair, Comm.), Adrian Burgos, Larry Hogan (courtesy Todd Bolton).

Former MLB Commissioner Fay Vincent acted as non-voting chair of the panel. Hall of Fame player Frank Robinson also served as an advisor to the voting panel, communicating by conference call on Sunday night of their deliberations. According to Fay Vincent, Robinson's advice was directed at reminding the committee of the Hall of Fame's high standards and urging them to vote on a person's performance, not to "rewrite American history."[9]

The final 12-member Voting Committee met for two days in Tampa, Florida, commencing on February 25, 2006. Also present in the room when the group met were representatives of the Hall of Fame: Chairman Jane Forbes Clark, President Dale Petroskey, Jeff Idelson, and publicist Brad Horn, although none of these individuals participated in the voting discussions. Clark addressed the voters and urged them to use high standards in making their decisions, although she was clear that there was no fixed quota on the number of candidates they could elect.

The voters were seated around a conference table and were led in their discussions by Fay Vincent.[10] Voting was held using secret paper ballots, with a candidate requiring an affirmative 75 percent vote of all committee members (9 votes) to be elected to the Hall of Fame.[11] Committee member Robert Peterson had died on February 11 but had submitted a ballot to the Hall of Fame in an envelope postmarked February 10. Robert Peterson was the author of the 1970 groundbreaking work *Only the Ball Was White*, which is generally credited with opening the door to public awareness of the Negro Leagues. The committee members unanimously voted to accept Peterson's ballot. In a tribute to Peterson, an empty chair was placed at the conference table used by the voting panel, with a copy of *Only the Ball Was White* placed on the table in front of it.[12]

Voting took place as follows. The discussion began with the candidates who had received the highest total of votes from the screening committee and then proceeded for subsequent candidates in descending order. Thus, the group of candidates receiving all five votes from the screening committee were discussed first. Fay Vincent kept the discussions moving along. After a discussion was completed on each group, a straw vote was taken by secret paper ballot. The ballots were taken out of the room by Hall of Fame publicist Brad Horn and tabulated.[13] In this manner, no committee member's vote was known to the others except as may have been expressed during discussion. After the completion of the straw votes, two candidates who had presumably fallen just short, Louis Santop and Buck O'Neil, were resubmitted to the group for further discussion. Santop eventually achieved a 75 percent vote.[14] Buck O'Neil did not, although Fay Vincent strongly urged his selection.[15] (The Hall of Fame publicity apparatus had anticipated and planned for O'Neil's selection.)[16]

On February 27, 2006, the committee's final results were made public. The committee's vote had added 17 individuals to the Hall of Fame, nearly doubling the Negro League members to 35. The new members were:

Ray Brown	Willard Brown	Andy Cooper
Frank Grant	Pete Hill	Biz Mackey
Effa Manley	José Méndez	Alex Pompez
Cum Posey	Louis Santop	Mule Suttles
Ben Taylor	Cristóbal Torriente	Sol White
J.L. Wilkinson	Jud Wilson	

Although aggregate voting results for the Hall of Fame are generally made public, the Hall of Fame had required the Negro Leagues committee to conduct their voting tabulations by secret written ballot and declined to release them.[17] While the Hall of Fame apparently never instructed the voting participants not to disclose their own votes, Fay Vincent announced that the voters had agreed not to do so. As a result, although full and open discussions had been held with respect to all candidates, none of the committee members ultimately knew exactly who had voted for any nominee or which candidates may have fallen just short. However, someone certainly knew the tabulations, because Fay Vincent acknowledged at the post-election press conference that a number of candidates received unanimous votes.[18] Pressed for vote totals, Vincent could only respond that announcing the voting results could somehow be "held against" those elected who did not receive a unanimous vote.[19]

Although the vote count was never revealed to the public, we can establish from the results that the 12-person committee cast at least 153 "yes" votes (17 new members times 9 required votes), or an average of 13 positive votes per committee member. Committee member Jim Overmyer was under the impression from the open discussions that Dick Lundy, John Donaldson, Minnie Minoso, and Buck O'Neil were the candidates who probably fell just short of the required 75 percent vote.[20] As stated, the voting ballots were retained by the Hall of Fame, which has declined to release them.

Almost as soon as the vote was announced, a firestorm erupted over the failure of the Hall of Fame's Special Committee to elect Buck O'Neil, who was waiting for word on the vote in a conference room in Kansas City. O'Neil took a phone call from Jeff Idelson of the Hall of Fame advising him that he had not received the requisite nine votes of the Voting Committee. O'Neil's immediate and generous response was to rejoice in the 17 players selected and to offer to speak for them at their induction ceremony, as none of them were still alive.[21] Buck O'Neil's Hall of Fame induction speech for the voiceless 17 selected is regarded as one of the best ever proffered and was the last public speaking appearance of his life. He died months later.

Officials at the Negro Leagues Baseball Museum (NLBM) fanned the flames of the controversy when NLBM Executive Director Bob Motley contended that historian Larry Lester and certain others aligned with him on the Voting Committee had worked together to block O'Neil's admission. Motley suggested that certain past litigation between Larry Lester and the NLBM, where Lester once worked, had created a bias against O'Neil, who was the NLBM chairman and its most visible personage.[22] While it was true that three members of the Voting Committee (Clark, Miller, and Heaphy) had taken public positions against Motley and in favor of Lester, Lester denied that he had coordinated any effort against O'Neil and stated that, in his mind, Motley had nothing to do with O'Neil. Although Lester has also been quoted as alluding to Buck's election being "a hard sell because people who study the history don't think Buck O'Neil is in the top 1 percent,"[23] he has also stated that he was saddened that Buck did not make the Hall and noted that he voted for a number of candidates who did not make the cut.[24] Unfortunately, Lester was unduly cryptic when directly asked if he had voted for O'Neil by responding "Buck knows how I voted." When questioned, Buck O'Neil stated that he had no idea how Lester voted.[25]

Buck O'Neil, passed over by the Hall of Fame voters in the 2006 Negro Leagues Special Election, gave the induction speech that summer on behalf of the 17 selected Negro Leaguers. It was the last public speech he would ever make. (National Baseball Hall of Fame, Cooperstown, New York.)

Doswell claims to have been startled by the final vote because no one said anything negative about O'Neil during the discussions.[26] In fact, when Fay Vincent took a straw vote on O'Neil and realized he was short of votes, he urged the committee to reconsider Buck's ambassadorship for Negro League ball in addition to his career as a player and manager. Vincent also claimed to be surprised by O'Neil's failure to make the final cut. When a story circulated that O'Neil had fallen one vote short, Vincent shot it down by noting that neither he nor the any of the other committee members knew the final tallies. Of course, that position is slightly inconsistent with his acknowledgment that certain players had received a unanimous tally and his admission that O'Neil had fallen short in a preliminary straw vote. Vincent added that he would have been surprised if there had been any bloc voting against O'Neil.[27] Committee member Jim Overmyer has similarly stated that he was unaware of any vote trading or bloc voting.[28]

The entire controversy was further confused by use of the secret ballot and the confidentiality imposed by the committee members upon the voting results. The Baseball Writers' Association of America (BBWAA) also uses written ballots, but the Hall of Fame does not impose confidentiality on the voters and always reveals its annual Hall of Fame voting tabulations. The controversy the BBWAA voting stirs up is advantageous to the Hall of Fame because it keeps the Hall in the public eye. The confidentiality as to the final vote in the 2006 special election for the Negro Leagues, which was imposed upon the voters by the Hall of Fame, and the reason for confidentiality, which was never adequately explained, allowed many to speculate that something fishy had occurred with respect to O'Neil.

Of course, whether Lester or anyone else voted against O'Neil is not the point. Even if Lester voted for him, and he may well have, O'Neil did not get in. There are always underlying politics in all aspects of life and historians are just as susceptible to it as anyone. Even one voter with a grudge against the NLBM could have affected the outcome. The real issue to be determined is whether O'Neil objectively belongs in the Hall of Fame (see Chapter 19).

Aside from the O'Neil controversy, Hall of Fame Chairman Jane Forbes Clark was very clear to state that no quota was established by the Hall of Fame with respect to the number of Negro Leaguers who could be elected.[29] Yet the fact that the final ballot contained only 39 names might have suggested to the voting panel that they would be expected to select a reasonable number of those 39 names rather than some larger group, which might have been selected if they had all considered the initial 94 name ballot. This suggestion was confirmed by voting panel member Todd Bolton, who acknowledged that the voting panel took its obligation seriously to limit the admissions to a reasonable number of candidates from the final ballot so as not to create the perception that the committee had overstepped its bounds.

Thus, although no one from the Hall of Fame ever expressly limited the number of candidates to be elected, there was an implied process at work. By the same token, Bolton noted that the committee was well aware that this might have been the last chance to elect Negro Leaguers and that, if the voting process had been part of a recurring review process of the Negro Leagues, the group might have made fewer selections knowing that the process would be renewed. The uncertainty of whether this would be the final Negro League election, counterbalanced by the belief in the committee that it should not appear to have been unreasonable in making too many selections, altered the final voting results.[30]

It is worth noting that it is the 94-name preliminary ballot, but not the 39-name final ballot, that contains the names of every one of the 24 individuals listed in this volume as being entitled to future Hall of Fame admission. The 94-name ballot had been prepared by the Hall of Fame, not the historians. However, since the screening panel was not allowed to expand the 94-name preliminary ballot, it is unknown if they would have included other viable candidates, such as catcher Quincy Trouppe, if given the chance.

It is also interesting to speculate on the composition of the voting panel and how it may have affected the vote. The core five-person screening panel was particularly distinguished. A few on the larger, 12-person voting panel were not the preeminent Negro League historians at that time. Left off the voting panel were some of the field's most significant Negro League researchers, men such as Phil S. Dixon, James A. Riley, William F. McNeil, John B. Holway, and Frederico Brillhart. Each of these five had published leading original work in the field, and two of them had won the distinguished Casey Award for the best baseball book of the year. (Committee member Leslie Heaphy has noted that Dixon, Riley, and McNeil had not chosen to submit materials to the 2006 committee despite an open invitation to the field to do so.[31]) In any event, the committee could have benefited from their presence.

John B. Holway, who did submit material to the committee but was still left off it, was particularly critical of the composition of the committee, referring to it as being composed of both "noted scholars and unknown fans"[32] and over-represented by Kansas City.[33] As a result, he felt that while all of the selections could be justified, only 11 of the 17 persons elected represented bona fide superstars and that six other of the chosen were not the best choices available. (Holway named four of those elected whom he regarded as more marginal: Effa Manley, Pete Hill, Louis Santop, and Alex Pompez.) He believes that a larger committee representing wider interests would have produced a better result.

As but one example of how the inclusion of others might have affected the vote, Phil S. Dixon is on record as supporting the Hall of Fame candidacies of John Donaldson, Chet Brewer, and Grant "Home Run" Johnson, none of whom were elected. Frederico Brillhart was a strong supporter of John Donaldson and Spottswood Poles. John B. Holway has stated that he believes that Dick Lundy, John Beckwith, Alejandro Oms, Ed Bolden, Buck O'Neil, and Abe Manley would have been better choices than some made by the 2006 committee. Voting committee member Todd Bolton has revealed that there was strong support in the discussions for Dick Redding, Dick Lundy, John Beckwith, and Alejandro Oms, suggesting that all of these players might have fallen just a vote or two short.[34] Certainly, it is fair to conclude that a committee comprising different historians would have come up with different results.

Screening and voting committee member Jim Overmyer acknowledged that the committee was mostly focused on the official Negro League era, beginning in 1920, for which the official Hall of Fame study had been compiled, and not as much on the pre–Negro League period. He believes that this may well have affected the outcomes for some pre–Negro League candidates such as Dick Redding and Home Run Johnson. He reported that, after the selection of pre–Negro Leaguer Frank Grant, there seemed to be a feeling in the room that it was more important to concentrate on the official Negro League era beginning in 1920, for which the statistical database had been collected.[35] As a result, pre–Negro Leaguers, for whom there were far fewer statistics available at the time, may have been shortchanged.

It is self-evident that even objective historians will have their favorite players and may hold inherent biases toward their fields of specialty. A specialist on the 19th century, Jim Overmyer readily acknowledges that he made a forceful argument in favor of pre–Negro Leaguer Frank Grant.[36] Of course, this was well warranted by his particular expertise and the reason why there were specialists on the committee. Committee member Todd Bolton reports that Andy Cooper was a dark horse candidate who seemed to be pushed over the top when one committee member analogized him to recent Hall of Fame selection Bert

Blyleven.[37] Of course, there is nothing wrong with voters arguing for their favored candidates during the open discussions. The point is that the areas of specialty included in the committee, and the fields of knowledge that may have been underrepresented, might have affected the final votes.

Leading sabermetrician Bill James has leveled criticism at the 2006 Hall of Fame voting, noting that the mass induction of 17 members at one time, no matter how well intentioned, was a "catastrophe for the research community" because the limited name recognition of the many players selected would undermine the seriousness of the Hall of Fame discussion itself.[38] Journalist Rob Centorani was another of those who bemoaned the mass election, but for a different reason. He noted that the 17 Negro League inductees were honored with "little more than fast-food service" at their induction, their entire dedication taking less than 37 minutes. How much better, Centorani noted, would it have been to spread their inductions over a five-year period so each could be properly honored for his or her individual contributions.[39]

In the final analysis, despite the objections, the historians' panel appears to have been a creative and warranted method for dealing with the dearth of survivors (players or writers) from the Negro Leagues. The researchers and historians certainly took their task to heart and seem to have made their decisions to the best of their judgment. Therefore, while one can conclude that the historians' panel did a solid overall job in electing 17 worthy candidates, it is also a fair assumption to accept that another panel of historians would have elected some different candidates, suggesting that the job may not be finished.

Committee members Todd Bolton and James Overmyer both expressed their opinions that Hall of Fame qualified Negro Leaguers still remain unchosen after the 2006 election and they hope the Hall will reopen the process in the future.[40]

After the election, the Hall of Fame and Major League Baseball issued glowing public statements about the results achieved by the 2005–6 Special Committee on Negro Leagues. Yet a careful review of Major League Baseball Commissioner Bud Selig's statement at the time included a subtle acknowledgment that the process might not yet be complete: "Eighteen Negro League stars had been elected prior to today's vote, but previous committees had overlooked many who were deserving. Major League Baseball is proud to have played a part in a process that has corrected *some of those omissions* [emphasis added]."[41]

PART TWO

Determining Hall of Fame Qualification of the Negro Leagues

CHAPTER 5

The Twelve Rules

Having now reviewed the often haphazard manner in which the Hall of Fame voting for the Negro Leagues actually unfolded, we have a basis for establishing more uniform criteria that should be applied in deciding of Hall of Fame eligibility. The basic standard of Hall of Fame eligibility for Major League players is relatively straightforward. A player needs to have competed in all or part of ten Major League seasons, be retired for at least five seasons, not be on the ineligible list (banned from baseball) and be elected by 75 percent of all ballots cast in a Hall of Fame election. Sportsmanship, character, and contribution to one's team and the game of baseball have always had some bearing as well. These fundamental guidelines are only the springboard for a discussion of a more complicated analysis of Negro League eligibility, leagues which operated in an entirely different manner on the other side of the color line. The fact that there have been no uniform guidelines for Negro League selection to the Hall of Fame has resulted in each voter's establishing his own. I believe that there are 12 rules that are logical outgrowths of the Negro League multiverse and which should be consistently applied with respect to the Negro League players to fairly determine their eligibility for the Hall of Fame.

Rule 1: The Entire Span of the Pre–Negro League and Negro League Eras from 1878 to 1949 Needs to Be Fully Assessed.

There was a tendency for voters in the Negro League Hall of Fame elections to focus on the names they were more familiar with from the 1920s through the 1940s. As students of the Major Leagues, most baseball aficionados whose interests cross over to the Negro Leagues find it more comfortable, understandable as it may be, to emphasize the period when formal major Negro Leagues were in existence, starting in the 1920s. In the 2006 Negro Leagues Special Election for the Hall of Fame, the voters did in fact concentrate primarily on the formal Negro Leagues era, which began in 1920, the earliest year used by the Hall of Fame in compiling its database.[1] The Hall database for that election was strictly limited to Negro League sanctioned games between 1920 and 1948, an era representing only a portion of the actual games played by Negro League teams. The voters' bias in this respect was logical in that almost all of the voting committee members had also been members of the Hall of Fame's Researchers and Authors Group, which had participated in the collection of that data.

However, the pre–Negro League era was vibrant and full of some of the greatest figures in the black ball game, players who often went head to head with white Major Leaguers in exhibition games and in Cuba during the winter. There were significant African American players in action as far back as 1878, when Bud Fowler became the first recognized African

33

American professional. He was followed in the 1880s by Moses Fleet Walker and his brother Welday, who played at the Major League level in the American Association. All of these African American players, and others who came after them, soon faced extreme prejudice, which drove them away from any further chance at the Major Leagues. Not many of these early figures had Hall of Fame talent, but some of them led varied and fascinating baseball careers that contributed in large measure to the betterment of the game.

While no player should be admitted to the Hall of Fame simply because he was the "first" at something, neither should any player be excluded because he was denied full participation if his overall accomplishments are Hall of Fame worthy. Nor should these early players be excluded simply because a full bank of verifiable statistics is not available for their time and place. In many instances, we have no more than scant data on some of these early players, but they still need to be evaluated as best we can. As we shall see, early players such as Bud Fowler and Grant "Home Run" Johnson had amazing baseball careers that, on careful analysis, may well entitle them to Hall of Fame entry.

On the flip side, few would argue that significant Negro League ball was played after 1949. The quality of black ball deteriorated quickly and dramatically effective with integration of the Major Leagues in 1947. And 1949 is used as an end date for proper Negro Leagues analysis only because a few of the long-time stars (such as Bill Byrd), who were then too old for the Major Leagues, hung on that long. By that time, the Negro Leagues had been stripped of their top talent by the Major Leagues and their minor league affiliates. Although a few youngsters such as Hank Aaron and Ernie Banks technically got their start with short stints in the Negro Leagues during the early 1950s, the quality of ball was not high and neither of them made significant contributions to those leagues. In the post–1949 era, even their most fervent advocates would acknowledge that the Negro Leagues would be considered the equivalent of low minor league ball, at best. The Negro Leagues actually continued with lesser players and in greatly diminished form until 1962,[2] but the truth is that nothing happened in those leagues after 1949 that would have any real bearing on whether a player should qualify for the Hall of Fame.

Rule 2: The Correct Definition of the Negro Leagues Encompasses Any League That Allowed Dark-Skinned Players to Play Baseball.

The Negro Leagues were not simply a Major League equivalent. They were any league that allowed dark-skinned players to play baseball. These leagues included the highest level of black ball, represented by

- Negro Leagues located in the United States, Caribbean, and South American winter leagues, to which the better players gravitated each winter,
- Barnstorming teams that operated independent of any league but which played black and white teams at all levels,
- Industrial and local league teams, which were omnipresent in pre–World War II America,
- The Californian Winter League, which integrated in the 1920s,
- The Mexican League of the late 1930s and 1940s,[3]
- High minor leagues such as the Pacific Coast League, which integrated prior to Major League baseball, and
- Elite military teams, which gave many African American players their start in the World War I era.

But, even if this expansive definition of the Negro Leagues corresponds to their reality, it does not solve the question of how much time should have been played, and where the games should have been played, to establish eligibility for the National Baseball Hall of Fame.

Rule 3: Any Player Who Played All or Part of 10 Years for Any Black Ball or Integrated Team in the United States Should Be Eligible for Admission to the National Baseball Hall of Fame.

No matter the forum electing members, the Hall of Fame has always required 10 full or partial years of performance in the United States. Historian William F. McNeil has argued that the 10-year rule should not be fully applicable to the Negro Leagues. McNeil points out that Negro League infielder Dobie Moore was one of the greatest players of his time and "could have sat on the bench for three or four years" and still had a Hall of Fame caliber career.[4] I disagree since what we should be talking about are fairness and equality—not preferential treatment. Once you accept the principle that all American baseball should count towards the 10-year rule, I believe we should accept that the 10-year rule is a correct and fair standard to be applied to all candidates for the National Hall of Fame.

Rule 4: Once Any Player Has Met the 10-Year Standard of Play in the United States, a Player Who Has Had His Career Disrupted by the Color Line Should Be Eligible to Have His Career Performance in the Entire Negro League Universe Judged as the Basis of His Admission to the Hall of Fame.

Let's demonstrate this rule using concrete examples.

Quincy Trouppe, Wild Bill Wright, and Chet Brewer were all American players who spent substantial parts of their productive playing years abroad. Each was reputed as one of the leading players of his time, and each was highly sought after by teams operating over the entire Negro League spectrum. Each of these men played at least part of 10 seasons in the Negro Leagues based in the United States, but their domestic statistics alone have not yet granted them Hall of Fame entry. In each instance, these players only left the country because of the racism they experienced or because they were offered a fairer level of pay in a foreign venue, usually both. Each of these players should be more fully evaluated based upon their entire careers.

John Donaldson was an American barnstorming pitcher in the pre–Negro League era. He spent the bulk of his career going from town to town taking on all comers. He was probably the greatest black ball drawing card of his time. His legendary status warranted far more pay in a barnstorming role than if he had performed full time for the black ball teams of his era. His career needs to be assessed based upon both his Negro League performance and his full accomplishments in the world he lived in.

Dobie Moore played four and a half years of top-level baseball in the Army during the World War I era prior to the founding of the Negro National League (NNL), which he joined in its first year of existence, in 1920. The Army team he played for was one of the strongest baseball units in the country. As a result of his time in the service (albeit as a baseball player), his career in the formal Negro Leagues was less than 10 years. His entire career performance in American ball should count towards the 10-year requirement.

Artie Wilson, although he spent significant time in the Negro Leagues, was paid more to play in industrial baseball leagues and in the Pacific Coast League (high minors) than he was ever offered by the Negro Leagues. In the era in which he played, the semi-pro and minor leagues he participated in played high quality ball. He was also the last .400 hitter in organized baseball. His entire career should be up for consideration.

Luke Easter was one of the great sluggers of the Negro Leagues in the last years of its existence, yet he also had a solid career in the Major Leagues after integration. He should be judged neither as a Negro League entrant, nor simply as a Major League entrant, but as a player whose entire career should be considered. Whether or not he is a Hall of Fame caliber player, and he may well not be, requires a full assessment of his entire baseball life. He should not fall between the cracks because his accomplishments on either side of the color divide are not sufficient in and of themselves.

Minnie Minoso spent three seasons with the Cuban Giants of the Negro Leagues before spending 17 years in Major League ball. When the Special Committee on Negro Leagues Election Committee convened in 2006, Minoso's name was on the final ballot. However, according to Committee member Adrian Burgos, the Hall of Fame forbade the committee from considering anything Minoso did in the Major Leagues.[5] Obviously, it would have been hard for him to have been admitted under that guideline. While Minoso has subsequently appeared on the ballot of the Hall of Fame's Golden Era Committee, it is not permitted to consider his Negro League performance. Minoso is entitled to be judged on his full career on both sides of the color divide.

Rule 5: Foreign-Born Latino Players Who Played the Principal Portion of Their Careers Overseas Should Be Judged Primarily on Their Performance in the United States.

Perhaps the hardest judgment is how to handle those extraordinarily talented Latino players who played in the American Negro Leagues, sometimes for all or part of 10 years, but the bulk of whose accomplishments occurred overseas in their homelands. This list is lengthy and includes some of the greatest ballplayers of all time: Alejandro Oms, Valentín Dreke, Eustaquio Pedroso, Luis Tiant, Sr., Bernardo Baró, Luis Padrón, Pancho Coimbre, Luis "Canena" Márquez, Horacio Martínez, Ramón Bragaña, Tetelo Vargas, Silvio García, Carlos Morán, Lázaro Salazar, Pelayo Chacón, Bienvenido Jiménez, José Fernández, Regino García, José Junco, Gervasio González, José Muñoz, Carlos Royer, Julián Castillo, and Isidro Fabré among others.

Certainly, there has been no overt prejudice against Latinos in the Negro League Hall of Fame voting. Cristóbal Torriente, José Méndez, Alex Pompez, and Martín Dihigo are all Latinos who accomplished enough in the domestic Negro Leagues to be voted into the Hall of Fame. But it is appropriate to understand that very few of these elite Latino players spent the requisite 10 years playing in the United States, which is the Hall of Fame standard. And some of them who did meet the 10-year requirement, such as Alejandro Oms, barely met it. These foreign-born players, whose careers were principally played abroad, should ultimately be judged in the Hall of Fame voting on their performance in the United States as this, after all, is an American baseball Hall of Fame. Ty Cobb played winter ball in Cuba, but he is deservedly not a member of the Cuban Hall of Fame.

In the modern era, one can reasonably concede that all of the major Latino players of the pre-integration era would have had Major League careers, and many might have ended up in the Hall of Fame. Yet, in their world, the focus of these Latino players was generally their home countries, where the competition was often equal to that in the American Negro Leagues and where they were treated as heroes. Most of these Latino players are already members of the Halls of Fame in their respective home countries, which is appropriate. Perhaps that is where we should leave it unless their performance in the United States for a 10-year period also warrants opening the door of the (U.S.) Hall of Fame to them.

Consider the career of Pancho Coimbre. The Puerto Rican–born Coimbre was a five-tool player who combined a natural swing with power, strong fielding, and speed on the bases. Coimbre starred for the New York Cubans in the early 1940s and was a two-time selection to the East-West All-Star Game. Overseas, Coimbre won the Puerto Rico winter batting titles in 1942–43 with a .342 average and again in 1944–45 with a .425 average. He did not strike out even once in the 1939–40, 1941–42 or 1942–43 Puerto Rican League seasons.[6] Widely regarded as the best Puerto Rican player ever before Roberto Clemente, he holds the record for hitting safely in the most consecutive Puerto Rican games (22) and was once called by Satchel Paige the best hitter he ever faced.[7] In the American Negro Leagues, he hit .382 in 1943 and .357 in 1946 in league games and compiled a lifetime average of .345 over five seasons.[8] Coimbre's Wins Above Replacement (WAR) per 162 games in the Negro Leagues was a solid 4.7, but only tenth all-time among right fielders. One of the greatest players ever to play on American shores, Coimbre's five years of play in the United States, consisting of only 151 league games, should not fairly qualify him for admission to the National Hall of Fame.

Rule 6: *There Is Statistical Equivalence Between the Negro Leagues and the Major Leagues.*

The fundamental question in fairly analyzing Negro League statistics is how they compare to those of the Major Leagues. Is a .300 batting average or a 2.95 ERA in one league comparable to that of the other? How does more advanced Negro League analytical data such as WAR, Similarity Scores and Total Runs Saved (TRS) reasonably equate to their Major League equivalents? The answer to these questions begins with a determination as to how player performance in Negro Leagues compared to that of the Major Leagues. Fortunately, research gathered in Todd Peterson's *The Negro Leagues Were Major Leagues* sets forth important analytical data on this issue. Three observations from that volume are particularly striking:

Negro League Statistics Correlate to Those of the Major Leagues

Researcher William F. McNeil, in his comparison of various levels of leagues to each other, observed that batting average tended to fall off in relationship to the quality of the league, with lower batting averages indicating a higher, more difficult level of play. McNeil determined the historical batting average of certain leagues to be as follows[9]:

Major Leagues	.260	AAA Minor Leagues	.287
Japanese Leagues	.278	AA Minor Leagues	.306

Applying this methodology, researcher Todd Peterson has determined that, for the pre-integration period 1929–1948, the Major Leagues and the Negro League composite batting statistics were remarkably consistent[10]:

	BA	OBP	SLG	OPS
NLB	.270	.331	.372	.703
MLB	.275	.340	.388	.728
% Difference	1.7	2.7	4.3	3.6

The pitching comparison is also intriguing. Two of the most important indicators of effective pitching in sabermetrics are walks plus hits per inning pitched (WHIP) and strikeout rate (K/9). Peterson has calculated the comparative data between the Major Leagues and the Negro Leagues to be[11]:

	WHIP	K/9
NLB	1.382	4.222
MLB	1.368	3.241
% Difference	3.4	26.3

Based upon these criteria, one could credibly argue that the quality of play in the Negro Leagues was actually higher than that of the Major Leagues because the Negro Leagues' collective batting average was lower and the strikeout rate was higher. For our purposes, let us simply acknowledge that the statistical correlation was closer between the Major Leagues and the Negro Leagues than any other level of play. This conclusion furnishes important objective evidence that Negro League statistics can be fairly compared to those of the Major Leagues.

The Negro Leagues Competed Successfully Against the Major Leagues

Researcher Ted Knorr has noted that various researchers have compiled the overall record for games played between Negro League teams and teams fully or partially comprised of Major League players. Ken Burns concluded that the Negro League teams had a winning percentage of .705 in those contests. Leading historians William F. McNeil and John B. Holway determined the Negro League teams won .698 and .571, respectively, of these games.[12] In his study of how the Negro League's Homestead Grays fared against minor league clubs during the period 1924–1948, researcher Scott Simkus found the results even more lopsided, with the Grays establishing a won-loss record of 83–25 against the minor league ball clubs.[13]

While the games played by the Negro League clubs against teams with Major Leaguers were barnstorming exhibitions, it would be a mistake to think that they were not hard-fought battles by two sides with much to prove. The blacks were out to prove that they were as talented as their foes and the Major Leaguers were trying to establish their superiority as ball players.[14] The participants in these games were hard-nosed professionals who held themselves to a high standard and were trying to give the fans their money's worth. As the 20th century progressed into the 1930s, the Major Leaguers began to accord the Negro Leaguers the respect they had earned. Dizzy Dean acknowledged such during his famous 1934 barnstorming tour against Negro League opposition, in a year he won the MVP award and led his St. Louis Cardinals to a World Series victory, "Don't expect me to strike out the [Negro League Kansas City] Monarchs. They are really a Major League ballclub."[15]

Again, the point is not that Negro League clubs were necessarily better than Major League clubs. However, the results of inter-league competition definitely suggest that the talent of the Negro League players was equivalent to that of their Major League counterparts and far superior to minor league players.

African Americans Competed Effectively Once Integration Occurred

The principal argument used to keep African Americans from Major League ball prior to 1947 was that they could not successfully compete at the Major League level. Here is a summary set forth by Todd Peterson as to what transpired in the Major Leagues once integration occurred:

> Despite being greatly outnumbered, the former Negro Leaguers captured several major and minor league batting and pitching titles while garnering numerous awards and honors. Nine of these players were eventually elected to the National Baseball Hall of Fame. Included in this group are Willie Mays and Hank Aaron, generally acknowledged as two of the five greatest players of all time. In the 40 years after Jackie Robinson's breakthrough, non-whites won 18 percent of the MLB Cy Young awards, 25 percent of the ERA titles, 39 percent of the home run crowns, and 48 percent of the batting championships, despite comprising less than 25 percent of the big league population during this period. After Robinson was named the Major League Rookie of the Year in 1947, black players received eight of the first 11 National League freshman awards. Nine of the 11 men voted the National League MVP between 1949 and 1959 were former Negro Leaguers.[16]

Peterson also notes that by 1967, when integration was more established in the Major Leagues, black players, then comprising fewer than 6 percent of all Major League players, accounted for more than half of the base hits in the Major Leagues. Further, 9 of the 10 leading hitters in the National League in 1967 (which integrated faster than the American League) were either African American or Latinos who would have been barred from Major League ball prior to 1947.[17]

All of these factors more than lend credence to the proposition that the Negro Leagues were major leagues and that one can fairly compare Negro League analytics to those of the Major Leagues.

Rule 7: The "Addie Joss Exception" Must Apply Equally to the Negro Leagues.

In the context of the Negro Leagues, the 10-year minimum requirement should be employed in the same manner applied by the Hall of Fame to the Major Leagues. There has been one exception already adopted by the Hall of Fame with respect to the 10-year service rule that is directly relevant to the Negro Leagues. In 1977, the Hall's Board of Directors waived the 10-year rule to allow the eligibility of Addie Joss, who had died of tuberculosis before he had participated in 10 seasons. This limited waiver occurred only because illness cut short what was judged to be a Hall of Fame career. It has never been extended beyond illness to other factors. This "Addie Joss Exception" should therefore be available to the Negro Leagues, and it directly applies in analyzing the career of outfielder Charlie "Chino" Smith, who died of cancer before he could achieve the 10-year standard. I am not advocating that the Addie Joss exception be applied to players who had Hall of Fame talent but who failed to meet the 10-year rule because of their own actions. An example of this kind might be pitcher Dave Brown, whose Negro League career ended abruptly when he killed a man and fled New York.

Rule 8: Championships Are Important.

In constructing a formula to predict which Major League players would be elected to the Hall of Fame, Bill James created a Hall of Fame monitor system in which 100 points would predict eventual Hall of Fame membership.[18] In so doing, he discovered that a player earned as much as 5 points each time he was a regular player on a championship team.

It is undoubtedly true that Negro League championships were not conducted on as regular a basis as Major League championships. In the pre–Negro League era, they tended to be self-declared affairs between two leading teams who both deemed themselves to be champions of their particular geographic location, often by a city or a region. In fact, formal Negro League World Series were only held from 1924 through 1927 between the winners of the Eastern Colored League and the first Negro National League and from 1942 through 1948 between the Negro American League and the second Negro National League. Even when they were held, these Negro World Series were not treated with great significance by the press or in the African American community. The Negro League World Series were often poorly attended and functioned almost more as exhibitions. However, the fact that they were only held sporadically or poorly attended did not diminish their importance to the players or their management, as these championships were important calling cards in stirring up the fans for the barnstorming games that were the lifeblood of many teams.

What is fascinating is the fact that certain top players seem to have continually ended up on "championship" teams, whether officially sanctioned or not. Newt Allen is a case in point. Allen was the regular second baseman on five Negro National League championship teams, six Negro American League championship teams, and 12 additional post-season and winter league championship teams, for a total of 23 championship teams.[19] This was neither luck nor coincidence. Newt Allen was sought after and played for the best teams because he was regarded as a premier second baseman. Home Run Johnson, a middle infielder who played in the pre–Negro League era, played both summer and winter ball and was able to play a part on 26 championship teams in his 21-year career.[20]

In the Negro Leagues, players could feely move from team to team in a time when their contracts were neither highly respected nor enforced. In this respect, the Negro Leagues were more analogous to modern free agency than Major League ball at that time, which was governed by a strong reserve clause. One can therefore draw the conclusion that the players who moved from championship team to championship team were, like the elite free agents in the 21st century, the most highly sought-after stars and therefore the glory of their times.

It is also imperative to recognize that the championships which should be considered by the voters are not just the rarely held Negro League World Series, but all of the championships available in the world of black ball, whether they be league titles, accomplished in Cuba winter ball, the Denver Post tournament, the California Winter League, or elsewhere. These championships were hotly contested and bitterly fought even if they did not receive the attention accorded to the Major League World Series. The integrated 1935 Bismarck semi-pro team put together by Neil Churchill consisted of an even number of white and black players. The four leading black players on that team were Satchel Paige, Hilton Smith, Ted "Double Duty" Radcliffe, and Quincy Trouppe—all recruited away from top Negro League franchises with an offer of better pay. That team blew away the competition in the National Semi-Pro Championship that year and was generally recognized as the best team outside of the Major Leagues.

The championships at stake in these alternative baseball worlds were often played for far more than money. When Satchel Paige led his team of All-Stars to the Dominican Republic in 1937, they feared for their safety if they did not win the Dominican championship representing the team of Dominican dictator Rafael Trujillo.[21] Needless to say, Paige's team won the Dominican title that year. Again, it is important to emphasize that the players who were recruited to these alternative Major Leagues were the best players of their time and often turned out to be the very players whose performance led their teams to the championship.

Rule 9: Character Counts.

It's not all about statistics and on-field performance. Often overlooked by sabermetricians in assessing Hall of Fame eligibility, character and contribution to the game have always been important considerations. Simply ask Pete Rose, Joe Jackson, or Mark McGwire. As early as the initial 1971 Negro Leagues election to the Hall of Fame, the Special Committee on the Negro Leagues was given written guidelines to select candidates not only on the basis of their playing ability, but also on their "integrity, sportsmanship, character and contribution to the team on which they played and to baseball in general."[22]

Truth be told, the Negro Leagues had its share of tough characters. Dave Brown fled the game when he killed a man. "Weasel" Warfield earned his nickname even before he bit off the nose of a fellow player in a fight. Oliver Marcelle was a hard fighter, on the field and off, who once settled a fight with Oscar Charleston by hitting him over the head with a bat. John Beckwith was a hard-drinking, surly, hot-tempered individual who pummeled both umpires and players alike, often players on his own team.

Conversely, "Gentleman" Dave Malarcher, Buck O'Neil, and C.I. Taylor were known for their outstanding characters and were well respected throughout baseball. They contributed far more to their sport than their playing abilities. Of course, personality and behavioral issues, even where they affect on-field performance, should never be dispositive. For example, how other players felt about Ty Cobb's aggressiveness on the base paths, or the fact that he once went into the stands to beat up a fan, hardly prevented his election to the Hall of Fame.

It should also be recognized that reputations are often exaggerated and subject to distortion so, unlike statistics, they must be measured in context. But these factors, pro and con, should all be fairly considered in making an overall assessment of a player's Hall of Fame eligibility.

Rule 10: The Full Scope of a Player's Baseball Career Needs to Be Considered.

There is an important distinction between the Major Leagues and the Negro Leagues that has never been fully appreciated. In the Major Leagues, there was always a clear line of demarcation between ownership, management, and players. Sure, there were player-managers in the Major Leagues and players occasionally became managers. And while some Hall of Fame managers had solid careers (e.g., Joe Torre), it was usually the less illustrious players (e.g., Casey Stengel, Leo Durocher, Tom Lasorda) who crossed over to management most successfully. There have been even fewer Major League Hall of Fame players who made the jump to successful ownership.

The Negro Leagues operated differently. There were many player-managers. Numerous top players became managers when their playing careers came to an end, and other players and managers went on to become successful owners. Rube Foster of the Negro Leagues was a Hall of Fame caliber player, manager, and owner. He can even be regarded as a Hall of Fame caliber pioneer. A glance at the list of the top 21 Negro League managers (see Chapter 17) reveals that seven of them were subsequently admitted to the Hall of Fame as players, and that another 11 of them were major stars in their primes. Moreover, other pivotal owners such as Cum Posey and Sol White had been leading players who segued into ownership.

While a Major League Hall of Fame candidate is generally evaluated solely in his role as a player, manager, or owner, the careers of Negro League candidates often cover multiple categories and these men should not be pigeonholed. Dave Malarcher and Dick Lundy were two of the greatest Negro League managers of all time. But both were also superb infielders with seasonal WARs higher than multiple Negro League infielders who have been admitted to the Hall of Fame. It's almost as though the voters forgot about their playing days. Buck O'Neil was a strong first baseman, a solid manager, a top Major League scout, the first African American coach in the Major Leagues, and a leading advocate in bringing the Negro League game to the attention of the American public. He was not just one of those things, but all of those things. They all need to be factored in. Negro Leaguers lived in a multitasking world brought about by the economics of their times. A player-manager saved the owner the cost of a roster spot without giving up anything on the diamond. No Negro League candidate should be compartmentalized just because it is customary to do so when assessing Major League candidates.

Rule 11: There Should Be No Fixed Number Limitation on Negro League Admissions.

Another consideration is determining the correct number of Negro Leaguers who should be admitted to the Hall of Fame. Some commentators and historians have tried to calculate an answer by assessing the country's population. Robert Peterson, in his groundbreaking work *Only the Ball Was White*, suggested that the number of African Americans in the Hall of Fame should correspond to the country's population—approximately 10 percent African Americans.[23] Negro League historian John B. Holway has noted that approximately one-third of all post–1947 Hall of Fame players admitted to the Hall of Fame have been African American and there is no reason that this percentage should not be the same for the pre-integration era.[24] The Hall of Miller and Eric, a website established by a group of stat heads that has focused its attention on the Negro Leagues, applied a proportional test to determine the correct number of Negro Leaguers by comparing the percentage of Major Leaguers in the Hall of Fame to the percentage of Negro Leaguers so honored. Their calculations indicate that, based upon this standard, 19 to 21 additional Negro Leaguers should still be admitted to the Hall of Fame. Their calculations even used percentages to break down the number of positions missing: 9 hitters, 4 pitchers, 6 managers, and 1 or 2 pioneers/executives.[25]

Yet even a proportional test misses the mark because African Americans have had an effect disproportionate to their numbers. Can anyone still think that it is a coincidence that the first three teams to integrate in any significant manner, the Brooklyn Dodgers, New York Giants, and Cleveland Indians, achieved their greatest pennant and World Series runs between 1947 and 1956?

Nor were the Negro Leagues a small operation. In his *Biographical Encyclopedia of the Negro Baseball Leagues*, researcher James A. Riley presents the biographies of over 4,000 Negro League players from 1872 through 1950. The Negro Leagues Researchers and Authors Group, which compiled the Hall of Fame database used in the 2006 Hall of Fame election, discovered more than 6,000 players participating in official Negro League sanctioned games between 1920 and 1948.

Through January 2020, there were 333 elected members of the Hall of Fame. Of these, there were 35 Negro Leaguers. I suggest in this book that there are at least 24 more Negro Leaguers who clearly belong in the Hall of Fame. That would bring the total of Negro Leaguers to 59 out of 355 members, or less than 17 percent. Another way of looking at this calculation is that there would then be approximately one Negro Leaguer admitted to the Hall of Fame for each year of the 60 + year existence of the Pre-Negro League and Negro League eras before the color barrier fell. This result, if justified by the players' records and deeds, would still be far less than the pro-rated number of Major Leaguers admitted to the Hall of Fame over the same period, and does not seem excessive.

Many historians have repudiated any quantitative or quota system as illogical. At the end of the day, any sort of quota operates either as a discriminatory cap or reverse discrimination, forcing open the doors to the unworthy. After all, what percentage of African Americans are elected each year to the Basketball Hall of Fame? The answer to this question is as many as deserve it. The Baseball Hall of Fame should also be open to admitting as many Negro Leaguers as deserve it. This has always been the standard applied by the Baseball Hall of Fame for the Major Leagues and it needs to apply to the Negro Leagues as well.

When Satchel Paige was first admitted to the Hall of Fame, it was to be with a separate plaque in a separate section of the Hall as a symbol for all Negro Leaguers. The time for symbolism is over. It is time to admit everyone who truly belongs. The Hall of Fame is not only for the Babe Ruths and Ty Cobbs. It also has room for the Ryne Sandbergs and the Barry Larkins. Not every player in the Negro Leagues was a Satchel Paige. But more than a handful were truly great.

Rule 12: Only the Best Should Be Admitted.

You cannot assess the Hall of Fame eligibility of any player simply by comparing him, as many have done, to the weakest existing Hall of Famers. Every knowledgeable baseball fan is well aware that pitcher Jesse Haines, outfielder Chick Hafey, and infielder Fred Lindstrom are in the Hall of Fame and don't belong there. And let's not get started on Lloyd Waner, who hit a grand total of 27 homers in his career and appeared in a single All-Star

Game. Lloyd Waner was lucky enough to have played alongside his brother, and true Hall of Famer, Paul Waner. The Waner brothers comprised an infamous duo nicknamed "Big Poison" and "Little Poison," demonstrating that a celebrated nickname and proximity to one's brother can alone open the door to the Hall of Fame. If the lowest common denominator were the correct standard, the Hall of Fame doors would be wide open. No, the 75 percent vote required for admission is a high standard and it should be high, even if a few oddball selections have slipped through. We should be willing to compare the Negro League players discussed here with baseball's greats, not the Hall of Fame's mistakes.

CHAPTER 6

The Sources for Hall of Fame Analysis of the Negro Leagues Are Hiding in Plain Sight

In 1936, the National Baseball Hall of Fame began admitting members to its not yet opened museum in Cooperstown, New York. Virtually from its inception, baseball enthusiasts have debated who should be eligible for admission. In a 2008 poll conducted on the Bill James Online website, 73 percent of those polled agreed with the proposition that "the Baseball Hall of Fame is the highest honor in American sports."[1] The debate as to Hall of Fame potential now begins with the entrance of any hot rookie into Major League Baseball and reaches a fever pitch as a player achieves eligibility for admission by a vote of the baseball writers. Since Major League statistics are officially kept and widely accessible to all, a player's value can be assessed by anyone based upon generally accepted uniform data. Even so, the voters and pundits continually reach many different conclusions. Admission to the Hall of Fame has spawned its own sub-genre in baseball literature, with books and websites dedicated to such subjects as the rationale behind the Hall of Fame ineligibility of Joe Jackson and Pete Rose. In fact, Pete Rose may be more widely known today for his Hall of Fame ineligibility than for his holding the Major League record for total hits.

Looking back on the advent of the civil rights movement, and the ongoing research on the role of the Negro Leagues which began about the same time, both movements began to reach maturity in the late 1960s and 1970s. There were literally only a few scattered books on the Negro Leagues (mostly memoirs with little overview of the Negro League history) until the issuance of Robert Peterson's *Only the Ball Was White* in 1970, which was followed by a slowly growing legion of serious studies over the past fifty years. In retrospect, it now seems inevitable that attention would eventually focus on the extent to which the stars of the Negro Leagues should participate in the Hall of Fame. After all, despite their close relationship, the Hall of Fame is a baseball institution, not a Major League establishment. With the selection of 17 men and women from the Negro and pre–Negro Leagues in February 2006, a total of 35 members of the Hall of Fame have now been chosen by the various Negro League selection committees. (Roy Campanella, who played eight seasons in the Negro Leagues, was selected for the Hall of Fame by the Baseball Writers' Association of America [BBWAA] based upon his Major League performance.)

Given the perennial significance of these issues to fans and players, the time has now come for an overall assessment of the Hall of Fame selection process for the Negro Leagues. How well has it worked? In what ways has it has fallen short? Have those selected been the most qualified for induction? Have the selectors already chosen too many members or are others still qualified for induction? Finally, if others are qualified, who are they and what would be an equitable process for the Hall of Fame to use in order to move forward in the future?

Fortunately, the extensive and ever-expanding body of research and analysis developed since the early 1970s serves as an objective basis for answering these questions. Many of these materials focus on the quality and performance of the great players throughout Negro League history. Among these materials are hard statistical data compiled by individual historians and the Hall of Fame, as well as biographies, oral histories, polls and autobiographical writings of Negro League veterans. Many of the more advanced analytical sources did not even exist when the Hall of Fame held its last Negro Leagues Special Election in 2006. By relying on the reputation of players among their contemporaries, the opinions of well-respected researchers, and available statistical evidence, a more complete portrait of the players and their performance can now be assembled.

The principal bases of analysis arise from three primary sources, as described below:

Statistics

When the first Negro Leagues committee met in 1971, it had no statistics it could refer to. None. It based its decisions solely upon players' reputations in the memories of the committee members. By the time the 2006 committee convened, Major League baseball had granted a $250,000 payment to the Negro Leagues Researchers and Authors Group (NLRAG) under the coordination of researchers and historians Dick Clark, Dr. Larry Hogan and Larry Lester to conduct a two-year study of all available Negro League statistics. As of the present, many different persons and groups have used their best efforts to further compile Negro League statistics. All of these sources vary from one another, but they are generally consistent enough to draw some solid conclusions. Some of the leading databases are those collected and published in and by the *Macmillan Baseball Encyclopedia of 1991*, the Center for Negro League Baseball Research, the Dick Clark/Larry Lester/Wayne Stivers directed survey conducted for the Hall of Fame under the auspices of NLRAG (which can be found at Baseball-Reference.com), and statistics compiled separately by leading historians John B. Holway and James A. Riley. The most intriguing online statistical banks for the Negro Leagues are described in the following.

The Seamheads Negro Leagues Database: The most unique source is the extraordinary Seamheads Negro League database, spearheaded by Gary Ashwill and produced by The Baseball Gauge, which can be found online at www.seamheads.com/NegroLgs. This site seeks to compile all verifiable statistics for the entire pre–Negro League and more formal Negro League history through 1948. The statistics residing in the Seamheads database range back to the pre–Negro League era, including games played by independent black teams as early as 1887, games between black teams and Major League groups, Cuban and Mexican League games, exhibition series between Negro League teams and U.S. Major League and Cuban teams, and independent black teams of substantial quality that played outside the Negro League universe. For the official Negro League era that began officially operating in 1920, Seamheads also includes the East-West Classic All Star and World Series games, as well as the in-season Negro League games from the entire 1920–1948 period. The Seamheads database is an ongoing project that is continually updated. Seamheads has also integrated certain data supplied by other leading historians such as Larry Lester and Scott Simkus.

Seamheads is a particularly important source because it gathers in one easily accessible location the verified statistics from other authoritative sources and is readily sortable by category by online users. The database includes the ability to sort statistics not just by the traditional categories such as batting average, home runs, and RBIs, but also by modern sabermetric indices such as WAR, Win Shares, and Similarity Scores. Nothing like this revolutionary database was available at the time of the previous Hall of Fame elections and it allows a fuller evaluation of a player's relevant contributions on the field. All references to WAR, Similarity Scores, and other statistics that are cited herein as coming from the Seamheads database are current through July 2020. As of that date, Seamheads had aggregated coverage of all of the traditional major Negro Leagues from 1920 through 1948, including the rarely considered 1932 Negro Southern League, the only year that circuit was regarded as "major league."

The National Baseball Hall of Fame and Museum Study (2000–2006): A second online, easily accessible database is the aforementioned NLRAG study conducted for the 2006 Hall of Fame Negro League election. This study compiled more than 3,000 day-to-day records and box scores from sanctioned games during the 1920–1948 period, an effort that was led by Dr. Larry Hogan, Dick Clark, and Larry Lester. These were the actual data collected and commissioned by the Hall of Fame for its 2006 Special Election for the Negro Leagues (available at *www.baseball-reference.com*). Many baseball statisticians believe that this is the most meaningful gauge of actual player performance because it was limited to the highest-level games of the Negro Leagues. Since no formal or official Negro League statistics were kept, this database of over 3,000 games may be as close as we can get. The NLRAG study purports to have included 100 percent of the games from the 1920s, over 90 percent of the games from the 1930s, and over 50 percent of the games from the 1940s. Of course, its most glaring omissions are all data prior to 1920 and the failure to include any independent games—which comprised the large majority of the Negro League universe.

Center for Negro League Baseball Research: Another invaluable repository of statistical data is maintained by the Center for Negro League Baseball Research (CNLBR) (www.cnlbr.org), a nonprofit foundation founded in 1990 by Dr. Layton Revel. Dr. Revel's website provides wide-ranging analyses of Negro League reference materials as well as detailed biographies of many forgotten Negro Leaguers. In those biographies, all available online, Dr. Revel sets forth and compares the statistics from several different sources (listed above). In most instances, those biographies are more detailed than those provided anywhere else.

BaseballReference.com: This website provides the advantage of combining all of the data from the NLRAG research compiled by the Hall of Fame study for 1920 through 1948 with the statistics compiled in the Seamheads Negro Leagues database for the pre–Negro League era from 1902 through 1919.

Compilations on the Negro Leagues: Leading historians, including John B. Holway, James A. Riley, Jorge Figueredo, Dick Clark, and Phil S. Dixon, have also compiled their own statistics, which can be found in their various published works.[2] Holway's statistics are an interesting counterpart to the abovementioned sources because he accumulates all known games regardless of competition, which may be an even more accurate gauge of the Negro League world as it was. Other researchers have gathered league data that are rarely found such as Thomas Aiello's treatise *The Kings of Casino Park, Black Baseball in The Lost Season of 1932* which provides statistics for the 1932 Negro Southern League, the one year that league achieved major league status, and Jorge S. Figueredo's *Cuban Baseball: A Statistical History 1878–1961*. Studies of individual Negro League teams, such as Mitch Lutzke's *The*

Page Fence Giants: A History of Black Baseball's Pioneering Champions, James E. Overmyer's *Black Ball and the Boardwalk: The Bacharach Giants of Atlantic City, 1916–1929*, and Phil Dixon's *Phil Dixon's American Baseball Chronicles: Great Teams: The 1931 Homestead Grays Volume I*, contain comprehensive team data which supplement the above sources with information not readily available.

Overall, the discrepancies between the various statistics gathered by the foregoing sources are hardly staggering and are generally consistent. One example would be the batting average of outfielder Oscar "Heavy" Johnson. Seamheads has Johnson amassing a .369 lifetime batting average in the Negro Leagues and a .366 average against all levels of competition. Lester and Clark list him as having a .369 average in Negro League games. John B. Holway records him at a .350 lifetime clip, and the *Macmillan Baseball Encyclopedia* records him at a .363 career average. Certainly, these are not the same total batting averages, but they do paint a consistent picture of performance for the player.

The 1952 *Pittsburgh Courier* Experts' Poll

In 1952, Pittsburgh's leading African American newspaper, the *Pittsburgh Courier*, selected a panel of 31 black baseball veterans and sports writers to compile a list of the two greatest teams in Negro League history.[3] In many ways, the 1952 *Pittsburgh Courier* All-Time Negro Leagues All-Star Teams Experts' Poll (*Courier* Poll) is extremely important to any analysis. The 31 voters were extremely familiar with the Negro Leagues and constituted some of its leading lights. Among the voters were five major owner/executives of the Negro Leagues: Tom Baird (Kansas City Monarchs), Lloyd Thompson (Hilldale Athletic Club), Eddie Gottlieb (Philadelphia Stars), Syd Pollack (Indianapolis Clowns), and Abe Saperstein (Birmingham Black Barons and others). Five leading sportswriters from the nation's various African American newspapers were also among the voters: Dan Burley (*Amsterdam News*), Fay Young (*Chicago Defender*), Alvin Moses (*Pittsburgh Courier*), Dr. Rollo Wilson (*Pittsburgh Courier*), and Ric Roberts (*Pittsburgh Courier*). The final contingent of 21 voters included some of the Negro League's leading veterans: Cool Papa Bell, Larry Brown, Oscar Charleston, Jimmie Crutchfield, Dizzy Dismukes, Bunny Downs, Frank Forbes, Vic Harris, Jesse Hubbard, Judy Johnson, Fats Jenkins, Pop Lloyd, Dave Malarcher, Jack Marshall, Ted Page, Bill Pierce, Jake Stephens, Willie Wells, Chaney White, Bobby Williams, and Bill Yancey (four of these voters would survive to one day serve on the 10-person voting panel of the initial 1971 Committee on Negro Baseball Leagues of the Hall of Fame).

What is particularly significant about this poll, compiled at just about the moment that the Negro Leagues were dying, is that it was compiled by many Negro League luminaries who lived or played in the Negro Leagues and personally remembered them during their glory years. As such, the *Courier* Poll constitutes an extremely valuable ranking of all-time greats created at the tail end of the Negro Leagues' existence by experts who had been intimately involved in its final decades. It is also regarded with great significance because, frankly, the voters did a great job. The *Courier* Poll sets forth ranked first and second teams of All Time Negro League greats together with a Roll of Honor including the names of all others receiving "admirable showings" with the voters ("Roll of Honor"). The results of the original 1952 Pittsburgh *Courier* Experts' Poll are set forth in Appendix C and will be referred to as the *Courier* Poll.

Since 1952, the *Courier* Poll has taken on a life of its own. Although the *Courier* Poll itself presents only the top two all-time Negro League teams, some sources have chosen to enhance the *Courier* Poll to include third, fourth and fifth ranked teams.[4] This version has sometimes been referred to by secondary sources and researchers as a separate *Courier* "Fan Poll." The enhanced *Courier* "Fan Poll," which includes the full five teams of Negro League greats in tiered order, is set forth for reference purposes in Appendix D.

In some cases, researchers have even referred to or adopted the so-called "Fan Poll" as the *Courier* Poll. In point of fact, there is no evidence whatsoever that a distinct "Fan Poll" ever existed. Upon closer examination, the so-called "Fan Poll" is nothing more than a reconstruction of the names provided on the *Courier's* Roll of Honor, based upon the order in which the names are listed on the Roll, presented as third, fourth and fifth ranked All-Time Great teams. Thus, on the "Fan Poll," the first name listed on the Roll of Honor at each position was deemed a third team starter, the second name on the Roll was deemed a fourth team starter, and so forth down the line. What is fascinating is that this methodology, used to construct a five tiered list of All-Time Great Negro League teams, and which seems to have been first utilized by researcher John B. Holway in his *Blackball Stars*,[5] may well be correct.

First, the narrative accompanying the *Courier* Experts' Poll occasionally names players who finished just out of the first or second tier. Where it does so with respect to position players, the names of the additional tiers on the Roll of Honor usually line up with the prose. For example, the narrative portion of the *Courier* Poll states that Dick Lundy and Dobie Moore just missed out in the vote for shortstop from making the first two tiered teams. Lundy and Moore are then subsequently listed as the first names at shortstop on the Roll of Honor. One seeming inconsistency in this regard is actually logical. The text portion of the Poll refers to Ray Dandridge as having come in third place in the voting for third base, although Jud Wilson's name is listed first on the Roll of Honor at third base and before that of Dandridge (which would seem to place Jud Wilson in third place in the overall voting). Yet, since the multi-positional Jud Wilson is listed as the first name on the Roll of Honor both at first and third base, and since a player cannot play two positions at once, it is certainly possible that the writer of the *Courier* Poll narrative treated Jud Wilson as a first baseman. Therefore, Dandridge might sensibly have been regarded by the writer as being deemed the third place finisher at third base.

Also, the names of the players set forth on the Roll of Honor roughly correspond to the overall prominence of the players. For example, superstars Jud Wilson (1b) and Dick Lundy (ss) are the first names listed first at their positions in the Experts' Roll of Honor and would reasonably have been the third team starters in the *Courier* Experts' Poll. Negro League great Bill Monroe, who is listed first on the Roll of Honor at second base, is an obvious third team choice at his position as opposed to Harry Williams who is listed last. Many of the later listed names on the Roll of Honor (e.g., shortstops Martin Clark and Bobby Williams, catcher Specks Webster) would hardly be candidates for the top tiers. In other words, the Roll of Honor appears to be seeded by quality and is not random. As such, it would plausibly constitute the order of the actual voting.

Other Negro League researchers, such as J. Fred Brillhart, maintain that only the first two tiers of the original list can be considered authentic because that is how it was presented, and that, since there is no affirmative proof that the Roll of Honor is presented in order of finish, the five tiered analysis set forth in the "Fan Poll" should be treated as moot.[6] To support this contention, Brillhart points to certain inconsistencies in the narrative portion of the *Courier* Poll relating to pitchers. He notes that Rube Foster and Walter Ball are mentioned in the prose as having received votes as pitchers but are not listed in the Roll of Honor. (The Rube Foster omission as a pitcher on the Roll of Honor is conceivably explained by the fact that he is already listed in the *Courier* Poll as the first team manager; the reason for the Walter Ball omission is not readily apparent.)

Ultimately, despite certain irregularities and possible errors, it remains a distinct possibility that the order of names set forth in the *Courier* Poll's Roll of Honor may indeed furnish an accurate ordering of the entire vote in that poll. Although the issue cannot be free from doubt, the consistency between the limited narrative relating to the position players, and the order in which the players are set forth in the Roll of Honor, furnishes evidence which should not be disregarded. Again, this issue is important to researchers because the 1952 *Courier* Poll is the paramount poll taken by true experts during the Negro League era and, as such, is an invaluable resource. As a result of the *Courier* Poll's significance, I think it appropriate to disregard the actual team tiers as artificially constructed in the nonexistent *Courier* "Fan Poll" (Appendix D), but to treat the order of ranking in the *Courier* Poll's Roll of Honor (Appendix C) as having some merit.

Polls of Historians and Negro League Veterans

One difference between the Major Leagues and the Negro Leagues is that full statistics have always been available for the Major Leagues. Baseball statistics are so well standardized that it is a major event in the baseball world when a person uncovers an extra hit for a baseball Hall of Famer. Of course, even now that we have collected a decent amount of statistics for the Negro Leagues era, this does not mean that the voters for the Hall of Fame always rely on them. Opinions and favoritism have always played a significant part in all of the Hall of Fame voting. With respect to the Negro Leagues, the opinions of Negro League veterans and historians are even more significant because statistics are spotty and incomplete. (Many people forget that the Major League players and managers controlled the vote for the All-Star game for a dozen years between 1958 and 1969 and that they did an excellent job until it was given back to the fans after 1969 for publicity purposes.) Although most major Negro League figures have themselves passed on, many left behind their selections for the All-Time Greats of the Negro Leagues. Similarly, the picks of virtually all major Negro League historians are readily available. Some of these sources are extraordinary. The principal ones relied on in this book are:

- William F. McNeil's books *Cool Papas and Double Duties* (2002)[7] and *Baseball's Other All-Stars* (2000)[8] containing:
  - ◊ Poll of 28 Negro League Veterans to determine greatest Negro Leaguers (McNeil Players' Poll).
  - ◊ Poll of 26 Negro League Historians to determine greatest Negro Leaguers (McNeil Historians' Poll).
  - ◊ Poll of 10 Pioneer Negro League Historians to determine greatest pre–Negro Leaguers (McNeil Pioneers Poll).
  - ◊ Ultimate All-Time Negro League All-Star Team compiled from the above surveys.
  - ◊ McNeil's personal All-Time Negro League All-Star team, containing a separate breakdown by era.
  - ◊ McNeil's proposed Negro League Hall of Fame ballot.
- *Top 100 Black Baseball/Negro League Players* (2006)[9] and *The All-Time All–Stars of Black Baseball* (1983),[10] both ranked lists compiled by Negro Leagues Baseball Museum historian James A. Riley.

- Cum Posey's All-Time Negro League All-Star Teams (1936–1938).[11]
- John B. Holway's *The Complete Book of Baseball's Negro Leagues: The Other Half of Baseball History* (2001)[12] which contains the following lists:
  ◊ All-Time Negro League All-Star Team
  ◊ Proposed Negro League Hall of Fame Nominees
  ◊ Season-by-Season Picks of Most Outstanding Players and Pitchers
- The Negro Leagues Baseball Museum All-Time Negro League All-Star Team (1993).[13]
- The SABR Negro Leagues Committee Poll of Greatest Negro Baseball Figures (1999).[14]
- *The New Bill James Historical Abstract* (2001),[15] with ordered rankings of the greatest Negro League position players.
- Negro League dream teams and Hall of Fame selections of Negro League veterans contained within the writings or reminiscences of such veterans as Monte Irvin, Buck O'Neil, Buck Leonard, Cool Papa Bell, Willie Foster, Quincy Trouppe, and Double Duty Radcliffe.[16]
- Published Hall of Fame and all-time great selections of leading Negro League historians.[17]

Hypothetical MVP, Cy Young, and All-Star Selections by Leading Historians

In addition to any picks they may have made for their All-Time Great teams, several knowledgeable researchers and historians have selected retroactive picks for year by year All-Star, MVP, and Cy Young award winners in the Negro Leagues. It is arguable that these picks are actually more accurate than their Major League equivalent picks because history has a way of removing the prejudices of the day. The most significant of these are John B. Holway's year-by-year selections for both the Eastern and Western conferences of his Fleet Walker Award (MVP) and George Stovey Award (Cy Young); Gary Ashwill's yearly selections on the Seamheads Negro Leagues Database of top position player, top pitcher, and yearly all-star picks for each position (only one award issued for all of the Negro Leagues); James A. Riley's selections for hypothetical MVP and Cy Young award winners in the 2006 ESPN Baseball Encyclopedia; and Bill James' yearly selections for Best Player and Best Pitcher in *The New Bill James Historical Abstract*. John B. Holway has also designated all-star teams on a sporadic seasonal basis from 1906 through 1948.[18] Holway's awards have particular importance because he names only one all-star player at each position for each respective league. While these awards are hardly dispositive of Hall of Fame eligibility, they furnish important standards directly comparable to modern-day all-star designations and MVP and Cy Young awards.

Selection to the East-West All-Star Games Between 1933 and 1948

Also available are the selections to the East-West All-Star Games, which can be referenced for the years 1933 through 1948. The East-West All-Star Game, conceived in 1933 by Gus Greenlee and others, was the pinnacle event in Negro League baseball. It was far grander and more significant than the sporadically played Negro League World Series. Games were played annually except for five years in which two games were played at different venues. Rosters were voted on by the fans and gathered by newspapers serving the African American community. It was a great honor to be chosen for the games, which were highly contested by players who seized the spotlight to showcase their talents. The 1933 game alone featured 13 future Hall of Famers: Josh Gibson, Oscar Charleston, Cool Papa Bell, Judy Johnson, Biz Mackey, Mule Suttles, Satchel Paige, Jud Wilson, Andy Cooper, Turkey Stearnes, Willie Wells, Willie Foster, and Pop Lloyd (as manager). Selection to this game is a meaningful standard for the time period.

Blogs and Fan Sites

It would be a mistake to overlook some of the work done by dedicated sabermetricians and the fans of Negro League ball. Some of these sources contain vital and original insights. Among the best are:

- *Baseball Think Factory—The Negro Leagues Home Page.* This website was founded by Jim Furtado and Sean Forman, who had previously worked on the now defunct *Big Bad Baseball Annual.* It has established a Hall of Merit, which is intended to correct the mistakes of the Hall of Fame based upon the analysis and vote of its members. The Hall of Merit consists of a group of more than 50 baseball enthusiasts and researchers who have undertaken a lengthy deliberative and fully debated process to determine the true greats of baseball. The players elected to the Hall of Merit parallel but do not replicate the results of the Hall of Fame voting. There are currently five Negro League players admitted to the Hall of Merit who are not in the Hall of Fame. The website contains online debates and discussions concerning many of the players analyzed in this book. Those discussions are lengthy (sometimes running over 20 pages) and smart, and they contain much new research gathered by its members. The threads of these discussions can be found at www.baseballthinkfactory.org/hall_of_merit/discussion.
- *The Hall of Miller and Eric.* This website was developed by two self-described baseball obsessives who analyze Negro League Hall of Fame candidates based upon their own statistical analysis, principally using the calculation of Major League equivalencies. The Hall of Miller and Eric has elected its own "Negro League Hall of Miller and Eric" consisting of the 29 leading Negro League players. The guru behind the site is Eric, a.k.a. Dr. Chaleeko, who also participates in the Hall of Merit analysis. Truly opinionated and fun: https://homemlb.wordpress.com.
- *Baseball Fever.* A website that collects fan polls and their rankings of Negro League players, with lengthy threads and discussions on many: www.baseball-fever.com/forum/general-baseball/the-negro-leagues
- *Legends on Deck* A detailed and ordered analysis of the top 100 Negro League players of all time by Kevin Larkin: http://legendsondeck.com/cream-crop-negro-leagues-100-best-player

WAR, Similarity Scores and Fielding Analysis Are Available for the Negro Leagues

What makes the Seamheads Negro Leagues Database particularly valuable is that the Baseball Gauge has created a website at Seamheads.com that is not only easily accessible but allows players to be compared on a position by position basis by all of the standard measures of batting average, RBIs, home runs, etc. More importantly, that site also allows players to be compared in accordance with either Wins Above Replacement (WAR) or Win Shares, standards that many sabermetricians have utilized as the key matrices for determining a player's ultimate value.

WAR is a non-standardized sabermetric-analysis baseball statistic developed to sum up a player's total contribution to a team in a single statistic. WAR seeks to measure how much better a player is than a player who would typically be available to replace that player. WAR is now commonly accepted as the most valuable objective indicator of whether a player belongs in the Hall of Fame, as it measures the importance of a player in comparison to a hypothetical average random player.[1] WAR for position players factors in runs created in any manner through batting, baserunning, or fielding. WAR for pitchers is basically calculated based upon runs allowed (earned and unearned) over innings pitched, with adjustments for team defense and custom park factors. WAR is particularly useful as a comparative measurement of the value of players—which is of course exactly what one is doing when assessing Hall of Fame eligibility. WAR gets to the heart of the fundamental question, expressed in an objective single statistic, as to how good any given player is in comparison to his peers. This book uses WAR as the primary tool to compare players with each other, and all references to actual WAR values presented herein are those calculated on the Seamheads Negro Leagues Database.

Of course, the Negro Leagues were not a single cohesive league; so, some further explanation is required as to how to most effectively apply WAR. Statistics for official Negro League games are the most readily accessible in the black ball world, and the Hall of Fame compilation made for the 2006 special election for the Negro Leagues chose to limit itself to these records. That methodology is understandable but hardly the only way to go about this process. Official Negro League games represented only small portion of the black ball world and, although they are more difficult to locate, even partial statistics from non–League games are valuable in analyzing comparable WAR. Why shouldn't performance in the Cuban Winter League or the California Winter League be included when they are available? To paraphrase researcher John B. Holway when he gathered his statistical base, if you can find it, you should count it.[2] While I will occasionally refer to WAR accumulated in the American-based Negro Leagues alone as the context requires, I will generally utilize statistics and WAR accumulated in all of the black ball leagues to the extent they are available to assess and compare players. WAR calculations determined by Seamheads are set forth at the conclusion of each position-by-position chapter in Part Three.

It is important to note that the calculation of WAR by Seamheads is an ongoing process and has only recently begun incorporating Mexican League data from 1940 when the Mexican Leagues upgraded the quality of their play by adding major Negro League players. Seamheads also does not currently include any results from Puerto Rico Winter Ball, where many of the leading players spent substantial time. (Alternatively, WAR as accumulated solely in Negro League games played in the United States is also set forth in Appendixes F and G for those who may believe that the Hall of Fame's own gathering of Negro League statistics, which was limited to the American-based Negro Leagues, is the correct methodology.)

Based upon the WAR of the players already admitted to the Hall of Fame, it would appear that any career WAR of 15 or better indicates a possible Hall of Fame candidate, and any WAR in excess of 20 requires explanation as to why a player is not in the Hall of Fame. For example, there are no catchers with a WAR in excess of 15 who are not in the Hall of Fame, which furnishes evidence that the voters have achieved the correct result in this category. Conversely, pitcher Dick Redding is the only player with a career WAR in excess of 37 who is not in the Hall of Fame—indicating that either further analysis is necessary or there has been a glaring omission. (Spoiler alert: It's the latter.)

While WAR established over a full career is probably the best tool for comparing Major League players to each other, it is not necessarily the best form of WAR analysis for evaluating the Negro Leagues. Major leaguers all played in one of two leagues each of which played a uniform number of games each year against similar competition. All of those statistics were fully accounted for. As a result, there was enough uniformity in the Major Leagues so that career WAR is a fairly complete record of a player's net worth.

Negro Leaguers, on the other hand, often played with no official league in operation or in leagues that only represented a portion (usually a small minority) of the games they played each year. In years when formal leagues did operate, statistics were not well kept, and teams played different numbers of games. Most Negro League seasons consisted of 50 to 60 official league games as opposed to the standard major league 154 games at that time. The best players also engaged in winter ball in various high-quality leagues around the hemisphere. Thus, when comparing players head to head, it is necessary to make allowance for the shorter official seasons, the fact that so many players are missing statistics for all or part of given years, and for seasons played abroad where statistics are even more elusive.

Accordingly, any comprehensive analysis must utilize both career WAR and WAR per 162 games in contrasting players. The more significant criteria may well be WAR per 162 games (the measure of a hypothetical modern season) over the course of a player's career, so at least the comparison of player to player is based upon an equal number of games. Of course, WAR per 162 games has its own inherent drawbacks as an analytical tool. It tends to favor players with shorter brilliant careers with higher peaks than those players who achieved fuller performance over a more sustained period of time (e.g., Luke Easter's WAR per 162 games of 5.5, achieved in only two seasons, exceeds that of Hall of Famer Ben Taylor; however, Taylor's career WAR is ten times higher than that of Easter). WAR per 162 games also prejudices some great players who hung on too long past their peaks, which resulted in dragging down their 162 game averages. Nonetheless, by comparing players on the basis of both career and seasonal WAR, there now exist objective criteria that are likely to determine who was the superior ballplayer.

Satchel Paige's WAR furnishes a solid example of this methodology. Generally regarded as the Negro League's greatest pitcher, Paige's career WAR of 50.8 is great but would only place him third in the pitcher rankings. This result follows from the fact that Paige, black-ball's greatest gate draw, spent so much of his career playing outside of the formal Negro Leagues wherever the highest payday would take him. On the other hand, his WAR per 162 games is 7.1, the highest of any starting pitcher in Negro League history, suggesting that Satchel Paige is truly at the head of the list in terms of quality performance on the mound.

Conversely, Oscar Charleston is generally acknowledged as the greatest overall player in Negro League history. Due to his lengthy playing career stretching from 1915 to 1941, his WAR per 162 games was averaged down to only the fourteenth highest of all time. Yet his career WAR of 79.5 is not only the all-time highest of any Negro League player, but it also exceeds that of any other player by more than 15 points. In this instance, career WAR confirms Charleston's place in the pantheon.

In addition to WAR, there is another truly entertaining tool available for Hall of Fame analysis: Similarity Scores. Perhaps the most basic of all arguments made when assessing the Hall of Fame qualifications of a player is to compare a player to existing Hall of Famers. In his *1986 Baseball Abstract*, Bill James stated the concept behind Similarity Scores as follows: "One of the most common arguments for any Hall of Fame candidate is the argument that Joe is comparable to Jim and Jim is in the Hall of Fame, so Joe should be, too. Similarity scores are a way of assessing the objective elements of an If-A-then-B argument."[3]

James went on to create a formula that compared relative players based upon their common offensive statistics and defensive value. The formula, which is quite extensive, can be found at Seamheads.com. Seamheads uses the Bill James's Similarity Scores formula as a means of comparing all players on a 162-game hypothetical season spread over the course of a player's career. In this way, any Negro Leaguer can be measured head-to-head against Major Leaguers based upon a common number of games. Of course, Similarity Scores are only one measure of a player's value. They do not measure factors such as the quality of the opposition, ballpark factors, length of career, championships won, or character. Further, there are certainly players in the Hall of Fame who do not belong, and one always wants to make sure the comparable players are the more deserving Hall of Famers, not the slipups. That said, Similarity Scores provide some astounding comparisons.

The value of Similarity Scores can be readily seen. As stated earlier, Oscar Charleston is generally regarded as the greatest player in Negro League history. According to Seamheads, among the closest 15 Major League players in all of baseball history most similar to Charleston based upon their Similarity Scores are Joe DiMaggio, Joe Jackson, Mike Trout, Ty Cobb, Ted Williams, Lefty O'Doul, and Stan Musial. That tells you all you really need to know about Charleston's greatness—and it suggests that those who are advocating Hall of Fame status for Lefty O'Doul may be on to something.

On the other side of the coin we have Frank "Weasel" Warfield. In his case, none of the 40 Major League players with the closest Similarity Scores to Warfield are Hall of Famers, with the exception of Johnny Evers. And Evers is widely regarded as one of the Hall of Fame's lesser members, an admission that was probably partially based upon his inclusion in the famous refrain, "Tinkers to Evers to Chance." In Warfield's case, Similarity Scores work against him.

Again, Similarity Scores are only one measure as they do not consider many of the important character and leadership issues integral to ballplayer's worth. But they sure are intriguing. All Similarity Scores used in this book were calculated by the Seamheads Negro Leagues Database.

Finally, Seamheads also provides fielding analysis for Negro Leaguers in the form of Total Runs Saved Above Average (TRS), a formula which is computed using categories such as outs made by a player (fielding range), any assists, and (for catchers) passed balls saved and runners thrown out, and then comparing the total to that of an average player. With respect to a pitcher's fielding abilities, we will use the category of Range (Putouts + Assists × 9 / Innings), a simpler measurement that reflects how many outs the pitcher participated in after the ball was put in play. These measurements are intended to gauge defensive effectiveness among players. For example, among second baseman, Bingo DeMoss has a TRS of 100.8 (the highest rating of any second baseman) compared with that of Charlie Grant (17.6), confirming lore that DeMoss was a superior fielder. We have already seen that Oscar Charleston had the highest career WAR of any Negro player ever. Statistics also rate Charleston with the highest TRS of any outfielder in Negro League history, providing even more objective proof of his overall excellence. So that there are some reasonable minimum criteria, we will only refer to fielding statistics for players with at least 1,000 recorded innings. All calculations of Total Runs Saved Above Average (for fielders) and Range (for pitchers) are those of Seamheads and are accurate for statistical data gathered through July 2020.

CHAPTER 8

Overview of Analytical Sources

Each of the available sources of information have unique advantages, and all are subject to some difficulties. Even the well-researched statistics are not complete and never will be. Aside from missing many of the official Negro League games, they will never include most of the independent games which were the true lifeblood of most Negro League teams. Recall that the NBHFM study commissioned by the MLB for the 2006 Hall of Fame Negro League election was limited to actual box scores which could be located in newspapers. As a result, it suffers from such flaws as games for which box scores could not be found, illegible box scores, and misspelled or missing names. RBIs, extra base hits, errors, stolen bases, runs, strikeouts, innings pitched, losing pitchers, and walks were regularly missing from these box scores. If that were not bad enough, fielding and pitching statistics were often omitted entirely from box scores.

The anecdotal evidence of players is often idiosyncratic and subject to exaggeration. The group opinion polls are inherently prejudiced by the era in which they were taken and subject to the likes and dislikes of the individual voters. The East-West All-Star Game selections cover only one limited period of time. Leading historians such as James A. Riley and John B. Holway seem at times to have fallen too much in love with their subject. The fan obsessives often get carried away with their analytical methodologies and fail to assess the leadership and other important attributes of athletes.

Even WAR, while an all-encompassing single statistic and perhaps the most valuable tool available in assessing a player's value, is only one standard. WAR always needs to be evaluated alongside intangibles such as team leadership on and off the field. One must also be vigilant to assess whether the player spent substantial time playing in the integrated leagues, which could be found abroad and in independent or minor league ball, or sometimes in leagues for which no or few statistics are available.

Even with their inherent deficiencies, I believe that all of these sources taken together furnish abundant evidence to help determine Hall of Fame eligibility. The partial statistics gathered over time now cover enough ballgames against elite competition to furnish an objective basis for comparison. Negro League player and fan polls taken in the past and contemporary historians' polls are of particular importance. When combined with even spotty and partial statistics, these polls can present a compelling case pointing to individuals who have been properly elected or who may have been overlooked by the Hall of Fame voters. Keeping in mind that the Negro League players and the sportswriters who covered them are virtually all gone, these collective sources still point to some solid conclusions. WAR analysis buttresses these other sources by furnishing a single tool to confirm or disprove any conclusions. Total Runs Saved, even if compiled on incomplete data, furnishes some reasonable objective standard for measuring a player's defensive prowess, either confirming or disproving their reputations among their peers. Similarity Scores can be particularly intriguing because they conjure up many fascinating analogies, either favorable or not. That WAR values and Similarity Scores were not available at the time of the prior Hall of Fame elections to the Hall of Fame is reason enough to reconsider that voting process.

Every Negro League veteran, historian and fan will have his or her own preferences, and many have unusual selections not mirrored by others. Yet these multiple sources do point to a core group of Negro Leaguers who are recognized as the elite of the Negro Leagues and who warrant election to the Hall of Fame. Taken together, these sources suggest that, while the 35 members of the Negro Leagues elected to the Hall of Fame to date may be highly qualified, the work is not finished. At least 24 individuals from the Negro Leagues also have strong evidentiary support for having earned induction to the Hall of Fame based upon objective analytical date. Part Three of this volume visits and reviews the résumés of many forgotten stars of the Negro Major Leagues. These overlooked players, managers, and executives are identified, and their qualifications are summarized. Assessments are made as to why they may have been passed over to date. These players are not analogous to the Hall of Fame's mistakes. They are equal in every measure to the Hall of Fame's true stars.

Part Three

24 Men Out—
A Position by Position Analysis
of the Voting to Date

Through an ad hoc voting system consisting of four separate phases spread over 50 years, a total of 35 Negro League members have been admitted to the Hall of Fame. Ongoing compilations of Negro League statistics and research in the 14 years since 2006 now furnish a significant foundation for determining how well the process has worked. This information creates a solid basis for establishing which Negro Leaguers may have been overlooked or, conversely, improperly voted into the Hall of Fame. It is time to assess the overall results on a position-by-position basis.

CHAPTER 9

Catcher

Perhaps because the smaller Negro League roster of players and coaches often required a catcher to act as de facto field manager, there may have been more outstanding catchers in the Negro Leagues than at any other position. Four Negro League players who were principally catchers are now in the Hall of Fame. Josh Gibson was the second Negro League Hall of Fame selection. Roy Campanella, who spent nine years in the Negro Leagues, and was rated by Seamheads as the top position player in all of Negro League ball in 1945, was elected to the Hall of Fame based upon his Major League service. With the addition of Biz Mackey and Louis Santop to the Hall of Fame by the 2006 Historian's Committee, the four Negro League catchers now enshrined are clearly the four best choices. WAR per 162 games in fact confirms Josh Gibson, Louis Santop, Biz Mackey and Roy Campanella (in that order) as the four highest rated catchers in the domestic Negro Leagues. The *Pittsburgh Courier* Experts' Poll, Cum Posey's All-Time All-Star selections, the 1999 SABR Poll Top 31, the 1993 Poll of Members of the Negro League Baseball Museum, Bill James' Negro League ratings, the McNeil Negro League All-Star Team, and both the McNeil Historians' Poll and the McNeil Players' Poll are all consistent with this conclusion. According to Seamheads, the group of four catchers admitted to the Hall of Fame also have the four highest slugging percentages of any catchers in U.S. Negro League history.

In fact, Josh Gibson, Biz Mackey, Roy Campanella and Louis Santop are arguably a higher quality grouping than their four best white counterparts in the Hall of Fame: Yogi Berra, Johnny Bench, Mickey Cochrane, and Mike Piazza. In the *New Bill James Historical Baseball Abstract*, Bill James, observing that catcher was probably the strongest overall position in the Negro Leagues, opined that he has no doubt that Josh Gibson was the greatest catcher in all of baseball history and concurs that the top Negro League catchers of their era were a greater combination than their white counterparts.[1] Correspondingly, leading historian John B. Holway concluded that Josh Gibson and Biz Mackey were the two greatest catchers in baseball history, white or black.[2]

As the Negro Leagues placed a high value on catchers, many of their best athletes played at that position. On-field, many Negro League catchers (like pitchers) were also expected to play other positions when they were given a day's rest, which increased their overall value. It is important to recognize that catchers also suffered more extensive wear and tear than Major League catchers, resulting from a relentless schedule of travel and play against independent teams.

Because of the overall importance and excellence of Negro League catchers, it is imperative to fully evaluate this position. While it would be more than fair to conclude that the four Negro League catchers currently in the Hall of Fame are the best who belong there, there were other catchers who deserve serious attention.

Worthy of Further Discussion

Bruce Petway is generally regarded as the premier Negro League catcher from its early days.[3] Over a 20-year span from 1906 through 1925, Petway was a defensive marvel, with a superb arm, one of the best ever.[4] He generally caught games on his knees but was still able to throw out runners with ease. He "instilled fear into the hearts of […] runners by his pegging, holding [them] close to the bags at all times."[5] He was one of the first Negro League catchers to fashion the trick of intentionally dropping the ball to entice runners off the base.[6]

James A. Riley reports that Petway's claim to fame was having thrown out Ty Cobb three times in one game in Cuba in 1910[7]; however, the box scores are ambiguous in that they reflect only one time he threw him out and that Cobb recorded no further steals in two games against Petway.[8] Solely in terms of defensive ability, Seamheads ranks Petway as the second best all-time Negro League catcher, ranking behind only Frank Duncan.

His reputation among his peers was topmost. It is reported that John McGraw and Connie Mack each called Petway the finest catcher in baseball, white or black.[9] Walter Mc-Credie, manager of the Portland Beavers stated in 1914: "There are two ballplayers of black color whom I think are, in their respective positions, as good as anyone else in the world. These two are [Pop] Lloyd … and Petway…. I think Lloyd is another Hans Wagner, while Petway is easily one of the greatest backstops in the game."[10] In his early days, Petway was also a speedy runner and led the Cuban Winter League with 21 stolen bases in 1911–12. According to Seamheads, Petway recorded 101 stolen bases over his career as opposed to the three times he was caught stealing. Petway actually had enough speed, combined with bat control, to hit leadoff for Rube Foster's Chicago American Giants' fast-paced style of ball when they were at the pinnacle of Negro League baseball from 1910 to 1918. At the same time, he learned enough working under Rube Foster that he was able to serve out his career as player-manager of the Detroit Stars from 1919 to 1925.

Petway was a decent switch-hitter, who James A. Riley reports had a batting average as high as .393 for the Leland Giants in 1910, when he played alongside Pop Lloyd and Frank Duncan for a team that Rube Foster regarded as the greatest team of all time.[11] However, despite sporadic seasons when he hit over .300, there were also many seasons when he hit below the Mendoza line of .200. He also struggled with injury, losing major playing time during three seasons from 1914 to 1916.[12] According to Seamheads, his overall lifetime batting average was only .231. In the Cuban Winter League, he batted .187 over six seasons and his batting average against Major League pitching was .227. The issue to be framed with Petway is whether a defensive specialist, regarded by some as the greatest pure catcher of his time, but coupled with little power (seven lifetime home runs) and only a mediocre batting average, warrants Hall of Fame inclusion. Petway's career WAR (13.3), accumulated over 20 years, would rank him seventh among all Negro League catchers, yet his modest seasonal WAR per 162 games of 2.7 does not place him in even the top fifteen of all-time catchers.

Bruce Petway had seven retroactive All-Star selections by John B. Holway, tied with Louis Santop for third all-time among catchers. Early Negro League players such as Pop Lloyd (one of Petway's best friends), Dizzy Dismukes, Ben Taylor, and Chappie Johnson include Petway as one of the two catchers on their All-Time Negro League teams. The 1999 SABR Poll included Petway among the 40 top Negro Leaguers of the 20th century. The *Courier* Poll and Quincy Trouppe, another Negro League catching stalwart, each included Petway as one of the two catchers on the second team of their All-Time Negro League teams.

Leading historian Robert Peterson placed Petway on this third All-Time team. Petway generates some Hall of Fame support by players and historians in the McNeil Polls, including such historians as Larry Lester, Dick Clark, and John B. Holway. James A. Riley calls him an all-time great, but below Hall of Fame caliber. Bill James and William F. McNeil each rank him lower than Double Duty Radcliffe (Radcliffe gets extra credit for also being a pitcher). Petway's early acclaim seems to have eroded as better hitting catchers evolved in the 1930s and 1940s. Altogether, Petway garnered less than 50 percent overall support from either the historians or players in the McNeil Polls—far less than the 75 percent vote required for Hall of Fame inclusion.

The online Hall of Miller and Eric compares the good-fielding, weak-hitting Petway to the likes of Major Leaguers Jerry Grote or Ray Schalk, calling him the type of durable, competent catcher who could help a championship team, but who "wouldn't make a dent in anyone's Halls of Fame."[13] Petway made the 94 name pre-ballot in the 2006 Hall of Fame Special Election for the Negro Leagues, but not the final ballot. Not a single one of the 100 Major League catchers with the closest Similarity Scores to Petway are in the Hall of Fame. He appears to rank as roughly the eighth best all-time catcher in Negro League history, which probably places him near or at the top of the second tier. Bruce Petway does not really have the all-around statistics to merit Hall of Fame selection.

Frank Duncan, Jr., was a Kansas City Monarch catcher starting in the 1920s who handled Satchel Paige, Bullet Rogan, John Donaldson, Chet Brewer, and José Méndez in their primes. Historian John B. Holway regards Duncan as one of the two greatest catchers in Negro League history, and Negro League star Art "Superman" Pennington even listed Duncan as one of his candidates for the greatest Negro League player of all time.[14] Seamheads ranks him as the single best fielding catcher in Negro League history. He was a strong-armed receiver reputed for his ability to handle pitchers. Dizzy Dean once recruited him out of a poolroom to act as his catcher for an exhibition game.[15] A tough player on the field, Duncan started a bench clearing brawl in 1926 that ended when a policeman knocked him unconscious with a pistol, after which Jelly Gardner kicked him in the head for good measure.[16] It is not recorded whether he got up and finished the game.

Duncan was also a winner. He was the catcher for the Kansas City Monarchs during their first dynasty, from 1923 to 1925, when they won three consecutive pennants and the first Negro League World Series, in 1924. He played in the California Winter League after the 1926 season and joined a group of African American players on their tour of the Orient in 1927, resulting in a dearth of statistics for his play during this period. In 1932, he was a member of both of the legendary Pittsburgh Crawfords and Homestead Grays teams. A line drive hitter, James A. Riley believes that Duncan's best seasons at bat were 1929 and 1930, when he hit .346 and .372, respectively, for the Monarchs. John B. Holway awarded Duncan his Fleet Walker award as the best player in Negro League ball for 1931. Duncan still had enough left in the tank to be named as an All-Star to the East-West Classic in 1938. According to Seamheads, Duncan's lifetime batting average was .254, but he hit only 15 recorded home runs over a 25-year career. In 1942, he took over as manager of the Kansas City Monarchs, in which capacity he won multiple pennants and the 1942 Negro World Series. His managerial stint from 1942 to 1947 produced a .565 winning percentage (Seamheads). As a manager, he continued to take occasional at-bats through 1945. After turning over managerial duties to Buck O'Neil in 1948, he ended his career umpiring Monarchs' games for a number of years.[17]

Generally regarded as the greatest Negro League backstop for his work behind the plate, Duncan was listed third on the *Pittsburgh Courier* Experts' Roll of Honor. He was also named a six-time all-star by John B. Holway. James A. Riley has declared Duncan an all-time great and Bill James ranked him 10th on his all-time catcher list. John B. Holway even named Duncan as the third catcher on his all-time all-star team. Yet, Duncan had virtually no support in the McNeil Historians' and Players' Polls and is only sporadically mentioned on all-time lists prepared by Negro League veterans. In terms of Similarity Scores, the only Hall of Fame match by Duncan among the 100 closest Major League catchers is Ray Schalk, as the 30th most similar player. Duncan's recorded lifetime batting average of .254 (Seamheads), with no real power, and his WAR per 162 games of 2.3 (twenty-third place among catchers in Negro League history), demonstrate that his defensive prowess alone is not sufficient for Hall of Fame inclusion.

George "Chappie" or *"Rat" Johnson* was a legendary Negro League catcher from the first two decades of the 20th century. Once called the greatest catcher in America by Hall of Famer Frank Chance, Johnson was reputed for his fast accurate throws down to second base, which would "discourage all attempts to steal."[18] Playing all around the diamond, but principally behind the plate, he was yet another of those players who seem to have always landed on the leading teams of his era. He developed a reputation as a skilled handler of pitchers and trained many of the other catchers of his time.[19] Johnson was also known for telling batters what pitch was coming in order to psych them out.[20]

He began his career playing semi-pro ball at the age of 13. In 1896, the 20-year-old joined the Page Fence Giants for three seasons, playing in the outfield, at first base, and behind the plate. By his third season, he was mostly a catcher. After the Page Fence Giants folded, he joined Home Run Johnson in 1899 and played for the Columbia Giants. His best season was in 1900, when recorded games show he batted .308 and formed the top battery in the pre–Negro Leagues with pitcher Lefty Wilson. He then topped that with an even better year in 1904, when Seamheads records him as hitting at a .367 clip for the Philadelphia Giants. In a 1904 playoff with the Cuban X-Giants, the betting was so heavy that Johnson bet "his underwear" on the outcome of one game. Johnson hit .352 for the series and kept his undergarments.[21] In 1905, he again teamed up with Lefty Wilson to take Renville, Minnesota, to the state title.

Over a playing career spanning from 1896 through 1919, Chappie Johnson was a member of such other legendary teams as 1906–07 Havana (Cuban Winter League), 1908–09 St. Paul Colored Gophers, 1909 Leland Giants, 1913 Royal Poinciana Hotel (Palm Beach Winter League), and the 1913–14 Mohawk Giants. However, his overall lifetime batting average was only .213, with six recorded home runs.

Johnson was particularly known as an innovator who popularized one-handed catching and also taught other catchers to line the inside of their gloves with goose feathers.[22] In 1910, he was, reputedly, the first Negro League catcher to wear shin guards on a full-time basis.[23] He is also very likely the first African American coach in Major League history, as he coached pitchers in spring training for such teams as the Boston Nationals, Cincinnati Reds, and the Washington Senators. One source pegs him as having taught Rube Waddell how to pitch effectively.[24] He is credited with helping to develop Nip Winters, Webster McDonald, Ted Page, and others. Page called him "better than any manager I played under."[25] No less an authority than Cum Posey designated Chappie Johnson as a coach on his all-time team. When asked in 1927 by writer Rollo Smith to designate his own all-time Negro League team, Chappie Johnson picked Biz Mackey and Bruce Petway as catchers rather than himself. He also noted that the Negro League squad "could clean up the National league, the American league."[26]

As his playing skills diminished, Johnson assumed a role as mentor, co-owner and manager of numerous teams, the last of which were variously named "Chappie Johnson All-Star" teams from 1924 to 1936. John Craig's 1979 fictionalized memoir *Chappie and Me,* which tells the story of how a player named "Chappie" trained a white first baseman to take the place of an injured Negro Leaguer for his All-Star team in 1939, may well be based upon fact.[27] By 1940, Johnson assumed the role of the first black trainer for Clemson University, where he often reminisced with the cadets about his playing days and where he remained until his death at age 73.

Despite his long and distinguished career, and his well-recognized skill in handling pitchers, he did not receive any votes in the 1952 *Courier* Poll or the McNeil Polls, and was not included on any Hall of Fame ballot. His 100 closest Major League Similarity Scores among catchers do not match any Hall of Famers. His lifetime batting average of .213 (Seamheads) with negligible power, and WAR per 162 games of 1.4, also do not amount to Hall of Fame statistics. Chappie Johnson nevertheless remains one of the most interesting and colorful figures in black ball history.

Wabishaw "Doc" Wiley. Once statistics began to be accumulated for the Negro Leagues, there were bound to be a few players who would be shown to be unappreciated stars. Aside from being included on the 94-name pre-ballot in the 2006 Hall of Fame Negro Leagues Special Election, Wabishaw "Doc" Wiley has not received the respect he deserves. Wiley, a practicing dentist, was also one of the leading Negro League catchers over a 14-year career from 1909 through 1923, with time off for military service during World War I. His WAR per 162 games of 3.1, ranks him twelfth all-time among catchers. According to Seamheads, his lifetime batting average was .310, with an OPS (on-base percentage plus slugging average) of .764. The college- and dental-school educated Wiley was regarded as an intelligent handler of pitchers, as well a clutch hitter with solid power.[28]

In the early part of his career, Wiley played with the West Baden Sprudels (1910) under the watch of legendary manager C.I. Taylor. The part–Indian Wiley then moved to New York (his dental practice was in New Jersey) and became a longtime member (1913–23) of the New York Lincoln Giants. Wiley generally hit in the heart of the order alongside Pop Lloyd, Spot Poles, Home Run Johnson, and Dick Redding. In 1913, Seamheads records him as batting .339 while catching for Lincoln Giants, who won the Eastern championship. He had another extraordinary year in 1914 when, according to James A. Riley, he batted third in the lineup and hit .418, while also catching Smokey Joe Williams in his prime. John B. Holway reports that Wiley exceeded that total in 1916, as he hit .481. In 1914 and again 1916, John B. Holway awarded Wiley his Fleet Walker Award (MVP) as the best player in all of the East. Holway has also deemed Wiley an all-star each year from 1913 through 1915. (As MVP, Wiley would certainly have also been an all-star in 1916, but Holway did not name an all-star team for the East in 1916.)

Seamheads' data reflect eight separate seasons in which Wiley hit over .300, in one of which he exceeded the .400 mark. John B. Holway has located 13 at bats Wiley compiled against top-flight Major League pitching in 1913, in which he batted a collective .385.[29] After he served in World War I, in the Dental Corps, he began spending more of his time on dentistry, which presumably paid better. Thereafter, he played only sporadically through 1923, when the New York Lincoln Giants released him in a housecleaning.

Wiley was regarded as a skilled handler of pitchers as well as a clutch hitter with decent power.[30] Who wouldn't love a catcher who regularly hit over .300 and was twice named an MVP? The Hall of Miller and Eric website (HME) analogizes Wiley's skills to those of Chief Myers, another catcher with Indian heritage who hit well and was an underappreciated mainstay of John McGraw's New York Giants teams of the same era.[31] The HME ranks Wiley's Major League Equivalency behind that of all of the Negro League Hall of Fame catchers and Quincy Trouppe, but ahead of that of Bruce Petway. Similarity Score analysis is truly intriguing for Wiley. There are a total 17 Hall of Famers among his top 100 matches, the large majority of whom are middle infielders, including Pee Wee Reese, Frankie Frisch and Barry Larkin. His closest Major League match is Hall of Fame shortstop Luke Appling. Generally ignored in the historians' and veterans' polls, Wiley was on the preliminary ballot in the 2006 Hall of Fame special election for the Negro Leagues. He was also listed fifth among catchers on the 1952 *Courier* Poll Roll of Honor. Maybe the 1952 voters were the smart ones.

Larry "Iron Man" Brown is generally included in any list of leading Negro League catchers. He was an outstanding defensive receiver with a strong arm he used to keep runners in check. In his own words: "Well, I could throw, I could throw pretty good. The crowd used to roar to see me throw men out. And I used to boot the ball and let it roll about eight or ten feet and go get it and then throw the guy out. Make him run. You don't see that stuff anymore."[32]

Brown claimed that he once threw out Ty Cobb five times stealing in a Cuban winter game, a feat that caused Cobb to think about passing off the light-skinned Brown as a Cuban in the majors.[33] Whether or not that story is factual, Brown was a smart, durable receiver who became a fan favorite, although he was also noted for being rough on umpires. In 1930, the durable Brown was credited with catching 234 games for the New York Lincoln Giants, including three games on one day, acquiring the nickname "Iron Man."[34] His best year was 1931, when he hit .318 (Seamheads) for the Memphis Red Sox and was named the retroactive winner of the Fleet Walker Award (MVP) for the Southern League.[35] Brown played a remarkable 29 years in the Negro Leagues, from 1919 through 1947. During his career, he was named as a catcher to seven East-West All-Star Games between 1931 and 1939 and played on three championship teams. In the 1927 Negro World Series, playing for the Chicago American Giants, he threw out four of eight players attempting to steal on him.[36] However, Seamheads ranks his defensive prowess as only 9th all-time among Negro League catchers. In the 1940s, he segued into a playing-manager.

At the plate, Brown was a switch hitter whose batting skills were never more than mediocre. Despite four seasons when his batting averages were over .300, Seamheads lists his lifetime batting average as .253 and he had no real power. Overall, his WAR per 162 lifetime games of 1.1 is not impressive and, despite his lengthy tenure, his career WAR of 6.3 does not rank him among the all-time top 15 Negro League catchers. James A. Riley lists Larry Brown as an all-time great, but also reports that his performance was adversely impacted, and his frequent uniform changes were caused, by his heavy drinking.[37] Infielder Sammy T. Hughes relates an incident that occurred when Brown had been named to the East-West game. He was carried in dead drunk on the shoulders of his teammates at 2 a.m. on the night before the game, having lost all of his catching gear. He played the next day with a new store-bought glove, but impressed Hughes because Brown only dropped one ball with a mitt that had not been broken in.[38]

Brown did receive some Hall of Fame support when he was included on the All-Time

Teams of players Double Duty Radcliffe, Bobby Robinson, Art "Superman" Pennington, and historian Sammy J. Miller. However, Brown did not receive any votes in the 1952 *Courier* Poll. Included on the preliminary 94-name ballot in the 2006 Negro League Hall of Fame Special Election, Brown did not make the final ballot. Larry Brown's Similarity Scores do not match him with any significant Major Leaguers. In ranking him as the ninth-best all time Negro League catcher, Bill James analogized Larry Brown's skills to those of modern Major League players Jim Sundberg and Benito Santiago.[39] Those players were solid catchers of their time but will never be Hall of Famers. Neither will Larry Brown.

Joe Greene was a solid receiver who caught the elite pitching staffs of the Kansas City Monarchs in the 1940s. Behind the plate, he had a strong throwing arm and a quick release.[40] At bat, he was a pull hitter with excellent power, often batting fifth behind Hall of Famer Willard Brown. Although noted for his lack of speed on the basepaths, he made up for it by leading the Negro American League with 33 home runs in 1940 (James A. Riley). Greene was the Fleet Walker Award (MVP) recipient for 1942 when John B. Holway credits him with a .366 batting average and he again led the league with 38 home runs (James A. Riley).

Greene always claimed that the Ted Williams shift was developed for him in the Negro Leagues and then adopted by the Major Leagues after they saw it used against him.[41] Like Ted Williams, he ignored the shift and just hit over it: "In Kansas City, center field was 400-something feet. Oh, my God, you've got to drive a ball almost 500 feet to get it out of center field over that wall. I hit over the scoreboard in left-center field. I've hit lots of home runs in Chicago's Comiskey Park way up in the stands. I hit a couple of long ones in Yankee Stadium.... Josh Gibson and I were the two most powerful hitters as catchers."[42]

In the 1942 Negro League World Series, Greene's Kansas City Monarchs were opposing Josh Gibson's Homestead Grays. Greene asserted: "Well, you've been talking 'bout the great Josh. I'm gonna let you know who's the great one."[43] Greene hit .500 with a home run to lead his team's offense to a four-game sweep. In the same series, Josh Gibson batted .077 with no home runs. Greene was named to three East-West All-Star Classics between 1940 and 1942, by which time he had become regarded as the best catcher in the Negro American League.[44] Greene capped 1942 with a game-winning double, leading his team to a 2–1 win over a Dizzy Dean Major League All-Star team before 29,000 fans in Wrigley Field.[45]

In 1943, when he was at his peak ability as a player, Greene was inducted into the military and served three years during World War II. Decorated for his combat experience after serving eight months on the front lines in North Africa and Italy, Greene was part of the military unit that cut down the bodies of Italian dictator Benito Mussolini and his mistress following their hanging by partisans.[46] In 1946, he was back in baseball catching for the Kansas City Monarchs as they won the pennant. John B. Holway has designated him the 1946 all-star catcher for the Western conference. The following year featured one of his career highlights when, at the age of 35, he blasted a long home run off Bob Feller (a game featuring a legendary nine-inning duel against Satchel Paige) in an exhibition game held in Los Angeles on November 3, 1947.[47]

Unfortunately, the hard truth is that he never really regained his prewar form.[48] His Negro League career was over by 1948, although he finished his playing days hitting .301 in the Canadian Mandak League in 1951.[49] His WAR per 162 games of 3.2 over the stretch of his career demonstrates his peak value and exceeds that of Bruce Petway, Double Duty Radcliffe, and Frank Duncan. Veteran pitcher Jim "Fireball" Cohen chose him as the catcher on his All-Time team. However, Greene was ignored in the *Courier* Poll and has never made any Hall of Fame ballot. Further, his Similarity Score does not match that of any noteworthy Major League catcher. World War II ended any chance Greene may have had to achieve Hall of Fame status over a full career.

Quincy Trouppe furnishes an intriguing Hall of Fame argument. This well-travelled catcher played for 23 years on a year-round basis all over the western hemisphere. He was a smart catcher and superior handler of pitchers, as well as a switch hitter who combined a good average with solid power from both sides of the plate.[50] He was nicknamed "Baby Face" or "Big Train." Bob Feller recalled him as "a very good receiver. He had an excellent arm, kind of like a Roy Campanella or Gabby Hartnett. He was very good calling pitches and blocked the bad pitches very well … there's no doubt in my mind that he would have been a very good major leaguer if blacks had been allowed into the big leagues."[51]

Just out of high school, he started in 1930 as a pitcher with the St. Louis Stars, for whom he once gave up a 400-foot home run to Josh Gibson.[52] By 1933, he had become friends with Satchel Paige after hammering a home run, triple, and single off him in a game.[53] From 1931 to 1935, he played with such leading teams as the Homestead Grays, Pittsburgh Crawfords, Kansas City Monarchs, Chicago American Giants, and the Detroit Wolves. Disgusted with the segregation that the Negro Leagues endured, Trouppe joined an integrated team in Bismarck, North Dakota, from 1933 to 1936 (together for a time with Satchel Paige). Some data from 1933 in Bismarck indicates he hit .438 against a league average of .238, hit for power and played great defense.[54] He appears to have been as popular as Satchel Paige in Bismarck and was honored by a "Quincy Trouppe Night" in 1933. It is important to recognize that Bismarck played high-level ball in those years. They played .500 ball against other Negro League franchises and generally beat up their minor league opposition.[55] In 1936, Bismarck entered the national Wichita tournament. Trouppe and Hilton Smith were the only two African Americans named to the all-tournament team, one scout reportedly saying he would pay $100,000 for Trouppe if he were white.[56]

After retiring to try his hand at boxing in 1937, Trouppe next shows up on the baseball radar in 1938–39 for a few games with the Indianapolis ABCs and St. Louis Giants of the Negro American League. However, in the middle of the 1939 season, he was recruited by Cool Papa Bell to play in Mexico, where he spent five years from 1939 through 1944, hitting over .300 each year and developing managerial skills.[57] The Mexican League at that time was raiding both the Major and the Negro leagues. In 1941, Trouppe was joined in Mexico by Josh Gibson, Ray Dandridge, Willie Wells and others. At the conclusion of 1941, he formed and managed an all-star barnstorming team to tour the United States with Josh Gibson, Cool Papa Bell, Ray Dandridge, Willie Wells, and other black stars. Trouppe claims in his autobiography that he was so much in demand in Mexico that in 1944, when he encountered trouble with his draft board about securing a passport to Mexico during World War II, Mexican League President Jorge Pasquel arranged for 80,000 Mexican workers to be exchanged for him and one other player so that they could play in Mexico.[58]

After the 1944 season, Trouppe was persuaded to return to the Negro League with an offer to play for and manage the Cleveland Buckeyes. He proceeded to lead his new team to a sweep of the 1945 Negro League World Series over the Homestead Grays, a series in which he hit .400. John B. Holway has designated Trouppe as the winner of the Rube Foster Award as the MVP of that 1945 World Series. At the end of the 1945 season, Trouppe organized and participated in a Negro League all-star barnstorming tour of Venezuela, a team that included Jackie Robinson, Roy Campanella, and Sam Jethroe. He continued on as player-manager with the Buckeyes for the next two seasons, leading them to a second NAL pennant in 1947 and at the same time batting .313 and .352, respectively.[59] A highlight of his career occurred in the Puerto Rico Winter League of 1947–48, when Trouppe, acting as player-manager, hit a home run in the seventh game of the playoff finals to push the game into extra innings, during which his team prevailed to win the championship for Caguas Criollas. When he told the story, he would report that he was made honorary mayor of the town and all of the schools were closed in tribute.[60]

The year 1948 found Trouppe back on the Chicago American Giants, where, according to James A. Riley, he hit .342 with 10 home runs. Over the course of his career, Trouppe played year-round in the summer and the winter, including spending extensive time not only in Mexico (1939–44, 1950–51), but also in Puerto Rico (three winter seasons), Cuba, Venezuela, and Colombia. According to John B. Holway, Trouppe hit .413 in Venezuelan winter ball in 1945. He also spent significant time in the off-seasons leading and playing exhibition games against Major League stars. From 1949 through 1951, Trouppe played for various teams in Canada and back in Mexico. Remarkably, he even had a cup of coffee in the Major Leagues, playing six games with the Cleveland Indians in 1951 at the age of 39 (the newspapers reported that he was 29).[61] As a result, he became the first African American catcher in the American League.

Trouppe concluded his formal baseball career as a scout for the St. Louis Cardinals, a position in which he found himself frustrated by the refusal of the higher-ups to accept his recommendations. Among the players he recommended who were declined by the Cardinals were Ernie Banks, Roberto Clemente, and Vic Power.[62] After baseball, he continued to make valuable contributions to the sport by writing his self-published memoir *20 Years Too Soon; Prelude to Major-League Integrated Baseball* (reissued by the Missouri Historical Society), probably the best book on Negro League baseball life written by a player. His extensive archive of photographs and motion pictures also served as the principal footage used by Ken Burns in the Negro League section of his documentary *Baseball*.[63]

As a result of all of his moving around, often outside of the official Negro League world, statistics for Trouppe in the prime years of his career are skimpy. Overall, James A. Riley lists his Negro League lifetime batting average as .311 and his lifetime Mexican League batting average was .304, although his Cuban Winter League average was only .254.[64] There is no uniformity of opinion on his defensive ability behind the plate. While Bob Feller and historian James A. Riley have praised his work, the limited statistics on Seamheads tend to show a catcher whose defensive abilities (based on a limited data sample) would have placed him only among the top 15 Negro League catchers, marginally above those of Negro League Hall of Fame catcher Josh Gibson. Trouppe seems to have been a durable workmanlike catcher whose principal contributions were based upon his ability with the bat, his acumen, and his character.

James A. Riley has determined that Trouppe played with about two dozen teams over 23 years, that he appeared in 17 seasonal all-star games in different countries during that period, and seven times assumed the role of catcher-manager.[65] Despite his limited time in the Negro Leagues, his all-star appearances included eight East-West All-Star Games, second only to Josh Gibson in appearances by a catcher. John B. Holway has deemed him as an all-star catcher in three separate Negro League seasons spanning from 1932 to 1947. Certainly, Jorge Pasqual would not have traded 80,000 Mexican workers (even if the number of workers is exaggerated) for a scrub.

Trouppe was also an unusually well-regarded and successful manager. Negro League veteran Riley Stewart stated: "He was one of the few managers who would fit into any era.... He was so far ahead in strategy than most managers.... He was a real gentleman. He was clean-cut, and well dressed. He was a model for the guys on the team. He might say 'dawg gone'.... And he knew the game—very well! I respected him more than any manager I ever had. Not even the great Candy Jim [Taylor] was the teacher that Trouppe was."[66]

Quincy Trouppe, driven abroad by segregation, just barely qualifies (but does qualify) for the 10-year minimum period in the Negro Leagues, which we have postulated is a proper minimum requirement. It is likely that this fact alone is responsible for Trouppe not even making the preliminary 94-name ballot in the 2006 Special Election for the Negro Leagues. Trouppe therefore becomes one of those American-born Negro Leaguers for whom it is appropriate to consult his overall record around the entire hemisphere in assessing his career. It is interesting that, despite his accomplishments being fresh in the mind of the voters, the experts in the 1952 *Pittsburgh Courier* Poll did not cast any votes for Trouppe. Perhaps the disappointment of his failed tryout with the Indians in that year was too recent in the voters' minds, even though he was almost 40 years old and not really given much of a chance to play. It is also likely that his lengthy tenure abroad weighed against him.

Yet, here is a player who was an all-star all over the world, was one of the leading catcher/managers of his era, hit over .300 lifetime, and whom Bob Feller claimed would have been another Roy Campanella if given the chance in white ball. Leading historians such as Lyle K. Wilson and Joe Posnanski have recognized his Hall of Fame credentials. The Hall of Eric and Miller, which calculates and often bases its rankings on Major League equivalencies, ranks Trouppe fourth all-time among Negro League catchers, just behind Roy Campanella but ahead of Biz Mackey. The SABR Poll named him as one of the top 40 Negro League players of all time. The sabermetricians at the Baseball Think Factory, after an extensive review of his record, elected him to their Hall of Merit in 1995, with one member noting that Trouppe was a superior catcher to Roy Campanella in 9 of the 11 years they played together in the Negro Leagues.[67] That designation made Trouppe one of only five Negro League players elected to the Hall of Merit but not the Hall of Fame. (Home Run Johnson, John Beckwith, Minnie Minoso and Alejandro Oms are the others.)

Similarity Score analysis is intriguing for Trouppe. Six Hall of Famers are included among his top ten matches, including Barry Larkin, Derek Jeter and Lou Boudreau (all infielders!). Since Trouppe does qualify for Hall of Fame consideration under the 10-year rule, but either chose or felt compelled to play most of his baseball life in an integrated world overseas, where he could be better respected, he is one of those players for whom it is more than fair to consider his overall accomplishments. While his recorded career WAR is not comparable to some others because of his lengthy time abroad, Trouppe's WAR per 162 games of 5.4 trails only that of Josh Gibson and exceeds that of the other leading Hall of Fame candidates at catcher. Major League equivalencies for catchers computed by sabermetrician Eric Chalek of the Hall of Miller and Eric rank Trouppe behind only the four Negro League catchers already admitted to the Hall of Fame. His record in the Western hemisphere over the span of the Negro League universe reflects a true standard of excellence. Because of the overall strength of catchers in the Negro Leagues, it would hardly be outrageous to elect another catcher to the Hall of Fame. The more one studies the entire record and accomplishments of this American ballplayer, the more he looks like a Hall of Famer.

WAR Comparison of Negro Hall of Famers and Candidates—Catchers.
All Leagues: Negro, Cuban, Mexican Leagues, vs. Major Leaguers and High Minors

Name	Years	WAR (per 162 games)	Career WAR
Josh Gibson	1930–46	10.1	57.1
Quincy Trouppe	1932–48	5.4	17.6
Louis Santop	1910–26	5.3	16.9
Roy Campanella*	1937–45	4.7	10.0
Biz Mackey	1920–47	4.4	30.8
Joe Greene	1936–48	3.2	4.4
Doc Wiley	1909–23	3.1	4.5
Bruce Petway	1906–25	2.7	13.3
Frank Duncan, Jr.	1920–45	2.3	14.7
Chappie Johnson	1899–1919	1.4	2.0
Larry Brown	1921–47	1.1	6.3

Hall of Famers in bold. WAR statistics courtesy of Seamheads.

*Admitted to Hall of Fame based upon Major League performance.

The table reflects a solid result for the Hall of Fame voters. The three Negro League catchers admitted to the Hall have the highest career WARs per 162 games in Negro League history. Bruce Petway had an admirable and lengthy career, but his WAR is not of Hall of Fame caliber. Any chance Joe Greene had to achieve the Hall of Fame was precluded by his service in World War II. The rarely mentioned Doc Wiley ranks higher than would have been expected.

Quincy Trouppe's outstanding WAR per 162 games, behind only that of Josh Gibson, suggests that he is the next man up if an additional Negro League catcher were to be selected for the Hall of Fame. If one also includes his lengthy and productive tenure outside of the U.S. Negro Leagues, Trouppe is a solid Hall of Fame candidate.

CHAPTER 10

First Base

Buck Leonard, Mule Suttles, and Ben Taylor, the three Negro League first basemen in the Hall of Fame, are regarded by most sources as the best Negro League players at their position. Not only do they have the highest career WAR of any Negro League first basemen, they are also the only players who played primarily at first base with career WAR in excess of 20. Any fair assessment would conclude that the Hall of Fame voting has achieved another collective bull's-eye at this position.

Worthy of Further Discussion

Edgar Wesley was a power-hitting lefty of the 1920s who hit over .400 in two seasons and, according to John B. Holway, led the western division of the Negro League in home run percentage in 1920 and again in 1925. He had been recruited out of the Texas All-Stars in 1918 by Rube Foster for his Chicago American Giants when his first baseman Leroy Grant was drafted. Wesley was already 27 years old when he moved up to major Negro League ball. In 1919, Foster moved him to help stock the Detroit Stars franchise, where he would spend his most productive years. Beginning with the lively ball era around 1919, Wesley proceeded to compile batting averages of .322, .287, .318, and .349 over the next four years (Seamheads). But he was also a solid fielder, renowned at first base for his proper footwork, handling of grounders, and fielding of bad throws. He had good speed on the bases and was well regarded for his quiet demeanor.[1] Seamheads' data confirm his defensive prowess, rating Wesley as the eighth all-time best first fielding baseman in Negro League history.

Seamheads designates him as the Negro Leagues All-Star first baseman in 1919. One of the earliest home run sluggers in Negro League history, Wesley led the National Negro League in home runs in both 1920 and 1925. He was also second in the league in home runs in 1919 and 1921.[2] Beginning in 1923, when Turkey Stearnes joined the team, Wesley generally batted cleanup behind Stearnes. The lefty duo proceeded to spark the Detroit Stars in 1923 as Stearnes and Wesley hit 18 home runs apiece (Seamheads).

In the summer of 1923, Wesley participated in a three-game post-season exhibition series with the Detroit Stars (supplemented by Oscar Charleston and John Beckwith),[3] playing against the Major League St. Louis Browns. In the first game, Wesley hit two home runs, including a walk-off shot in the ninth inning off 16-game winner Dave Danforth. After the Detroit Stars won two of the three games, Commissioner Landis barred future games between Major League and Negro League teams to avoid future embarrassment. (He did decree that Major League all-star units would be permitted to continue to play in the future.)[4]

After a year in the Eastern Colored League, in 1924, Wesley returned to the Stars in

1925 and led the league in batting average (.413), while finishing as the league runner-up to Stearnes in home runs and RBIs, all in a season cut short by a broken ankle.[5] Hobbled by injury and age, Wesley was traded to the Cleveland Hornets in 1927. John B. Holway deemed Wesley the All-Star first baseman for six of the nine years from 1919 through 1927. He spent the next few years wandering with teams in Cuba and South America as "just one more itinerant ballplayer past his prime … in desperate need of a paycheck."[6] He finished up his career in 1931 with the Atlantic City Bacharach Giants at the age of 40.

According to William F. McNeil's research, Wesley averaged 28 home runs and a .328 batting average for each 550 at bats over his life in baseball (a hypothetical Major League length season).[7] Author Richard Bak has calculated Wesley's batting average over his seven years with the Detroit Stars as .338.[8] John B. Holway ranks his overall home run total as the seventh highest, and his home run percentage as fourth highest, in Negro League history.[9] Wesley's WAR per 162 games of 4.7 barely trails that of Hall of Fame entrant Ben Taylor.

Historian William F. McNeil has deemed Wesley the All-Time Negro League First baseman for the era 1900–1925 and a solid candidate for Cooperstown. Other eminent historians (John B. Holway, David A. Lawrence) and great Negro League players (Larry Doby) have ranked Wesley among the best first basemen of all time. However, he achieved an aggregate vote of only 16 percent in the McNeil Historians' Poll and 4 percent in the McNeil Players' Poll. He did not receive a single vote from any of the experts in the 1952 *Pittsburgh Courier* Poll. He has never appeared on any Hall of Fame ballot; Bill James did not rank him among the top 10 first baseman in the Negro Leagues; and Cum Posey never included him on any of his all-time lists.

Yet, his performance as a high-average power hitter was more than solid. How many players had lifetime batting averages of .328, the fourth highest home run percentage in history, were solid defensively, and were deemed all-stars for six years? It is fascinating that his two closest Major League Similarity Score matches are current stars Todd Helton and Joey Votto. Hall of Famers Johnny Mize and Jim Bottomley also appear among his five closest Similarity Scores. However, because of his late start, his tenure in high-level Negro ball barely meets the 10-year requirement imposed by the Hall of Fame. Edgar Wesley was a Hall of Fame caliber player, but his longevity in the Negro Leagues may not warrant Hall of Fame admission.

George "Tank" Carr, who played primarily at first base, had a career WAR of 13.9. A rarity in Negro League ball, he grew up in Southern California, where he played baseball at Pasadena High School. The 6 ft. 2 in., 230 lb. Carr was a switch-hitting power hitter with speed who entered semi-pro ball with the Los Angeles White Sox in 1915. Photos of him often show his cap at an angle with a playful smile. His performance in California caught the attention of Smokey Joe Williams, who recruited him to play in the Florida Hotel League in 1916.[10] Carr then returned for a few years with the Los Angeles White Sox, a highly competitive semi-pro team that played some seasons in the California Winter League and some years as an independent. Although records for this period are sparse, Carr led the 1916–17 California Winter League in batting average (.458) and slugging percentage (.625).[11]

When J.L. Wilkinson founded the Kansas City Monarchs in 1920, he sought the best players available from many independent teams and he signed Carr. In the inaugural 1920 season of the Kansas City Monarchs, Tank Carr is credited by John B. Holway with a .336 batting average, 5 home runs, and 15 stolen bases (Seamheads credits him with 18 stolen bases), earning him a place on the *Kansas City Sun* 1920 Negro National League All-Star team.[12] In 1921, he hit .323, stole 22 bases, and his 14 home runs were second only to Oscar Charleston in the Negro National League.[13]

In 1923, Carr was recruited by Ed Bolden to join Hilldale of the Eastern Colored League. For the next three years, he was a key member of the Hilldale team, which won three consecutive Eastern Colored League titles. According to authors David A. Lawrence and Dom Denaro, "Carr was a tremendous hitter—good enough to hold down the number three position in the Hilldale batting order—plus he was either the best base-stealer in the league, or very close to it."[14] Carr played for Hilldale in the 1924 and 1925 Negro League World Series, batting .326 over both series. His best year was 1925, when he batted .351 and led the Eastern Colored League in doubles, triples, and stolen bases.[15] Carr was a Pittsburgh *Courier* and John B. Holway All-Star pick for 1925. In 1928, his last truly prolific year, he led the East with 14 home runs.[16]

During this entire time period, Carr returned to his home base in California most winters and was a member of seven championship teams between the winters of 1920–21 and 1930–31. He also led the California Winter League in home runs during the 1920–21 and 1925–26 seasons and spent one winter in Cuba, where he batted .416 as he helped lead Alacranes to the 1926–27 championship.[17] In 1932, Carr participated in a Far East exhibition tour by the Royal Giants who, according to the *Afro American* newspaper, compiled a won-loss record of 50–2 while spending two months playing in Japan, China, Korea, and the Philippines. Carr was one of the leading hitters on the tour, compiling a batting average of .355.[18]

Carr has been tarnished by several researchers who have mentioned his drinking problem and the resulting disciplinary issues, which affected his productivity and shortened his career.[19] Perhaps this explains the falloff in his play in the Negro Leagues, or perhaps it was the fact that he was already 25 when he joined the Negro National League in 1920. In any event, James A. Riley reports that by the late 1920s "his skills faded and he was only a shadow of his former self."[20] After his playing days were over, he managed the lower-level Philadelphia Black Meteors and the Philadelphia Colored Giants from 1935 to 1941. Carr died of a heart attack at the age of 53 while working as a cook for the Rock Island Railroad Company. His pallbearers included Biz Mackey, Jud Wilson and Dobie Moore.[21]

According to the Center for Negro League Baseball Research (CNLBR), Tank Carr compiled a career batting average of .321 and .475 slugging percentage in Negro League play and was consistently among the league leaders in stolen bases. He also played regularly in the California Winter League, where he compiled a lifetime batting average of .336, a career slugging average of .569, and led that league in home runs in two seasons. Over a 12-year Negro League career, Carr batted over .300 nine times. CNLBR has located box scores for 15 exhibition games Carr played against Major League pitching in which he compiled a .326 batting average.[22] Tank Carr was the rare player who combined his average and power with speed. According to the Seamheads Negro League Database, Carr is the all-time stolen base leader among Negro League first baseman.

As is true for many leading players, Carr seems to have brought a winning tradition to an extraordinary number of championship teams, having played on 15 championship teams in the Negro Leagues, the California Winter League, and in Cuba between 1920 and 1934.[23]

Tank Carr was cited third among first baseman on the Roll of Honor in the *Courier* Experts' Poll. Bill James also ranked him as the fifth all-time best Negro League first baseman. James A. Riley labeled Carr an all-time great but did not include him on his proposed Hall of Fame list. Only one player cited Carr in the McNeil Players' Poll, and he garnered no support whatsoever in the McNeil Historians' Poll. Moreover, his WAR per 162 games of 3.3 is not equivalent to that of the other candidates at his position. While his on-field performance demonstrates that he was a fine ballplayer, Carr's productive career in the Negro Leagues consisted of a limited high arc of performance from 1920 to 1928 (although he returned for short unproductive stints in 1933 and 1934). Among his top 10 Similarity Score matches from the Major Leagues are Hall of Famers Zack Wheat and Joe Kelley. In the final analysis, even when including his superb performance in the California Winter League, Carr simply did not sustain his high quality of play over a sufficient period of time to be seriously considered for the Hall of Fame.

Luke Easter was ranked by preeminent sabermetrician Bill James as the second best first baseman in Negro League history. James has said that, even in today's world, Easter might have had the potential to be the greatest power hitter in all of baseball history.[24] What's interesting about Bill James' comment is that he may not be exaggerating. Luke Easter was a 6 ft. 4½ in., 240 lb. colossus who was born in 1915 and rose from the sandlots of St. Louis. During his time in the Negro Leagues, his WAR per 162 games of 5.5 exceeds that of Hall of Famer Ben Taylor.

Easter spent his early career, in 1937 to 1941 (age 21 to 25), playing for the St. Louis Titanium Giants, an industrial team that so dominated the area that the Negro American League (NAL) was unable to re-establish a St. Louis franchise because of their success.[25] The Giants, for whom Easter batted cleanup, were a really good team that played, and often beat, other semi-professional and official Negro League teams. The Giants won 90 percent of their games and went 6–0 against NAL teams in 1940.[26] Understandably, records for the Giants from that time are virtually nonexistent, leaving a gaping statistical hole in Easter's résumé. Buck O'Neil, in listing Easter as his second team pick for his all-time Negro League team behind Buck Leonard, notes that Easter's many early years spent outside of the formal Negro Leagues were due to the fact that he was making a better living as a security guard than he would have made in the Negro Leagues.[27]

In 1941, Easter received the first of many serious injuries when he broke his ankle in a car accident in an auto being driven by teammate Sam Jethroe. Easter, ineligible for the Army because of that injury, spent the four-year period 1942–45 working in a defense plant.[28] When the war ended in 1945, Easter was sought out and signed by Abe Saperstein for his independent Cincinnati Crescents, with whom he barnstormed the country, often playing against NAL and NNL teams, and hitting home runs at an amazing rate. The March 30, 1949, *Sporting News* claims Easter batted .415, with 152 RBIs, in 1946. Another unverified report claims he also hit 74 home runs.[29]

After Josh Gibson's death in 1947, the Homestead Grays were looking to replace Gibson and signed Luke Easter, who had yet to play a game in the official Negro Leagues. The 240 lb. first baseman was touted in his 1947 Negro League rookie year, at the age of 31,[30] as the new Josh Gibson.[31] That year, James A. Riley reports that Easter hit .382, with 45 home runs against all levels of competition. John B. Holway has designated him as the 1947 all-star first baseman. In 1948, Easter hit .403, led the league in home runs, was named to the East-West All-Star Game, and was part of the Homestead Grays final pennant-winning team. In the Puerto Rican Winter League of 1948–49, Easter became the league MVP as he led the league in batting average (.402), RBIs, triples, doubles, and was even second in steals.[32]

Signed by the Cleveland Indians in the winter of 1949 (he told Indians owner Bill Veeck he was 27), he spent the next year becoming a phenomenon in the Pacific Coast

League, drawing crowds as he hit .363, with 25 home runs, in 80 games. Easter was finally called up to the Indians in 1949 as a 33-year-old rookie. In full seasons from 1950 through 1952, he hit between 27 and 31 home runs each year and averaged over 100 RBIs per year for the three-year span. His June 27, 1950, blast (estimated at 477 feet) is regarded as the longest home run ever hit at Cleveland's Municipal Stadium.[33] In 1953, he was batting .303, with seven home runs in 230 plate appearances for the Indians, when a bad pitch broke his foot. His Major League career ended in 1954 after an injury during his spring training (the Majors had little patience for older African American players).

Easter spent the next 12 years, through the age of 49, in the high minor leagues. In 1955 and again in 1956, aged 40–41, he led the International League in home runs (35 and 40) and RBIs (106 and 128). Altogether, between the ages of 39 to 48, Easter came to the plate 4,048 times, clouted 210 home runs, and batted .287.[34] One of his most famous home runs occurred on June 14, 1957, when he hit the first ball ever over the center field scoreboard in Buffalo's Offermann Stadium, which then broke a window across the street, an arc of approximately 550 feet.[35] James A. Riley sums up his career as having achieved a .336 Negro League batting average, a .274 Major League average, and a .296 minor league average, with a lifetime total of 385 home runs.[36] After he left baseball in 1964, Luke Easter died tragically in 1979 when he was killed in a payroll robbery while working as an armed guard.

Luke Easter is one of those players whose entire baseball life deserves scrutiny because, in addition to the Negro Leagues, he played in different baseball worlds for more than 10 years and had his career disrupted by the color line. He spent some of his prime years playing independent ball in St. Louis, and then performed at a high level in the Negro Leagues, the Major Leagues, and the high minors. Monte Irvin certainly appreciated Easter and ranked him as the fourth best first basemen in Negro League history.[37] His Similarity Scores to comparable Major Leaguers, based upon his Negro League performance, find Dave Winfield and Monte Irvin among his top 10 matches.

The amiable and fun-loving Easter was also a fan favorite who was often compared to Babe Ruth based upon his home run prowess and ability to relate to the fans. In the words of veteran player and manager Del Baker, "I've seen a lot of powerful hitters in my time but for sheer ability to knock the ball a great distance, I've never seen anybody better than Easter—and I'm not excepting Babe Ruth."[38] The Hall of Miller and Eric concludes: "Easter can probably claim to have had among the most interesting of careers with so many stops, starts, obstacles, and towering homers that a movie should be made about him."[39] One blogger on Baseball Think Factory's Hall of Merit discussion page, after studying Easter's career, said it well: "Holy Crap! If he had a normal career curve, all of it in the [Major Leagues], it sure seems like he might have hit 700 HR."[40] In a fairer and more equitable world, that result might have followed. But, while his body, talent, and home runs were prodigious, and his career fascinating, the four plagues of race, war, injury, and timing have conspired to deny him any true Hall of Fame possibilities.

Bill Pettus is a solid candidate for the most underappreciated player in Negro League history. Pettus was a left-handed power-hitting multi-position player who played principally at first base. His WAR per 162 games of 7.0 is exceeded in Negro League first base annals only by that of Buck Leonard. He was another of the Texas-born Negro Leaguers who actually began his career in New Mexico, in 1902. In 1905, while also making money boxing and working in a coal mine, he played for and managed a mixed team of Mexicans and African Americans that compiled a 48–1 record, taking on all clubs in that part of the country.

The knowledge of Spanish he picked up served him well later, when he played against the Cuban Stars; Pettus claimed always to know when they planned to steal bases.[41] By 1906, he was the catcher and only black player on the Albuquerque team, where he developed a reputation as a power hitter. During this period, Major League pitcher Babe Adams called him "one of the best catchers in the baseball world."[42] James A. Riley reports that, when playing for Santa Fe, Pettus once had 15 hits in 20 at bats, including three home runs, against Las Vegas, New Mexico.[43]

In 1909, he joined the Negro Leagues, playing first base for the Kansas City Giants. Pettus was also a solid fielder and fine baserunner, who could steal a base when necessary. According to Seamheads, he rates as the second best fielding first baseman of the Negro Leagues. The Hall of Miller and Eric declares his fielding prowess alone was statistically strong enough to rate as 75 percent as good as that of defensive stalwart Keith Hernandez.[44] By 1910, he was hitting cleanup for Frank Leland's Chicago Giants, batting .385 for the season.[45] Spending his career moving from team to team, Pettus was well regarded as a smart ballplayer and acquired the nickname "Old Reliable."[46] From 1912 on, his primary position switched from catcher to first base. Usually batting fifth behind Pop Lloyd on the Lincoln Stars, Pettus helped lead the team to the Eastern championship in 1916. Seamheads records his 1918 batting average as .432, when he played for multiple teams and, according to James A. Riley, he hit as high as .434 in 1920. In 1923, while still an active ballplayer, he contracted tuberculosis. His fans raised $230 to send him to a desert climate but he died within a year and never made it.[47] Bill Pettus was 40 years old.

While no significant statistics are available from his early vibrant days in the West, Seamheads credits Pettus with a lifetime batting average of .317 and an OPS of .869 in Negro League and one year of Cuban League action between 1909 and 1923. In seven games recorded against Major League competition, he hit .393 (Seamheads). There are four strong Hall of Fame matches among his five closest Major League Similarity Scores: Kirby Puckett, George Brett, Kiki Cuyler, and Roberto Clemente. Ignored in the *Courier* Poll, the McNeil Polls, and the Hall of Fame balloting, Pettus seems to have been lost in the fog of the dead-ball era. Maybe his nickname of "Old Reliable" didn't sparkle enough. But he was quite a player.

Buck O'Neil (see analysis in Chapter 19).

WAR Comparison of Negro League Hall of Famers and Candidates—First Base
All Leagues: Negro, Cuban, Mexican Leagues, vs. Major Leaguers and High Minors

Name	Years	WAR (per 162 games)	Career WAR
Buck Leonard	1933–48	7.8	31.1
Bill Pettus	1909–23	7.0	17.7
Mule Suttles	1923–44	6.4	34.6
Luke Easter	1947–48	5.5	3.5
Ben Taylor	1909–28	4.9	35.0
Edgar Wesley	1917–25	4.7	17.1

Name	Years	WAR (per 162 games)	Career WAR
George Carr	1920–34	3.3	13.9
*Buck O'Neil**	1937–48	1.4	3.1

Hall of Famers in bold. *24 Men Out candidates in italics.* WAR statistics courtesy of Seamheads.
*Buck O'Neil is proposed as one of *24 Men Out* by reason of his overall contribution to baseball.

WAR Summary—First Base: The Hall of Fame voters collectively nailed the voting for first base. All first basemen who have career WARs in excess of 20 are in the Hall of Fame. Luke Easter's short tenure in the Negro Leagues was brilliant, but the bulk of his career was spent in the Major League and high minor leagues. Neither Edgar Wesley nor Tank Carr had the longevity of high caliber play normally associated with the Hall of Fame. Bill Pettus is one of the Negro League's truly underrated stars and worthy of Hall of Fame consideration. While Buck O'Neil's WAR is set forth for comparative purposes, his Hall of Fame résumé is clearly not based upon his performance at first base alone (see Chapter 19).

CHAPTER 11

Second Base

It is ironic that Jackie Robinson became renowned at second base. He was actually the last in a long line of remarkable Negro League second basemen whose skill set, focused on great fielding and speed, granted them less consideration by the Hall of Fame voters than that of the other Negro Leaguers admitted to date. It has been theorized that the lesser talent pool available to the Negro Leagues led the best infielders with the strongest arms to play the left side of the infield. However, that is also true of Major League baseball. The keystone position was a strong one in the Negro Leagues and a smooth-fielding second baseman was much appreciated by the public. It is not often remembered that future Major League Hall of Famer Larry Doby started out as a second baseman in the Negro Leagues. Yet, pre–Negro Leaguer Frank Grant is the only second basemen from the Negro Leagues admitted to the Hall of Fame (other than super-utility player Martin Dihigo, who played second base as well as all of the other fielding positions, pitcher, and catcher). It is time to fill in this cavernous gap with three great players who sequentially succeeded each other as the paramount second sackers over the span of modern Negro League history:

Elwood "Bingo" DeMoss

Years	Games	Runs	Hits	HR	RBI	SB	BA	SLG	WAR per 162g	WAR Career
1910–30	934	617	789	4	315	190	.238	.289	3.5	19.9

Career statistics and WAR (Seamheads).

According to historian James A. Riley, DeMoss was "Unquestionably the greatest second baseman in black ball baseball for its first quarter century."[1] Playing with a toothpick in his mouth, Bingo DeMoss combined tremendous speed, agile hands, and clutch hitting. His career WAR of 19.9 is the second highest of any Negro League second baseman. Between 1920 and 1923, DeMoss also established three of the six highest WAR ratings accumulated by a Negro League second baseman in a single season.

Playing from 1910 through 1928, DeMoss fashioned a smooth fielding style (including a trademark "no look" throw to first base on the double play), which was emulated by those who came after him. A quick-handed and sure defender, DeMoss established the best Runs Saved Above Average (RSA) of any defensive player at second base in Negro League history—and the competition wasn't even close. He began his career playing on marginal teams as a shortstop but switched to second base after he hurt his arm pitching.[2] He was also a skilled contact hitter who developed a reputation as a player who could execute the hit-and-run play in the clutch as well as anyone.[3] According to historian John B. Holway, DeMoss is generally acknowledged as the best bunter in the history of the Negro League game. In the dead-ball era, this was an invaluable attribute. Hall of Fame umpire Jocko Conlon claimed he could "drop a bunt on a dime" and could drive the other team crazy with his ability to place the ball exactly where he wanted.[4]

Once he got on base, the fleet-footed DeMoss was a leading base stealer in his prime. On the basepaths, Seamheads ranks him second all-time for number of stolen bases and runs scored by a second baseman (behind only Weasel Warfield for whom Seamheads located almost 200 more games than DeMoss). He stole 34 bases in 50 games with the Indianapolis ABCs in 1915 (Riley), led the Western conference league in stolen bases in 1917 (Holway), and averaged 38

Bingo DeMoss, a preeminent second baseman during the 1920s, established the best defensive rating of any player in Negro League history. (Courtesy Helmar Brewing. Artist Sanjay Verma.)

stolen bases for each 162 games played over the course of his career (Seamheads).

DeMoss was also an aggressive leader who played for many championship teams, including the Indianapolis ABCs, whom he helped spark to the 1916 championship. Subsequently, he served six years as team captain for Rube Foster's Chicago American Giants as he led them to the first three Negro National League pennants in the early 1920s. Seamheads designated DeMoss the all-star second baseman a remarkable seven times: 1915, 1918, 1920, 1921, 1923, and in the Cuban winter leagues of 1916–17 and 1917–18. John B. Holway deemed DeMoss an all-star in four of the five years from 1915 to 1919. On a combined basis, that would make DeMoss an All Star for seven of the nine years from 1915 to 1923. After the 1924 season, Rube Foster sent DeMoss to the Indianapolis ABCs to stabilize a franchise which had lost too many players to raids. After his playing days, he became a tough, respected manager in the Negro Leagues for 15 years. He managed the Detroit Stars from 1926 to 1931 and later assumed that role with lesser quality teams.[5]

The rap on DeMoss is his low lifetime batting average, which according to Seamheads was a modest .238. However, there were seasons in which he hit over .300. James A. Riley calculates that he hit .316 in 1915 and over .300 in three other years between 1919 and 1929, although these statistics probably include batting against all competition. John B. Holway's statistics reflect that he hit .328 in 1915–16 Cuban winter ball and .308 against Major League competition in 1923. DeMoss's offensive numbers may also be underinflated by the fact that he spent much of his career in the dead-ball era, many of his prime statistics are lost because they occurred before the advent of the formal Negro Leagues in 1920, and by the fact that he played much of his career in an extreme pitcher's park, Chicago's Schorling Park.[6]

William F. McNeil ranks sometime second baseman Bill Monroe (see Chapter 16) above DeMoss at the keystone position solely based upon batting, while acknowledging that DeMoss was probably "the greatest defensive second baseman in Negro league history."[7] Because of his performance at the plate, DeMoss is also derided as a "poor man's Bill Mazeroski" on the stat heads' Hall of Merit website.[8] Moreover, his Similarity Score analysis does not provide any matches to Hall of Famers among the top 100 comparable Major League players.

Other pundits take a far more favorable view, recognizing that DeMoss was a critical component throughout his career of some of black ball's leading teams. Bill James, Negro League Hall of Famers Oscar Charleston and Pop Lloyd, as well as leading historians Dick Clark, Tweed Webb, Todd Bolton, and Robert W. Peterson, all regard DeMoss as the all-time best second baseman in black ball history. Veteran catcher Quincy Trouppe also includes DeMoss on his number one all-time team. In the McNeil Historians' Poll, DeMoss tied with Newt Allen as the greatest second baseman in Negro League history. Historians John B. Holway, James A. Riley, Brent Kelley, Chris Jensen, Larry Lester, Sammy J. Miller, Jim Overmyer, and the *Courier* Poll all deem DeMoss as one of the top two second basemen in Negro League history. (The *Courier* Poll, taken in 1952, ranked DeMoss behind only behind Jackie Robinson at second base. Robinson, who had played just one year in the Negro Leagues, was then at the height of his fame. In 1952, DeMoss had been retired for 20 years.) The SABR Poll included DeMoss as one of the top 40 Negro Leaguers of the 20th century.

While his offensive numbers may not be flashy, DeMoss was the type of core player whose fielding prowess served as the glue for many championship teams. As was true with Bill Mazeroski, defense and leadership can sometimes take a while to be recognized. Unlike Mazeroski, DeMoss' speed also allowed him to sparkplug a team more in the manner of a Lou Brock. His standing in career WAR among all Negro League second basemen, and rating as greatest fielding second baseman in Negro League history, are analytical evidence of his overall value. Deemed a retroactive All Star seven years in the Negro Leagues, it is time to put Bingo DeMoss in the Hall of Fame.

Newton "Newt" Allen

Years	Games	Runs	Hits	HR	RBI	SB	BA	SLG*	WAR per 162g	WAR Career
1922–47	1177	681	1465	29	290	154	.300	.382	4.1	26.8

Career Statistics (CNLBR), WAR (Seamheads). *Negro League games only.

One of the unsolvable quandaries of Negro League baseball is determining whether Newt Allen or Bingo DeMoss was the greater second baseman. Beginning in the early 1920s, Newt Allen would succeed DeMoss as the Negro game's leading defensive second sacker.[9] He was a fluid fielder and a speedy base runner who generally batted second for the

Kansas City Monarchs. During his 23 years with the Kansas City Monarchs, Newt Allen served as the heart and leader of a team that won 11 Negro League championships. For most of that period, Allen was the team captain, and his role further evolved when he assumed command and led the Monarchs to a championship in 1941 after their manager Andy Cooper suffered a stroke.

Bill James regards Allen as the all-time greatest Negro League fielder at the keystone position. Hall of Famer J.L. Wilkinson called him "the greatest second baseman who ever wore a spiked shoe. In his prime he never had an equal."[10] Buck O'Neil believed Allen had the best throwing arm ever of any Negro League second baseman. O'Neil claimed "He [Allen] could stand in center field and throw a ball over the grandstand behind home plate. I've never seen anyone throw that far."[11] His longtime Kansas City Monarch teammate Chet Brewer stated: "Newt was a real slick second baseman … he could catch the ball and throw it without looking. Newt used to catch the ball, throw it under his left

Newton "Newt" Allen, the Kansas City Monarchs' second baseman, played on 23 Negro League championship teams, more than any other player. He accumulated the highest career WAR of any Negro League second baseman. (Courtesy Helmar Brewing. Artist Scott Pedley.)

arm; it was just a strike to first. He was something! Got that ball out of his glove faster than anybody you ever saw."[12]

Seamheads' defensive statistics actually rate him in fourth place in terms of all-time fielding prowess among Negro League second basemen. Allen teamed up with Dobie Moore and later with Willie Wells to form two of the best double-play combinations in Negro League history. After a tragic accident ended Moore's career, Newt Allen even played a few years at shortstop.[13]

Allen was always proud of being a hard-nosed player who played by the rough rules of Negro League ball. In an interview in John B. Holway's *Voices from the Great Black Baseball Leagues* (2010), Allen talked about pitchers throwing at batters, routine fisticuffs on the field, and how players often used their spikes to take out an opposing fielder. He spoke of the time when he was permanently scarred by Oscar Charleston kicking a ball out of his hand. Allen told another story about receiving 18 stitches after Dave Malarcher spiked him and then, on a subsequent force-out play at second, throwing the ball directly into Malarcher's forehead, proving that he could give as well as he could take.[14]

At the plate, Allen was a line-drive hitter who, according to CNLBR, had a lifetime batting average of .300 against all levels of competition. He seems to have started his career as a switch-hitter, but then batted exclusively from the right side later on.[15] In his prime, he was regarded as one of the fastest players in Negro League ball, a consistent threat to steal. He knew how to get on base and was reputed for his ability to score runs.[16]

Later in his career, he was named to the East-West All-Star Game six times (1933, 1934, 1936, 1937, 1938, and 1941). This achievement is particularly astounding because the Monarchs played an independent schedule and were not even in the Negro National League in 1933, 1934 or 1936. John B. Holway has designated Allen an all-star in eight seasons between 1925 and 1939. ESPN named Newt Allen as their league MVP selection for 1937. Newt Allen was also selected to the Americanos All Star team in Cuba, in 1937–38.[17]

Most importantly, he played a key role on more Negro League championship teams than any other player. As captain of the Monarchs for most of his career, Allen played on five Negro National League championship teams and six Negro American League championship teams. He was also a member of 12 additional post-season and winter league championship teams.[18] In 34 Negro League World Series games, he compiled a .295 batting average.[19]

Newt Allen's recorded lifetime statistics are materially and adversely impacted by the fact that the Monarchs played a largely independent schedule from 1931 through 1936. The CNLBR estimates that 90 percent of his statistics are lost for 1933 and that thousands of his at-bats are missing for this entire period,[20] a period during which his selection to the East-West All-Star Game demonstrates that he was in his prime. Allen also played games in Mexico and joined a 10-month tour to the Orient, for which no statistics can be located.

Some have suggested that Newt Allen's lifetime batting average of .300 is too low to qualify for the Hall of Fame. Still, Allen hit .371 in the 1930 Negro League season and batted .361 in non-league games uncovered by the CNLBR. His batting average was .365 in the 1928–29 California Winter League and .423 in the 1929–30 California Winter League.[21] He also led the California Winter League in hits, doubles, and triples in 1929–30. In 19 games discovered by CNLBR against Major League pitching, Allen batted .367. As noted, many of his statistics for the prime of his career are missing because the Monarchs spent so many years playing independent ball. Finally, Newt Allen played well beyond his productive years. From 1928 to 1947 (when he turned 46), his lifetime batting average dropped 41 points and his slugging percentage dropped 100 points.[22] Nonetheless, it was probably because of his higher career batting average that it was Newt Allen, and not Bingo DeMoss, who made the 39-name final ballot in the 2006 Hall of Fame election.

A secondary issue with Newt Allen is his low WAR per 162 games of only 4.1, probably lower than it should be because he hung on so long. Yet his career WAR of 26.8 is still sufficient to place him first on the all-time list among Negro League second basemen. Similarity Scores also weigh in Allen's favor, as two of his ten closest Major League matches are Hall of Famers Red Schoendienst and Nellie Fox. A correct summation of Newt Allen's overall career is that he was the consummate professional, combining great defensive skills, solid hitting, and top speed. Beyond that, his record reflects leadership skills that led the Monarchs to many championships. His rare longevity on one team over the course of his career demonstrates his loyalty and value to his team. In his later career, he also served as manager of the Kansas City Monarchs and the Indianapolis Clowns.

Cited by many historians as one of the top two Negro League second basemen of all time, Newt Allen was deemed a Hall of Fame caliber player by leading historians James A. Riley, Leslie Heaphy, John B. Holway, Lyle K. Wilson, Larry Lester, and 57 percent of the Negro League veterans surveyed by William F. McNeil. William F. McNeil's Historians' Poll has Newt Allen tied with Bingo DeMoss as the second greatest second baseman in Negro League history. Allen was regarded as the Negro League's all-time best second baseman by fellow players Willie Wells, Buck O'Neil, and Double Duty Radcliffe. Newt Allen was ranked as an all-time second team player in the *Courier* Poll, in Larry Lester's 1993 player's survey, and by leading historian Robert Peterson. William F. McNeil places Allen on his all-time Negro League all-star team. If one were to design a Hall of Fame career for a second baseman, it would look like that of Newt Allen.

Sammy T. Hughes

Years	Games	Runs	Hits	HR	RBI	SB	BA	SLG	WAR per 162g	WAR Career
1929–46	513	361	705	38	180	38	.316	.453	4.2	13.4

Career statistics (CNLBR), WAR (Seamheads).

In 1937, Cum Posey, who had seen them all, called Sammy T. Hughes the best second baseman in Negro League history.[23] According to CNLBR, "Sammy Hughes is considered by historians as one of the best, if not the best, second baseman in Negro League baseball history. He had extremely quick reactions, excellent range, an outstanding glove, possessed a cannon for a throwing arm and rarely made an error."[24] In a career spanning from 1929 through 1946, the 6'3" infielder was a sure-handed graceful fielder.

Usually batting second in the lineup, Hughes was a contact hitter with extra base power, usually doubles. He was considered one of the best bunters and hit-and-run batters of his time.[25] One of the smartest base runners in the Negro Leagues, Hughes could also steal a base when necessary.[26] Seamheads records Hughes with a .309 batting average in Negro League games, and CNLBR logs Hughes as having a lifetime batting average of .316 and slugging percentage of .453 against all levels of competition. The CNLBR summarizes his overall value well: "When you combine hitting, exceptional defensive skills and his intelligent style of play, Sammy T. Hughes was a 'complete ball player.' He had virtually no weaknesses on or off the field."[27]

Sammy T. Hughes, lifetime batting average of .316, was regarded by many Negro League veterans as one of the best second basemen in the Negro Leagues, if not the best. He was deemed a Hall of Fame qualified player by 80 percent of the historians on the 2001 McNeil Pioneers Panel. (Courtesy Helmar Brewing. Artist Scott Pedley.)

Sammy Hughes began his career with the Louisville Black Caps of the Negro Southern League in 1929. When his team joined the Negro National League in 1931, John B. Holway's research reflects that he hit .421 for the year.[28] However, Louisville joined the NNL too late for Hughes to secure enough bats to qualify for the league batting championship.[29] By 1934, he was regarded as the leading second baseman in the Negro Leagues and was selected for the first of his seven consecutive selections (1934–40 including two games played in 1939) in the East-West All-Star Classic. Cum Posey, who selected his own all-star teams most years, deemed Hughes the all-star second baseman for all of the Negro Leagues each year from 1934 to 1938. In 1936, he was a member of the Negro National All-Star team, which won the *Denver Post* tournament, a team so dominant that it was not invited back.[30] Hughes batted .379 in the tournament.

Hughes had his strongest season in 1939, when he led the Elite Giants with a .372 batting average and .512 slugging percentage (Seamheads). During the 1930s and early 1940s, Hughes also played offseason in the California Winter League. In seven California Winter League (CWL) seasons, Hughes hit .384 and played on six teams that won the championship. His CWL batting average is higher than that of Hall of Famers Babe Herman, Oscar Charleston, and Turkey Stearnes. The CNLBR has found 10 games in which Hughes played against Major League pitching and in which he went 18 for 36 at the plate for a .500 batting average.[31] In a five game exhibition series held in 1936 against a white barnstorming team including Bob Feller and Rogers Hornsby, Hughes had 13 hits in 26 at-bats to compile a .500 batting average.[32]

In 1941, he played in the Mexican League with teammates Hilton Smith and Wild Bill Wright, compiling a batting average of .324.[33] After returning to the Negro Leagues in 1942, Hughes led his team in batting average and was one of three players (together with Roy Campanella and Dave Barnhill) designated for a tryout with the Pittsburgh Pirates, a tryout that never happened.[34] In 1942, Hughes was squeezed out by Ray Dandridge in a narrow vote in an East-West All-Star election, the first year since 1934 that Hughes came in second. However, John B. Holway deems him the true all-star worthy player at the keystone position in 1942.

After 1942, Hughes lost three potentially productive years serving in the military during World War II. When he attempted a comeback in 1946, it was not successful, and he retired from baseball that year. During his final season in 1946, too old to be considered for the majors, he mentored Junior Gilliam as his replacement.[35] A particularly interesting fact about Hughes is that he played most of his Negro League career with one team, the Elite Giants, and became instrumental to their success. Unlike many Negro League stars who jumped from team to team, Hughes helped stabilize an important Negro League franchise.

The list of world class veterans and historians who have included Hughes on their all-time teams is particularly impressive. In selecting Hughes first at the keystone position when he picked his all-time team in 1937, Cum Posey gave his reasoning: "Sammy was a good hitter, crack fielder, and real baserunner. [George] Scales could not cover enough ground at second base; DeMoss and Warfield were mediocre hitters."[36] Researcher John B. Holway has also rated him as the top all-time second baseman in Negro League history. Hughes has been deemed a rightful Hall of Famer by leading historians James A. Riley, William F. McNeil, Todd Bolton, Brent Kelley, Larry Lester, Lyle K. Wilson, and Sammy J. Miller. Hughes was selected as a Hall of Famer by 80 percent of the historians on the McNeil Pioneers Panel and 57 percent of the Negro League veterans in the McNeil Players' Poll. William F. McNeil deemed Hughes a first team second baseman on both his McNeil All-Time Negro League and Non-Major League All-Star teams, noting that he was "one of the greatest defensive second baseman ever to step on a field: a master of the double play."[37] Hughes was also a Roll of Honor selection in the 1952 *Courier* Poll.

Hughes has also been selected to the dream teams of such superstars as Monte Irvin, Cool Papa Bell, Buck Leonard, Quincy Trouppe, Buck O'Neil, Wild Bill Wright, Louis

Santop, and Larry Doby. Roy Campanella, who played with Jackie Robinson, claimed "Sammy T was the best second baseman I've seen."[38] Bill James believes Sammy Hughes' skills on the ballfield were comparable to those of Hall of Famers Ryne Sandberg and Barry Larkin.[39]

It is intriguing how close Sammy T. Hughes has come to selection to the Hall of Fame to date. He is one of only four players remaining from both the original 1971 Hall of Fame Negro League ballot and the 39-person final ballot in 2006 Negro League Special Election who is not yet admitted to the Hall of Fame. Perhaps the answer lies in the fact that Sammy T. Hughes is one of those players who was neither flashy nor had great power. He is also bedeviled by a significant amount of missing statistics, both in his Negro League and California Winter League careers. Finally, he also lost numerous productive seasons serving in World War II. Because of these voids, his career WAR of 13.4 does not reflect his true abilities, but still ranks him among the elite infielders. That Hughes played mostly in the Western conference, which we have seen was at a disadvantage in the early Negro League voting, may not have helped.

Similarity Scores reveal Hughes' strength. A remarkable 10 of his 15 closest Major League matches are Hall of Famers, including Honus Wagner and Eddie Collins. Among his seven closest matches are Mike "King" Kelly, Joe Mauer, Frankie Frisch, Jose Altuve and Roberto Alomar, all well rounded players who played critical roles on their teams.

Hughes was highly regarded by his peers and had no true weakness. He was a lifetime .300 hitter, an outstanding fielder, a winner who played on 13 separate championship teams, and a perennial all-star. How many Major Leaguers with seven consecutive all-star selections and a .300 lifetime batting average are not in the Hall of Fame? Sammy T. Hughes has no holes in his résumé for the Hall of Fame.

Worthy of Further Discussion

Frank "The Weasel" Warfield. At first glance, it is surprising that Warfield has not received more Hall of Fame support. The 5 ft. 7 in. Warfield was generally regarded as the best fielding second baseman in the Negro League's Eastern Conference during the 1920s.[40] Over a 19-year career stretching from 1914 through 1932, Warfield carries the fifth highest career WAR (15.9) of any second sacker in Negro League history. Playing in the East, he formed leading double-play combinations with both Dick Lundy and Pop Lloyd. Warfield had great range at his position and was selected as an all-star by Seamheads in five seasons: 1919, 1922, 1924, 1926, and in the Cuban Winter League of 1923–24. John B. Holway named him an All-Star in four separate seasons from 1918 to 1923. Cum Posey made Warfield his all-star selection in 1924 and 1925. The *Afro American* named him to their all-star team in 1929. Bill James regards him as having been a "complete defensive wizard."[41]

While he only carried a .264 lifetime batting average and had little power, he had great lead-off skills and generated many runs because he was superb at using the sacrifice and hit-and-run at the plate combined with a great batting eye, which led to many walks. He was also regarded as a savvy baserunner who, rather than relying on speed, was adept at studying and taking advantage of the opposition's weaknesses.[42] He had actually carried a solid .285 batting average for the first 14 years of his career, which dropped precipitously when he hit 52 points lower over his last 5 years.[43]

Weasel Warfield certainly had some stellar career highlights. He hit .423 in 1918, hit over .300 in five separate seasons, had a .300 career batting average in four seasons of Cuban winter ball, batted .290 in 27 games against Major League opposition, and played on 12 championship teams.[44]

Warfield's modest size belied a tough and competitive mean streak. Known for carrying a knife, he was caustic and not well regarded by his teammates, leading to his "Weasel" nickname. He argued constantly with umpires, demeaned his teammates, and fought with opposing players. Acting as a manager, he once ordered a player who ignored his slide signal to remove his uniform and sit in the stands.[45] It was Warfield who disfigured Oliver Marcelle when he bit off his nose in a fight over $5.[46] Another example is a threat he made to kill infielder Jake Stephens, a threat Stephens took seriously.[47]

He later developed into a successful manager who led the Hilldale Club to three consecutive pennants from 1923 to 1925, as well as a World Series victory in 1925. He was the starting second baseman, as well as the manager, on all of these teams. In nine years at the helm of various clubs, CNLBR has calculated that he achieved a .668 winning percentage against all competition, one of the best records of all time. His won-loss record of 35–8–1 (.778) in leading teams against Major League competition is particularly impressive.[48] Some say he mellowed as a manager, but perhaps his players were just terrified to perform badly for him. He died in 1932 at the age of 34, probably of tuberculosis,[49] when his career as a player-manager would certainly have continued.

Weasel Warfield was a Roll of Honor selection of the 1952 *Courier* Poll. Owner Ed Bolden, one of the Negro League's most important Negro League owners, included him on his All-Time All-Star team. Warfield was a second all-time team selection of veteran catcher Quincy Trouppe and historian Todd Bolton. Historian James A. Riley has labeled the "hustling middle infielder" an all-time great but failed to include him as one of his Hall of Fame candidates. Perhaps a reflection of Weasel's unpopularity as an individual (even apart from his nickname) is that his name is listed only sixth on the Roll of Honor for second basemen in the *Courier* Poll, and that he failed to receive a single player vote in the McNeil Players' Poll. While Warfield did make the pre-ballot in the 2006 Hall of Fame Special Election for the Negro Leagues, he was not included on the final ballot.

It seems that either his mediocre hitting, or his reputation for a vicious temper, caused his Hall of Fame support to dissipate over time. Similarity Score analysis does not boost his cause. Warfield's only close Hall of Fame match is the marginal Hall of Famer Johnny Evers. Not quite a Hall of Fame player on the field, Warfield might have made a stronger all-around case as a manager if he had lived. If baseball conduct and contribution to one's team is a factor, and it certainly is a designated criterion in Hall of Fame voting, Warfield's violent actions towards his teammates also detract from his record.

Charlie Grant is often mentioned among the leading Negro League second basemen of the pre–Negro Leagues. He made the preliminary ballot in the 2006 Special Election for the Negro Leagues but was not on the final ballot. Grant played from 1896 through 1916. John McGraw discovered Grant in spring training in Hot Springs, Arkansas, probably in 1900.[50] At that time, white and black teams trained side by side at Hot Springs. It was the light-skinned Grant who McGraw eventually tried to pass off in the Major Leagues as an Indian named "Chief Tokahoma" when he managed the Baltimore Orioles in 1901. Charles Comiskey, alerted to the ruse by fans who had seen Grant play in Chicago with the Columbia Giants, exposed the plan and brought it to an end.[51]

The reasons why McGraw wanted Grant were manifold. Grant was a smooth-fielding, solid-hitting second baseman who would not draw too much attention to himself. *Sporting Life* called him "a phenomenal fielder."[52] Like many of the leading players of his time, he seemed to always be a member of the era's best teams. He was on the infamous Page Fence Giants (1896–98), the Columbia Giants (in 1901), the Philadelphia Giants (in 1902), and played for the 1903 champion Cuban X-Giants and the 1906 champion Philadelphia Giants. Certainly, he was in demand by the top clubs of his era.

Yet even the scant statistics from his dead-ball era do not support a strong Hall of Fame case. While he may be among the smoother-fielding infielders of the pre–Negro League era, Seamheads records that he had a lifetime batting average of only .211, with little power. His defensive statistics collected on Seamheads rank him only as the tenth best fielding second baseman in the Negro Leagues. The prime of his career was relatively short, and he had lost his starting position by 1908, after which he played a few years with lower-tier clubs. His career WAR and WAR per 162 games are both negligible. His Similarity Score produces no Hall of Fame matches among the 100 closest Major Leaguers. In fact, some early plaudits he received appear to have confused him with his contemporary, second baseman Frank Grant, who is a rightful Hall of Famer.[53] While Bill James calls him the best Negro League ballplayer from the period 1900–1903, he acknowledges that he has done so without the benefit of seeing any statistics.[54]

Charlie Grant's Hall of Fame candidacy has little or no support from leading historians. Grant received not a single vote in either the 1952 *Courier* Poll or the 1971 ballot of the Special Committee on the Negro Leagues. No player or historian taking part in the McNeil Polls mentions his name. I've been unable to locate a single all-time Negro Leagues best player list that includes him. While it is true that he played for some of the leading teams of his time, the best argument in his favor seems to be that, if McGraw wanted him, he must have been great. In fact, Grant's interesting backstory as "Chief Tokahoma" seems to have propelled a solid but unspectacular infielder from the dead-ball to greater notoriety than is warranted by the facts.

Lorenzo "Piper" Davis is a sporadic all-time great selection of some leading historians and players. Nicknamed for his hometown of Piper, Alabama, Davis began his career in 1939 in the strong Birmingham Industrial League, where he led his team to five straight championships with a career batting average of .410.[55] In 1942, Davis joined the Birmingham Black Barons, where he would spend his entire Negro League career (1942–1950) and become a seven-time selection to the East-West All-Star Game. With the Black Barons, he played first base, shortstop, second base, and occasionally in the outfield. Piper Davis could just as easily be categorized as a super-utility player. But we include him here at second base, the position at which he made his reputation teaming with Artie Wilson to form a strong double-play combination, and where he played during all of his East-West All-Star Classic appearances.

It was Piper Davis who was the addition to the Black Barons that sparked them to the Negro American League pennant in 1942 and 1943. His best season at the plate was 1943, when James A. Riley reports that he hit .386 with solid power. ESPN deemed him the MVP of the NAL for 1943. According to Seamheads, Davis also hit .385 in 1945 and .392 in 1947. John B. Holway deemed him an all-star in 1943, 1947, and 1948. In a remarkable seven appearances in the East-West All-Star Game in the 1940s, he hit .308. (He was actually named to play in an eighth East-West Classic in 1945 but had been suspended for a fight.)[56]

In 1947, Piper Davis joined Satchel Paige in playing for Chet Brewer's Stars in a series of games against Bob Feller's and Ewell Blackwell's All-Stars. In six of those games, he led his team in hitting, with a .300 batting average, including a home run off Ed Lopat.[57] Named as player-manager of the Black Barons in 1948, he led his team to the Negro League World Series with a rookie Willie Mays on his roster. Piper Davis was in fact the very person who scouted and recruited Willie Mays to play for the Black Barons. Davis knew Willie Mays' father and had heard about his high school play. He ran into Mays one day when Mays was about 17 to whom he remarked: "if your daddy lets you play, have him call me…. His daddy called me and said, 'if he wants to play, let him play.' I said, okay have him out at the ballpark at twelve o'clock. Now, I needed an outfielder…. I started him off in the outfield just to see if he had a good arm … and he handled that pretty good."[58] For two years, Piper Davis mentored and taught Mays all he knew about the game. Mays credits Davis with being the most important person in his baseball career.[59] Piper Davis was a hard-nosed player and manager who once ran out to Willie Mays, who was lying on the ground moaning after having been hit on the arm by a pitch. Davis asked Mays if he could see first base and Mays nodded. Piper told him to "then get up and go down there … and when you get there, steal second." And Mays did.[60]

In 1949, Piper Davis led the Negro Leagues in hitting with a .378 batting average[61] and won his second ESPN award as MVP of the NAL. He was one of those players who played year-round, including barnstorming and stints in the California Winter League and the Puerto Rico Winter League, both of which named him to their league all-star teams. Altogether, Piper Davis played 24 years in the United States, Mexico, and the Caribbean. If that were not enough, Davis was also a two-sport star who spent five years during his baseball career playing guard for the Harlem Globetrotters.[62]

Back in 1945, Piper Davis had been one of the names on Branch Rickey's secret short list compiled to pick the first player to integrate the Major Leagues, a distinction that eventually went to Jackie Robinson, who was only 18 months younger.[63] In 1948, he was scouted but not signed by the New York Yankees. In 1950, despite the fact that he was 33 years old, he became the first African American player signed by the Boston Red Sox. Yet, Davis's big break was a mirage. The Red Sox assigned him to their Scranton minor league affiliate, where he hit .333 in his first year. When Scranton released him after only 15 games, he was leading the team in every offensive category.[64]

Unfortunately for Davis, history would prove that neither the Yankees nor the Red Sox were seriously interested in promoting an African American at that time. A subsequent discovery of the original Yankees scouting report on Piper Davis focused on the fact that his double-play partner Artie Wilson was also so good that there would be undue pressure on the Yankees to hire both of them. That scouting report, given to Yankees President Lee MacPhail in 1948, reads in part: "They are both [Artie Wilson and Piper Davis] good players…. If you hire one … they [unidentified committees favoring integration] will want you to hire another one."[65] As for the Boston Red Sox, it would not be until 1959 that they became the last Major League team to integrate, with the unremarkable Pumpsie Green, a player who cannot be deemed comparable to Piper Davis on any reasonable basis.

Davis concluded his playing career with five solid years with the Oakland Oaks of the Pacific Coast League, where he was named to their league all-star teams in 1954 and 1956.[66] After his playing days, he acted as a longtime scout for various Major League teams before he retired in 1986. He was also well respected throughout baseball. Negro League veteran Bill Greason called Davis the greatest manager he played for and one of the finest men he knew. He required his players to dress well, refrain from profanity, and to give maximum professional effort on the field and act as gentlemen off the field.[67]

During his career, Piper Davis was a member of 16 championship teams, appeared in three Negro League World Series, and in three Caribbean World Series tournaments. The CNLBR calculates that his lifetime batting average in the Negro Leagues was .348. Davis also had decent power, having led the Birmingham Industrial League (1942) and the California Winter League (1947) in home runs, and the Negro American League (1948) in RBIs.[68] ESPN designated him as the MVP of the American Negro League in both 1943 and 1949. One of the top Negro League players of the 1940s era, Piper Davis was an all-time all-star selection of historians Brent Kelley, Lyle K. Wilson, Eric Newland, and of players Art "Superman" Pennington and Earl Wilson, Sr. Monte Irvin thought enough of Davis to name him as one of the five greatest shortstops in Negro League history. He was also named to the all-time Negro League All-Star first team in a 1993 poll by the members of the Negro League Baseball Museum.

Piper Davis's Similarity Score analysis reveals an amazing 28 Hall of Famers included among his closest 100 Major League matches, the closest of whom are Frankie Frisch, Home Run Baker and Jackie Robinson. Davis' career WAR per 162 games exceeds that of all Negro League second basemen other than Larry Doby and Bonnie Serrell. A leader and winner at all levels of ball at which he was permitted to play, it sure feels as though Piper Davis would have been as successful in the Major Leagues. In fact, author Allan Barra noted that most of the players and managers he talked to believed, if given a full opportunity in the Major Leagues, "Piper could have been a Hall of Famer."[69] Let's not forget that Piper Davis was also the man who discovered, recruited, and nurtured a guy named Willie Mays.

Bonnie a/k/a Barney Serrell. Prior to the integration of Major League ball in the 1940s, the Negro Leagues saw much of their talent lured away by foreign leagues. A case in point is Bonnie Serrell a/k/a "The Vacuum Cleaner" (before Brooks Robinson appropriated the nickname). The speedy, slender infielder anchored the Kansas City Monarchs infield in the early 1940s. John B. Holway asserts that in 1942 the line-drive hitter compiled a batting average of .400 and led the league in hitting. Serrell followed that up by batting .556 in the 1942 World Series victory over the Homestead Grays. In 1944, he compiled a .321 average and played in his only East-West Classic (he went 2 for 3). He also had great range and a strong arm, making him a valuable contributor in the field. Seamheads has designated Serrell as the all-star second baseman for all of the Negro Leagues in 1942 and 1944. According to James A. Riley, Bonnie Serrell was greatly disappointed when the Dodgers chose Jackie Robinson over him because Serrell was regarded as the better player.[70]

Serrell spent the next 12 years (except for a short return to the Monarchs) playing in Mexico, Cuba, Puerto Rico, and Cuba, with stops in the minor leagues. While many of his statistics are missing from this period, William F. McNeil has recorded his overall Mexican League batting average as .311. Having participated in multiple all-star games in various venues, Serrell finished his career batting .376 in the Arizona-Mexican League in 1958.[71] In only five years of play in the Negro Leagues, Seamheads has calculated his lifetime batting average as .323. His value as a player is demonstrated by the fact that his WAR per 162 games of 8.5 is the second highest of any second baseman in Negro League history, trailing only Larry Doby. Veterans Bill Cash and Art Pennington even picked Serrell as their all-time best second baseman. Still not convinced that this guy could play? His three closest Major League Similarity Scores (in order) are Hall of Famers Charlie Gehringer, Honus Wagner, and Nap Lajoie. If the Major Leagues had integrated five years earlier, we could be talking about a Hall of Fame player.

Marvin "Tex" Williams. Williams is an extremely intriguing and overlooked player who played primarily at second base, but also manned the corner infield slots and the outfield. Known mostly to Negro League obsessives, Williams was a solid hitter with power who played all over the Western hemisphere from 1943 through 1961. According to James A. Riley, he hit .388 in 1944 for the Philadelphia Stars in a year he was named to the East-West All-Star Classic. Together with Jackie Robinson and Sam Jethroe, Williams was one of the three players brought to Boston in 1945 for a "tryout" with the Boston Red Sox. When the Red Sox showed no interest in the three players, he resumed his play in the Negro Leagues. He was hitting .393 with a .732 slugging percentage when he jumped to the Mexican League during the middle of the 1945 season. In Mexico, Williams hit .362 and slugged .633 for the balance of the year.[72] Regarded as only an average fielder with normal speed, Williams' hitting nevertheless propelled him to be named an All Star in various leagues ranging from the minor leagues to Venezuela in at least 13 different seasons.[73]

He played for dozens of teams in Mexico, Venezuela, Canada and the minor leagues from 1945 through 1961. CNLBR has identified at least 57 teams Williams played for between 1943 and 1963.[74] Some highlights of his career include hitting .381 in Mexico in 1948, twice leading the Venezuelan Winter League in doubles, winning batting titles in Mexico in 1952 (.401) and in Vancouver in 1954 (.360), a home run and RBI championship in Mexico (1952), and batting .322 in the Texas League in 1956.[75] As late as 1959, he led the Mexican Pacific Coast League in home runs (29) and RBIs (109).[76] According to CNLBR, Williams compiled a career batting average of .326 as he won four batting championships, three home run titles and led his league in slugging percentage and RBIs four times each.[77] His lifetime batting average over only three seasons he played in the Negro Leagues was .360 and Williams averaged 147 RBIs for each 162 games played (Seamheads). Imagine this type of power from a second baseman. His WAR per 162 games of 6.5 established in three seasons of the Negro League play is truly elite.

One of only 29 men selected to the Hall of Eric and Miller as the best all-time Negro League players, Marvin Williams was also picked as an all-time Negro League selection by leading Puerto Rico baseball historian Eduardo Valero. His closest Major League Similarity Score match is another second baseman: Rogers Hornsby. Unfortunately, his few years in the American Negro Leagues, combined with his time in the minor leagues, do not meet the minimum 10-year Hall of Fame requirement for domestic play. But the talent which the Boston Red Sox passed over in 1945 was genuinely there.

WAR Comparison of Negro League Hall of Famers and Candidates—Second Base
All Leagues: Negro, Cuban, Mexican Leagues, vs. Major Leaguers and High Minors

Name	Years	WAR (per 162 games)	Career WAR
Larry Doby*	1942–47	9.8	8.8
Bonnie Serrell	1941–45	8.5	6.6

Name	Years	WAR (per 162 games)	Career WAR
Piper Davis	1942–48	7.1	7.1
Marvin Williams	1943–45	6.5	3.4
Frank Grant	1891–1907	4.9	1.6
Sammy T. Hughes	1932–46	4.2	13.4
Newt Allen	1922–47	4.1	26.8
Bingo DeMoss	1910–28	3.5	19.9
Charlie Grant	1897–1913	2.4	1.7
Frank Warfield	1914–32	2.3	15.9

Hall of Famers in bold. *24 Men Out candidates in Italics*. WAR statistics courtesy of Seamheads.
*Admitted to Hall of Fame based upon Major League performance.

WAR Summary—Second Base: Second base is the neglected orphan of the Negro Leagues. Larry Doby, who would be converted to an outfielder when he played in the Major Leagues, was well on his way to a Hall of Fame career as the best second baseman in Negro League history. Bingo DeMoss and Newt Allen, the only second baseman with career WAR ratings over 19, are the leading choices for Hall of Fame admission at the keystone position. The Hall of Fame candidacy of Newt Allen, who sported .300 lifetime batting average, is also based upon his overall contribution to winning teams and enhanced by his overall reputation among the public and fellow players. The extraordinary acclaim heaped upon Sammy T. Hughes by his peers and historians should not be ignored. Piper Davis, Marvin Williams and Bonnie Serrell clearly had Major League abilities but were unlucky not to be chosen as the color line fell in the late 1940s. Piper Davis had the dual misfortune to be signed by the Red Sox, a team paying only lip service to integration. As a result, their careers were split between the Negro Leagues and PCL/foreign venues, where they all became stars but never really had a chance to develop Hall of Fame credentials in a consistent forum.

CHAPTER 12

Shortstop

The greatest Negro League shortstops are (with apologies to Honus Wagner) a stronger collective grouping than their counterparts from the Major Leagues in the pre–World War II era. In fact, the postwar assemblage continued this tradition. Ernie Banks, a Negro League youngster who played most of his career in the Major Leagues, would become the prototype for the power-hitting shortstop of the modern era. Hank Aaron was a skinny 18-year-old shortstop for the Indianapolis Clowns of the Negro Leagues in 1952 before the Braves bought his contract and converted him to an outfielder. Willie Mays began his career in sandlot ball as a shortstop before the Birmingham Black Barons moved him to the outfield. As such, these future Major League stars were simply representative of the best shortstops from Negro League history. Only two Negro League shortstops, Pop Lloyd and Willie Wells, are currently in Cooperstown. Those shortstops who should join them are discussed in the following.

Richard "Dick" Lundy

Years	Games	Runs	Hits	HR	RBI	SB	BA	SLG	WAR Per 162g	WAR Career
1916–37	948	615	1116	51	653	110	.319	.454	6.4	37.4

Career statistics and WAR (Seamheads).

"King Richard," in the recorded opinion of John McGraw, was the greatest shortstop who ever lived, save Honus Wagner.[1] Playing in the 1920s, squeezed between the eras of Pop Lloyd and Willie Wells, Dick Lundy was regarded as one of a triumvirate of great Negro League shortstops in the modern era. Seamheads ranks his overall fielding ability at shortstop as second only to Dobie Moore

John McGraw regarded "King Richard" Lundy as the game's greatest shortstop, after Honus Wagner. Lundy was a defensive marvel who also sported a .319 lifetime batting average. He has the highest career WAR of any Negro League position player not in the Hall of Fame. (Courtesy Helmar Brewing. Artist Scott Pedley.)

in all of Negro League history. Lundy played deep in the hole, using his great range and strong arm to dazzle crowds by throwing out runners from short left field. In fact, when Lundy joined the Pop Lloyd–led Bacharachs in 1924, Lloyd moved himself to second base in recognition of Lundy's superior fielding prowess.[2] Satchel Paige regarded Lundy as the greatest defensive shortstop in Negro League history: "It looked like he knowed where you were going to hit the ball. He was just like Lou Boudreau."[3] In the words of Napoleon Cummings, Negro League pitcher: "Lundy could go behind second base and get a ball and throw you out, go behind third base and do the same thing. There was no one in the Big Leagues could beat Lundy playing shortstop. Nobody. Hans Wagner? Yeah, I've seen him play…. I've seen shortstops come and go, but Dick Lundy was my favorite."[4]

As a batter, Lundy was a switch-hitting contact hitter with moderate power, reputed for his wicked line drives.[5] Seamheads determined that during a 21-year playing career stretching from 1916 to 1937, he had a career batting average of .319. According to CNLBR, Lundy hit over .300 in 15 of his 21 seasons in the Negro Leagues. In 1921, he led the Eastern Colored League (ECL) in hitting with a .361 average and then topped that with a .381 average in 1932. John B. Holway has deemed Lundy his 1921 Fleet Walker (MVP) award winner. Lundy also played extensively in the Cuban Winter League, where he compiled a lifetime batting average of .341 over nine seasons. That batting average is the third-highest lifetime batting average in Cuban Winter League history, trailing only those of Cristóbal Torriente and Alejandro Oms.[6] In 1926–27 in the Cuban Winter League, Lundy batted .410. In 16 exhibition games against Major League competition over the course of his career, Lundy hit .396.[7] Lundy was not just a slap hitter, as he had enough power to lead the ECL with 24 home runs in 1924. He was also a competent base stealer who led the Cuban Winter League in stolen bases in 1924–25.[8]

Dick Lundy's career WAR of 37.4, which includes only two of his nine Cuban Winter League seasons, is the highest of any Negro League position player not in the Hall of Fame.

Between 1920 and 1935, Dick Lundy played on 10 different championship teams in the United States and Cuba, including the Atlantic City Bacharachs in 1926 and 1927,[9] where he paired with Oliver Marcelle to form an impregnable left side of the infield. In the 1926 Negro League World Series, Lundy hit .325 and stole 6 bases in 11 games. In 1929, he joined the Baltimore Black Sox as a player-manager to create the infamous "Million Dollar Infield" (because that's what they were worth, not what they were paid) with Jud Wilson (1b), Frank Warfield (2b) and Oliver Marcelle (3b), a team he led to the Negro American League championship.

Seamheads has deemed Lundy an all-star four times. John B. Holway regards him as an all-star in seven years between 1919 and 1931. John B. Holway also awarded Lundy his Fleet Walker Award as his league's MVP in both 1921 and 1926. Lundy was also deemed the MVP of the ECL by ESPN for 1926. He was tagged as an all-star by the Pittsburgh *Courier* in 1925 and 1929. Cum Posey, who did not make selections every year, named Lundy to his All-Star units in 1931 and 1932. That he was also well respected by his peers is demonstrated by the fact that he was named team captain as early as 1923 and was a player-manager from 1926 to 1928. He led his team to two Negro League World Series during that time, with his team falling short both times. When the East-West All-Star Game began in 1933, Lundy was selected to the first two games as his career reached its denouement.

His last playing season was 1937 when he hit .310 for the Newark Eagles at the age of 39.[10] He concluded his baseball career as a full-time manager of the Newark ball club, serving a total of 33 years in Negro ball. In Newark, he mentored youngsters Monte Irvin and Ray Dandridge, among others. He managed as he played, with the full respect of the players.

According to veteran "Bunny" Downs, "On and off the field he was the type of fellow everybody took a liking to, always a gentleman, with real baseball courage and fighting instinct."[11] His performance as a manager was beyond solid. In 10 seasons, he had a winning percentage as a manager of .613 in Negro League games and won three pennants. His 293 wins as a manager ranks him seventh all-time in that category. Only Vic Harris, Oscar Charleston, and Andy Cooper managed their teams to more Negro League pennants. In 1940, Effa Manley fired Dick Lundy from Newark to save expenses,[12] after which he managed several lesser teams through 1955.

After his health failed, Lundy returned to his home state of Florida where he became a shoeshine man in the Jacksonville train station. Veteran Nap Cummings, who regarded Lundy as better than Pop Lloyd, stated that he once tipped him $5 for a shine.[13] Dick Lundy died broke in 1965 and Effa Manley, the former co-owner of the Newark Eagles, who had fired Lundy, sent the $50 necessary to bury the shortstop from the Negro League's "Million Dollar Infield."[14]

Cum Posey selected Dick Lundy as a first team player on his 1937 All-Time Negro League team. Lundy was selected as a Hall of Famer by 96 percent of the voters in the McNeil Historians' Poll and 84 percent of the voters in the McNeil Players' Poll. He was cited first on the Roll of Honor in the *Courier* Poll, and was one of two shortstops selected to William F. McNeil's 1926–1950 All-Time Negro League team. Leading historians James A. Riley, Dick Clark, Todd Bolton, Leslie Heaphy, John B. Holway, Brent Kelley, Larry Lester, Jerry Malloy, William F. McNeil, Lawrence Hogan, and Robert F. Peterson have all opined that Dick Lundy is Hall of Fame qualified. Great Negro League veterans such as Chappie Johnson, Monte Irvin, Quincy Trouppe, Larry Doby, and Buck O'Neil have deemed Lundy one of the top shortstops in Negro League history.

Lundy is one of only four players, both the original 1971 Negro League Hall of Fame ballot and the final 2006 Negro League Special Hall of Fame ballot, who have not been inducted to the Hall of Fame. Screening and Voting member of the 2006 Hall of Fame ballot Jim Overmyer acknowledges that he was surprised that Lundy was not selected at that time.[15] Another committee member believed that, based upon the discussions, Lundy should have been selected and probably achieved at least a 50 percent vote on the committee.[16] Lundy's two closest matches in terms of Major League Similarity Scores are those of Hall of Famers Arky Vaughan and Derek Jeter. Honus Wagner and Barry Larkin are also among his ten closest matches.

Lundy was summed up by Bill James: "Probably a better fielder than Lloyd, certainly a better fielder than Wells, and regarded by some as a better all-around player."[17] Buck O'Neil was more succinct in his view of Dick Lundy: "Great shortstop. Great, great shortstop."[18]

So let's summarize the baseball career of Dick Lundy: one of the greatest defensive shortstops in Negro League history, a .319 lifetime hitter, won a batting championship and a home run crown, a perpetual winner, esteemed in player and historian polls (96 percent in the McNeil Historians' Poll!!), all-star selection in almost every year between 1919 and 1932, designated league MVP four times, 37.4 WAR rating (even with a massive amount of missing statistics),[19] selected to Cum Posey's all-time first team, and one of the best managers in the Negro Leagues. Moreover, he often toiled from 1926 through 1937 in the dual role of player-manager, a versatility that saved his team a roster spot. Aside from the scandal and steroid-tarnished players, "King Richard" Lundy is probably the greatest American ballplayer eligible for Cooperstown who is not currently enshrined. This result represents a truly shocking omission from the Hall of Fame.

Grant "Home Run" Johnson

Years	Games	Runs	Hits	HR	RBI	SB	BA	SLG	WAR per 162g	WAR Career
1893–1922*	590	483	763	99	333	74	.316	.506	10.1	25.2

Career statistics (CNLBR), WAR (Seamheads). *Johnson's regular career ended in 1914 but he played three games with Buffalo in 1922.

Before there was a Pop Lloyd, Grant "Home Run" Johnson was the greatest shortstop in black ball history. A right-handed contact hitter at the turn of the century, the 5 ft. 10 in. Johnson started his career as a shortstop and segued to second base in the latter portion of his career. While he was good fielder with excellent range, he was mostly known as a natural hitter with a disciplined swing and for the fact that he rarely struck out.[20] A crowd favorite, he was regarded as a hustling and unselfish teammate who rarely argued with umpires. By at least 1893, Johnson was starting at shortstop for the semi-professional Findlay Sluggers, an outstanding regional team in the Midwest. It was while playing for Findlay that Johnson, as a 20-year-old minor leaguer, acquired the nickname "Home Run" when he himself reported that he hit 40 home runs.[21]

In a short stint with the Columbia Giants in 1894, he batted .356, with a .567 slugging percentage.[22] Together with Bud Fowler, Johnson formed the Page Fence Giants in

Grant "Home Run" Johnson was probably the greatest Negro League player in the early 20th century. His WAR per 162 games is second highest of any Negro League player ever, trailing only that of Dobie Moove. (Courtesy Helmar Brewing. Artist Scott Pedley.)

1895, batting .471 for a team that won at a .766 clip.[23] Fowler became the player/manager and Johnson served as shortstop/captain for what became the greatest Negro League team up to that time. In 1896, the Page Fence Giants defeated the other leading black team in the Midwest, the Cuban X-Giants, in 10 of the 15 meetings and claimed the title of "Colored World's Champions."[24] In 1897, the Page Fence Giants stepped it up even more and dominated all opposition with an astounding win-loss record of 125–12 (.912). While statistics from this era are virtually nonexistent, researcher Ray Nemec did uncover 11 games played by Grant Johnson for the Page Fence Giants in 1895, in which he led the team with a .636 batting average.[25] Johnson was also not averse to taking a turn on the mound. He was reputed to be an exceptional submarine-type pitcher who compiled a known record of 11–2 for the Page Fence team.[26]

When Page Fence dropped their sponsorship after 1898, Johnson continued to perform for many great Negro League teams through 1916, sometimes compiling a batting average in the .400 range. In 1899, many of the Page Fence Giants followed Johnson to the Chicago Columbia Giants, which team proceeded to win the Western Championship but lost a one-game playoff to the Cuban X-Giants despite Johnson's home run. In 1903, Johnson jumped to the Cuban X-Giants, who won the Eastern Championship that year, although they subsequently lost a championship series to Sol White's Philadelphia Giants, in 1904. He next played for the Philadelphia Giants who won the Eastern Championship in 1905 and 1906. In 1909, Johnson captained the Brooklyn Royal Giants to the Eastern Championship.

From 1910 to 1913, Johnson played for the Leland Giants and the Chicago American Giants and was on the winning championship team each year. In 1913, he switched to second base for the New York Lincoln Giants to form one of the great shortstop–second base combinations in baseball history with a young John Henry Lloyd. He batted cleanup behind Lloyd as they won the Eastern championship and topped Rube Foster's Chicago American Giants in a 12-game playoff. According to CNLBR, Johnson's batting average in the 1913 season was .452, and he then helped lead the Lincoln Giants to victory in the Championship Series. By that time, his nickname had morphed into "Dad."

While few would maintain Johnson was a better all-around player than Pop Lloyd, Chris Cobb of the Hall of Merit has pointed out[27] that a comparison of their batting averages when they were teammates for four seasons is instructive (because they faced the same opponents):

1910	Johnson .397	Lloyd .417
1911	Johnson .374	Lloyd .476
1912	Johnson .413	Lloyd .376
1913	Johnson .371	Lloyd .363

Johnson played again for the Lincoln Giants in 1914 and moved on to the Mohawk Colored Giants in 1915. After a failed attempt with Sol White to form a "Negro Baseball League" in 1917,[28] Johnson, who always kept himself in great shape, continued to play and manage professionally for lesser teams until 1932, when he was 58 years old. Having become blind in his old age, he died at age 88 of heart failure after surgery.[29]

In addition to his summers in American ball, Johnson also played in the Cuban Winter League on a regular basis from 1903 to 1912. Twice he participated in an American-Cuban series, playing against Major League stars. In 1910, he became notorious in Cuba when he hit .412 for Habana playing a series against the Detroit Tigers, outhitting Ty Cobb and Sam Crawford.[30] His best Cuban year was 1912, when he hit .410, led the league in hits, and captained the Habana Reds to the Cuban winter ball championship.[31]

Despite his sobriquet, "Home Run" Johnson demonstrated little power during the many years he played Negro League ball. It was as a consistent batsman that he excelled. The CNLBR reports that Johnson had a lifetime batting average of .316 against all opposition, .327 against top level Negro League teams, and .325 in the Cuban Winter League. Seamheads records five years that Johnson hit over .400 for a team, including for the New York Lincoln Giants in 1914, when he was 41 years old. His performance against Major League competition was consistent with his performance in black ball. In ten exhibition games against the Philadelphia Athletics, he hit .457, with the majority of his at-bats against Chief Bender and Eddie Plank.[32]

Such was Grant Johnson's renown as a hitter that Sol White asked him to contribute the chapter on hitting to his legendary *History of Colored Baseball*. (Rube Foster was asked to write the chapter on pitching.) Johnson's principal advice was to be patient and wait for a good pitch.[33]

As was true of many great players of the pre–Negro Leagues era, Grant Johnson left few verifiable statistics. According to CNLBR calculations, when he was in the prime years of his 20s, Johnson played at least 2,500 games from 1893 to 1914. During this period, box scores for only 569 games have been located. His entire performance in the Florida Hotel League, most data from the early 1890s, and all games after 1914 are also missing.[34] In an interview with this author, 2006 Hall of Fame voter Todd Bolton opined that Johnson's candidacy for the Hall was adversely affected because the statistics supporting his case were not as solidly documented as those of other candidates.[35] As noted on the Hall of Eric and Miller website: "Sadly, however, Johnson appears to have received scant attention from the Hall voters, and his absence is glaring. He played a very long time ago, and the lore from his days didn't travel nearly as well as that from those still alive to tell the tales."[36]

Yet, even with the limited statistics available from his era, his career WAR of 25.2 is one of the highest of any Negro League infielder not in the Hall of Fame. And his WAR per 162 games on the collected data is 10.1, tied with Josh Gibson for the second highest WAR rating of any player in Negro League history.

Even more importantly, Grant Johnson was a key part of five of the greatest teams in Negro League history. These teams were the 1895–1898 Page Fence Giants, the 1903 Cuban X-Giants, the 1905 Philadelphia Giants, the 1910 Chicago Leland Giants, and the 1913 New York Lincoln Giants. All of these teams won championships. During his career, Johnson played for 26 championship teams, often serving as captain for those teams. In seven of those years, he served a dual capacity as manager, winning a championship in every one of those years.[37]

Seamheads declared Home Run Johnson an all-star at his position in 1897, 1899, 1902, 1905, 1906, 1907–08 (Cuba), 1908–1909 (Cuba), and 1910. Seamheads also designated him as the Top Position Player (MVP) for all of black ball in four separate seasons between 1906 and 1910. Grant Johnson was selected as an all-time Negro League all-star by leading historians John B. Holway and William F. McNeil and Negro League veterans Ben Taylor and Dizzy Dismukes. He has been deemed a Hall of Fame caliber player by historians James A. Riley, James E. Overmyer, Jerry Malloy and 28 percent of those voting in the McNeil Historians' Poll. Grant Johnson's closest match to a Major Leaguer under Similarity Scores calculated by Seamheads is Hall of Famer Luke Appling.

Home Run Johnson was one of the few players selected to the statistician's Hall of Merit at the time of the 2006 Negro League Special Election who was not eventually selected for the Hall of Fame. When the Hall of Merit submitted their letter of recommendation to the Hall of Fame voters in the 2006 Negro League Special Election, they strongly argued in support of Grant Johnson:

> We believe that Grant Johnson was the first great shortstop in black baseball. Parlaying his ample athleticism into good defense and combining it with one of the most potent bats of his generation, Johnson blazed the trail that John Henry Lloyd and John Beckwith would soon follow. Because of the lack of published documentation of his early career, our deliberations relied heavily on anecdote and reputation. But the oral record, and what little data exist, are very clear: Johnson was … a strong, clutch player who shone in all aspects of the game and provided leadership to match his accomplishments. Grant Johnson won election to the Hall of Merit … placing 44 of the 48 ballots cast.[38]

The Hall of Fame voters ignored this advice.

Grant "Home Run" Johnson was one of the greatest players of the black dead-ball era and one of the game's first true superstars in the pre–Negro Leagues. He was a consummate professional, a true leader, and a consistent winner. Joe Dimino of the Hall of Merit: "Johnson was *arguably the finest player at the turn of the 20th century*, a terrific slugger during the dead-ball era, he also possessed impressive strike zone judgment, was an outstanding contact hitter and an excellent fielder [italics added]."[39] Johnson was a perennial all-star, one of the great line-drive hitters of his time, always hustled, and was a leading infielder at his position who was sought out and signed by all of the best teams of the early 1900s. He played 21 seasons at the highest level of black ball available to him from the age of 21 through 42. He was one of the best at his position from 1893 right through 1914. Teamed with a young John Henry Lloyd at shortstop, their keystone combination may have well been the best in all of Negro League history. His role as player, manager, and even as a pioneer in the pre–Negro League era is astounding.

Again, the man was either a starting shortstop or second baseman, and often captain or manager, for 26 championship teams in 21 years. Johnson is one of only three pre–Negro League finalists on the 39-name final ballot of the 2006 Negro League Special election who was not elected to the Hall of Fame. Johnson seems to have been a victim of the fact that some on the 2006 Committee felt it had admitted enough pre–Negro Leaguers (Sol White, Frank Grant) and needed to focus on the players from the Negro League era, for which more verifiable statistics were available.[40] The documentary evidence supporting Grant Johnson may not be as extensive as that which exists for other players, but it is more than sufficient. There is no convincing reason why Grant "Home Run" Johnson does not belong in the Hall of Fame.

Walter "Dobie" Moore

Years	Games	Runs	Hits	HR	RBI	SB	BA	SLG	WAR per 162g	WAR Career
1920–26	576+	407	920	50	377	58	.352	.526	10.2	35.6

Career statistics (CNLBR), WAR (Seamheads).

Walter "Dobie" Moore was a power hitter with a lifetime .352 average. Bill James calls him "the best 230-pound shortstop in baseball history." Born in 1896 and growing up on the sandlots of Atlanta, Dobie Moore joined the Army and was recruited to play for the 25th Infantry Regiment in 1916 at the age of 20. There, he played for four and a half years on the infamous "Buffalo Soldiers," an all-black military team assigned to the 25th Infantry Regiment. That team, commonly known as the "Wreckers," included future Hall of Famers Andy Cooper and Bullet Rogan, as well as coming Negro League stars Hurley McNair, Oscar "Heavy" Johnson, and William "Big C" Johnson. The Wreckers played in the Post League (a military league), the Honolulu City League, against barnstorming Pacific Coast League teams, and against all-star teams comprised of Major League and minor league players.[41]

The Wreckers constituted a dominating dynasty in amateur and military baseball, with their results carried in black newspapers throughout the country.[42] They were not only the best team in the Armed Forces, but possibly the best baseball club in the nation. Between 1916 and 1922, the Wreckers team fielded 16 players who would go on to join the Negro National League after it was formed in 1920.[43] While only a few statistics survive from that team, it is known that Moore played a significant role. (Seamheads has uncovered only nine box scores for the Wreckers, hardly a representative sample.)

Although statistics may be lacking for the Wreckers, the oral testimony is not. According to Joe Taylor, an outfielder, Moore "was a sensation even then. He was a great hitter, base runner, and a *sensational* shortstop. I don't ever recall seeing Moore make an error. I never saw Honus Wagner play, but I don't think Wagner could have been any better than Moore."[44] Catcher Frank Duncan, commenting on the fact that Moore became a great bad ball hitter because umps called so many strikes against them when the Wreckers barnstormed: "I've seen them throw a curve ball to him and break in the ground, bounce up, and he hit it all upside the fence."[45]

After the regiment moved to Hawaii, they took on any team willing to play and won the undisputed Hawaiian championship every year through 1918. Casey Stengel, who saw the Wreckers play in New

Walter "Dobie" Moore compiled a .352 batting average and .526 slugging average. His career ended abruptly in 1926 when, after a fight, he was shot in the leg by his girlfriend as he jumped off a second story whorehouse balcony. (Courtesy Helmar Brewing. Artist Scott Pedley.)

Mexico, claimed that he thought they were as good as any Major Leaguer outfit. Stengel purportedly recommended several players to J.L. Wilkinson, who was then forming the Kansas City Monarchs for the newly established Negro National League.[46] In the summer of 1920, with the season already well under way, Dobie Moore allegedly paid $150 to secure his release from the Army and joined the inaugural season of the Kansas City Monarchs.[47] He was already 24 years old. And that's where the recorded magic began.

According to CNLBR, between the remaining part of the 1920 season and 1926, Moore established a career .352 batting average and .526 slugging percentage against all opposition.[48] In 1922 and 1923, Moore compiled WAR ratings of 5.9 and 6.7, respectively, two of the three highest WAR marks ever earned by a middle infielder in a single Negro League season. (From 1921 to 1924, Moore established four of the ten highest seasonal WAR ratings of any shortstop in Negro League history.) In 1922, in 76 Negro League games, Moore hit .383, with 8 home runs, 66 RBIs, with a .546 slugging average. The 1923 season was a replica, as Moore compiled a .366 batting average, 8 home runs, 82 RBIs, and a slugging percentage of .535 in 95 games.[49] From 1923 through 1926, Moore served as a critical cog in a Kansas City Monarchs team that won four straight National League championships, as well as the Colored World Series in 1924.

In the Cuban Winter League of 1923–24, Moore's team easily won the winter season championship, paced by his .386 batting average.[50] Playing in the California Winter League between the winters of 1920–21 and 1924–25, Moore compiled a career batting average of .385 and a slugging average of .631, including hitting .347 against Major League pitching.[51] In five winter league seasons (three in California and two in Cuba), his team won the championship every time.[52] Twice over this short time span he led his league in both hitting and slugging. He batted .453 (slugging .694) in the 1924 Negro National League and hit .487 (slugging .873) in the 1924–25 Californian Winter League.[53]

He was also a defensive stalwart at shortstop. Historian James A. Riley notes, "he was a superb fielder with outstanding range and a terrific arm, He could go in the hole, make a diving, backhand stab, stand up, and, flat-footed, throw the man out at first."[54] Veteran George Sweatt reports Moore "may not have been as agile as some of them but he had a rifle arm and made good plays … as far as fielding his position, and throwing and hitting, you couldn't beat him."[55] In the 1924 Negro League World Series, he combined with second baseman Newt Allen to make six double plays in one game.[56] Oh, he also hit .300 and .364, respectively, in the 1924 and 1925 World Series.[57]

Seamheads deemed Moore an all-star each year from 1920 through 1925, and in the Cuban Winter League of 1923–24. He was also the Seamheads' Top Position Player in all of blackball in 1923 and 1924. Cum Posey selected him to his All-Star unit in 1924. John B. Holway also regards him as an all-star for the entire six-year period from 1920 through 1925.

In 1926, Moore began his most torrid season yet and was performing at the peak of his abilities. John B. Holway's records reflect that he was hitting .548 through May 23.[58] Then the magic ended. While versions differ, the most credible account has Moore being shot in the leg by his girlfriend as he jumped out of a second story whorehouse balcony after a fight.[59] The jump (not so much the bullet) ended his career when his leg shattered badly in six places. Moore drifted away from baseball and neither his date nor place of death has ever been ascertained.[60]

Whether one believes that Moore is a Hall of Famer depends on many factors. If he is given credit for his four and a half years with the Wreckers in addition to his seven years in the Negro Leagues, and his multiple seasons playing California winter ball, it would put him well over the 10-year minimum requirement. In point of fact, the military team on which he served prior to 1920 was one of the leading venues for African American players in the pre–Negro League world. There is no reason it should not count. But if it does, how does one make up for the lost statistics of his Wrecker years? It hardly seems appropriate to ignore the anecdotal evidence of Moore's performance on such an outstanding team just because the statistics are largely missing for that period. Luckily, Moore's Cuban Winter League and California Winter League seasons furnish significant supplementary data.

Another complicating factor is the manner in which he left baseball. Do we hold against Moore the fact that he was shot in the leg by his girlfriend after a fight? This seems somewhat harsh in view of the fact that he was one who was shot while running away from her (albeit in a whorehouse after a fight in which she claimed he hit her). Aside from causing him to have lost a substantial portion of his productive career, it's hard to understand how a "Roy Hobbs" type of incident should reasonably be deemed to diminish his confirmed record.

Leading historians John B. Holway, William F. McNeil, Larry Lester, Jay Sanford, David A. Lawrence, and Tweed Webb all believe Dobie Moore should be a Hall of Famer. Hall of Fame shortstop Pop Lloyd listed Dobie Moore as the starting shortstop on his all-time all-star team. Top veterans such as Buck O'Neil and Chet Brewer agree.

Leading historian William F. McNeil, who was not on the 2006 Hall of Fame voting panel, regards him as "the best all-around shortstop in the annals of Negro League baseball."[61] He argues: "According to my calculations he would have hit .317 in the major leagues along with 32 doubles, 10 triples, and 20 home runs for every 550 at-bats." According to his contemporary Tweed Webb, "Moore was an outstanding defensive shortstop with big hands, wide range, and a powerful throwing arm. He was at least as good defensively, as best I can determine, as Lloyd and Lundy, and better than Willie Wells, who had a weak throwing arm. He outhit Lloyd by a least 12 points, and Lundy and Wells by more than 30. And he was the top power hitter of the three, with only Wells close to him."[62] The Seamheads statistics bear out his fielding prowess, ranking Moore as the single best all-time fielder among Negro League shortstops.

The overall statistics we do have for Dobie Moore's active career in the Negro Leagues confirm that he was one of the all-time greats. His career WAR of 35.6, which he produced in less than 10 years in the official Negro Leagues, is the second highest (trailing only Dick Lundy) of any Negro League position player not in the Hall of Fame. His career WAR per 162 games of 10.2 is the highest of any player in Negro League history.

Dobie Moore's Seamheads Similarity Scores reveal the following players among his closest 11 Major League matches: Hall of Famers Arky Vaughan, Charlie Gehringer, Joe Cronin, Honus Wagner, Nap Lajoie and Derek Jeter. One member of the 2006 Committee acknowledged that the theatrical manner in which Moore's career ended negatively impacted his vote, since the election was intended to emphasize what was best about the Negro Leagues.[63] Rather than focus upon the drama surrounding his life, or speculate as to what he might have accomplished in the years he lost after he broke his leg, perhaps it's more important to assess what Moore actually did achieve. If one does that, it is fair to conclude that Dobie Moore is one of the greatest players in the history of black ball and that he had a Hall of Fame worthy career.

Worthy of Further Discussion

Artie Wilson was perhaps the top Negro League shortstop of the 1940s. The 5 ft. 10 in., 162 lb., Wilson began his playing days at shortstop and then segued to second base later in his career. Wilson was a left-handed opposite-field spray hitter who specialized in wearing out pitchers by constantly fouling off pitches at the plate. Wilson hit over .400 (.402) in the Negro American League (NAL) in 1948, the last modern era player to do so in a top-level league.[64] (Subsequent research has uncovered that he actually hit .428 that season in official league games.[65]) For good measure, he also hit .405 in the 1947–48 Puerto Rico Winter League.[66] In 1948–49, acting as a player-manager, he led his team to the Puerto Rico championship, hit .373, and set an all-time season hits record (126) in Puerto Rico that has never been broken.[67]

Wilson was also a solid fielder and a constant stolen base threat[68] who had earlier won four Birmingham Industrial League batting titles at a time when it was a highly competitive league. The popular Wilson went on to win two NAL batting titles in the 1940s and both the Pacific Coast League (PCL) batting championship and stolen base title in 1949. In 1950, he led the PCL in hits and runs scored. Five other times in his career Wilson was the runner-up for league batting championships.[69]

Wilson compiled a Negro League career batting average of .376, second only to those of Chino Smith (.434) and Larry Doby (.384).[70] Wilson was named to four East-West All-Star Games during his five years in the Negro American League. He was also deemed the MVP of the 1944 East-West All-Star Game and the 1944 MVP of the Negro American League by the *ESPN Baseball Encyclopedia*. John B. Holway designated him an all-star in 1944 and again in 1947, when he won John Holway's Fleet Walker award as the league's MVP. He played on 10 championship teams during his career, including participating in the Negro League World Series in 1944 and 1948.[71] The CNLBR believes that the missing data on Wilson's batting prowess would show a hitter who amassed over 3,000 hits during his career.[72]

When integration arrived, Artie Wilson was particularly unlucky. Bill Veeck signed him to the Indians in 1948, asserting "he is the best prospect in the Negro Leagues today."[73] The Yankees then protested his signing for the sole purpose of blocking the Indians. When Major League baseball upheld its protest, the Yankees, who had no intention of promoting an African American to the Majors at that time, relegated him to their Newark farm club.[74] Wilson signed instead with the Oakland Oaks of the PCL, who, after his strong performances in the PCL, eventually sold his contract in 1951 to the New York Giants. It was Artie Wilson who, when he finally received his cup of coffee in the Major Leagues with the New York Giants in 1951 (a mere 19 games, mostly on the bench), volunteered to be demoted to make room for Willie Mays' debut that year, most likely due to the fact that the Giants already had too many African Americans.[75] (At that time, Major League teams would retain only an even number of African American players so they could room together. Wilson would have been the fifth African American on the Giants after the Mays call-up.)[76]

Artie Wilson spent the rest of his career as one of the all-time greats in the Pacific Coast League and never returned to the Majors. All he did in the PCL was collect over 200 hits in five different years and be named to the PCL all-star team in 1949, 1950, 1952, and 1953.[77] At that time the PCL, which operated almost as a third Major League, paid salaries to its top stars in excess of Major League salaries.[78] Wilson became one of their top earners.

Artie Wilson was clearly one of those Negro League players whose timing was just off and could have been a Major League star if integration had occurred sooner. To those who discounted his being the last player to hit over .400 in a top-level modern league, Wilson responded: "Well, if I hit .400 in the Negro Leagues, I probably would have hit more in the majors, because I'd have gotten better pitches to hit."[79]

His winning personality and team camaraderie suggest that he may have been the best alternative to Jackie Robinson as a candidate to successfully integrate Major League Baseball in 1947. However, it was not to be. Ignoring his short stint in Major League ball, Dodger Hall of Fame manager Tommy Lasorda once opined that Artie was "the greatest player never to have played in the Major Leagues."[80]

In the McNeil Negro League Players' Poll, Artie Wilson and Dick Lundy were the only two shortstops to amass at least 50 percent of the ballots.[81] Artie Wilson and Willie Wells were the two Hall of Fame shortstops selected by the 1993 Negro League Hall of Fame Poll of its members.[82] Larry Lester's 1993 player survey named Wilson as the second team shortstop, behind only Willie Wells. Historian John B. Holway, commenting on the fact that Wilson was not selected for the Hall of Fame in 2006, noted that Artie Wilson, as baseball's last .400 hitter, would have given the Hall of Fame a vibrant living presence at the July 2006 induction ceremonies.[83]

Statistics bear out Wilson's prowess. His WAR per 162 games of 9.5 ranks third highest of all time among Negro League shortstops. His Seamheads Similarity Scores are equally eye-popping. Artie Wilson's six closest matches to Major League players (in order) are Ross Barnes, Arky Vaughan, Derek Jeter, Eddie Collins, Honus Wagner, and Barry Larkin.

Wilson's short stint in the official Negro Leagues was probably responsible for his not even making the preliminary 2006 Negro League Hall of Fame ballot. This result reflects the myopia of relying exclusively on official Negro League statistics. Artie Wilson won batting championships at virtually every level that he played: Birmingham Industrial League, Negro American League, Puerto Rico Winter League, and Pacific Coast League. He was a perennial all-star in all four of those leagues and played on 10 championship teams. He has the highest career batting average at his position in Negro League history. He was one of the most charismatic and popular Negro League players during its glory days. In retrospect, his 26-year career in American baseball (1937–1962) demonstrates that he is a worthy Hall of Fame candidate.

James "Bus" ("Buz" or "Buzz") Clarkson does not receive enough respect. As implied, by his nickname, this 5 ft. 11 in., 210 lb. former football player was built like a tank. He played all around the diamond, but mostly at shortstop and third base. He began his black ball career with Oscar Charleston's Pittsburgh Crawfords in 1937. Clarkson was a fine fielder with a strong arm who was developed into one the Negro League's feared hitters. At the plate, he was a right-handed pull hitter with better than average speed on the basepaths.[84] In 1940, according to Seamheads, he hit .339, with a .997 OPS, and was named to the all-star team in the East-West All-Star Game. In 1941, he joined a group of top players in the Mexican League and hit .334, with 19 home runs, to trail only Josh Gibson.[85] He returned to the United States the next year and was retroactively designated the Top Position Player in all of black ball by Seamheads for 1942, when he hit .339 with an OPS of 1.011.

Clarkson was then drafted into the military and served three years (1943–45) in the service, years in which he would have been in prime playing condition. In 1946, he was back with the Philadelphia Stars at age 31 where, according to James A. Riley, he batted cleanup and hit .308. He spent the next few years ping-ponging between the Mexican League, the Canadian Provincial League (CPL), and the Philadelphia Stars, for whom he was again named an all-star in 1949. His 1948 stint in the CPL produced a .399 average and 28 home runs in 80 games.[86]

In 1949, he was signed by the minor league Milwaukee Brewers at the age of 35. He hit over .300 with them (in 1951, .341) for the next two years. He was even called up to the Major League Boston Braves for a few games in 1952 as a placeholder for a young Eddie Mathews. Reassigned to the Texas League, he was the best player in the league for the next two seasons, hitting over .300 each year and outperforming future Hall of Famer Willard Brown. His 1954 Texas League season was amazing: .324 batting average, 42 home runs, 135 RBIs, and 104 walks.[87]

All the while he was playing summer ball on the continent, Clarkson played 11 winters in Puerto Rico between 1940 and 1955 where he tore up that league. He accumulated a .310 lifetime batting average while averaging 27 home runs a year. On May 1, 1941, he hit for the cycle in the Puerto Rico Winter League and the next day he hit two home runs in a single inning. To augment his résumé in Puerto Rico, he led the league in stolen bases in 1941–42, led the league in runs scored in 1940–41, led the league in home runs in 1950–51, and led the league in RBIs in 1954–55.[88] Clarkson finished up in the Pacific Coast League in 1955 and 1956, having played at virtually every level of ball over the course of his career.[89]

Mostly due to his service in World War II, Clarkson spent less than 10 years in the American Negro Leagues. His possible entrance to the Major Leagues was adversely affected by the fact that Clarkson was already 32 years old when Jackie Robinson broke the color barrier. But Bus Clarkson was one impressive player. The Hall of Eric and Miller has determined that in the 4,690 at bats they could find for him, Clarkson hit 172 home runs, 191 doubles, walked 621 times, and stole about 12 bases a year.[90]

James A. Riley claims he had a .359 batting average over the course of his Negro League career. William F. McNeil has included Bus Clarkson as a shortstop on both his all-time Puerto Rico Winter League team and his all-time Negro League all-star team. Despite his short tenure in the Negro Leagues, historians William F. McNeil, Eduardo Valero, and Robert Cottrell deemed Clarkson a Hall of Fame qualified player. Negro League veterans Art "Superman" Pennington, Herbert Simpson, James "Lefty" Turner, and Earl Wilson, Sr., have also included him on their all-time teams. However, Clarkson's closest Major League Similarity Score matches on Seamheads are Nomar Garciaparra, Charlie Gehringer, Robinson Cano and Corey Seager, a fine grouping of players who will mostly fall short of the Hall of Fame.

In the final analysis, Clarkson's limited tenure in the official Negro Leagues, and the fact that his strongest performances were in the Puerto Rico Winter League, were probably the reasons that he did not make the either the preliminary ballot in the 2006 Negro League Special Election for the Hall of Fame or the 1952 *Courier* Poll. It is still clear that he was consistently one of the best players in black ball during the 1940s era. In another and more equitable time, Bus Clarkson would have been a more than successful ballplayer in the Major Leagues. He is also one of those players, like Quincy Trouppe and Wild Bill Wright, whose extensive time playing abroad in Mexico, Puerto Rico, Canada, and the minor leagues reflects the fact at he was an in-demand hired gun with plenty of talent. The Hall of Merit discussion thread on Clarkson concludes that he was similar in many respects to Hall of Famer Barry Larkin.[91] Based upon the available evidence, I would have selected Clarkson over Larkin in their primes.

WAR Comparison of Negro League Hall of Famers and Candidates—Shortstop
All Leagues: Negro, Cuban, Mexican Leagues, vs. Major Leaguers and High Minors

Name	Years	WAR (per 162 games)	Career WAR
Dobie Moore	1916–25	10.2	35.6
Grant Johnson	1895–1914	10.1	25.2
Artie Wilson	1944–48	9.5	7.3
Willie Wells	1924–48	7.4	63.0
John Henry Lloyd	1906–32	6.4	53.0
Dick Lundy	1916–37	6.4	37.4
Bus Clarkson	1938–46	6.4	10.5

Hall of Famers in bold. *24 Men Out candidates in italics*. WAR statistics courtesy of Seamheads.

WAR Summary–Shortstop: Infield position players have been shortchanged by the Hall of Fame voters, probably because defensive contributions are not fully recognized by the collected statistical data. Pop Lloyd and Willie Wells had great careers, and their staggering career WAR's establish that they were deserving to be the first shortstops voted in. Yet they were only two of a handful of worthy alternate choices. Grant "Home Run" Johnson, Dick Lundy and Dobie Moore are all Hall of Fame qualified players. While Moore has issues relating to his character and career longevity, Home Run Johnson and Dick Lundy should be among the first future Negro League inductees. Artie Wilson's overall career spanning the Negro Leagues, industrial leagues and the Pacific Coast League also presents a serious case for Hall of Fame scrutiny. Wilson's WAR per 162 games is third all-time at shortstop and exceeds that of the current Hall of Famers. Bus Clarkson was a truly great shortstop whose career WAR does not match those of the other candidates, probably because his greatest accomplishments occurred in the Puerto Rico Winter League.

CHAPTER 13

Third Base

Negro Leaguers currently in the Hall of Fame who played substantial time at third base are Ray Dandridge, Jud Wilson, and Judy Johnson. Yet there were two other third baseman of comparable merit who seem to have been overlooked by the vagaries of the selection process. They are:

Oliver "The Ghost" Marcelle

Years	Games	Runs	Hits	HR	RBI	SB	BA	SLG*	WAR per 162g	WAR Career
1918–30	NA	523	1034	19	257	59	.305	.373	3.9	18.5

Career statistics (CNLBR), WAR (Seamheads), *Negro League games only.

In 1953, John Henry Lloyd picked Oliver Marcelle (sometimes spelled Marcell) as his choice for the top third baseman in Negro League history.[1] Buck O'Neil said people nicknamed him "the Ghost" because he would disappear after the game, not use his hotel room, and then suddenly reappear the next day.[2] In the 12 year period from 1918 through 1930, the quick and graceful Marcelle used his speed, range and a strong arm to knock down balls at third and throw out runners from deep in the hole. According to veteran Bobby Robinson, Marcelle had strong nerves and quick reflexes, which allowed him to play 10 feet closer to the plate than any other third baseman.[3] Widely regarded as the best fielding third baseman of the Negro Leagues of the 1920s, he charged bunts with élan and protected the hot corner. This reputation is confirmed by the Seamheads defensive data, which ranks him as the sixth best fielding third baseman of all time in the Negro Leagues, trailing Judy Johnson, but ahead of Jud Wilson.

The handsome Marcelle was a fan and media favorite; the latter branded him as having the "ability of Frisch" and being "as brainy as Herzog."[4] It is extremely significant that Marcelle was named as the first team starting third baseman in the 1952 *Courier* Poll over Judy Johnson, Jud Wilson, and Ray Dandridge, long after Marcelle's career had ended. The *Courier* Poll narrative noted: "Oliver Marcelle could do everything! A fielding gem he could go to his right or his left with equal facility. He was a ballplayer's ballplayer and the idol of fandom."

Forming a left side infield with Dick Lundy at short, the two of them led the Bacharach Giants to pennants in 1926 and 1927. Earlier he had teamed with Pop Lloyd at shortstop, in 1918–19 and 1923, and with Walter "Dobie" Moore, in 1923–24. Marcelle was therefore part of three of the greatest left infield combinations in Negro League history. In 1929, he was also a member of the Baltimore Black Sox "Million Dollar Infield" with Jud Wilson, Frank Warfield, and Dick Lundy. Clearly, he was his era's preeminent third baseman.

According to Negro League veteran Buddy Burbage (1928–51), "There was nobody else like him [Marcelle]. He was legendary at his position and other players regarded him with awe."[5] He was also smart and aggressive on the base paths, leading the Eastern league in stolen bases in 1921. Nor was he a slouch at the plate, often batting second or third for quality teams. According to CNLBR, his lifetime batting average compiled against all competition was .305 and his highest reported seasonal batting average was .354 in 1922.

During eight winters in Cuba (years in which teammate Judy Johnson always ceded third base to him in deference to his fielding)[6] he hit for a .305 average, including a league leading .393 in 1923–24. In 19 career games against Major League pitching, his batting average was .325.[7] Particularly interesting is the fact that he compiled a cumulative batting average of .417, and a slugging percentage of .556, when he faced

OLIVER MARCELL

BIG LEAGUE BREW

Oliver "The Ghost" Marcelle was deemed the greatest third baseman in Negro League history in the 1952 *Pittsburgh Courier* Experts' Poll. He left the game shortly after he had his nose bitten off in a 1929 fight with Frank "Weasel" Warfield. (Courtesy Helmar Brewing. Artist Sanjay Verma.)

Adolfo Luque of the Cincinnati Reds 36 times in the Cuban Winter League.[8] A Seamheads all-star in the Cuban Winter League of 1923–24, Marcelle was elected to the Cuban Baseball Hall of Fame in 2007 for his overall performance in that country.

His career WAR of 18.5 is solid, but seems lower than it should be because of the fewer statistics available from his era. The CNLBR estimates that the 3,394 reported at bats for Marcelle do not include hundreds of games, and thousands of his at bats, from 1917 to 1934.[9] Yet, despite his reputation as a defensive specialist, his overall WAR still places him among the top all-time Negro League third basemen. Of further note is the statistic that Marcelle's WAR per 162 games (3.9) exceeds that of Hall of Fame third baseman Judy Johnson. He was deemed an all-star by John B. Holway in four years between 1919 and 1927.

Oliver Marcelle was also a winner. He was a member of the 1920 Atlantic City Bacharach Giants self-proclaimed "Champions of the East" and the 1923–24 Cuban Winter League champion Santa Clara Leopards, played for Atlantic City in both the 1926 and 1927 Negro League World Series, and was a member of the 1929 American Negro League Championship Baltimore Black Sox.

Marcelle had a few other traits as well. Behind this handsome veneer lay a vain, fiery, combative individual, whose emotions and drinking led him into reckless behavior. Many players regarded Marcelle as having a virtually uncontrollable temper. He constantly fought with opposing players, umpires, teammates, and sometimes fans.[10] On May 25, 1925, after a night of drinking, Marcelle was involved in an episode with legendary pitcher Dave Brown when Brown killed a man. In another incident, he hit Oscar Charleston over the head with a bat to settle a dispute. Later, Marcelle had his nose bitten off in a fight with Frank Warfield over a dice game in the winter of 1929. Taunted by the fans over his disfigurement in an era before plastic surgery, he soon left the game, psychologically defeated.[11]

After leaving the upper echelon of Negro League baseball, Marcelle lived in Denver, where, according to Chet Brewer, he played a major role in integrating the Denver Post tournament in 1934 by convincing Charles "Poss" Parsons to send an invitation to the Kansas City Monarchs.[12] The integration of that tournament, which was the top independent team tournament in the country, subsequently became an important calling card for the Negro Leaguers (and specifically Satchel Paige) to show off their talents in an integrated setting. As such, it was an important stepping-stone to Major League integration in the 1940s. Although Marcelle did some barnstorming for lesser teams through around 1934, he spent the balance of his life as a house painter and doing odd jobs in the Denver area. Oliver "The Ghost" Marcelle died in abject poverty at age 53 in 1949 and was buried in an unmarked grave.[13]

There seems little reason, aside from his temper, not to deem Marcelle a Hall of Famer based upon his on-field performance. One of the best defensive third baseman in Negro League history, he was also a lifetime .300 hitter and one of the more popular players of his time. His Seamheads Similarity Scores reflect two Major League Hall of Famers among his top six matches: Jimmy Collins and George Kell. Judged as the single best third baseman in Negro League history by the *Courier* Poll, he was also rated as the all-time best Negro League third baseman by veterans Oscar Charleston and Chappie Johnson. Quincy Trouppe and Buck O'Neil picked Marcelle on their number two all-time teams. Leading historians Jerry Malloy, William F. McNeil, Robert W. Peterson, John B. Holway, Dick Clark, James A. Riley, Leslie Heaphy, Brent Kelley, Sammy J. Miller, James E. Overmyer, Todd Bolton, Lawrence D. Hogan, and Bill James all included Marcelle among their top three picks for the best Negro League third basemen of all time. Marcelle was designated a rightful Hall of Famer by a remarkable 80 percent of the voters in the McNeil Historians' Poll and 90 percent of the voters in the McNeil Pioneers' Poll. Oliver Marcelle, a finalist in the 2006 Hall of Fame election for the Negro Leagues, is one of only three first team players from the *Courier* Poll not currently enshrined in Cooperstown. It's time for him to join the Hall.

George "Tubby" Scales

Years	Games	Runs	Hits	HR	RBI	SB	BA	SLG*	WAR per 162g	WAR Career
1920–46	810	589	1,037	88	455	66	.328	.505	4.7	25.8

Career Statistics (CNLBR), WAR (Seamheads). *Negro Leagues games only.

Another infielder worthy of serious Hall of Fame consideration is George Scales, who played all over the infield during his 26-year Negro League career. We will consider him here as a third baseman, although others treat him as second baseman where he also spent much of his career. Well-travelled Quincy Trouppe, the veteran Negro League catcher, regarded Scales as the greatest second baseman he ever saw.[14] Cum Posey called him the best third baseman of his era.[15] Ted Page designated him as his selection for the best second baseman in the Negro Leagues.[16] Buck Leonard said he was the best curve ball hitter he ever saw play.[17] In his book *State by State*, Chris Jensen designates Scales as the all-time best second baseman from Alabama to play in any league, black or white.

Scales, who played in the Negro Leagues for over 20 years, hit well and possessed a cannon arm. Nicknamed "Tubby" because of his thickset build, he was a stocky, fast man who studied the hitters to compensate for his lack of range.[18] Scales was an excellent fielder and considered one of the best in Negro League baseball at turning a double play.[19] His Seamheads defensive statistics, which rank him 13th all-time in Negro League history (albeit at second base), confirm that his fielding was well above average.

George "Tubby" Scales was a seven-time All Star with a .328 lifetime batting average. The power hitting Scales hit .300 or better 14 times in his Negro League career and 35 percent of his recorded hits were for extra bases. (Courtesy Helmar Brewing. Artist Sanjay Verma.)

Scales greatest strength was his hitting prowess. He generally hit in the middle of the order, often cleanup, during a career that ran from 1920 through 1946. The Center for Negro League Baseball Research credits Scales with batting averages against Negro League teams of over .400 in two seasons and a lifetime batting average of .317, with a .505 slugging percentage. Scales compiled a .408 batting average in 1923 with a .772 slugging percentage, and a.446 batting average and .676 slugging percentage in 1927. In addition to his two .400+ seasons, CNLBR has uncovered six seasons in which his batting average was in the mid-.300 range (1924: .341; 1925: .348; 1929: .390; 1930: .373; 1940: .353; 1944: .345).

Scales also played hundreds of non-league games for which statistics are scant. The CNLBR has uncovered 51 non-league games for Scales in which he batted .519, with a .806 slugging percentage.[20] In one three game series against Indianapolis in 1923, he went 9 for 14, with two doubles, four home runs, and nine RBIs.[21] Although only an infielder, Scales is credited by Seamheads as being in 16th place on the Negro Leagues all-time home run list. His home run at New York's Protectory Oval on September 16, 1928, is regarded as the longest ever hit at that arena.[22] According to Seamheads, Scales amassed a .418 OBP (on-base percentage) and .924 OPS (on-base percentage plus slugging percentage) between 1921 and 1946. The Candidate profile prepared for Scales in the 2006 Hall of Fame Negro Leagues election notes that he hit .300 or better 14 times in his Negro League career and that 35 percent of his recorded hits were for extra bases. Seamheads calculates that Scales averaged an extraordinary 117 RBIs for each 162 games played during his career. Earlier in his career he also had some speed when, according to CNLBR, he swiped 13 bases in 1928 for the New York Lincoln Giants during their championship run.

During his prime years of 1923–29, Scales often played alongside Pop Lloyd with the New York Lincoln Giants. In 1931, he was lured away to the great 1931 Homestead Grays, where he hit behind Josh Gibson to give Gibson protection. Historian Phil S. Dixon's detailed study of the 1931 season reports that Scales had over 200 base hits, 20 home runs, and over 150 runs scored that year.[23] However, after 1931, when he turned 30, there was a substantial falloff in his offensive production. According to CNLBR, Scales' lifetime batting average dropped 85 points in the period 1932–38.[24] Whether this was due to aging, injury, or letting himself go physically is just speculation. He played on, somewhat productively through 1946, often as a player-manager. His best remaining year was 1943, for which John B. Holway's research shows he batted .303 in league and non-league games. Scales even appeared in the 1943 East-West All-Star Classic as a pinch hitter.[25] After that, he continued on as a manager in the Negro Leagues and Puerto Rico through the winter of 1959–60.

Scales' career WAR of 25.8 is the second highest WAR ever for any American Negro Leaguer at third base (trailing only Hall of Famer Jud Wilson). His career WAR exceeds that of both Hall of Fame third basemen Judy Johnson and Ray Dandridge.

Scales was also a fiery performer with a tough disposition. According to who was telling the story, he was either an ornery loudmouth or the tough glue that held a team together.[26] One story told about Scales is that he got into a fight with his roommate Ted Page when he challenged Page's on-field performance while both were with the Homestead Grays. By the time they were separated by teammates, Page had knocked out two of Scales' teeth and Scales had cut Page with a knife. That night, both players, who shared the same bed, slept with a weapon in their hands.[27]

Still, Scales was a perennial winner. He was a member of the 1930 and 1931 Homestead Grays, both of which won the "Colored Baseball Championship." In 1937, he became an integral member of the Negro all-stars (Trujillo All-Stars), which won the Denver Post tournament. He was also on the Baltimore Elite Giants team that won the Negro National League title in 1941 and 1942. As early as 1923, and as late as 1940, he was deemed an all-star at his position by Seamheads. Writer Rollo Wilson of the *Pittsburgh Courier* designated him an all-star in 1929 and Cum Posey selected Scales to his all-star unit in 1934. John B. Holway has deemed Scales an all-star in seven different seasons between 1922 and 1936.

It is interesting to observe how Scales, like many leading Negro Leaguers, played for so many different championship teams. Because of the lack of any effective reserve clause or strong Negro League leadership, the careers of players like Scales appear to reflect that of modern free agency. Most top Negro League players would think nothing of jumping from team to team in search of a larger paycheck, often in mid-season. And, as in the modern era, it was the better players who were so highly recruited to play for the leading teams, which were always in search of a missing piece. For this reason, players who were the most well-travelled were often the best. The classic example of this phenomenon was Satchel Paige, who would casually jump from team to team during a season, his notoriety and talent protecting him from any major repercussions.

In addition to his exploits in the American Negro Leagues, Scales played all over the hemisphere. He was a member of the Royal Poinciana team that won the Florida Hotel League in 1925. He spent three seasons from 1927 through 1930 playing in the Cuban Winter League, batting .282, .321, and .290 over that span. He participated in the legendary 1937 Dominican League, where he compiled a .295 average competing against dictator Rafael Trujillo's Satchel Paige/Josh Gibson–led team.[28]

Beginning in 1932, Scales served in a dual capacity as player-manager on many teams. He also spent over a decade playing and managing in the Puerto Rican Winter League. A hard-nosed taskmaster, Scales organized and managed the New York Black Yankees from 1932 through 1936, except for 1935, when he returned to the Homestead Grays as a player. He also managed the Baltimore Elite Giants, the Birmingham Black Barons, the East squad in both of the 1939 East-West All-Star Games, six Puerto Rican Winter League teams to league championship titles, and one team to a Caribbean Series title. Managing for 15 seasons in Puerto Rico, he was selected manager of the year four times in the Puerto Rico Winter League. Regarded by many Latin American baseball historians as the greatest manager in Puerto Rican baseball history,[29] Scales was elected to the Puerto Rico Baseball Hall of Fame in 1996.

Scales is credited as a teacher and mentor of many successful players including Joe Black, Sammy T. Hughes, Pee Wee Butts, Lenny Pearson, and Jim Gilliam.[30] It was Scales who is credited with having talked a reluctant Roy Campanella into joining the Brooklyn Dodgers. In 1945, Campanella had received a call from the Dodgers but was reluctant to leave the life he knew in the Negro Leagues. Scales sat him down and told him this was his chance to make real money. Campanella's response was to claim he did not know the way to Brooklyn. In Campanella's words: "George Scales took me [to Brooklyn] in the subway from the hotel in New York." When the subway ride was over, Scales had lost his star catcher, and the Major Leagues had secured a future Hall of Famer.[31]

Based upon the statistics, George Scales is one of the Negro League's most underappreciated stars. He was, however, appreciated by his peers. Scales was a Hall of Fame selection of 57 percent of the players voting in the McNeil Players' Poll, including such greats as Larry Doby, Double Duty Radcliffe, Harold Tinker, Sr., Tommy Sampson, Bobby Robinson, Red Moore, Max Manning, and Jimmie Armstead. Historian James A. Riley has labeled him an all-time great. John B. Holway and Bill James both regard him as the Negro League's third all-time best second baseman. He was named second on the Roll of Honor in the 1952 *Courier* Poll. Scales was also a finalist on the 39-name final ballot in the 2006 Hall of Fame election for the Negro Leagues, but he was not elected. Is it surprising to discover that his closest Major League player match under Seamheads' Similarity Scores is Jackie Robinson?

The pugnacious Scales combined power and batting average with excellent fielding. He appears to be another player who has not received the acclaim he deserves because he is not associated with a single position. Altogether, he compiled a 40-year career starting as a young infielder for the 1919 Montgomery Gray Sox and culminating in 1960 as a Puerto Rican League manager who had been named manager of the year four times. That much of his career was spent in high level Caribbean ball may not have helped his case either, although his winter ball exploits should, if anything, only enhance his résumé. Scales' overall record as a player and as a tough, well-respected manager when his playing days ended, mentor to many future Major Leaguers, buttressed by a lifetime batting average well over .300 with power, and a WAR exceeded by only one other American third baseman in Negro League history, warrants Hall of Fame selection.

Worthy of Further Discussion

Alec (Alex) Radcliffe. Ted "Double Duty" Radcliffe (see Chapter 16) was not even the best ballplayer in his own family. His brother Alec Radcliffe (Radcliff) was a consistent hitter and a perennial all-star. During a 15-year career from 1932 to 1946, Alec played in 11 All-Star games, second only to Buck Leonard in all-star game appearances. James A. Riley has deemed him the rookie of the year in 1932, when he helped his Negro Southern League American Giants to the title, batting second and accumulating a .283 batting average.[32] One of his career highlights occurred in 1932, when he broke up a no-hitter by his brother Ted in the ninth inning with a game-winning home run.[33] His lifetime all-star game batting average was .341 and he leads the All-Star Classics in all-time at-bats and hits. He was the true star of the 1938 All-Star Classic, driving in two runs to lead the West to victory.

Radcliffe was also a solid fielder whose brother Ted acknowledged as having one of the greatest arms anyone had ever seen. One longtime Chicago fan told how Alec would field the ball and tease the runner by holding it and "then cut loose."[34] But his true strength was as a great clutch hitter.[35] Seamheads calculates he compiled a .291 lifetime batting average and that he averaged 91 RBIs for each 162 games over the course of his career. According to James A. Riley, his highest yearly batting average was .431, in the 1933 Negro National League as his American Giants won the pennant. He also led the Negro American League in home runs in 1944 and 1945.[36] He was designated a Seamheads all-star in 1943. John B. Holway regards him as an all-star in 1932 and 1943.

Historian James A. Riley opines that Radcliffe was the best third baseman in Negro American League history, albeit one whose accomplishments were overlooked in view of his more colorful brother, Ted "Double Duty" Radcliffe.[37] He has also been designated the best third baseman in Negro League history by multiple players.[38] On the other hand, Bill James ranks Radcliffe as only the eighth best third baseman in Negro League history, and there is just a single Hall of Famer (Jimmy Collins, the sixth closest) who appears among his top thirty Seamheads' Major League Similarity Scores. Despite his popularity with the fans, who kept electing him to the All-Star Game, Radcliffe's career WAR calculates out as a modest 10.2. Yet, his WAR per 162 games of 3.9 exceeds that of Hall of Famer Judy Johnson. It makes one wonder which third baseman would have been selected if the early Hall of Fame voters had all of the statistics before them and if Alex Radcliffe had survived as long as Dandridge and Johnson.

Orestes "Minnie" Minoso. The failure of Orestes "Minnie" Minoso to be elected by the 2006 Negro League Special Negro Leagues Committee was the subject of much criticism. Nicknamed "The Cuban Comet" by the American press, Minoso combined a lethal combination of bat speed, natural speed, and power. According to CNLBR, Minoso collected 4,457 hits and a batting average of .298 at all levels of professional competition over the course of his lengthy career.[39] Of the thousands of ballplayers throughout history, only Pete Rose has recorded more hits at a professional level. Add to that gold glove defensive ability, a serious stolen base threat, four years in which he had over 100 RBIs, and seven appearances in the Major League All Star game, and you have a player who Bill James ranked as the 10th best left fielder of all time[40] (he often played the outfield in the Major Leagues).

Minoso started his professional career in his homeland of Cuba in 1945–46, where he hit .294 and was named Rookie of the Year.[41] Minoso then spent a few highly productive years in the Negro Leagues. From 1946 to 1948, he joined the Negro National League, where, according to Seamheads, he proceeded to hit a cumulative .314 for the New York Cubans. His best year was 1947, when he batted .346 (Seamheads) in the leadoff spot and helped lead the New York Cubans to the Negro National League pennant and a World Series win over the Cleveland Buckeyes. In his short Negro League career, he was voted onto and played in four East-West All-Star Games, batting .308. Minoso was designated the co–MVP of the second game of the All-Star Classic series played in 1948.

John B. Holway selected Minoso as an Eastern Conference All-Star in 1946, and Seamheads designated him as the best third baseman in all of the Negro Leagues in both 1947 and 1948. In the late 1940s through early 1960s, Minoso also played a total of 14 seasons in Cuban winter ball, with a lifetime .280 batting average.[42] Minoso was inducted into the Cuban Hall of Fame in 1983. He was finally given an everyday position in the Major Leagues by the Chicago White Sox in 1951, when he was already 28 years old. Nonetheless, he played 17 years in the Majors, amassing a .298 batting average and 186 home runs over an All-Star career. He led the American League in steals three times and ended up fourth in the MVP voting four times. Though one is tempted to say he should be his own Major League match on terms of Similarity Scores, the closest match to his Negro League performance is Jackie Robinson—furnishing even more evidence of how distinctive the performance of the Negro Leaguers was compared with that of the Major Leaguers. His high level of accomplishment in the Negro Leagues is well demonstrated by the fact that his WAR per 162 games (6.0) exceeds that of all of the other remaining Hall of Fame candidates at third base.

Minoso was a finalist in the 2006 Negro Leagues Special Election but was passed over by the electors, who were instructed by the Hall of Fame to not consider anything Minoso did in the Majors. Based upon this instruction, Minoso's failure to be named to the Hall of Fame in the 2006 Special Election is understandable. However, I believe that Minoso's entire career (including his three spectacular years in the Negro Leagues) should be considered by the electors as part of the regular Major League voting process.

The move to elect Minoso to the Hall as a Negro Leaguer seems to be a relatively recent phenomenon. Minoso received no support whatsoever as a Negro League Hall of Fame candidate from the veteran players in the McNeil Poll and was only the tenth name mentioned on the Roll of Honor in the 1952 *Courier* Poll. Minoso was considered by the Hall of Fame's Golden Era Committee in its 2011 and 2014 elections and garnered 56.3 percent and 50 percent of the votes, respectively. In supporting his candidacy in the Hall's 2006 Special Election for the Negro Leagues, voting member Todd Bolton supported his candidacy. Bolton argued that the Special Committee was the only forum that would be willing to assess the full scope of Minoso's career, from Cuban ball to the Negro Leagues to the Major Leagues.[43]

While Minnie Minoso has a strong overall Hall of Fame résumé, I believe the voters in the 2006 Hall of Fame election for the Negro Leagues showed proper discretion by not electing him through the "back door" of a Negro League vote. His three years in the Negro Leagues were by far the lesser part of his career, as reflected by his total career WAR in the American Negro Leagues of only 4.4. The issue is not whether Minoso belongs in the Hall of Fame (spoiler alert! he does), but that he deserves to be elected in the proper forum where he spent in his more productive years. He is again eligible for consideration in future Major League Golden Era elections—as well he should be, based upon his distinguished Major League service.

"Candy Jim" Taylor: see analysis in Chapter 17.

Dave Malarcher: see analysis in Chapter 17.

WAR Comparison of Negro League Hall of Famers and Candidates—Third Base
All Leagues: Negro, Cuban, Mexican Leagues, vs. Major Leaguers and High Minors

Name	Years	WAR (per 162 games)	Career WAR
Jud Wilson	1922–45	6.4	45.4
Minnie Minoso	1946–48	6.0	4.4
George Scales	1920–46	4.7	25.8
Ray Dandridge	1933–44	4.7	14.5
Oliver Marcelle	1918–30	3.9	18.5
Alec Radcliffe	1933–46	3.9	10.2
Dave Malarcher*	1916–34	3.8	18.8
Judy Johnson	1918–36	3.4	22.3
*Candy Jim Taylor**	1907–42	2.9	15.9

Hall of Famers in bold. *24 Men Out candidates in italics.* WAR statistics courtesy of Seamheads.
*Proposed for consideration for the Hall of Fame primarily in Manager category.

WAR Summary—Third Base: Jud Wilson, who could also be considered a first baseman, is clearly at the head of the field. After that, the Hall of Fame voting results for third base are not particularly impressive. Judy Johnson and Ray Dandridge were both solid players who may owe their early elections to the fact that they played in more recent times and were alive to accept their honors. (Judy Johnson was also a member of the 1971 Committee that elected him.) WAR analysis particularly points to George Scales, who equaled or exceeded Dandridge and Judy Johnson in both seasonal and career WAR value. Scales' candidacy is enhanced by his strong managerial tenure. Oliver Marcelle was a leading third baseman in Negro League history and is also a solid Hall of Fame choice. Alec Radcliffe, an 11-time All Star game selection, is another viable Hall of Fame candidate at the hot corner. "Candy Jim" Taylor and Dave Malarcher both made their most important contributions to the Negro Leagues as managers, as is discussed in Chapter 17. Yet both were also elite third basemen in their playing days. "Candy Jim" Taylor had a seasonal WAR just behind that of Judy Johnson and a higher career WAR than Ray Dandridge. Minnie Minoso was remarkable in his short time in the Negro Leagues, but he should be assessed in the Major League category, where he spent the vast majority of his playing career. Minoso's career WAR in the Negro Leagues is simply not Hall of Fame worthy in and of itself.

CHAPTER 14

Outfield

Seven Negro Leaguer outfielders have been selected for Cooperstown. They are Oscar Charleston, Cool Papa Bell, Monte Irvin, Turkey Stearnes, Pete Hill, Cristóbal Torriente, and Willard Brown. (This group does not include Martin Dihigo, who played outfield among many positions, but was a super-utility player also regarded as a pitcher and all-around infielder.) Since outfielders frequently consist of some of the best athletes and power hitters on a team, this grouping seems far too few for the Negro Leagues, which operated in one form or another for over 60 years. It is inadequate. The best of the rest are as follows.

Charlie "Chino" Smith

Years	Games	Runs	Hits	HR	RBI	SB	BA	SLG	WAR per 162g	WAR Career
1925–31	260	280	597	53	160	50	.388	.688*	9.7	15.2

Career Statistics (CNLBR), WAR (Seamheads), *Official Negro League games only.

Often called the greatest hitter the Negro Leagues ever produced, Charlie "Chino" Smith has the highest lifetime batting average of any player who ever played in any Major League, white or black. While CNLBR records his career batting average as .388, multiple credible researchers have calculated his lifetime batting average well over .400. Researcher John B. Holway lists it as .434; James A. Riley at .434, and Larry Lester and Dick Clark pin it as .402. Moreover, Charlie Smith combined a high batting average with substantial power. According to Seamheads, he established the highest OPS (On Base Percentage Plus Slugging Percentage) in Negro League history. Satchel Paige claimed that, aside from Josh Gibson, Chino Smith was the toughest hitter in Negro League history.[1] According to James A. Riley, he also was a strong outfield defender and a fine base runner. Veteran Jesse Hubbard reported that Smith played so well in right field that he could often trap a runner by throwing behind him as he made his turn at first base.[2] Determining why Smith is not already in the Hall of Fame requires additional analysis of his longevity and comportment.

Born in South Carolina in 1901, Charlie Smith spent his teenage years in a boarding school and began his working career as a redcap carrying luggage for terminal passengers. After playing sandlot ball, he joined the Pennsylvania Red Caps semi-professional team in 1923. By 1924 he had moved up to the Philadelphia Giants of the Negro National League. Ted Page recalled that he was nicknamed "Chino" in Cuba because of his slanted eyes, which gave a Chinese cast to his face.[3] He began his career as a second baseman and transitioned to the outfield. Moving over to the Brooklyn Royal Giants of the Eastern Colored League (ECL) in 1925, Smith became a starter and batted .339 including league and non-league games.[4] After hitting .349 in 1926 for the Brooklyn club, he truly broke out in 1927 when he became the leading batter in all of black ball. That year, he led the ECL batting championship, batting .451, with a .703 slugging percentage. His 10 home runs placed him just behind Oscar Charleston for the league lead.[5] Smith spent 1928 barnstorming with the Brooklyn Royal Giants, resulting in fewer verifiable statistics. Seamheads has located only nine games for that year, in which Smith hit .371.

Joining the New York Lincoln Giants of the new American Negro League (ANL) in 1929, he led the league in home runs (23), batting average (.464), runs scored, and even outfield assists.[6] ESPN designated Charlie Smith as the retroactive MVP for the 1929 ANL season. He followed that up in 1930 with a year for which John B. Holway credits him with his highest seasonal average of .492. Obviously, ESPN has also

Charlie "Chino" Smith's lifetime batting average of .388 was the highest of any player who played in any major league in the history of baseball. Only Babe Ruth had a higher career slugging percentage. Smith died of cancer at the age of 31. (Courtesy Helmar Brewing. Artist Scott Pedley.)

deemed Charlie Smith the league MVP for 1930. On July 5, 1930, Charlie Smith played for the New York Lincoln Giants in the first Negro League game ever in Yankee Stadium. That day, patrolling Babe Ruth's right field, Smith electrified a stadium crowd of 18,000–20,000 fans by hitting two home runs, tripling, and walking, in four plate appearances.[7] The game was so successful that Negro League ball became a staple at Yankee Stadium.

By that time, Smith had become a legend among players and fans. Pitcher Jesse Hubbard recalled one game when the team was facing Claude Hendrix, a particularly tough ex–Major League pitcher who was throwing an emery ball: "Charlie Smith told me, 'I'm going to hit a home run off this man.' I said 'If you hit a home run … here's a $10 bill.' I swear to God, Chino walked up to bat, and the first ball Hendrix threw him, Chino walked up on it and hit it a mile over the right field fence. When he came in, I handed him his ten."[8]

During his playing career, Charlie Smith also participated in five seasons in the Cuban Winter League. Playing against top-flight Negro League and Major League competition, Smith compiled a .335 lifetime batting average in Cuba, the third best ever, behind Cristóbal Torriente and Alejandro Oms.[9] He was a member of the 1927-28 and 1928-29 Habana teams, which won the Cuban Winter League Championships. John B. Holway's research has determined that, against the Major League pitching he faced in Cuba and in exhibition games, he batted .458 overall.

During the Cuban winter campaign of 1930, Charlie Smith felt weak and his skills began to diminish. Returning to the United States, he died suddenly at age 31. Although there has been confusion about Smith's cause of death, including reports of his having contracted yellow fever, Gary Ashwill of Seamheads located his death certificate and firmly established that he died of pancreatic and stomach cancer.[10]

Although Major League equivalencies are only hypothetical, historian William F. Mc-Neil calculated the Major League Equivalency of Charlie Smith. He concluded that, over the course of his entire career, Smith would have had an average annual batting average in the Major Leagues of .349, with 39 doubles, 12 triples, and 20 home runs.[11]

That the other players respected Charlie Smith would be an understatement. John B. Holway interviewed Negro League veterans and secured the following reflections[12]:

> I've faced two tough hitters. Josh Gibson was one. But the best hitter I think I ever faced was a boy named Chino Smith. That was the best man I ever faced. Smith hit me just like he knew what I was going to throw him. He hit it to all fields, and he would spit at the first two pitches and tell me, "Young man, you've got yourself in trouble."—Sug Cornelius, Negro League pitcher

> He and Pop Lloyd were two hitters of the same type, but I think Chino had better power than Lloyd. His line drives would go farther. Golly he hit line drives out of the park.—Ted Page, Negro League outfielder

> I've faced Jimmy Foxx, Oscar Charleston and Josh Gibson. But the greatest hitter I ever faced wasn't any of them. It was Chino Smith. It seemed like everything I throwed him, he could hit. He wasn't afraid of any pitcher.—Lamon Yokely, Negro League pitcher

Despite his talents, there are a few reasons Smith may not be in the Hall of Fame. First, he could be obnoxious and aggressive on the field. He loudly and regularly ragged the opposition players. He would taunt pitchers: "Is that all you gonna throw today? If that's all you gonna throw, I'm gonna kill you today."[13] He was also known for crowd baiting the fans, creating torrents of jeers and thrown debris. Pitcher Bill Holland reminisced to John B. Holway about Charlie Smith: "This guy could do more with the fans down on him. He'd get up to bat and spit at the first two pitches. If the fans booed, he pretended to charge them, making them boo even louder. Then he hit the ball out of the ballpark and would go around the bases waving his arms at the stands."[14]

In another incident, the *Chester Times* reported that on September 3, 1929, Smith had been ejected from a game because he hit an umpire squarely on the head with his bat.[15] But player Ted Page noted that his act was more for show than a result of bad temperament, claiming he certainly wasn't one of the game's brawlers like Oscar Charleston or Jud Wilson, "although he'd fight back if he was riled."[16]

Aside from his on-field demeanor, the principal issue concerning Smith's eligibility for the Hall of Fame is that he did not play a full 10 years in the Negro Leagues. If you count his initial year with the semi-professional Pennsylvania Red Caps, Charlie Smith played a total of eight seasons in American Negro League ball, from 1923 through 1931. In addition, he participated in five seasons of Cuban winter ball from 1926 through 1930. He was also involved in extensive barnstorming in the United States, including as a member of the opponent squad to Babe Ruth's and Lou Gehrig's all-star teams in 1926, 1927, and 1929.

The only significant bar to Charlie Smith's Hall of Fame admission would therefore seem to be his failure to have survived 10 years. However, the Hall of Fame waived the same 10-year rule in 1978 when Addie Joss was admitted despite playing less than 10 seasons due to his premature death from meningitis.[17] If any player is entitled to the application of the Addie Joss rule waiving the absolute 10-year requirement in the event of death, it is Smith. Smith did not self-destruct through drinking or a violent confrontation. He died of cancer at the height of his powers. Some Negro League players, such as Slim Jones or Dave Brown, possessed Hall of Fame talent but had their careers cut short by violence or alcohol. Charlie Smith's years of sustained brilliance in top-level black ball outshone their accomplishments both in terms of longevity and performance. He easily played the equivalent of ten years of ball if you add his five years of high-caliber Cuban winter ball to his eight years in the American Negro Leagues.

Let's summarize what Charlie Smith actually did accomplish during that time. He has the highest lifetime batting average in Negro League history. John B. Holway, who includes non–League games, records Smith's lifetime average as .434. In 1930, Smith hit .492 for the season. During his seven official Negro League seasons, he won three batting crowns, three slugging percentage titles, and two home run crowns. He was also a strong enough fielder to having led the league in outfield assists (1929) and speedy enough to have once won a stolen base crown (1930).[18] Charlie Smith's career WAR per 162 games of 9.7 is the highest of any Negro League outfielder of all time. Smith was deemed by John B. Holway the three-time winner of the Fleet Walker Award (MVP) as the best player in the Eastern Conference of the Negro League in 1927, 1929, and 1930. ESPN has accorded him their MVP designation for 1929 and 1930. Seamheads designated him the Top Position Player in the 1927–28 Cuban Winter League. Bill James regards him as the co–MVP in 1929.

Charlie Smith was included as a member of William F. McNeil's all-time Negro League all-star team, one of three starting outfielders on veteran Quincy Trouppe's all-time Negro League team, and a second team selection in both the *Pittsburgh Courier* Poll. Leading historians John B. Holway, Luis Alvelo, David A. Lawrence, and Jerry Malloy are all on record that they believe Smith has Hall of Fame credentials.

Still not convinced that we should break down the door to the Hall of Fame for this man? Of the over 19,000 individuals who have ever played in the Major Leagues, here are the six Major League players with the closest Similarity Scores to Charlie Smith (in order):

1. Babe Ruth
2. Ted Williams
3. Rogers Hornsby
4. Joe DiMaggio
5. Ty Cobb
6. Lou Gehrig

Mike Trout, Stan Musial, Joe Jackson, Tris Speaker and Jimmie Foxx are also among his top 20 Similarity Score matches.

Charlie Smith has the highest career batting average of any player who played in any major league in the history of baseball. Among Major League players, only Babe Ruth had a higher career slugging percentage and OPS than him. No matter how hard you try, it's pretty tough to disregard those facts. Charlie "Chino" Smith, the greatest hitter in Negro League history, belongs in the Hall of Fame under the Addie Joss exception.

Burnis "Wild Bill" Wright

Years	Games	Runs	Hits	HR	RBI	SB	BA	SLG	WAR per 162g	WAR Career
1932–56	1,337	861	1,783	119	774	182	.344	.488	6.3	25.8

Career statistics (CNLBR), WAR (Seamheads).

Picking "Wild Bill" Wright as the third best right fielder in Negro League history, Monte Irvin said: "If anybody belongs in the Hall of Fame, it's Bill Wright."[19] Often referred to in the press as the "Black DiMaggio," Wright stood 6 feet 4 inches tall, weighed 220 pounds, and possessed a powerful build.[20] He was an excellent fielder with a great arm, had superior speed, and was a powerful hitter. A switch-hitter noted for his clutch play, Wright often batted cleanup where he slashed the ball with a short, strong stroke.[21] As for his speed, he claimed that he had once been timed circling the bases in 13.2 seconds (at a time when the Major League record was 13.3).[22] Negro Leaguers of his era generally felt that only Cool Papa Bell was faster than Wright[23]: "Bill Wright was my roommate. The biggest, strongest, fastest, big man I've ever seen. I looked up to him in awe as a 15-year-old. He was 6–5 or 6–6, 230–240 pounds, could run as fast as anyone I've seen."—Roy Campanella[24]

Wright was signed by the Nashville Elites as a 17-year-old outfielder in 1932, although he occasionally drew "double duty" as a pitcher. It was as a pitcher in his youthful playing days that Wright secured the "Wild Bill" moniker because of his control problems.[25] In 1933, the Elites joined the Negro National League and Wright hit .340, with a .489 slugging percentage. That winter, the Elites played in the California Winter League and Wright batted .351, with a .517 slugging percentage. He was edged out for the batting championship that winter only by future Hall of Famers Cool Papa Bell and Willie Wells. In

B. Wright, BALT ELITE GIANTS

Burnis "Wild Bill" Wright, who had a lifetime batting average of .344, played on ten teams that won the California Winter League title. He spent much of his career in Mexico to escape the racism of his day. In 1943, he won the Mexican triple crown and missed the stolen base title by one base. Pitcher Bill Byrd regarded him as the best player in black ball. (Courtesy Helmar Brewing. Artist Sanjay Verma.)

the California Winter League of 1934–35, Wright won the batting championship with an astounding .481 batting average. He led the California Winter League in home runs in the winter of 1937–38. In 12 years of California winter ball, Wright compiled a career batting average of .375 and a slugging percentage of .599, and was a member of teams that won the California Winter League championship 10 times.[26]

In 1935, Wright was selected to the first of nine East-West All-Star Classics, a figure that is even more impressive in view of the substantial time Wright would later spend playing abroad. His lifetime batting average playing in the East-West All-Star Games was a cumulative .355. ESPN has designated Wright as the MVP of three separate East-West All-Star Games in the late 1930s. His best East-West All-Star Game performance occurred in the 1937 game, when he was the star of the game by going 3 for 5, driving in two runs, and making the fielding play of the game when he caught a blooper hit by Newt Allen.[27] After the 1936 season, Wright was chosen for the Negro National League All-Stars Team to play in the Denver Post Tournament. That team, containing five future Hall of Famers (Josh Gibson, Satchel Paige, Cool Papa Bell, Buck Leonard, and Ray Brown), proceeded to steamroll the tournament with seven consecutive victories.

Wright arguably had his best season in the Negro Leagues in 1937, when he hit .387, with nine home runs in 38 games, and was deemed a Seamheads all-star selection. John B. Holway regards him as a four-time all-star between 1936 and 1945. Cum Posey made him his all-star selection for 1936 and 1938. By 1939, he was the league's most feared hitter, with an official batting average that year of .371, while some newspaper accounts reported his 1939 average as high as .485.[28] He was labeled the NNL MVP for 1939 by ESPN.

In 1940, at the peak of his career, and after five consecutive appearance in the East-West All-Star Classic, Wright was recruited by and left to play in the Mexican League. In Mexico he discovered better pay, easier scheduling (usually three games a week) and greater respect.[29] It was here that his legend became even grander. In 1940, he finished fifth in the batting title (.360) and third in slugging percentage. In 1941, he led the Mexican league in stolen bases and batting average (.390) and finished third in home runs. His batting average exceeded that of former Negro Leaguers Josh Gibson (.374) and Ray Dandridge (.367), who joined him in Mexico that year.

After playing back in the United States in 1942 (because of his draft status)—where he hit .313, was among the league leaders in RBIs[30] and was named to both East-West Classics that year—he returned to Mexico in 1943. Bill Wright proceeded to win the 1943 Mexican Triple Crown, led the league in slugging percentage, and missed the stolen base crown by a single steal. His 1944 Mexican season featured a .335 batting average, with a .539 slugging percentage.[31] In 1945, when he came back to the United States, Wright hit .376, led the Negro National League in doubles, and was once again named to the East-West All-Star Game (his ninth time).[32]

There was certainly another side to Wright. He could be temperamental, and some regarded him as a "dirty" player. Pitcher Bull Harvey claimed that infielders were afraid of him and that Wright had a reputation that he would run over any player who got in front of him.[33] He became infamous in Mexico for one brawl in 1950 when his pitcher Lewis had been knocked unconscious by Lorenzo Cabrera's bat, after Cabrera had been hit by a pitch. With Cabrera ready to strike Lewis again, Wright rushed out of the dugout and knocked Cabrera unconscious with his own bat, possibly saving Lewis' life. Although Wright's actions were generally regarded as justifiable, the hubbub caused by this incident delayed Wright's eventual admission to the Mexican Hall of Fame.[34] Despite his disposition, Wright was well liked by the Mexican fans. Conceding that Wright could be volatile, Sammy Hughes and Roy Campanella both vouched for him as a nice fellow when you got to know him, with Campanella averring that he never saw Wright thrown out of a game.[35]

In 1946, "Wild Bill" returned to Mexico for good. He played in the Mexican League through 1951, then coached and played in the Mexican minor leagues, and retired as the owner of a successful Mexican bar and restaurant. Stung by the racism of his home country, Wright declined to return to the United States thereafter except for Negro League functions and tributes. Elected to the Mexican Baseball Hall of Fame in 1982, he lamented the fact that time had passed him by when his friend Roy Campanella finally made it to the big leagues. Wright believed that more than 50 percent of the Negro Leaguers could have played in the Major Leagues.[36] In an interview with Todd Bolton, he acknowledged: "It made you bitter, so many years you couldn't get in the major leagues, and now all the guys are getting in. So you start thinking about it all. You wonder about your life, all your good years behind you, up and down the highways. You think about all the talent in Negro baseball—it looked like it was just a waste."[37] "Wild Bill" Wright died in Aguascalientes, Mexico, in 1996 at the age of 82.

Various Negro League researchers have calculated that "Wild Bill" Wright had a lifetime batting average ranging between .341 and .361. With his speed, he led the Negro National League in triples three times. His California Winter League lifetime batting average was .375, including a home run title and one batting title. According to James A. Riley, he batted .371 in games against Major League pitching in Mexico and the California Winter League, including games in which he faced Dizzy Dean and Bob Feller. Wright was selected to nine East-West All-Star Games, chosen as a Mexican League All-Star three times, and picked as a Puerto Rican league all-star once. His career Mexican League batting average was .333, with 155 stolen bases in 905 games.[38] He won the Mexican batting crown twice and the Mexican League triple crown once. At multiple points of his career, he led his league in home runs, RBIs, batting average, slugging percentage, stolen bases, triples, and doubles. Between 1932 and 1955–56, CNLBR has determined that Wright played in season for at least seven Negro League teams in the United States, and for 12 teams in Mexico, participated in 20 Winter Leagues, and took part in major barnstorming tours.[39]

Bill Wright was deemed by historians James A. Riley and Dr. Lawrence Hogan to have had a Hall of Fame–worthy career. He was selected by leading historians John B. Holway, William F. McNeil, Todd Bolton, Lawrence D. Hogan, Brent Kelley, Larry Lester, and Jerry Malloy to their all-time Negro League all-star teams. He was picked as a rightful Hall of Famer by 68 percent of the voters in the McNeil Players' Poll. Significant Negro League veterans who placed him on their all-time all-star teams include Cum Posey, Buck Leonard, Willie Foster, Monte Irvin, Max Manning, Louis Santop, and Larry Doby. Pitcher Bill Byrd said bluntly that he was the best player in the black game.[40] He is one of six outfielders chosen to William F. McNeil's ultimate all-time Negro League all-star team based upon the votes of the veterans and historians in the McNeil Polls.

Wright's Similarity Scores are remarkable and demonstrate his true value. Seventeen of his closest 25 Major League matches are Hall of Famers, including such luminaries as Ty Cobb, Tris Speaker and Tony Gwynn.

It is apparent that the chief blemish that has kept Wild Bill Wright from the Hall of Fame was the fact that he "absconded" to Mexico and spent so much of his productive career there. Accordingly, his recorded WAR is not strictly comparable to other Negro League Hall of Fame candidates who spent the bulk of their careers in the United States. However, we have already postulated that, assuming a player meets the 10-year requirement for having played in American Negro League ball, a player who was driven abroad before the lifting of the color line by racism and the lure of better pay should have his entire career considered. Named on the pre-ballot for the 2006 Hall of Fame Negro League election, Wild Bill Wright is the "poster child" for this rule. His career WAR in only 10 years in the American Negro Leagues is the highest of any center fielder not in the Hall of Fame. His performance in Mexico only adds luster to that shine. His peers knew he had a Hall of Fame career. The voters should follow their lead.

Spottswood Poles

Years	Games	Runs	Hits	HR	RBI	SB	BA	SLG	WAR per 162g	WAR Career
1909–23	442	378	725	7	165	120	.328	.387	5.3	14.3

Career statistics (CNLBR), WAR (Seamheads).

First deemed the "The Black Ty Cobb" by Cuban sportswriter Abel Du-Breull in 1911,[41] Spot Poles was a switch-hitter and renowned superstar in both the United States and Cuba during the dead-ball era. Usually batting leadoff, he was a high-average line-drive hitter, which he coupled with superb defense in centerfield and blazing speed on the base paths. Poles claimed that he once ran 100 yards in less than 10 seconds in a track meet.[42] Veteran pitcher Sam Streeter declared that Poles was faster than Cool Papa Bell.[43]

According to historian James A. Riley, the speedy Spottswood Poles, known as the "Black Ty Cobb," had a lifetime batting average over .400 in Negro League competition. His speed is demonstrated by the fact that he is credited with 41 stolen bases in 60 games during his 1911 season with the New York Lincoln Giants. (Courtesy Helmar Brewing. Artist Scott Pedley.)

Growing up in Harrisburg, Pennsylvania, Spot Poles turned professional at age 19 as an outfielder for the 1906 Harrisburg Giants. Poles moved up the highest level of the Negro Leagues in 1909, when he joined Sol White's Philadelphia Giants as their center fielder.[44] That year, combined with Pop Lloyd and Bruce Petway, his team won the "Colored Championship of the World" from Rube Foster's Leland Giants. In 1911, he and Pop Lloyd jumped to the newly formed Lincoln Giants, where he spent much of his prime career. From 1911 through 1914, he became the foremost hitter in all of black baseball. According to Larry Lester and Dick Clark, who counted only games against high level competition, Poles' batting averages in those four seasons were .330, .313, .363, and .429 (a four-year average of .381). John B. Holway, who compiled games against all competition, credits Poles with a batting average of .481 in 1914.[45] Bill James regards Poles as the best player in all of the Negro Leagues for the span from 1914 through 1916. During the same era, he played four winters in the Cuban Winter League, with a cumulative batting average of .319.[46] Seamheads has designated him a Cuban Winter League all-star in all four of those winter seasons.

From 1914 to 1917, Poles was also a member of the legendary Breakers Hotel Team in the Florida Hotel League, where he played together with Hall of Famers Pop Lloyd, Smokey Joe Williams, and Pete Hill. Poles led the Florida Hotel League in batting average in 1914 and again in 1916.[47] He also is recorded as having a .405 average in 21 games against white Major League opposition, including three straight hits off Grover Cleveland Alexander.[48]

In 1918, he entered the military during World War I, during which he served with the Harlem Hell Fighters. In the service, he fought in the trenches and participated in the first Allied unit to cross the Rhine. Poles won five battlefield decorations and a Purple Heart[49] during what should have been one of his prime playing years. By 1919, he was back in the Negro Leagues and played through 1923, but with lesser success. It is probable that being wounded in action diminished his playing skills.[50] However, he did hit .365 for the Lincoln Giants during their 1920–21 California Winter League season, a campaign in which his team dominated the league with only two losses all season.[51]

One of the early game's legendary speedsters and stolen base mavens, much of Poles' stolen base statistical data is lost, but his speed is demonstrated by the fact that he is credited with 41 stolen bases in 60 games during his 1911 season with the New York Lincoln Giants.[52] The significant amount of missing records for Poles, who started his career in a pre–Negro League era, is reflected in the fact that Poles is only deemed 25th all-time in stolen bases in the statistics collected by Seamheads. Based upon the partial records uncovered, he is still listed as the stolen base leader in the Negro League East in 1911, 1913, 1914, and 1915.[53] John B. Holway, who deemed Poles an all-star in 1910, 1913, and 1914, states that in four games against Major Leaguers in which stolen bases were actually recorded, Poles stole five bases. He also used his speed to extend his range in order to become one of the game's best center fielders, which he complemented with a strong throwing arm.[54]

Poles was also considered a team leader on some of the greatest teams of his day. Between 1909 and 1921, CNLBR credits Poles with playing on 12 different teams that either won or self-proclaimed themselves championship teams, which was done commonly by teams in the times before there were formal playoffs. He was a member of eight teams that declared themselves "Colored Champion of the East" or "Colored Champion of the World." He was the spark plug of the Club Fé Championship team in the Cuban Winter League of 1913 and a member of the Breakers hotel team that won championships in 1915 and 1916.

Altogether, although he missed the 1918 season serving in the military, he had a lengthy career. Poles played 17 regular seasons of black ball from 1906 to 1923, and 10 years of winter ball (Cuba for four seasons; Florida for five; California for one). In 1923, Poles retired from the game: "I was still batting above .300 when I quit. The only thing was that I got tired of the train travel and carrying those bags around all the time. So I got out of baseball and bought myself five taxi cabs."[55]

The CNLBR estimates that Poles' recorded deeds are dwarfed by the number of games he played for which statistics are missing.[56] But one need not rely on the missing data to assess Spot Poles' career. James A. Riley has documented a .400 lifetime batting average for Poles in the Negro Leagues and .319 in the Cuban Winter League,[57] while CNLBR lists his career batting average against top level competition as somewhat lower, at .328. If you add his defensive prowess and speed to his batting ability, you are talking about one of the all-time greats of black ball. As for his lack of power, it needs to be remembered that Poles' career was played at the height of the dead-ball era. In terms of Major League Similarity Scores, Hall of Famer Richie Ashburn and future Hall of Famer Ichiro Suzuki are among his 10 closest matches.

Still it is the anecdotal evidence concerning Poles that truly stands out beyond the documented figures. John McGraw called him (with John Henry Lloyd, Dick Redding, and Smokey Joe Williams) one of the top four talents in the Negro Leagues.[58] The famous sportsman and entertainer Paul Robeson listed Spot Poles as one of the four greatest athletes he had ever seen, together with Jack Johnson, Joe Louis, and Jesse Owens.[59] Veteran Dizzy Dismukes included him as a starter on his all-time team.

Spot Poles was selected as a Hall of Famer by 70 percent of the historians in the McNeil Pioneers' Poll; an all-time Negro League all-star by William F. McNeil (including a first team all-star for the pre–1925 era); deemed a rightful Hall of Famer by leading historians Robert W. Peterson, James A. Riley, Jerry Malloy, Larry Lester, Brent Kelley, and Dick Clark; and picked as one of the top four all-time Negro League center fielders by Bill James. Bill James noted that he was "bothered by" his inability to find room for Poles on his all-time top 100 player list (which included Major League players), suggesting that he certainly has Hall of Fame credentials.[60] Spot Poles, whose career was long over, was listed sixth on the Roll of Honor for outfielders in the *Courier* Poll.

Poles is one of only three pre–Negro League player finalists on the 2006 final 39-name ballot of the Special Election for the Negro Leagues not yet admitted to the Hall of Fame. As properly summed up by the CNLBR, Spot Poles "was not only one of the best players of his day but also one of the best players in the history of black baseball."[61] Possibly the most famous African American ballplayer during his era not currently admitted to Cooperstown, the "Black Ty Cobb" appears to have been victimized by the Hall of Fame voters because of the long-ago period in which he played and the relative dearth of verifiable statistics available from his playing days.

Herbert "Rap" Dixon

Years	Games	Runs	Hits	HR	RBI	SB	BA	SLG	WAR per 162g	WAR Career
1922–37	607	512	706	77	468	110	.325	.538	5.8	21.8

Career Statistics and WAR (Seamheads)

When a player is named to the all-time Negro League outfield by no less than six Negro League Hall of Famers (Oscar Charleston, Cool Papa Bell, Leon Day, Larry Doby, Monte Irvin, and Ben Taylor), attention must be paid. Herbert "Rap" Dixon was a five-tool player who was both a leading hitter and one of the top defensive fielders in the 1920s and 1930s. Dixon could hit for average and power, was regarded as one of the fastest players in black ball, and possessed an extraordinary throwing arm. Working at a local area steel mill during summers in high school, Dixon is reputed to have developed his arm and shoulder strength by "throwing pig billets at the crane operators."[62] Dixon claimed he earned his nickname in high school back in 1919 from the manner in which he consistently "rapped" the ball all over the field when at the plate.[63]

After beginning his career with the independent Keystone Giants in the mid–1910s, Dixon stepped up to higher level professional ball with the Harrisburg Giants in 1922. After Harrisburg joined the Eastern Colored League in 1924, he often batted cleanup behind Oscar Charleston.[64] For the next four seasons, Dixon formed one of the greatest Negro League outfields of all time, playing alongside Oscar Charleston and "Fats" Jenkins. (Researcher Ted Knorr has argued that this triumvirate may well have been the single greatest outfield in baseball history.)[65]

Along with his speed, which gave him great range in the outfield, the *Afro American* reported that his throws were as though "shot from a rifle."[66] In fact, when he toured Japan with the Philadelphia Royal Giants in 1927, he would en-

Sporting a .325 lifetime batting average, Herbert "Rap" Dixon averaged 21 home runs and 38 stolen bases for each 162 games played during his career. In July 1929, Dixon had 14 hits in 14 consecutive at-bats in major league professional competition, a record which will probably never be broken. (Courtesy Helmar Brewing. Artist Scott Pedley.)

tertain the Japanese fans by standing on home plate and throwing the ball over the outfield fence during skills exhibitions.[67] Dixon's overall prowess in the field is confirmed by his Seamheads statistical ranking as the fourth best defensive right fielder in Negro League history, with 300 games or more in right field, when measured by Runs Saved Above Average.

And the man could hit. He was a line-drive-type hitter with power who was noted for his ability to hit with two strikes and to effectively handle curve balls.[68] In 1928, he had a 21-game hitting streak, later followed by a 19-game hitting streak.[69] Altogether he hit .398 for the Baltimore Black Sox in 1928, with a .701 slugging percentage. The next year he was even better; he led the Black Sox to the 1929 pennant as he hit .415 with 16 HRs, 22 SBs, and a .722 slugging average (Seamheads). In late July of 1929, Rap Dixon set a professional record of 14 straight hits in 14 "official" at-bats. His streak included two walks so that he reached base in 16 consecutive plate appearances. Both records have never been broken in any modern major league.[70] Moreover, this fully-documented streak (by box scores in multiple African American newspapers) was accomplished over a span of four games while facing some of black ball's leading pitchers: Smokey Joe Williams, Phil Cockrell and Sam Streeter.[71]

Dixon's seasonal WAR of 5.1 in 1929 is the fourth highest WAR that any Negro League left fielder (where he played most of that year) ever accumulated in a single season. In 1930, Dixon inaugurated the first Negro League games (a doubleheader) ever played in Yankee Stadium by hitting the first home run by an African American in Yankee Stadium in his initial at bat. That day, he hit a total of three home runs,[72] a Yankee Stadium record which would stand until Bobby Mercer hit four home runs in a 1970 doubleheader. When owner Gus Greenlee invited Pittsburgh Crawfords manager Oscar Charleston to assemble the best players in black ball in 1932, it was Rap Dixon who he selected as his right fielder. According to Seamheads, he proceeded to hit .318 and .359 in 1932 and 1933, respectively.

Over the course of his career, Rap Dixon had four or more hits in a game 12 times, four or more RBIs in a game eight times, and two home runs in a game six times.[73] Rap Dixon led the California Winter League in slugging percentage, triples, and hits, in 1927–28, and the Cuban Winter League in steals, in 1929–30.[74] In a 1927 goodwill tour of Japan with the Philadelphia Royal Giants, Dixon hit the longest ball ever recorded in Koshien Stadium and was awarded a trophy cup by Emperor Hirohito.[75] In the winter of 1934, Dixon and Josh Gibson replaced Johnny Mize on the 1934 Venezuelan Concordia team, which sparked them to the Caribbean title.[76] Limited statistics available from that winter campaign show that he batted .381 (CNLBR).

Rap Dixon is credited by CNLBR with a career batting average of .333 and a .530 slugging percentage against all competition. In official Negro League games and games against top levels of competition, he maintained an amazingly consistent lifetime batting average of .325 and a .538 slugging average (Seamheads). His career batting average in the California Winter League was .326. In 23 games against Major League pitching, CNLBR has compiled his batting average as .410. Aside from his high batting average, according to Seamheads, Dixon averaged 21 home runs and 38 stolen bases for each 162 games played over the course of his career. His career WAR of 21.8 and WAR per 162 games of 5.8 place him second and fourth respectively all-time among Negro League players who primarily played right field.

Dixon was a member of at least ten championship teams during his era, including the 1929 American Negro League title-winning Baltimore Black Sox, the 1934 Concordia team which won the Copa Trujillo Cup, and even played a single game with the 1934 Pittsburgh Crawfords. Off-season, he also played in five California Winter League seasons and one Cuban Winter League campaign. All five of Dixon's California Winter League teams won the winter league championship between 1925 and 1926 and 1930 and 1931.

Later on, Dixon's career was impacted by a severe back injury he suffered playing winter ball in Puerto Rico in 1933–34. Truth be told, he also had drinking and behavioral problems, which limited the teams willing to sign him. He developed a "hard case" reputation and was regarded by many as having become temperamental and lackadaisical.[77] In the winter of 1930, he found himself stranded and broke in California, probably due to drinking,[78] and only Hilldale was willing to take a chance on signing him.[79] In the mid–1930s, he also suffered from severe dental problems and developed pulmonary tuberculosis. His last hurrah came in 1935 as he drove the New York Cubans to the 2nd half title of the Negro National League, and then led his team in batting average and on base percentage in the playoffs.

Dixon never played at the major league level after 1937, although his "bad" reputation seems to have faded since he successfully served as a manager and general manager of various Negro League teams through 1944. Some of the highlights of his post–playing career were managing the Trujillo All-Stars to the 1937 Denver Post title and serving as business manager of the 1943 Harrisburg Stars. The Stars were noteworthy in that they played teams skippered by Honus Wagner and Dizzy Dean in 1943 to raise money for War Bonds. Rap Dixon died in 1944, after suffering a heart attack on a Detroit trolley, at the relatively young age of 41.[80]

Rap Dixon was selected to the 1925 and 1929 *Pittsburgh Courier* East All-Star Teams,

Cum Posey's all-star teams in 1925, 1929, 1933, and 1935, and to the *Afro American* all-star teams in 1926 and 1929. Seamheads has named him an all-star in 1928, 1929, 1931, 1932 and 1933; John B. Holway deemed him an all-star in 1928, 1929, and 1935. He was picked by the fans to play in the first two East-West All-Star Games in 1933 and 1934. That made him an all-star selection by at least one leading authority in nine of the 11 years between 1925 and 1935.

Dixon was the first outfielder listed on the Roll of Honor in the 1952 *Courier* Poll. Rap Dixon is included on William F. McNeil's all-time Negro League all-star team, historian Robert Peterson's second all-time team, and was deemed an all-time great by James A. Riley. He is a Hall of Fame selection of leading historians Jerry Malloy, Dick Clark, David A. Lawrence, Ted Knorr and Lou Hunsinger, Jr. His 20 closest Seamheads' Major League Similarity Scores include a stunning 14 Hall of Famers, Stan Musial, Joe DiMaggio, Hank Aaron and Mel Ott among them. Modern major leaguers among his 20 closest Similarity Scores also include Miguel Cabrera, Vladimir Guerrero and Ryan Braun.

Rap Dixon was included on the 39-name final ballot in the 2006 Hall of Fame election. Despite significant Hall of Fame support from the six Negro League Hall of Fame veterans mentioned above, Rap Dixon failed to garner the necessary 75 percent vote from the historians in the 2006 election. His health problems, which may well have led to his drinking and curtailed his career in the mid–1930s, seem to have affected his reputation and therefore his Hall of Fame vote. Nonetheless, Rap Dixon was one impressive ballplayer in the 1920s and mid–1930s and a perennial all-star for more than a decade. His .325 lifetime batting average, coupled with power at the plate and strong defensive skills, clearly evidence Hall of Fame ability. Dixon was a member of numerous championship teams wherever he played. His record of 14 straight hits in major league professional ball will probably stand forever. The record he left makes him a solid Hall of Fame selection. Can all of those Negro League Hall of Famers and historians who included Rap Dixon on their all-time teams be wrong?

Worthy of Further Discussion

Oscar *"Heavy" Johnson* was a Kansas City Monarchs slugger in the 1920s who consistently hit over .300. Big for his era, he was six feet tall and weighed in at approximately 250 lbs. In 1913, Johnson claimed he was three years older than his actual age and joined the Army.[81] Between 1913 and 1922, he spent somewhere between six and eight of his most productive seasons serving on the all black military baseball team, the 25th Infantry Regiment Wreckers. The Wreckers were a dominant team in amateur and military baseball because their players were specially recruited and paid to play baseball as entertainment for the Army. Symbolic of their strength was a 1917 series they swept against the Portland Beavers of the Pacific Coast League, a Portland team containing seven former and future Major Leaguers.[82] The CNLBR has uncovered a mere six Wreckers games played by Johnson, but in that small sample he batted .500, hit two home runs, scored at least five runs, and had one stolen base.[83]

As is true with respect to Dobie Moore, who was also on the Wreckers, this presents a quandary to his assessment for the Hall of Fame. The Wreckers were probably the best black ball team in the country, but few statistics remain from its heyday. At the suggestion of Casey Stengel, who saw them play in the Army, Johnson joined four of his military teammates (including Bullet Rogan, Andy Cooper, Walter "Dobie" Moore, and Hurley McNair) on the Kansas City Monarchs in 1922.[84] By that time, Johnson was already 27 years old. According to John B. Holway, Johnson proceeded to amass a .451 batting average and a .644 slugging percentage in 1922 in both league and non-league games.[85] In league games alone, he won the 1922 Negro National League batting championship by hitting .389. He then led the Los Angeles White Sox to the California Winter League championship during the 1922–23 season while winning that league's batting championship with a .340 average.

But Heavy Johnson is even better known for his 1923 season, in which he won the Negro National League triple crown with a .406 batting average, 20 home runs, and 120 RBIs (CNLBR). He also led the league that year in slugging, hits, total bases, and doubles. John B. Holway has awarded Heavy Johnson his Fleet Walker Award (MVP) for 1923. That winter he hit .345 and led the Santa Clara Leopards to the Cuban Winter League title.[86]

In 1924, James A. Riley's statistics show he hit .411 in National League action (although other sources show him as low as .361) and reputedly hit more than 60 home runs against all opposition in a schedule that probably ran to over 250 games.[87] He then capped that season off by leading the Monarchs to win the 1924 Colored World Championship with a .296 batting average. An unpolished fielder,[88] "Heavy" Johnson's true position was hitter. Jocko Conlon, who barnstormed with Johnson, claimed that "Heavy" Johnson could hit the ball out of any park.[89] According to John B. Holway, Johnson was 8–16 lifetime against Major League pitching. CNLBR has located only two exhibition games he played against Major Leaguers, in which he batted .500 and hit one home run.

"Heavy" Johnson remained a star through around 1928, when he was 33 years old, leading the Eastern Colored League in triples in 1927[90] and, according to Seamheads, batting .379 and .348 respectively in 1927 and 1928. Whatever the reason for his diminished powers at that point, he continued playing ball for various Negro League teams, at lower and lower levels, through 1935. Few significant statistics exist for him after 1928.

Seamheads designated Johnson an all-star in 1922 and 1923. John B. Holway deemed him an all-star in 1922, 1923, 1924, and 1926. Overall, Johnson compiled a lifetime .369 batting average in the Negro Leagues and won three batting titles.[91] Twice he batted higher than .400 over the course of a season (1922 and 1923). His slugging percentage was consistently over .500 over the course of his career.[92] As stated, he was the league MVP in 1923. Heavy Johnson's lifetime WAR of 17.7 accumulated in a short official career, and his WAR per 162 games of 5.4 places him among the all-time leaders not yet in the Hall of Fame. (His aggregate offensive WAR is actually 23.3 but was reduced by his woeful defensive contributions.)

"Heavy" Johnson's Seamheads Similarity Scores are more than intriguing. His three closest Major League matches (in order) are Ty Cobb, Joe DiMaggio, and Joe Jackson. His 20 closest Major League matches also include Mike Trout, Ted Williams, Tris Speaker, Stan Musial, and Rogers Hornsby. Clearly his peak value was astonishing, but the period of his high performance in recorded black ball was not lengthy (although he does meet the overall 10-year minimum requirement even excluding his early career with the Wreckers). Probably as a result, he is only mentioned sporadically in historian and player polls and was not cited at all in the 1952 *Courier* Poll. "Heavy" Johnson was included on the 2006 Hall of Fame pre-ballot, but he did not make the final ballot. What he might have accomplished if he had played the entire early portion of his career in the Negro Major Leagues is only speculation. Historian William F. McNeil has calculated Major League equivalencies that estimate, if given the chance, Heavy Johnson would have averaged .302, with 21 home runs each year over the course of a full Major League career.[93] That would certainly have made him a Hall of Famer.

Hurley McNair is the leading candidate for the most underappreciated outfielder in Negro League history. McNair has the highest career WAR (31.1) of any Negro League outfielder not in the Hall of Fame. For years, the lack of Negro League statistics was used as an excuse to keep Negro Leaguers out of the Hall of Fame. Now that a significant amount of statistics, however incomplete, have been compiled, Hurley McNair has been revealed as an unacknowledged jewel.

McNair was one of the early Negro National League's great stars who had a productive 27-year career. He initially was a dual threat who could pitch and hit for high average. Standing only 5 ft. 6 in. tall and weighing approximately 150 lbs., McNair came out of the sandlots in Texas. A contact hitter with a reputation for delivering in the clutch, he was reputed to be the best two strike hitter in baseball. His teammate George Giles once said: "Mac could have taken two strikes against Jesus Christ and base hit the next pitch."[94]

He was also a strong defensive outfielder with a robust arm and excellent speed on the base paths. Unfortunately, McNair also had a reputation for being moody and self-centered. Historian James A. Riley called him "a little man with a big head" and reports that he would refuse to play if things were not to his liking.[95] Others, however, credited him with teaching them the game. Willie Wells told John B. Holway that McNair taught him how to hit a curve ball by tying his front leg to home plate and throwing him curve after curve.[96]

Starting in 1910, McNair spent his first 10 years playing independent ball. During that decade, he played for such legendary teams as the Minnesota Keystones (1911), Frank Leland's Chicago Giants (1912), Chicago Union Giants (1913–14), Rube Foster's American Giants (1915), J.L. Wilkinson's All Nations team (1917), the Army's 25th Infantry Wreckers (1918), and the Detroit Stars (1919). The bottom line is that he was sought out by and played for many of the legendary teams of his era. Relatively few statistics have been uncovered for this earlier (and presumably most productive) part of his career. According to James A. Riley, McNair batted cleanup for Rube Foster's American Giants in 1915 and hit .288.[97] overall, CNLBR has found only box scores for 116 games Hurley played before 1920, in which he collectively batted .348, with a .500 slugging percentage.[98]

McNair was already 31 when he joined the Kansas City Monarchs of the fledgling Negro National League in 1920. Over the next six years, he proceeded to hit .348 in league action. His best recorded season was 1922, when he hit .374, with a slugging percentage of .553, and helped the Monarchs win the City Championship of Kansas City over the Kansas City Blues.[99] McNair's seasonal WAR of 5.4 in 1922 is the second highest ever accumulated by any Negro League left fielder (where he mostly played that year) in a single season.

As a pitcher in the earlier part of his career, Seamheads records that he had a .636 winning percentage and a 3.73 ERA. The highlight of his pitching career seems to be a 10-inning game in which he out-dueled Rube Foster in 1911.[100] His pitching duties, largely successful, ceased in 1924. While one might assume his WAR is inflated by his pitching, only 0.8 of his total WAR of 30.9 is based upon his performance on the mound.

Seamheads has deemed McNair a hypothetical all-star (if such had existed) in 1915, 1916, 1920, 1922, 1923, and 1924. Defensively, Seamheads also awards McNair a retroactive Golden Glove in 1915 and second place in 1920, 1922, 1923, 1924, and 1928. He also finished in the top four places of their Silver Slugger award in 1915 and each year from 1920 through 1923. The *Kansas City Star* named him an all-star in 1920. John B. Holway designated McNair an all-star in 1922, and 1923. Cum Posey named him to his all-star unit in 1924. According to Seamheads, McNair had the highest WAR of any Kansas City Monarch for the period of 1920 to 1934.[101]

Most importantly, he was a winner. CNLBR has determined that he played on 10 championship teams on which he played from 1911 to 1925, including three consecutive Negro National League titles that he won with the great Kansas City Monarchs teams of the 1920s. McNair also played four seasons in the California Winter League between 1920 and 1925, accumulating an overall batting average of .322.[102] Each of his California Winter League teams won the league championship. In 23 games against Major League pitchers, he compiled a .303 batting average and a .485 slugging percentage.[103]

According to CNLBR, McNair batted .424 in 1932 at the age of 43 as a member of John Donaldson's All Stars. He continued to play until 1937 when he was 48 years old. As a result, Hurley McNair's playing career extended at least 18 years, from 1910 through 1937. The CNLBR reports he compiled a .331 career batting average and a .486 career slugging average in Negro League play.[104] He ended his career as a Negro League umpire, officiating in the 1941 Negro League World Series. Legend claims he once ended an argument by pulling a knife on a group of players who disagreed with his umpiring call and had come after him with their bats.[105] McNair, rarely mentioned by historians or players as their proposed all-time or Hall of Fame selection, was properly included in the initial pool of 94 candidates selected by the 2006 Hall of Fame Special Committee on the Negro Leagues Election. But he did not make the final ballot that year.

Perhaps his attitude affected how others valued him. Based upon his on-field offensive and defensive performance, it seems remarkable that his name does not appear at all in the McNeil Polls or in the 1952 *Courier* Poll. Surely, even the limited statistical record compiled by McNair after the age of 30, combined with the longevity of his career, appear to build a thought-provoking Hall of Fame case. The stat heads at the Hall of Eric and Miller included McNair as one of their selections to their list of the 29 greatest Negro League players. This conclusion is buttressed by his Similarity Scores, which include six Hall of Famers among his closest ten matches, including Kiki Cuyler and Roberto Clemente. One of the truly great Negro League outfielders whose statistics from the prime of his career are lost to time, Hurley McNair died in 1948 at age 60.

Clarence "Fats" Jenkins is already an inductee of the Basketball Hall of Fame based upon his role as captain of the legendary New York Renaissance. Nicknamed "Fats" by his younger brother, Jenkins was a short, stocky speed demon. Jenkins stood only 5 feet 7 inches tall and weighed roughly 165 to 180 pounds during his playing days.[106] As a baseball player, he was a fleet-footed leadoff hitter who John B. Holway reports averaged .337 at the plate over an 18-year career stretching from 1920 through 1938. Jenkins was also an excellent defender, his speed giving him extraordinary range. Because of his range, he played plenty of center field, but was mostly in the left field corner. However, Seamheads ranks his fielding prowess only eleventh all-time among Negro League left fielders.

Although he had little power, researcher John B. Holway lists him among the top 10 hitters in Negro League history, ranked by batting average.[107] He was a lefty who was exceptionally fast starting out of the batter's box and running the bases. A slap hitter, he was able to get on base often and stole bases with abandon.[108] From 1923 to 1927, he served as the lead-off hitter for Oscar Charleston's Harrisburg Giants, never batting less than .300 each year.[109] Jenkins' best season for Harrisburg was 1927, when, according to John B. Holway, he hit .413 and led the league in stolen bases. Seamheads' data reveals that he averaged 45 stolen bases for each 162 games played during his career. In 540 league games reviewed by CNLBR, he got two or more hits in 215 games and three or more hits in 68 games.[110] He was designated a Seamheads all-star in 1930 and was selected to the East-West All-Star Game in 1932 and 1935. Jenkins was also a four-time John B. Holway all-star selection, a *Pittsburgh Courier* all-star pick in 1925, and a Cum Posey all-star selection in 1932.

Playing mostly for second division and independent teams during his prime years from 1924 through 1932, many of Jenkins' statistics are lost. His performance also suffered from his always skipping spring training due to his basketball schedule, which appears to have been his priority.[111] He played basketball on the best black teams in the country for 25 years from 1916 through 1941. Basketball teams for which he either played or coached won 10 "World Championships."[112] (He also excelled at boxing, just missing out on being designated an Olympic boxer in 1920.)

Still, his career WAR of 17.8 in his secondary sport of baseball ranks him among the top two left fielders in Negro League history. Jenkins was listed third on the Roll of Honor for outfielders in the 1952 *Courier* Poll (in which he was a voter). A player whose slap-and-run skills relate back to the dead-ball era, it is fascinating that his four closest Major League Similarity Scores are those of old time Hall of Famers Jesse Burkett, Cap Anson, Billy Hamilton and Wee Willie Keeler.

Fats Jenkins was a third team all-time pick of historian John B. Holway and earned honorable mention on William F. McNeil's all-time Negro League team, who called him a world-class outfielder. Jenkins was designated by James A. Riley as an all-time great and was a finalist on the 39-name 2006 Hall of Fame Negro Leagues ballot. Fats Jenkins has also been listed on the All-Time best teams of numerous historians, including Todd Bolton, Lou Hunsinger, Jr., and Lyle K. Wilson. Possibly the greatest two-sports athlete in American professional sports history, Jenkins was also included on the all-time all-star outfields selected by numerous Negro Leagues players, including Buck Leonard, "Double Duty" Radcliffe, Ted Burnett, and Josh Johnson.

Alejandro "El Caballero" (The Gentleman) Oms.

No Latino player who has failed to make the National Hall of Fame has received more support from historians than Alejandro "El Caballero" Oms, support not really mirrored in the polls of Negro League veterans. Oms was, together with Cristóbal Torriente, probably one of the two best Cuban-born players in the first half of the 20th century.[113] He was nicknamed "The Gentleman" due to his non-argumentative behavior on the field, but in point of fact he would pretend not to understand English with umpires when it was to his advantage.[114] Legend has it that his cover was eventually blown when he was hit by a pitch and yelled out "give me some water."[115]

Oms began his career in 1910, playing in local sandlot and sugar-mill leagues in Cuba. He moved up the ladder until he was playing for his local Santa Clara team and spent one undistinguished year moonlighting with New York's independent Cuban Stars, in 1917.[116] Returning to the Cuban Stars in 1921, Oms was now ready for the big time and formed one of the greatest outfields in Eastern Colored League (ECL) history, playing for the Cuban Stars alongside Bernardo Baro and Pablo Mesa. He had great range as a fielder but was known for having a weak arm. He also was a bit of a showman. When games were not close, he would catch balls behind his back or execute a 720-degree spin before throwing the ball.[117]

Oms was also an exceptionally fast runner who excelled at stealing bases. But it was at the plate that he shone. When the Cuban Stars entered the ECL in 1923, James A. Riley's stats, which include both league and non-league games, reflect that he hit .400.[118] Throughout his career, he consistently hit in the mid-.300 range, and he was able to spray the ball to all fields with power. Oms reportedly hit a record 40 home runs against all competition in 1922,[119] becoming widely known as the "Cuban Babe Ruth."[120] He generally batted third or cleanup for Cuban Stars teams, which unfortunately for him often played mediocre baseball. In 1935, at the age of 39, he hit .354 for the New York Cubans and was named to the East-West All-Star Game, where he went 2 for 4. After 1935, he ceased playing in the domestic Negro Leagues and spent the rest of his career in Cuba, the Dominican Republic, and Venezuela. According to Seamheads, his lifetime batting average in the American-based Negro Leagues was .328 over a 15-year career.

Yet it was in Cuba and Venezuela that Oms truly outclassed the field. Playing in Cuba from 1922 through 1941, he was the second leading batter (.343) in Cuban League history, behind only Cristóbal Torriente (.352).[121] He won five batting titles and led that league in slugging five times. Oms hit over .300 in 11 of the 13 full winter league seasons he played in Cuba. He was the Cuban Winter League MVP in the 1928–29 season. Historian Dr. Layton Revel has pointed out that, if one factors out his last two seasons in Cuba, when he was in his mid–40s, his career batting average in Cuba would have been .372.[122] Later in his career, beginning in the mid–1930s, Oms began playing in Venezuela, where he won two batting championships, hit over .400 in two seasons with Concordia in 1934 and 1935, and was voted the top defensive player in the league in 1943, at the age of 48.[123] He died suddenly in 1946 shortly after completing another Venezuelan season.

Oms was fittingly elected to the Cuban Hall of Fame in 1944. Analyzing whether Oms belongs in the American Hall of Fame is more problematic. On the one hand, Oms is undisputedly one of the top ballplayers of his era who participated in the American Negro Leagues in excess of the Hall of Fame's 10-year minimum requirement. His lifetime batting average of .328 and overall performance in the United States were outstanding—but not as exceptional as those of his fellow Cubans Cristóbal Torriente or José Méndez, who were elected to the Hall of Fame in 2006. His Seamheads Similarity Scores are also strong, featuring eight Hall of Famers among his top ten Major League matches, the closest of whom are Tris Speaker and Sam Thompson.

If one takes a broad view of the Negro Leagues as including the Caribbean venues where players spent their winters, Oms should be a Hall of Famer. However, we need to keep in mind that we are assessing whether a candidate should be elected to the American Hall of Fame. Oms' cumulative WAR over the course of 15 seasons played in the American Negro Leagues was only 13.8 (89th all-time), which does not truly place him among the elite players in the United States. His defensive statistics on Seamheads show him as a negative factor compared to an average center fielder. He played on four championship teams, won five batting championships, five slugging percentage championships, a home run title, a stolen base title, one MVP award, and a top defensive player of the Year award, but never in the United States.

We have earlier postulated that American players who met the minimum 10-year entry requirement should have their records abroad considered for Hall of Fame eligibility because they were not permitted to play in the Major Leagues and went wherever they could earn their best pay. This reasoning is supported by the fact that it was the better Negro League players who were generally recruited to play abroad. It is not as clear that this rule should be applied in reverse for foreign-born players who played the principal portion of their careers abroad and also participated for the lesser part of their careers in the United States.

Conceding that Oms was one of the all-time greats of the sport, and would have played in the Major Leagues had he not been prevented from doing so because of racism, it still does not seem as though his accomplishments in the United States truly warrant inclusion in the National Hall of Fame. Seamheads never designated him an all-star in any year in the United States, although John B. Holway regards him as an all-star for three years in the United States during the period 1922–1930. As stated, Oms was selected for one East-West All-Star Classic (1934).

Of the 92 former players who participated in the 2001 McNeil Players' Poll, fewer than 10 cited Oms for Hall of Fame consideration. Only 20 percent of the historians voted for Oms in the McNeil Historians' Poll. His name also does not appear at all in the 1952 *Courier* Poll. Though leading historians such as William F. McNeil and John B. Holway (who count games from all venues in gathering his statistics) have argued for Oms' admission to the Hall of Fame,[124] preeminent sabermetrician Bill James concluded that, aside from his high batting average, Oms did not do "anything special."[125] It appears that the voters in the 2006 Hall of Fame Special Election on the Negro Leagues struggled with this issue and collectively reached the same conclusion as James. Oms was included on the 39-name final ballot in 2006 but was not one of the 17 players elected. Still, 2006 voting committee member Todd Bolton believed that, based upon the discussions, Oms may have garnered at least 50 percent of the vote.[126]

In his book *Baseball's Other All-Stars*, historian William F. McNeil designates Oms as a starter on the Cuban All-Time Winter League Team and even as a member of the truly elite Non–Major League All-World All-Time All-Star Team. Those designations are appropriate, as is Oms' 1944 election to the Cuban Hall of Fame. Perhaps it should be left at that.

Valentin Dreke. Although not receiving as much attention as Alejandro Oms, Valentin Dreke was one of the best Cuban stars spending time in Negro Leagues of the United States. Playing in the era from 1918 to 1928, he was a speedy leadoff hitter who could spray the ball around the diamond, lay down and beat out drag bunts, and get himself into scoring position once he was on base.[127] According to Seamheads, the left-handed hitter's lifetime batting average in the American Negro Leagues over the nine years he played in the United States was .326. He began his stateside career with the Cuban Stars in 1918 and continued with them after they joined the Negro National League in 1920, playing alongside other Cuban legends Eustaquio Pedroso and Bernardo Baro. According to James A. Riley, he tormented pitchers as he hit .353 in 1920 and then had his best year in 1924, when he hit .429, with a slugging average of .538. For the next three years, he batted cleanup and hit over .300 each year, and averaged over 100 runs scored each year.[128] According to James A. Riley, he was also an excellent fielding outfielder with a strong throwing arm.[129]

Dreke was a major star in Cuban Winter Ball over the same period, accumulating a .334 lifetime batting average[130] and leading that league in stolen bases in 1923–24. Dreke retired from baseball in 1928, when he was only 30 years old. William F. McNeil included Dreke as a member of his All-Time Cuban Winter League Team but only as an honorable mention on his All-Time Negro League Team. Dreke's play in the United States fails to meet the 10-year minimum requirement for American Hall of Fame admission, as reflected in his credible but hardly remarkable career WAR of 12.3 and WAR per 162 games of 3.2. Only one of the 20 Major Leaguers with his closest Similarity Scores is a Hall of Famer: marginal selection Lloyd Waner. Perhaps this, combined with his lack of power, is the reason he has received virtually no Hall of Fame support from veterans or historians. Valentin Dreke was elected to the Cuban Hall of Fame in 1945.

Chaney White was a star center fielder for the Eastern Colored League champion-ship Bacharach Giants in the 1920s. According to Seamheads, in a 17-year career from 1920 through 1936, White accumulated a .312 lifetime batting average and a WAR of 15.6. Known for his quiet personality off the field, on the diamond he featured blazing speed and an aggressive no-holds-barred style of play, White was described by one player as "built like King Kong but runs like Jesse Owens."[131] White liked to lean into a pitch, get hit, and then steal second. On the bases, he was a spikes-up slider who once sliced off Josh Gibson's chest protector.[132] According to Buck Leonard, White was a player "a fella was afraid to tag. He came in pretty high."[133]

White often played left field because of his weak throwing arm, but he compensated for his arm with good range, which came from his speed. Overall, his defense was a major asset and his fielding statistics on Seamheads rate him as the all-time 11th best defensive left fielder in Negro League history. Chaney White first made his mark in the Eastern Colored League in the early 1920s, where, according to James A. Riley, he batted over .300 every season from 1921 through 1925. After battling leg injuries for a few years, he became the regular center fielder for the Bacharachs, batting in the heart of the order and helping them to league titles in 1926 and 1927 (they lost the World Series in each of those years).[134] In the 1926 World Series, he stole five bases in six attempts. In 1930, he became a member of the legendary Homestead Grays, although he switched to Hilldale by the end of the season.

The *Pittsburgh Courier* deemed him an all-star in 1925 and Seamheads designated White an all-star outfielder in 1931. John B. Holway regards him as an all-star in 1933. White's Similarity Scores turn up no Hall of Famers among his closest ten Major League matches, and his WAR per 162 games of 2.9 is not particularly strong. An interesting side note is that Chaney White was himself one of the expert voters in the 1952 *Courier* Poll, but neither he nor any of the other voters cast ballots for him in that poll.

The respect of his peers may be the strongest factor in favor of Chaney White's can-didacy. Chaney White was selected by both Pop Lloyd and Willie Foster as the starting left fielder on their All-Time Negro League All-Star teams, by ECL founder Ed Bolden in 1950 to his all-time team, and by historian Robert Peterson to this third team all-star team. Bill James ranked him as the seventh all-time Negro League left fielder. Of particular interest is Satchel Paige's 1950s memoir *Maybe I'll Pitch Forever*. In that book, Paige ranks the top hitters he ever saw in order as Josh Gibson, Ted Williams, Joe DiMaggio, Stan Musial, and Chaney White (who he calls a close fifth). Perhaps anecdotal evidence is not dispositive, but the collective opinions of Pop Lloyd, Willie Foster, and Satchel Paige cannot be entirely discounted. They actually played against the guy.

There were other exceptional Negro League outfielders who evidenced a sufficient skill set but whose overall career performance might not quite rise to the Hall of Fame standard:

Clint "Hawk" Thomas was an extremely popular .300 power hitter in the 1920s; good speed, a superb fielder; WAR of 21.4 is second highest of any Negro League center fielder not currently in the Hall of Fame; defensive standout who covered the outfield with such grace that he became known as "The Black DiMaggio"; Seamheads statistics rank him as the 14th best defensive center fielder in Negro League history; according to James A. Riley, in 1923 Thomas hit .373, with 23 home runs and 56 stolen bases, to lead Hilldale to the first Eastern Colored League pennant, and then batted averages of .363 and .351 the following two years; lifetime batting average of .301 (Seamheads); John B. Holway's All-Star pick in 1925, 1930, and 1933; played on three consecutive Cuban winter ball championship teams; Seamheads all-star in Cuban Winter League in 1922–23 and in the United States in 1926; hit a home run off of a young Fidel Castro in Cuba[135]; his stolen base total ranks eleventh in Negro League history; alleged to have hit 367 home runs before he retired in 1938[136]; Similarity Scores reflect no Major League Hall of Famers among his top 10 matches; Bill James ranked him as sixth best Negro League center fielder; despite solid credentials, Hawk has received little support in player or historian polls.

Sam "The Jet" Jethroe had world class speed; played seven torrid years in the Negro Leagues before entering the Major Leagues in 1948; led the league in batting average in 1944 and 1945 and in stolen bases in 1944, 1945, and 1946; career Negro League batting average of .314 through 1948 (Seamheads); hit a grand slam home run off Dizzy Dean in a 1943 exhibition game[137]; winner of John B. Holway's Fleet Walker Award as the best player in the Negro League West in both 1944 and 1945; winner of ESPN's retroactive MVP award in both 1945 and 1947; named to seven East-West All-Star Classics; John B. Holway deemed him a four-time all-star between 1942 and 1947; at age 33 took a pay cut to play Major League ball from 1950 to 1954; earned Rookie of the Year in the National League in 1950, when he hit .273 and led the league in stolen bases; WAR per 162 games of 7.5 is among the top 15 in Negro League history; best Major League season was 1951, when he hit .280, with 18 home runs and 35 stolen bases.

Jimmie Lyons. Before there was a Cool Papa Bell there was a Jimmie Lyons; according to James A. Riley, "one of the fastest men ever to wear a baseball uniform"[138]; career WAR of 17.0 is third highest all-time among Negro League left fielders; according to CNLBR, career batting average of .310, with a slugging percentage of .431 against top competition; one of the fastest players of his era (1910–25) who would often bunt his way on base; top base stealer of his time, who played for 13 championship winning teams over an 18-year career from 1910 to 1925; led his league twice in batting, with .325 average in 1911 and .399 average in 1920; awarded John B. Holway's Fleet Walker Award as the best player in 1911 and again in 1920, when he coupled his .399 batting average with 39 steals and 10 home runs in 164 at bats; a three-time Seamheads all-star in the Cuban Winter League of 1911–12, 1918, and 1921; two-time all-star pick of John B. Holway; abilities adversely impacted by a 25-foot fall down an elevator shaft in 1921[139]; member of three Negro League championship teams from 1921 to 1923; when he played in an Allied Expeditionary Force League during World War I, he played against Ty Cobb's brother, who remarked that Lyons was better than Cobb[140]; no power, often injured; Seamheads' defensive statistics rank him fourth among all-time among Negro League center fielders; there are no Hall of Famers among his top five Similarity Score matches; his skills were designed for his dead-ball era; an all-time outfield selection of multiple players (e.g., Buck O'Neil and Dave Malarcher) and of historians (Tweed Webb, Sammy J. Miller, and Jerry Malloy; listed fourth on the Roll of Honor for outfielders on the 1952 *Courier* Poll); Bill James ranked him as fifth best Negro League center fielder.

Charlie Blackwell had a career WAR of 16.2, placing him squarely among the elite outfielders; an excellent contact hitter with solid power and a drinking problem[141]; in a 13-year career from 1915 to 1929, he hit .313 with an OPS (on base percentage plus slugging percentage) of .873 (Seamheads); Seamheads' outstanding position player for black ball in 1921, when he established the highest seasonal WAR (6.8) for right fielders in Negro League history, as led the league with an outstanding .402 batting average, 13 home runs and 26 stolen bases in 84 games; followed it up in 1922 with a .353 average; John B. Holway all-star selection for 1921 and 1922, whom Holway placed on his third all-time team; closest Major League player pursuant to Similarity Score analysis is Hall of Famer Roberto Clemente; skills faded as he fell more and more under the influence of alcohol; Bill James ranked him ninth among all-time Negro League center fielders; died from drink-related issues in 1935.

Ted Strong. High average switch-hitting power .300 hitter who won HR and RBI crowns; solid defensive player who played in seven East-West All-Star Games and started all-star games at three different positions (shortstop, right field, and first base); hit .348 in all-star competition; played in Mexico in 1940, where he finished second in slugging average and home runs[142]; ESPN's MVP of the Negro American League in 1941; lost three years serving in World War II and then returned to drive his team to the pennant in 1946 by leading the league in home runs and RBIs; ranked by Bill James as one of the top three all-time Negro League right fielders; two-sport star who played for the original Harlem Globetrotters basketball team; career [1936–1948] batting average was .322 (Seamheads); career OPS of .926 is 19th highest in Negro League history; WAR per 162 games of 6.7 is best all-time among right fielders with at least ten years of play; closest Major Leaguer in terms of Similarity Scores is Jackie Robinson (it is remarkable that, out of all of the thousands of Major Leaguers who have played the game, how many Negro League players have their closest Similarity Score match as Jackie Robinson—leading one to suspect that the Negro Leagues were filled with many players with a unique skill set established in Negro League play); bad reputation for being an undisciplined free swinger at the plate and undisciplined in life; career and productivity probably shortened by drinking and womanizing.[143]

Bernardo Baro. Five-tool left-hander who hit to all fields for average and with power; smaller player who relied more on speed than power; played alongside Alejandro Oms and Pablo Mesa on the Cuban Stars in the 1920s to create one of black ball's greatest outfields; lifetime Negro League batting average of .298 over 15 American Negro League seasons (Seamheads); selected as an all-star by John B. Holway in 1915, 1919, and 1923; taking a turn on the mound in a doubleheader, pitched a no-hitter against the Indianapolis ABCs in 1921; overly sensitive and quick-tempered player who fought often[144]; suffered a mental breakdown in 1929 and died at 37; superstar of Cuban Winter League who was the Seamheads' Top Position Player in Cuba in 1922–23, when he hit .401; elected a member of Cuban Hall of Fame; Similarity Scores show Frank Chance as the only Hall of Famer among his top 40 Major League matches; cited by only a single player and one historian in the McNeil Polls; not mentioned in the 1952 *Courier* Poll; although he was on the 2006 Hall of Fame preliminary ballot, career WAR of 8.0 in American Negro League competition does not seem sufficient for serious Hall of Fame consideration.

Roy "Red" Parnell. Spent most of his career patrolling the outfield in the lower quality Negro Southern League, which is generally regarded as a Negro Major League only in 1932; accumulated the highest career WAR (18.9) of any Negro League left fielder playing in a lesser Negro League circuit; solid hitter and good fielder without much power; excellent range in the outfield but weak throwing arm; won batting championships when he hit .467 for New Orleans in 1926[145] and .426 for the Birmingham Black Barons in 1927; according to CNLBR, led the Negro Southern League in eight offensive categories in 1932, including hitting (.384), runs batted in, slugging percentage (.801) and hits, the one season in which the Southern League is accorded major league status by historians; career batting average of .326 (Seamheads); played on 17 championship teams (mostly in the South)[146]; Seamheads fielding statistics rank him as an overall negative factor in comparison to an average Negro League left fielder; elected to two East-West All-Star Games; named a John B. Holway all-star and Top Position Player in all of black ball by Seamheads in 1927; Cum Posey all-star in 1932 and 1936, although Posey acknowledged his fielding prowess was subpar[147]; played 18 years despite drinking problem[148]; managed successfully from 1929 to 1941, guiding his teams to 11 championships[149]; Hall of Famer Willie Foster selected him as an outfielder on his all-time Negro League team; seven Hall of Famers among his top ten Similarity Score matches, including Kirby Puckett; received one lone player vote in the McNeil Polls and no citation whatsoever in the *Courier* Poll; his inclusion on the final 2006 Special Committee ballot for the Negro Leagues seems more of a tribute to the Negro Southern League, by including its greatest player, than may be justified by his career WAR of 18.9 (although the paucity of Southern League statistics doubtless lowers his actual WAR).

George "Rabbit" Shively. Speedy lead-off left fielder and great bunter with outstanding defensive outfield range; played from 1910 to 1925; career WAR of 12.3 is the eighth highest of any Negro League left fielder; teamed with Oscar Charleston and Jimmie Lyons on the 1918 Indianapolis ABCs to form one of the great outfields in Negro League history; twice a winner of John B. Holway's Fleet Walker Award as the MVP of the Western Conference, in 1914 and 1917; two-time batting champion with a lifetime Negro Leagues batting average of .306; designated an all-star by either John B. Holway or Seamheads (usually by both) each year from 1913 through 1918; superstitious left-handed hitter who would not let a right-handed batter borrow his bat[150]; recorded stolen-base total of 123 ranks him 20th all-time in American Negro League action despite reams of missing statistics form his era; only Major League Hall of Famer with matching Similarity Scores among the his top 25 matches is the marginal HoF selection Tommy McCarthy; similar in talent to Jimmie Lyons but may have been better; another of the underrated stars of the Negro Leagues.

Vic Harris (See Analysis in Chapter 17).

WAR Comparison of Negro League Hall of Famers and Candidates—Outfield
All Leagues: Negro, Cuban, Mexican Leagues, vs. Major Leaguers and High Minors

Name	Years	WAR (per 162 games)	Career WAR
Charlie "Chino" Smith	1925–31	9.7	15.2
Willard Brown	1935–48	8.5	25.8
Turkey Stearnes	1923–40	8.1	52.4
Pete Hill	1904–25	7.8	47.7
Monte Irvin	1938–48	7.8	16.9
Oscar Charleston	1915–41	7.7	79.5
Sam Jethroe	1942–48	7.5	7.6
Cristóbal Torriente	1912–28	6.9	61.6
Ted Strong	1936–48	6.7	14.5
Wild Bill Wright	1933–45	6.3	25.8

Name	Years	WAR (per 162 games)	Career WAR
"Rap" Dixon	1924–37	5.8	21.8
Alejandro Oms	1917–35	5.6	17.3
Heavy Johnson	1916–32	5.4	17.7
Spottswood Poles	1909–23	5.3	14.3
Hurley McNair	1910–37	5.4	31.1
Cool Papa Bell	1922–46	4.9	48.5
Roy Parnell	1928–43	4.8	18.9
Jimmie Lyons	1911–24	4.6	17.0
Fats Jenkins	1920–40	4.6	17.8
Charlie Blackwell	1915–28	4.1	16.2
Clint Thomas	1920–38	3.6	21.4
George Shively	1911–24	3.4	12.3
Vic Harris	1923–47	3.3	16.6
Valentin Dreke	1919–27	3.2	12.3
Chaney White	1920–36	2.9	15.6
Bernardo Baro	1915–28	2.5	13.5

Hall of Famers in bold. *24 Men Out candidates in Italics*. WAR statistics courtesy of Seamheads.

WAR Summary—Outfield: The Hall of Fame voters have done an excellent job in electing the six of the seven outfielders in Negro League history who had the top career WAR. The seventh selection, Monte Irvin, spent much of his productive career in the Major Leagues but his Negro League War per 162 games was outstanding. Chino Smith, with the highest WAR per 162 games of any outfielder in Negro League history, clearly had a Hall of Fame career if one applies the Addie Joss death exception. "Wild Bill" Wright's performance in the Negro Leagues created a solid WAR rating despite his lengthy career abroad. Spotswood Poles is the leading Hall of Fame candidate from the dead-ball era. Herbert "Rap" Dixon also has Hall of Fame stats, but his candidacy may have suffered from health issues which curtailed his career. Hurley McNair can be viewed as the most underappreciated outfielder in Negro League history.

CHAPTER 15

Pitcher

The ten Negro League pitchers enshrined in Cooperstown from the more than fifty years of black baseball's segregated existence are an extraordinary grouping: Satchel Paige, Bullet Joe Rogan, Smokey Joe Williams, Rube Foster, Willie Foster, Leon Day, Ray Brown, José Méndez, Andy Cooper, and Hilton Smith. They include every Negro League pitcher (save Dick Redding and William Bell) with a WAR in excess of 35. But the process is not complete, as a total of ten pitchers over five decades is hardly an excessive number. At least four (and probably more) pitching entries are clearly warranted.

Dick "Cannonball" Redding

Years	Games	W–L	Pct.	SO*	ERA*	WAR per 162g	WAR Career
1911–38	NA	346–152	.695	1,515	2.55	4.4	38.8

Career Statistics (CNLBR), WAR (Seamheads). *Negro League games only

Dick "Cannonball" Redding was a 6 ft. 4 in. pitcher with an overpowering fastball whose career spanned from the dead-ball era in 1911 to 1938. To complement his speed, Redding did not hesitate to aggressively brush back batters. He is also credited with developing a "hesitation pitch" long before Satchel Paige.[1] Redding is attributed with having pitched 12 no-hitters against black teams and as many as 30 no-hitters against all

Dick "Cannonball" Redding's recorded lifetime WAR of 38.8 is the highest of any Negro Leaguer not currently in the Hall of Fame. An overpowering fastball pitcher, he is credited with having pitched 12 no-hitters against black teams and as many as 30 no-hitters against all opposition. (Courtesy Helmar Brewing. Artist Scott Pedley.)

opposition.[2] Two of his verified no-hitters both occurred in August of 1912. The first was against the Cuban Stars in Atlantic City, and the second was a perfect game against the Cherokee Indians during a barnstorming tour.[3] Redding, regarded in his time as one of the game's true superstars, often jumped from team to team. He could be found playing in top level pre–Negro League games and also playing against semi-pro teams, leaving a less than full statistical trail but a blazing legend.

In his rookie year of 1911, pitching for the Philadelphia Giants and the New York Lincoln Giants, he is credited with 17 straight victories.[4] Incidentally, he also batted .323 that year.[5] In 1912, he compiled a record of 43–12 for the Lincoln Giants, including several no-hitters, one of which, against the Cuban Stars, was the first documented no-hitter between two high-level black teams.[6] He appeared in only a few games for the Lincoln Giants in 1913, likely because of injury, but he was still a member of the squad which won the "Colored Championship of the World" that year.[7] In 1914, he went 12–3, with 101 strikeouts in 18 games. In 1915, he won his first 20 games in a season, including several against Major Leaguers.[8]

His teammate Frank Forbes, who played with Redding on the 1914 Lincoln Giants, claimed, "Dick Redding was like Walter Johnson. Nothing but speed. That's the reason they called him Cannonball. He just blew the ball by you. I've seen Redding knock the bat out of a man's hand."[9] After facing him, Casey Stengel said, "If he was on a club in the big leagues, he wouldn't lose any games at all!"[10] Old-time outfielder-pitcher Jesse Hubbard insisted that Redding was a better pitcher than Satchel Paige: "Now Satchel didn't throw the ball as hard as Dick Redding. You should have seen him turn the ball loose."[11]

Moreover, he was a consummate winner. The research of Larry Lester and Dick Clark shows that Redding, when pitching at the highest level of Negro League ball, had a winning percentage of 73 percent. Redding led his teams to 15 separate championships, among them the New York Lincoln Giants (1911–13); New York Lincoln Stars (1915–16); 1917 Chicago American Giants, and the 1919 and 1921 Atlantic City Bacharachs.[12] In the 1915 Negro League World Series against Pop Lloyd's Chicago American Giants, which ended in a tie, Redding won three games, including a shutout, and hit .385 for good measure.[13]

In 1917, Redding led his Chicago Americans to the pennant with a 17–5 record and a 0.97 ERA for the season.[14] On the mound, he had a powerful control of his fastball and managed to achieve four times as many strikeouts as walks during his prime years of 1911–1919.[15] It is important to take note that Redding could help himself at the plate as well, generating, according to CNLBR, a decent .249 lifetime batting average against all opposition.[16] He was also an excellent defensive player, holding the 14th highest fielding rating (Range Factor) of any pitcher in Negro League history with 1,000 or more innings pitched (Seamheads).

An interesting and illuminating incident occurred on October 8, 1917, during barnstorming season, when Redding was scheduled to face the New Haven Colonials, who had hired the great Ty Cobb to play first base. When Redding was brought in the game to pitch in relief, Cobb left the game, presumably fulfilling the vow he had made in Cuba in 1910 never to face black players again. Redding pitched four innings of relief, striking out the first seven men he faced, and doubled to help score the game's only run. The Norwich Bulletin reported that Redding was a greater gate attraction than Cobb.[17]

During his career, Redding also pitched in five winter league seasons, including the Florida Hotel League, and four American series in Cuba. Tough and hard-working, he played for many of the leading teams and managers of his era. He spent 1918 serving combat duty overseas during World War I, when his skills were at their highest. After the war, he segued into a player-manager for the balance of his career, pitching somewhat less effectively until his skills really began to fade around 1923.

Yet, he still retained bursts of brilliance after the war. On July 20, 1920, he outdueled Smokey Joe Williams 5–0 before 16,000 fans in the first black game ever played at Ebbets Field.[18] On August 22, 1920, Redding pitched the first no-hitter in Negro National League history, against the Chicago Giants.[19] He was deemed the top pitcher in all of black ball by Seamheads for 1922. The *Afro American* newspaper reported in 1927 that Redding had once pitched 22 scoreless innings in a game for the Bacharach Giants.[20] And he still managed to throw one last no-hitter against Port Jervis (New York) in 1927, when he was 37 years old.[21] The CNLBR has established that Redding was also a truly durable workhorse pitcher, who would often pitch on back-to-back days and sometimes both ends of a doubleheader. Their research has revealed that he completed an astounding 91 percent of games he started against top level competition during the period 1911–1921, 22 percent of which were shutouts.[22] According to Seamheads, over the course of all recorded Negro League history, only Smokey Joe Williams and Willie Foster had more career wins, only Williams and Satchel Paige had more strikeouts, and only José Méndez, Satchel Paige and Willie Foster had more shutouts, than Dick "Cannonball" Redding.

In his prime period (up till about 1923), he was regarded as particularly effective against Major League opposition and is credited with securing wins over the New York Giants, Boston Braves, Major League All-Stars, Jersey City, a Carl Mays all-star team, Jack Scott's all-stars, and the Babe Ruth All-Stars.[23] According to CNLBR, legend has it that Ty Cobb refused to bat against Redding on yet a second occasion after watching him pitch batting practice against the Detroit Tigers.[24] Redding is said by John B. Holway to have once struck out Babe Ruth three times on nine consecutive pitches.[25]

Of course, exhibition games against white Major Leaguers were sometimes subject to other factors. In 1927, the year Ruth hit 60 homers, an exhibition game was advertised as Ruth against Redding's all black team. After being reminded by the promoter that the fans were there to see the Babe hit home runs, Redding responded "Gotcha … right down the pike." That afternoon, Babe hit three monster home runs off Redding in five at bats. In the words of one historian, "the fans went home happy, and both Ruth and Redding went home richer."[26] An interesting footnote to his career is that John McGraw hired Redding in 1911 to pitch batting practice against the New York Giants, and the New York Yankees paid Redding to pitch batting practice to Lou Gehrig when the latter was still at Columbia University.[27]

Redding continued to manage and pitch occasionally through 1937, when he retired. Redding's career as a manager was moderately successful, as he compiled a known record of 279–246 (.531 winning percentage). Redding died of an unknown malady in a Long Island mental hospital in 1948.[28]

Redding's pre–Negro League career record is subject to a significant amount of missing statistics. While many of his league games during his later official league career are now available, there remain many, many games against independent and semi-pro clubs that will never be located. The CNLBR believes he won at least 140 games as a pitcher against this lower level opposition during the period 1930–34, for which there are no records.[29]

A huge name in the United States and Cuba during his reign, Redding is generally regarded as one of the four greatest pitchers of the Negro Leagues, together with Satchel Paige, Joe Williams (with whom he was teammates), and Bullet Joe Rogan.[30] Even with a significant number of missing statistics, Dick Redding's recorded career WAR of 38.8 is the highest of any Negro Leaguer not currently in the Hall of Fame. His career WAR exceeds that of four of the ten Negro League pitchers in the Hall of Fame, and that's in spite of the missing data.

Bill James claims Redding was the best Negro League pitcher for the period from 1917 to 1919. John B. Holway has awarded him his George Stovey Award as the best pitcher in the Eastern Negro Leagues in four separate years from 1915 through 1922. ESPN (James A. Riley) lists him as the best pitcher of his Negro League in 1911, 1912, and 1920. Seamheads regards Redding as the top Negro League pitcher in the 1912–13 Cuban Winter League and in 1922.

"Cannonball" Redding was designated a rightful Hall of Famer by 80 percent of the historians and 50 percent of the Negro League veterans (even though many of them had never seen him pitch) in the McNeil Polls, and chosen by William F. McNeil to his all-time Negro League all-star team. Significantly, Redding was selected by Cum Posey as second-best pitcher of all-time on his 1952 All-Time Negro League Team (behind only Smokey Joe Williams but ahead of Satchel Paige). Eastern League founder Ed Bolden and leading historian Robert Peterson both named Redding as one of the top four pitchers on their all-time Negro League teams. James A. Riley has labeled him a Hall of Fame caliber player. Noteworthy veterans Quincy Trouppe, Buck O'Neil, and Dizzy Dismukes, together with Hall of Famers Buck Leonard, Willie Foster, and Ben Taylor, all selected Redding to their all-time Negro League teams. Dick Redding's closest Hall of Fame Similarity Score matches among major leaguers are Gaylord Perry (16th closest) and Bob Gibson (19th closest).

Redding was named a second team pitcher in the 1952 *Courier* Poll. Eric Chalek of the Hall of Miller and Eric, after crunching the numbers for years, concluded that Redding was indeed, together with Satchel Paige, Smokey Joe Williams, and Bullet Rogan, one of the Negro League's four greatest pitchers.[31] Again, the man won four George Stovey (Cy Young) awards over an eight-year span.

Dick Redding is one of only four unelected candidates remaining from the Hall of Fame Negro League's original candidates list in 1971. He is one of two unelected candidates from the final pre–Negro League finalist's list in the 2006 Hall of Fame voting. This star of the pre–Negro League era was doubtless held back in the Hall of Fame voting in 2006 by a large quantity of statistics missing for his career. Committee member James Overmyer was surprised that Redding was not elected in 2006 and also offered his assessment that Redding's election was negatively impacted because his prime career was over before the advent of the official Negro Leagues in 1920.[32] Hall of Fame voting member Todd Bolton felt that Redding probably received at least 50 percent of the vote in 2006.[33] This would mean that he fell only three or fewer votes (possibly only a single vote) short of election. Aside from players who were tarnished in the MLB steroids era, he is probably the greatest American pitcher eligible for admission to the Hall of Fame who is not currently inducted. That he is not in the Hall of Fame is unacceptable.

John Donaldson

Years	Games	W–L	Pct.	SO	ERA	WAR per 162g	WAR Career
1908–41	NA	401–N/A	N/A	5,002	2.96	3.6	11.8

Career statistics (The Donaldson Network); ERA and WAR (Seamheads).

"This is the West, sir. When the legend becomes fact, print the legend." —from John Ford's movie *The Man Who Shot Liberty Valance*

John Wesley Donaldson was a truly enigmatic figure. For 30 years, he evolved into a legend as he crossed the backroads of America pitching against semi-pro and small-town teams. In doing so, he created a record shrouded in myth and hard to verify. The tall, thin left-hander was known for a curveball that was reputed to be comparable to other pitcher's fastballs. Born in Glasgow, Missouri, in 1891, Donaldson emerged in the pre–Negro League era in 1911 as a barnstorming pitcher for the Tennessee Minstrels, a team also referred to as the Rats. The Minstrels would play a game against a local town team during the day, followed up by putting on a minstrel show at night. He immediately became their leading pitcher, with a reported record of 44–3.[34]

In 1912, Donaldson was recruited to J.L. Wilkinson's All Nations traveling team, a multiracial team with a woman player that barnstormed the Upper Midwest. This was a step up from the Rats as they travelled by train in their private Pullman car. The team even carried their own bleachers and portable lights. From 1912 through 1917, Donaldson entered his prime starring for the All Nations team. Hall of Famer J.L. Wilkinson, who would later found the Kansas City Monarchs of the Negro Leagues, claimed that Donaldson was the most amazing pitcher he had ever seen.[35] In 1913, he pitched a 12-inning game in Marshall, Minnesota, striking out 27 batters. In both 1913 and 1914, he is said to have pitched 100 consecutive shutout innings.[36] In 1915, he pitched 30 consecutive innings of no-hit ball,[37] averaged 18 strikeouts a game, and struck out 500 batters.[38] In 1915, he is credited with whiffing 35 batters in an 18-inning game at Sioux Falls.[39] In 1916, he was again credited with having struck out 500 batters and had become commonly regarded as the best pitcher then competing in the pre–Negro League era. That season, he is reputed to have pitched his All Nations team to series victories over Rube Foster's Chicago American Giants and C.I. Taylor's Indianapolis ABCs.[40] Donaldson was named the winner of ESPN's Pitcher of the Year and John B. Holway's George Stovey (Cy Young) Award for 1916.

Generally pitching every third game for the All Nations squad (and playing outfield when not on the mound), he is credited with 11 documented no-hitters and 2,332 documented strikeouts between 1912 and 1917.[41] The press had begun to refer to Donaldson as the world's best colored pitcher.[42] Newspaper stories spoke of his changeup as comparable to that of Christy Mathewson and a fastball like that of Rube Waddell.[43] John McGraw recognized his talent when he was quoted

John Donaldson, a legendary barnstormer, is reputed to have won over 400 games and tossed 5,000 strikeouts over a 30+ year span in the early 20th century. (Courtesy Helmar Brewing. Artist Scott Pedley.)

during this time period as stating, "If Donaldson were a white man … I would give $50,000 for him."[44]

After the All Nations team disbanded in 1917, Donaldson joined the Indianapolis ABCs in 1918, and then jumped to the Brooklyn Royal Giants to assist in their title drive. In his first year with a more traditional Negro League team, Donaldson was designated the best pitcher in all of black ball by Seamheads for 1918. After being recruited by Rube Foster to the Detroit Stars in 1919, Donaldson joined J.L. Wilkinson's Kansas City Monarchs of the newly formed Negro National League, in 1920–21. (Wilkinson even credits Donaldson with coming up with the Monarchs team name.)[45] Already 30 years old, and with his arm either fatigued or injured, he played mostly center field, batted leadoff and hit .320 for the 1920 season. He averaged .294 at the plate from the third slot in 1921.[46] In 1922, with his arm in better shape, Wilkinson arranged for Donaldson to split his time between playing the field for the Monarchs and headlining as a pitcher for a newly formed version of the All Nations barnstorming team.

Sometime in 1924, Donaldson seems to have segued into an almost-exclusive barnstorming hurler (although he briefly pitched again for the Monarchs in the 1930s). He performed for hire with local teams and became a huge star throughout the Midwest, making upwards of $750 a month.[47] He was still playing on semi-pro teams through the 1930s (he turned 40 in 1931), with his last known competitive game having occurred in 1940, when he was 49 years old.[48] According to the John Donaldson website, he played in over 500 towns and 25 states over his lifetime, most often as the major gate attraction.[49] After his playing days were over, Donaldson concluded his long baseball career in 1949 as a Chicago White Sox scout. According to Buck O'Neil, he resigned in disgust after the White Sox rejected his recommendation of a young Ernie Banks.[50] In his post baseball life, Donaldson worked for the post office and spent time coaching youngsters. He died from bronchial pneumonia on April 14, 1970, and was buried in an unmarked grave in Alsip, Illinois.[51]

In a career spanning four decades, Donaldson spent much of his time barnstorming against semi-pro teams to receive a bigger pay day based upon his reputation. He was probably the highest-paid black pitcher of his day. As a barnstormer, he is said to have thrown three straight no-hitters in 1915 and to have struck out 20 batters in a game on multiple occasions. Historian Phil S. Dixon claims that Donaldson recorded almost 5,000 strikeouts in his lifetime.[52] The John Donaldson website claims to have located records showing that he had 121 wins against only 8 losses between 1911 and 1913, was credited with 13 no-hitters, won 73 percent of the games he started as a pitcher, and achieved at least 401 lifetime wins (even taking into account that over 200 of his pitching performances have no recorded pitcher of record). His performance certainly seems Paul Bunyanesque.

Elden Auker was a Major League pitcher who actually saw Donaldson in action. He relates a story that, before a game, Donaldson went out to center field and assumed catcher's squat position. Then, to entertain the fans, he had catch with the regular catcher located behind home plate. Auker, saying he would not have believed it had he not seen it, says Donaldson then repeatedly threw the ball from his squat position 300 feet on a straight line to the catcher behind the plate.[53]

Yet, although his performances were in the large part against semi-pro and amateur teams, the legend seemed to fit the man.

Federal League Park Sept 24–5–6… Heralding the First Appearance of the Worlds All-Nations…. The Great Donaldson will positively pitch one of these games. JOHN DONALDSON. The Greatest Colored

Pitcher in the World. Donaldson pitched 65 games last season, winning 60 of them.—from a pre–World War I poster[54]

Donaldson's more limited but solid statistics against Negro League teams were less astounding and presumably not sufficient to earn admission to the Hall of Fame by the 2006 Historian's Panel. In his forays into the integrated 1917 and 1918 California Winter Leagues, the Florida Hotel League in 1915–16, and two stints with the Kansas City Monarchs in 1920 and 1921, black baseball expert Scott Simkus has him recording 22 wins against 23 losses, albeit with a solid 2.88 ERA.[55]

Even Donaldson's rarer performances against Major League opposition are the subject of debate in the fog of Negro League history. James A. Riley claims Donaldson lost a 1–0 duel against John McGraw's New York Giants in 1918.[56] Scott Simkus says he was bombed in the same game, allowing 7 runs and 10 hits over 9 innings.[57]

The issue to be framed with Donaldson is simply whether he chose to pursue his fame and fortune as an exhibitor striking out lower level competition because that's the best he could do, or whether he was a superstar who felt motivated to do so because of racism and higher pay. Many of Donaldson's supporters have argued that he was the true forerunner of Satchel Paige, the paramount fireballer and star of his era who always chased the biggest payday, which was rarely in the Negro Leagues. In his autobiography, Buck O'Neil said, "John Donaldson showed Satchel the way, and the fact is, there are many people who saw them both who say John Donaldson was just as good as Satchel."[58]

Others, such as Scott Simkus, have argued that, unlike Donaldson, Satchel Paige never ducked first rate competition, and he thrived when he faced it. For example, Donaldson's record in the California Winter League shows he won four of six recorded decisions and struck out 6.9 men per game. Solid stuff. In the same Winter League, a generation later, Paige had a 56–7 record with 12.1 strikeouts per nine innings pitched. Spectacular stuff. Simkus concludes that Donaldson only truly thrived being the big fish in the little pond because he was simply not successful enough against top-flight competition. Simkus opines: "Take a man with a major league arm and pitch him against teams which were probably no better than junior varsity high school teams today … and he's going to notch dozens of no-hitters and strikeout more than 20 batters dozens of times, just the way Donaldson did."[59]

It is certainly possible that Buck O'Neil and Scot Simkus are each a little correct in their assessment of Donaldson. On the one hand, Donaldson's prime occurred in the pre–Negro League era and he starred for the country's leading barnstorming teams, for which records are virtually nonexistent. By 1920, when the Negro National League was formed, Donaldson's arm was worn out. Thus, his recorded statistics do not reflect his peak. Yet, the limited statistics gathered for Donaldson by Seamheads for the period 1915–1919, before his arm gave out, seem to confirm that he was something special. He is listed in Seamheads as having the fourth leading strikeout rate (14.4 percent) and as the fourth overall best pitcher for this period (trailing only Smokey Joe Williams, Dick Redding, and Juan Padrón). Later on, when his skills had faded, he became the highest paid barnstormer in the country, a hurler who could still mow down local and semi-pro opposition.

So, how does one fairly sum up the Hall of Fame credentials of John Donaldson? A finalist on the 2006 Historian's Hall of Fame ballot, it seems that Donaldson's verifiable statistics were not sufficient for election at that time. In fact, one 2016 committee member stated that Donaldson's decision to leave the Negro Leagues in the 1920s to play semi-pro ball was a major factor discussed before the vote on Donaldson was taken.[60] This result ensued despite the fact that Donaldson had the strong support of the historians committee chair

Fay Vincent, who was a non-voting member.[61] The data relied upon by the 2006 Historians' Committee reflected only 146 known wins and 2,245 documented strikeouts for Donaldson. Since that time, the Donaldson Network website, founded by a group of researchers dedicated to finding out more about John Donaldson, reports his total documented wins are up to 401 with over 5,000 documented strikeouts, albeit against all opposition.[62]

Donaldson is generally regarded as the first great left-hander in Negro League history. John Henry Lloyd called him the toughest pitcher he had ever faced, J.L. Wilkinson (for whom Satchel Paige was a star) said Donaldson was the best pitcher he ever saw, and John McGraw claimed he would have been worth $50,000 if permitted to play in the white Major Leagues. Bill James believes Donaldson and Smokey Joe Williams were the two best pitchers in Negro League ball from 1914 to 1916. John B. Holway awarded him his George Stovey Award as the best pitcher in Negro League ball in 1916. Hall of Fame pitcher Willie Foster included Donaldson as the left-hand pitcher on his second all-time team. Monte Irvin lists him among the top five left-handers in Negro League history. Hall of Famer Ben Taylor and veteran Dizzy Dismukes included him on their all-time teams. Leading historians such as Dick Clark, William F. McNeil, and James Overmyer all designate Donaldson as one of the game's all-time greats. Donaldson remains the only pitcher selected to the first team in the *Courier* Poll not yet elected to the Hall of Fame. As a first team pitcher in the *Courier* Poll, and the fifth greatest pitcher in Negro League history according to the McNeil Historians' Poll, Donaldson was arguably the Negro League's best all-time lefty hurler.[63]

A pitcher who overwhelmed his opposition in his prime, and became the preeminent barnstorming legend of his time, John Donaldson could hardly be faulted for the fact that his best years came before the advent of the formal Negro Leagues in 1920. Nor can he be criticized for choosing the highest payday available once the official Negro League era commenced. Often pitching in small towns where statistics were rarely kept, he still managed to create an enduring legacy. It is important to remember that, despite their close association, the Hall of Fame is not merely an MLB Hall of Fame, but the Hall of Fame for all of American baseball. As summed up by J. Fred Brillhart in his detailed analysis of the 1952 *Pittsburgh Courier* Experts' Poll, "Donaldson should be a no brainer shoo-in [for the Hall of Fame]."[64] That assessment is spot on. When Fay Vincent was interviewed by *The New York Times* in connection with the impending 2006 Hall of Fame special election for the Negro Leagues, which he chaired, he noted that he could not foretell the results but referred to the one candidate he was confident would get in: John Donaldson.[65] He was wrong. Whether 75 percent of the voters in any Hall of Fame balloting process will ever agree with Fay Vincent's assessment remains an open issue. It should not be.

Bill Byrd

Years	Games	W–L	Pct.	SO	ERA	WAR per 162g	WAR Career
1933–50	248	156–96	.618	724	3.30	5.2	33.0

Career statistics (John B. Holway); ERA and WAR (Seamheads).

A spitball, knuckleball, and curveball specialist who played from 1932 through 1950, Bill Byrd is the best pitcher of the Negro League's final decade not currently enshrined in Cooperstown. He was the Baltimore Elite Giants' "money pitcher," who was usually held in reserve by his team for their more important opponents.[66] At a time when the Negro Leagues played only three official games a week and many other games against semi-pro teams, it was Byrd who pitched the "Sunday" games which truly counted in the standings. He hooked up in numerous pitching duels against Hall of Famer Leon Day in the Negro Leagues and in Latin America. Byrd was a true workhorse pitcher who once pitched and won both ends of a doubleheader.[67] A quiet and modest man, his record as uncovered over the past few years speaks for itself. According to Seamheads, he completed 115 of 158 games he started from 1933 through 1948, a remarkable 73 percent.

One of the last pitchers legally permitted to continue use of a spitter, he was actually more of a control pitcher who lived on his roundhouse curve, mixed in with a fastball, changeup, and knuckleball.[68] On the other hand, Buck Leonard says that when Byrd did load up, "I wouldn't watch the ball, I'd watch

Bill Byrd was probably the last great Negro League pitcher. He was named as the best pitcher in Negro League ball in seven different seasons from 1936 through 1949. He completed a remarkable 73 percent of the games he started. (Courtesy Helmar Brewing. Artist Scott Pedley.)

the spit."[69] And Byrd has acknowledged that, for psychological reasons, he faked throwing the spit ball far more than he used it, as had been taught him by his first manager, Candy Jim Taylor.[70] Monte Irvin recalls how Byrd would go to his mouth, and then when Irvin looked for the spitball, "here would come that fastball or something."[71]

Byrd's lifetime winning percentage was in excess of .600 from 1932 through 1950, during which he had only one losing season. His career WAR of 33.0 through 1948 is higher than that of four other Negro League Hall of Fame pitchers, including his contemporaries Leon Day and Hilton Smith. In games limited to the U.S. Negro Leagues, he has the third highest WAR of any Negro League candidate not yet admitted to the Hall of Fame (trailing only Dick Redding and William Bell). According to Seamheads, he accumulated the ninth highest number of wins of any pitcher in official American Negro League games, even though Byrd often pitched for lesser teams. As his teammate Roy Campanella put it when arguing for Byrd's admission to the Hall of Fame, "He was a good pitcher and he was good for a long time!"[72]

Byrd also spent substantial time playing winter ball overseas. Pitching in Puerto Rico in the winter of 1939–40, Byrd had 14 wins and an ERA of 1.97,[73] earning the nickname "el maestro Beely (Billy)." In 1940, he joined Josh Gibson in Venezuela, where he played in the outfield or first base when not on the mound. Records for that season have not yet been found.[74] Returning to Puerto Rico in the winter of 1940–41, he compiled a record of 15–5,[75] leading his team to the pennant.

In 1942, Byrd was back with the Baltimore Elites, where Byrd served as the Elites' mound ace for the remainder of his career through 1950. He led the league in winning percentage in 1942 (.818) and 1949 (.800), and in total run average (2.85) in 1943. In 1949, a year not included in most statistical databases, which end a year earlier, he may have had his best season at age 42, when he compiled a 12–3 record.[76]

Byrd led the East in wins four separate years and, according to John B. Holway, was the George Stovey (Cy Young) Award winner top Negro League East pitcher in 1942, 1948, and 1949. Seamheads has also deemed him as either the leading Negro League starting or relief pitcher in 1936, 1939, and 1943. Bill James believes he was also the best pitcher in all of the Negro Leagues in three separate years (1944, 1948, 1949). ESPN (James A. Riley) regards him as the best pitcher in all of Negro League baseball in 1939 and 1949. Put it all together and at least one significant historian has concluded that Bill Byrd was the leading pitcher in Negro League ball in seven different seasons from 1936 through 1949.

Byrd's perennial participation in the East-West All-Star Game demonstrates how highly he was esteemed by the fans. He was named to eight East-West All-Star Games, the most of any pitcher other than Leon Day. His two starts and two wins in the East-West All-Star Game were equaled, but never exceeded, by others.

Bill Byrd was also a good enough hitter to play the outfield between starts[77] and to appear as a pinch hitter in the 1945 East-West All-Star Game. In an era when a full team roster might not exceed 17 players, his ability to play outfield made him even more valuable. He would often pitch one game of a doubleheader and then play the field in the other contest. He was extremely proud of his hitting. Seamheads lists seven seasons in which he hit over .300. According to Seamheads, his lifetime batting average was .261 although John B. Holway lists it as high as .319.[78] In an oral biography, Byrd remembered: "They always played me [as a hitter] in Yankee Stadium, because I could drop that ball right in there [into the right field stands]. I think I hit six or seven homers in Yankee Stadium. I just missed another. They used to have a sign '467 feet.' I dented that thing for a triple, five or six inches from going over. Hit the sign and dented it."[79]

Bill Byrd also deserves substantial credit for mentoring many future stars, who referred to him as "Daddy." Byrd took Roy Campanella under his wing, converted Joe Black from a thrower to a pitcher, and helped foster Jim Gilliam. Campanella was never shy about crediting Byrd with teaching him how to catch a spitball, enabling him to effectively handle Preacher Roe's spitball when he joined the Brooklyn Dodgers.[80] Campanella, who should know, claimed Byrd would have been a consistent 15–20 game winner in the majors.[81]

Bill Byrd was one of eight pitchers named to the all-time Negro League all-star team of historian John B. Holway. He was deemed a Hall of Fame caliber player by leading historians James A. Riley, Jerry Malloy, Tweed Webb, Sammy J. Miller, Luis Alvelo, and Todd Bolton. William F. McNeil included Byrd on his all-time Negro League team. Many prominent Negro League veterans, such as Larry Doby, "Double Duty" Radcliffe, Rodolfo Fernandez, and James "Red" Moore, have deemed Byrd a Hall of Fame qualified player. The Hall of Miller and Eric has concluded that Byrd's career closely parallels that of Bob Feller, an obvious Hall of Famer. Byrd's closest Similarity Score match among Hall of Famers is (you won't guess this one) old-time Hall of Famer Clark Griffith. Hall of Famers Catfish Hunter, Ferguson Jenkins, Bert Blyleven, Don Sutton and Greg Maddux (all of whom are somewhat analogous to Byrd in their sustained performance over a long period of time) are also among his top 35 matches. Byrd was listed fifth among pitchers on the Roll of Honor in the 1952 *Courier* Poll.

A finalist in the 2006 Negro Leagues Hall of Fame balloting, one can actually surmise how this three-time George Stovey (Cy Young) Award winner has failed to be named to the Hall of Fame to date. He was neither flashy nor notorious. John B. Holway once quipped that Byrd would have been in the Hall of Fame if he had been the one to utter Satchel Paige's famous phrase, "Don't look back. Something maybe gaining on you."[82] He may have been under the radar because he was the ace of a Baltimore franchise that was not one of the leading Negro League teams. Byrd's statistics were also not fully developed at the time of the most recent Hall of Fame Negro League election. Politically, he had never been a teammate of Monte Irvin, who was so instrumental in the selection process.[83] However, we do know that Monte Irvin feared Byrd: "The first time I faced Bill Byrd, I went 5-for-5. I don't ever remember getting another hit off him. I used to say, 'I know he's gonna throw a curve, I'm not gonna pull away.' But I couldn't hit a thing."[84]

Another mark against Byrd is that he used a spitball. First, his use of that pitch was authorized by the Negro Leagues as he was "grandfathered" under the same rules applied in the Major Leagues.[85] Secondly, the occasional use of a spitball certainly did not hamper Gaylord Perry or Burleigh Grimes from being admitted to the Hall.

In 1949, Byrd, at the age of 42, won his final George Stovey (Cy Young) Award as the best pitcher Negro ball. That year, although the Negro League had admittedly been denuded of much of its talent, he went 12–3 and led his team to a Negro League World Series championship. Yet his 1949 statistics for one of his best seasons are not included in most databanks, which customarily end in 1948 because the black press had stopped posting most box scores with the post–Jackie Robinson fading of interest in the Negro Leagues. Too old to receive a call from the majors, Byrd called it quits in early 1950 as the Negro Leagues slowly folded. He lived on in the players he mentored: Campanella, Joe Black, and Jim Gilliam. By any fair measure, Bill Byrd's lengthy and distinguished career has earned him entry into the National Hall of Fame.

Chet Brewer

Years	Games	W–L	Pct.	SO	ERA	WAR per 162g	WAR Career
1925–52	485	311–147	.679	1,424	3.23	4.2	20.4

Career statistics (CNLBR); ERA and WAR (Seamheads).

Chet Brewer may be the leading exception to the rule that performance in the United States–based Negro Leagues is the single most important requirement to assess Hall of Fame eligibility. The well-travelled Brewer was an arm-for-hire who pitched for 30 years in a span running from 1923 to 1953. He credited his reputation for endurance and control to the endless games he pitched as a youth, and to a mound and home plate he built in his back yard at which he hurled hundreds of pitches at a time.[86] He pitched for teams in the United States, Canada, China, Cuba, the Dominican Republic, Hawaii, Japan, Mexico, Panama, the Philippines, and Puerto Rico, often playing 12 months a year. The Center for Negro League Baseball Research has compiled a three-page single-spaced list of teams he played for over the course of his career.[87] Brewer claimed at the end of his career that he played in 44 of the then 48 States.[88] In the United States, he pitched parts of 14 seasons with the Kansas City Monarchs, with whom he is generally associated.

Here is what Brewer has to say about his own Hall of Fame eligibility: "I know I should be up there in that Hall of Fame. I played with Satchel Paige, and I beat him as many times as he beat me. My biggest thrill was when I beat Satchel a no-hitter in Santo Domingo in 1936…. I played on the Kansas City Monarchs with Satchel. None of us got any publicity when Satchel was there, because he got all of it. I was unfortunate, because when I came up to the Monarchs in 1926, Bullet Joe Rogan got all of the publicity. Then later Satchel got it. But I beat everyone the rest of them did."[89]

Brewer's record lends support to his contention. Brewer was a true stylist who used a variety of curves, sliders, screwballs, and fastballs to get batters out. He was particularly noted for his curve ball and outstanding control, for which he was described as "like Koufax, only right handed."[90] Brewer also had a well-earned reputation for using a cut ball.[91] Buck O'Neil called Brewer more of a finesse pitcher: "Cut the ball? In the later years they say he roughed it up a bit, but during his prime he didn't have to cut it. Good curve ball, good control,

Chet Brewer, the Cleveland Buckeyes' ace in the 1940s, played on 21 championship teams during his career and is reported to have thrown 31 consecutive scoreless innings in 1929. (Courtesy Helmar Brewing. Artist Scott Pedley.)

spotted the ball."[92] Despite a legion of missing statistics arising from the fact that he was so well travelled, the Center for Negro League Baseball Research credits him with a winning percentage of .614 and an overall ERA as 3.00 against top level Negro League competition. According to CNLBR, his lifetime winning percentage against all competition was an extremely high 67.4 percent, and his full game completion rate stood at 69.9 percent—even more impressive when you consider that he pitched virtually 12 months a year.

His true breakout year was 1926, when, according to James A. Riley, he secured 20 victories against all competition for the Negro National League (NNL) champion Kansas City Monarchs. John B. Holway picked him as an all-star in 1925 and 1928. The ESPN rates Brewer as the best pitcher in the Negro National League in 1929, and Bill James opines that he was the best pitcher in all of Negro ball in 1933. His best year with the Monarchs was 1929, when he went 17–3, a year for which John B. Holway designated him as his George Stovey Award (Cy Young) winner in the Negro League West. James A. Riley credits him with winning 30 or more games against all competition at least three times in the 1930s. Brewer led the Negro American League and the California Winter League in wins twice each. Twice he also led the California Winter League in strikeouts and shutouts. Three times he led his league in winning percentage.[93] The CNLBR has located 311 career wins accumulated by Brewer over the course of his career in all leagues and has speculated that he might have won over 500 games if all of his data could be found.[94] And the man could hit as well. CNLBR data shows he had a lifetime batting average of .273 in all venues. He won his own game when he drove in the winning run in the bottom of the ninth in the second game of the 1945 World Series.

In 1929, Brewer threw 31 consecutive scoreless innings in Negro National League competition and combined with Army Cooper to throw a no-hitter on June 29, 1929, against the Chicago American Giants.[95] Seamheads regards Brewer as the top pitcher in all of black ball in 1929. Brewer became infamous for a 12-inning hookup with Smokey Joe Williams in 1930, when he struck out 19 men—including 10 in a row.[96] A 1931 highlight was a 12-inning 1–1 tie against the Colored House of David in a faceoff against the legendary Negro League pitcher John Donaldson.[97] In 1934, Brewer, pitching for the North Dakota All Stars, threw a 11–0 shutout against a Major League all-star team that included Jimmie Foxx, Bill Dickey, and Heinie Manush.[98] In the prestigious 1934 *Denver Post* tournament, he set the tournament record by striking out 19 batters in one game.[99] His career record against Major League teams in exhibition games was 13–2.[100] In 1937, Brewer outdueled Satchel Paige by throwing a one hitter in the Dominican League tournament against the Ciudad Trujillo, a team which included Josh Gibson and Cool Papa Bell.[101]

Assessing Brewer's record is particularly challenging because so much of his career is undocumented, resulting in a misleadingly low career WAR. We have few or none of his statistics from his early days (1922–1925) or the middle 1930s, the hundreds of non-league games he pitched, his Kansas City Monarchs barnstorming games, his later years in the Negro American League, the California Winter League, the Denver Post Tournament (1934 and 1937), Cuba (1930), his two tours of the Far East, and many of his prime years playing in the Dominican Republic, Puerto Rico, Panama, Mexico, and Canada. For one example, the "official" Negro League games that Brewer played in during 1933 and 1934 only reflect records of 4–1 and 2–4 respectively.[102] Yet Bill James recognized him as the best pitcher in Negro League ball in 1933. James A. Riley, who counts all games, credits Brewer with 34 wins in 1933 and 33 wins (including 16 in a row)[103] in 1934.[104] The latter unofficial record seems more meaningful since Brewer was named to the All Star Classic in both 1933 and 1934, and finished second to Bill Foster in the voting for pitchers for the 1934 Classic, even though Brewer wasn't even in the league. As late as 1947, he was the ace of the Negro American League champion Cleveland Buckeyes as he led the league in wins.

Over the course of his 30-year career, Brewer was also a perpetual winner, whose presence brought success to his team. He played on at least 21 championship teams, including those winning six Negro League titles, nine California Winter League championships, and the Caribbean World Series. Brewer also participated as a leader on teams that won the 1935 National Baseball Congress Tournament, the 1937 *Denver Post* tournament, and six Canadian baseball tournaments.[105]

He was the very first major Negro Leaguer recruited to Mexico, in 1938.[106] In 1939 and 1949, he compiled records of 18–3 (ERA 1.82) and 16–6 (ERA 2.50) in Mexico, which included two no-hitters.[107] Brewer, despite all of his time playing in other venues, was named to the East-West All-Star Game four times, in 1933, 1934, 1947, and 1948.[108] At the tail end of his career, he spent 11 years as a manager at various levels of black and independent ball, twice leading teams to the California Winter League championship.

Brewer was particularly venerated by his peers. According to Cool Papa Bell, "There was no better teammate. He'll do anything to win. All of the fellows respected him for that…. There were games he just refused to lose…. He had total concentration on the mound."[109] In a survey of 28 Negro League veterans who played between 1926 and 1947 taken by historian William F. McNeil, Brewer was one of only four pitchers who appeared on over 50 percent of the player ballots as to who belongs in the Hall of Fame. Negro League Hall of Famers Willie Foster and Louis Santop both list Brewer on their all-time Negro League greats teams. Among the other leading players citing Brewer for their Hall of Fame ballot were Larry Doby, Max Manning, Red Moore, and Double Duty Radcliffe. In fact, Brewer is the only pitcher listed by 50 percent or more of the players in the McNeil Poll who is not yet in the Hall of Fame. The McNeil survey of historians reveals that Brewer appears on 64 percent of their ballots, also the highest vote total of any player not yet selected for the Hall of Fame.

Chet Brewer was included on the initial 1971 Hall of Fame ballot. Joe Reichler, who served on the 1971 committee, called Chet Brewer, Leon Day, and Willie Wells the most outstanding Negro League candidates still alive.[110] The other two candidates eventually made it, but Chet Brewer is one of only four players on that ballot who has not yet been elected.

Brewer also made the cut for the final ballot used by the 2006 Hall of Fame Negro League historians. Since the historians' voting results have been kept confidential, it is not known how close Brewer came to securing the requisite 75 percent vote. However, it can be reasonably inferred that his candidacy was adversely impacted because his overall statistics were skinnier than those of other candidates as a result of so many of his accomplishments having occurred overseas. Chet Brewer was an outspoken advocate for integration in the 1930s and 1940s, one whose frustrations let him to pitch abroad, where he could earn the respect he deserved. In effect, pitching in foreign lands was his own form of social protest.[111] The irony, of course, is that he pitched abroad only because he was more valued in those venues than in his own country. William F. McNeil, who included Brewer on his All-Time Negro League All Star Team, believes he had the potential to have been a 300-game winning pitcher in the Majors. The fact that CNLBR has located at least 300 wins which Brewer did in fact accumulate (on limited data) over the course of his lifetime is evidence that McNeil is correct. Brewer was one of the very best pitchers of his era and it is time to honor him in his homeland with the Hall of Fame plaque he deserves.

Worthy of Further Discussion

Several other pitchers warrant serious Hall of Fame consideration. Many of these pitchers may well have been of Hall of Fame caliber but were robbed of their full performance potential because of the color of their skin.

William Bell. A remarkable one-half of the 10 Negro League pitchers currently admitted to the Hall of Fame are from Texas (Rube Foster, Willie Foster, Smokey Joe Williams, Hilton Smith, and Andy Cooper). What is even more startling is that there is a sixth Texan pitcher who should arguably join them. According to John B. Holway, William Bell's 141 wins ranks fifth in all-time Negro League history, over a 14-year career that spanned from 1923 to 1937. Most sources concur that Bell also sported the highest winning percentage in all of Negro League history.[112] The Center for Negro League Baseball Research lists his winning percentage as .723 (the best in Negro League history), his lifetime ERA as 3.05, and his game-completion percentage as 75.3 percent. According to Seamheads, Bell averaged 21 wins during each 162-game span over the course of his entire career and completed 73 percent of the games he started. Research by CNLBR indicates that his winning percentage against lower level teams was .913, making him virtually unbeatable at that level. Both his career WAR and WAR per 162 games are extraordinary, and each is equal to or higher than that of four Negro League pitchers admitted to the Hall of Fame. Throughout his career, Bell was a workhorse who had a reputation for being at his best under pressure and being able to deliver in the clutch. He mixed excellent control with an extensive variety of pitches, including a moving fastball, curve, slider, and change of pace.[113]

Bell began his professional career in 1921 with the Galveston Black Sand Crabs of the Texas League. In 1922 and 1923, he played for the legendary All Nations barnstorming team managed by John Donaldson while also making occasional starts for the Kansas City Monarchs in 1923. By this time, he was already 25 years old and his late start in the game, together with years of having played lower level and barnstorming ball, has resulted in significant missing statistics for a period of four to five years in which he seems to have been very effective on the mound.[114]

In 1924, Bell became a starter with the Monarchs and proceeded to reel off 10 straight wins to start the season.[115] That year, he led the Negro National League in winning percentage (.846). In 1925, he went 11–5 in league games. He started five games in the 1924 and 1925 World Series, sporting a 2.63 ERA and 1.13 ERA, respectively. Bell was designated as both a John B. Holway and Seamheads All-Star in 1926 when he led the Negro National League in wins with 16. Bell also won John B. Holway's George Stovey (Cy Young) Award as the best pitcher in the Negro League West in 1926. In 1927, he led the Negro National League in earned run average (2.09) and pitched four shutouts among 12 complete games. In 1930, he served as the Monarchs' ace, completing 12 of 13 games he started with a 2.96 ERA. He played on five Kansas City Monarchs teams (1923, 1924, 1925, 1926, and 1929), which won the Negro National League pennant. Playing most of his career for the Monarchs and the Pittsburgh Crawfords, he pitched in the shadow of Bullet Rogan, Satchel Paige and José Méndez, never receiving much publicity or his proper recognition.[116] Between 1924 and 1930, he never won fewer than 10 league games a year in a much shorter season than utilized in the Major Leagues.

Bell was also the leading pitcher for the Habana Leones team that won the Cuban Winter League championships in 1927–28 and 1928–29. Pitching for the 1928–29 Habana Leones, he led Cuban Winter League in wins and complete games. He moved to the Pittsburgh Crawfords in 1932 where he won nine straight games between July 12 and August 26, compiling a record of 11–4.[117] In 1932, he also secured three wins in a seven-game exhibition series against the Major League Casey Stengel All-Stars.[118] Altogether, he was a key member of 12 separate championship teams, including the legendary 1929 Kansas City Monarchs and the 1933 and 1935 Pittsburgh Crawfords. When he ended his career in 1937, with the Newark Eagles, Bell completed 17 consecutive years of pitching without ever having had a losing record.[119] He was also a really good hitter who occasionally filled in at an outfield position. According to CNLBR, he hit as high as .296 in 1929 and .295 in 1932, although his lifetime batting average was .237. Bell concluded his career serving two years as a successful manager of the Newark Eagles.

Ignored in leading veterans' polls and the *Courier* Poll, Bell was justifiably on the 39-name final ballot in the 2006 Negro League special election for the Hall of Fame. Hall of Fame voter Todd Bolton reports that Bell garnered strong support in the discussions in 2006 and probably accumulated at least a 50 percent vote.[120] William Bell's closest Hall of Fame Similarity Score is Hall of Famer Clark Griffith. There are a total of eight Hall of Famers among Bell's 25 closest Major League matches, including Bob Lemon, Greg Maddux, Bob Feller, Kid Nichols and Catfish Hunter. Although Bell was often not the most renowned pitcher on his own team, he may well have Hall of Fame credentials. Certainly, if one had to choose a starting pitcher for a big game between Bell and Hall of Famer Jesse Haines, the choice would go to Bell. The man's overall record is extraordinary.

George Stovey was, according to historian Robert Peterson, the 19th-century's greatest African American pitcher. The southpaw is credited with striking out more than 300 batters and winning 50 games over his first two seasons.[121] Probably born in Williamsport, Pennsylvania, in 1866, Stovey played amateur ball starting in the 1880s. After building a reputation playing semi-pro ball in Elmira, New York, and Canada, he was recruited in 1886 to join the Cuban Giants just as overhand pitching became legal.[122] The Cuban Giants were the first great black team in baseball history. Using its connections with bookers, Jersey City of the Independent League was able to threaten the Giants and secure the rights to Stovey after he pitched only one game with the Cuban Giants.[123] Stovey pitched 31 games for Jersey City in 1886, accumulating a 16–15 record, with a 1.13 ERA over 270 innings. In one game against Bridgeport he struck out a remarkable 22 batters.[124]

Stovey's reputation was so outstanding during this time period that *Sporting Life* reported in September 1886 that the New York Giants were interested in acquiring the light-skinned Stovey for help in their pennant race.[125] Whether that rumor was true or not, Stovey was signed in 1887 by the white Newark Little Giants, who were the defending Eastern League champions. Adding African American catcher Fleetwood Walker to its roster, Newark created a duo it marketed to the public as "our Spanish Beauties." Pitching for Newark, Stovey is credited with leading the league in 1887 with between 33 and 35 wins and a 2.46 ERA.[126]

In a game on April 7, 1887, Stovey pitched against Tim Keefe and the New York Giants at the Polo Grounds. While he lost that game by 3–2, the *Newark Daily Journal* reported that the New York Giants had offered to purchase Stovey's contract.[127] It was Stovey who was scheduled to pitch in an exhibition game in July 1887 against the Chicago White Stockings, that led to Cap Anson's infamous refusal to play that day if Stovey took the field.[128] The International League adopted an official ban on further signings of African American players on July 14, 1887, the same day Cap Anson refused to play against Stovey and his battery mate Fleet Walker.[129] The ban was dually motivated by racial animus and the fact that African Americans in the International League were performing so well. Aside from Stovey's stellar record, Bud Fowler was hitting .350, and African American Frank Grant led the International League in home runs, even though many umpires and players had conspired against them. After 1887, African American players were not permitted to play in organized white ball again until 1947.

After the ban on black players was adopted as of the end of that season, Stovey played with Worcester, of the New England League, in 1888, and then rejoined the Cuban Giants. He garnered a winning percentage of .600, with a 2.17 ERA over his remaining six seasons in organized ball, playing for such leading black teams as the Big Gorhams, Cuban X-Giants, and the Brooklyn Colored Giants.[130] Stovey pitched sporadically at various levels of ball until he was 50 years old. He also umpired and organized youth teams and leagues for decades in Williamsport, Pennsylvania, which would become the future birthplace of Little League. Stovey died of a heart attack at age 70. Black ball's greatest 19th-century pitcher was buried by the city in a pauper's grave.[131]

The only 19th-century Major League pitcher who had a better ERA than Stovey was John Montgomery Ward.[132] Seamheads has recognized Stovey as the Top Pitcher in all of black ball in 1888. His WAR per 162 games of 6.5 exceeds that of all but two Negro League pitchers admitted to the Hall of Fame. Stovey's limited amount of statistics have still generated a Similarity Score that lists two of this three closest Major League matches as Hall of Famers Ed Walsh and Rube Waddell. In tribute to him, historian John B. Holway created the

George Stovey Award, his Cy Young Award equivalent, which he has retroactively awarded each year to the best Negro League pitcher in the Eastern and Western conferences. Unfairly banned from organized white ball, it will remain forever unanswered whether Stovey's minimal recorded statistics would have translated into a Hall of Fame career in the Major Leagues. But, then again, maybe the evidence is already sufficient for the 19th century's best black ball hurler.

Jesse "Nip" Winters was the greatest pitcher in Eastern Colored League history. If Hall of Fame selection were based upon peak value, Winters would be a surefire Hall of Famer. He was a left-handed curve baller who led his team to three straight pennants and a World Series victory, in 1925. Over the period from 1923 through 1927, Winters dominated opponents in league games and games against top level opponents with a record of 91–33, a winning percentage of 73.4 percent.[133] He led the ECL in wins each year from 1923 through 1927 and in strikeouts four of those five years. He pitched a no-hitter in 1922 and then followed it up with the first no-hitter in ECL history on September 3, 1924. In the 1924 World Series, Winters pitched four complete games, winning three (including a shutout) for a composite ERA of 1.16. His single-season WAR of 7.9 established in 1924 is the twelfth highest single season WAR of any position player or pitcher in domestic Negro League history. He was also a great hitter, compiling a lifetime .296 batting average and a .468 slugging percentage.[134] He was often chosen to pitch in exhibition games against Major League all-star units, including Babe Ruth's All Stars. In those games, he split two decisions against Lefty Grove.[135] His three seasons in Cuban Winter Ball were less impressive, where, according to CNLBR, he posted an aggregate won-loss record of 4–12.

Winters was deemed the hypothetical "Cy Young" award winner in 1924 by Seamheads, in all three seasons from 1923 through 1925 by ESPN, and in 1923, 1924, and 1926 by John B. Holway. Bill James has tagged him as the best Negro League pitcher in 1924 and 1926. The Pittsburgh *Courier* named him to their all-star unit in 1925. John B. Holway designated Winters an all-star pitcher for five seasons between 1918 and 1926 and the winner of his Fleet Walker Award as the league's MVP in 1924. In 1926 and 1927, he won 15 and then 14 games for Hilldale, before he was suspended late in the 1927 season for insufficient effort.[136] By then, his fastball was no longer effective, although he hung on until 1933 as a marginal pitcher and then pitched for lower level Canadian teams until 1940.[137]

Yet, Winters' lifetime Negro League WAR of 31.0 is still among the four highest of any Negro League pitcher not in the Hall of Fame. Between 1923 and 1927, he led the ECL in complete games and wins five times, in shutouts three times, and in strikeouts four times. During that five-year span, according to CNLBR, his ECL record was 91–33 for a winning percentage of 73.4 percent. Veteran catchers Chappie Johnson and Quincy Trouppe included Winters on their all-time teams. He scored as an impressive second team pitcher in both the 1952 *Courier* Poll. Leading researchers William F. McNeil, Tweed Webb, Larry Lester, and John B. Holway have all included Nip Winters on their Negro League all-time teams. Among his ten closest Hall of Fame Major League Similarity Score matches are Herb Pennock, Tom Glavine and Lefty Gomez. Winters was named on the pre-ballot but not the final ballot in the 2006 Negro Leagues election for the Hall of Fame.

Ultimately, Winters had two problems that led to his downfall. He struggled with control of his fastball and suffered serious drinking problems. It is more than probable that these two issues were related.[138] As a result, his effectiveness was limited to a five-year period, after which he became a journeyman drifting from team to team, where he played for anyone who would pay him.[139] In William F. McNeil's Negro League historian's vote, he garnered substantial support (seventh place among pitchers), but less than 15 percent of the total votes.[140] In terms of Hall of Fame eligibility, he lasted only 10 years in the top-level American Negro Leagues, making him barely eligible for Cooperstown under the criteria we have laid out. Major League history is replete with pitchers like Nip Winters who dominated for a couple of years (e.g., Smokey Joe Wood) but could not sustain their success. While very few of them make the Hall of Fame, some do.

William "Dizzy" Dismukes spent a 40-year career in the Negro Leagues as submarine pitcher, manager, club officer, and league executive. Regarded as one of the best pitchers of the 1910–1920 era, he is credited with teaching his submarine pitch to Carl Mays.[141] His best years were 1915 and 1916 when he went 19–5 and 17–6, respectively. He pitched a no-hitter against the Indianapolis ABCs on May 15, 1915.[142] He was also designated John B. Holway's hypothetical George Stovey (Cy Young) Award winner in 1915 and named top Negro League pitcher of that year by both ESPN and Seamheads. Dismukes was deemed an all-star pitcher by John B. Holway in 1915 and in 1916. John B. Holway has also deemed him the MVP of the 1916 end-of-season playoff series between his Indianapolis ABCs and the Chicago Giants. In that series, Dismukes won three of the five games, giving up a Total Run Average of only 2.74. Defensively, he was rated by Seamheads as the all-time fourth best pitcher at fielding his position.

Despite a career interrupted by service in World War I, he was selected as a both a first team coach and a second team pitcher in the 1952 *Courier* Poll. The *Courier* Poll consequently places Dismukes among its top 10 Negro League pitching selections, in addition to his coaching role. The *Courier* Poll is of particular significance because it demonstrates that Dismukes was still revered in 1952, long after his active playing days had ended.

From 1919 until 1952, Dismukes served variously as a manager, in the front office of numerous teams, and as an officer of the Negro National League. In his capacity as personnel director for the Kansas City Monarchs, it was Dismukes who participated in signing Jackie Robinson, and he was instrumental in switching Robinson out of the shortstop position, which he preferred.[143] From 1953 to 1956, Dismukes concluded his career as a scout for the New York Yankees (he scouted and signed Elston Howard)[144] and the Chicago White Sox. No less a luminary than Harold Tinker, the manager of the Pittsburgh Crawfords who signed Josh Gibson and played with Satchel Paige, named Dismukes as one of his Hall of Fame selections. Major Negro League historians Tweed Webb, Leslie Heaphy, and Robert Cottrell have deemed Dismukes a Hall of Fame caliber player. William F. McNeil included him as one of the pitchers on his all-time Negro League team and James A. Riley labeled him as an all-time Negro League great. However, despite his longevity and multifaceted contribution to Negro League ball, Dismukes' effectiveness as a pitcher covered less than a decade, demonstrated by his modest WAR per 162 games of 2.1. Seamheads compiled his career WAR as only 11.5, which would not rank him among the top 50 Negro League pitchers in that category. Dismukes may have been a Negro League stalwart, but he is not a Hall of Famer.

Juan Padrón. For years the Hall of Fame used the lack of verifiable statistics as a primary reason for excluding Negro Leaguers. Once statistics were compiled, there were bound to be some surprises. Perhaps the biggest shock was the discovery of a virtually unknown and underappreciated pitcher who had the one of the highest career WARs of any starting pitcher in Negro League history (32.7). This pitcher was also a Seamheads designated top pitcher in all of Negro League ball for two seasons (1916 and 1917), and the best pitcher in Cuban Winter Ball in another season (1916–17).

His name is Juan Padrón, and he is a bit of an enigma. As pointed out in Hall of Miller and Eric, much of the confusion arises from the fact that James A. Riley mistakenly combined the statistics of Luis Padrón, another Cuban ace, with those of Juan Padrón.[145] The combined player conceived by Riley hit .403 in the 1902 Cuban Winter League, taught Willie Foster to throw a changeup in 1908, played against Ty Cobb's Tigers in 1910 in Cuba, became a dominant pitcher in the United States in the 1920s, and defeated both Major League pennant winners in exhibition games in 1931—which would have made him the Paul Bunyan of Negro League ball.[146] Another anomaly is that it is generally assumed that Padrón is a Cuban because of his name and his affiliation with the Cuban Stars, when he was in fact an American of Cuban heritage. Juan Padrón was born in Key West, spent the bulk of his career in the United States, and lived his post-baseball life in Michigan.[147]

In any event, the real Juan Padrón was a top pitcher who combined a good fastball, a solid curveball, and an overpowering changeup. Over 12 years starting in 1915, in a career spanning the Negro Leagues, Cuban winter ball, and the Florida Hotel Leagues, he compiled a lifetime ERA of 2.69. Padrón dominated for the Cuban Stars West in 1916 and 1917, when, according to Seamheads, he compiled ERAs of 1.58 and 1.55, respectively. His 1916 seasonal WAR (9.4) is the second highest of any player in domestic Negro League history. After a few off years, Padrón had regained his form by 1922 and was even regarded that year as the Chicago American Giants' ace over fellow star Dave Brown. Seamheads' data reflects that he pitched great ball from 1922 through 1925 and then disappeared from their radar. The Hall of Miller and Eric blog speculates (probably correctly) that his arm gave out, although he continued to pitch with semi-pro and industrial teams through 1938.[148]

According to Seamheads, Juan Padrón still was able to accumulate the ninth highest number of strikeouts in Negro League history, more strikeouts than of Hall of Famers Hilton Smith or Ray Brown. In 12 years of pitching for which records exist, his WAR per 162 games of 5.4 was also higher than three Negro League Hall of Fame pitchers. However, his period of sustained high-level performance was short and his win-loss record in Negro League ball stands only at 81–82 (Seamheads). Probably as a result, Padrón's name does not appear in the McNeil surveys or in the 1952 *Courier* Poll. Interestingly, Padrón's top 10 Major League Similarity Score matches do include Hall of Famers Sandy Koufax and Whitey Ford. And Cum Posey, in his 1943 column about the selection of his all-time Negro League team, mentions that Juan Padrón needs to be in the discussion.[149] All things considered, Padrón, a true all-star quality player in his prime, does not rise to the level of a viable Hall of Fame candidate.

Eustaquio "Bombin" Pedroso. When speaking of great pitchers of Cuban heritage, one cannot fairly skip over the fabulous Eustaquio "Bombin" Pedroso. Pedroso was a true Cuban who split his career between the U.S.-based Negro Leagues and the Cuban leagues. Pedroso, his nickname "Bombin" acquired because of the type of hat he wore, was also a solid batter who played the field, mostly first base, when he was not pitching. In fact, Seamheads lists him primarily as a first baseman even though his true value was as a pitcher. From 1907 to 1925, Pedroso compiled an extraordinary WAR of 37.6, playing at all positions in the United States and Cuba. To put that in perspective, Pedroso has the second highest career WAR of any Negro League player not in the Hall of Fame.

As a pitcher, this big right hander combined an outstanding fastball with great control.

Facing the Tigers in Cuba in 1909, he pitched a no-hitter and then followed that up in 1910 by splitting two decisions against Ty Cobb's Tigers.[150] In the winter of 1911–12, he went 2–1 against John McGraw's National League Champion Giants. He led the Cuban League in wins in 1913–14 and 1914–15, a year in which he was also the league's best pitcher.[151] Gervasio González, a great Cuban catcher, actually regarded Pedroso as a better pitcher in his prime than either José Méndez or another Cuban pitching great, Adolfo Luque.[152] By 1921, he was basically done as an effective pitcher, although he did manage to throw a perfect game on November 6, 1932, against the Bulls of Parades.

Pedroso was also a good hitter, leading the Cuban League in batting in 1915–1916 with a .413 average. In 10 separate seasons, he batted over .300 and had a decent lifetime batting average of .264. Later in his career, he gravitated more toward playing first base and even catching.[153]

The initial problem with fairly assessing his credentials for the National Hall of Fame is that Pedroso's best performances were in Cuba. He was designated an All-Star by Seamheads in the 1913–14, 1914–15, and 1915–16 Cuban Winter League seasons and in the United States only in 1914. The only year John B. Holway deems him an all-star in the United States was in 1921. Although he played in parts of 16 U.S. Negro League seasons, his WAR in the American Negro Leagues was only 11.5, less than a third of his overall WAR, which would not place him in the top echelon of pitchers or first baseman in the United States. According to Seamheads, as a pitcher, he sported a lifetime losing won-loss record in the U.S. Negro Leagues of 50–63 and an ERA of 4.16.

Cum Posey once included Pedroso as one of the seven pitchers on one of his numerous all-time Negro League all-star teams, and historian William F. McNeil selected Pedroso as a pitcher on his all-time all-star Cuban Winter League team. However, overall Pedroso was an above-average pitcher and a below-average position player. There are no Hall of Famers among Pedroso's top 40 Similarity Score matches, and he was not cited even once in the McNeil or the *Courier* Polls. Despite his accumulated WAR, Pedroso does not emerge as a solid candidate for the National Hall of Fame. The Federation of Cuban Professional Players in Exile elected Pedroso to the Cuban Hall of Fame in 1962, which is where he rightfully belongs.

Dave "Impo" Barnhill was a 5 ft. 7 in., 126 lb. fireballer who grew up playing ball on the sandlots of North Carolina side by side with future Hall of Famers Buck Leonard and Ray Dandridge. He got his start in black ball at the age of 22, with the barnstorming Miami Giants in 1936, a team that later evolved into the Ethiopian Clowns. Barnhill developed into their star attraction in his role as "Impo" the clown. The name Impo stuck with him for his entire career, although others called him "Skinny."[154] These teams "clowned" for the fans, often in ridiculous stereotypical African costumes, and are now regarded by history as the baseball equivalent of basketball's Harlem Globetrotters. In point of fact, the Clowns were composed of some truly talented players who also barnstormed successfully against local teams. The Clowns played hard when the game started because the usual arrangement was that the winning team would earn the higher share of a 60–40 split of the gate.[155] After they built a lead, they would switch to entertainment mode. Barnhill spent four years traveling with the Clowns (and their rival, Zulu Giants) entertaining the fans with clowning skits in the United States, but also pitching effectively offseason in Puerto Rico. In the Puerto Rico Winter League of 1940–41, Barnhill proved his worth as a real ballplayer by leading the league with 193 strikeouts.

Buck Leonard, who knew Barnhill from their youth, wanted to sign him for the Homestead Grays, but the team was dissuaded by his small stature.[156] Alex Pompez was impressed enough, however, to sign him to the Cuban Stars, for whom he would pitch from 1941 through 1949. He soon became their leading moundsman by going 18–3 in 1941 and winning 26 games in 1943. John B. Holway named Barnhill the George Stovey (Cy Young) Award winner for 1941, and ESPN also deemed him the outstanding pitcher of that year. According to Buck O'Neil, "He had a live fast ball. It was amazing. He'd throw it around your waist, it would come up to your armpits."[157] Another of the solid hitting pitchers who seem to have populated the Negro League game, Barnhill accumulated a .255 career batting average with a .324 OBP (on-base percentage) (Seamheads).

By 1942, Barnhill had built enough of a reputation to be one of three Negro League players (with Roy Campanella and Sammy T. Hughes) designated for an announced tryout with the Pittsburgh Pirates. The tryout never took place when the Pirates reneged on their commitment. Barnhill always felt that "Benswanger [the Pirates president] was scared to take a chance."[158] It's hard to conceive of any other motivation for the Pirates' decision, since they finished 36½ games out of first place in the National League in 1942. Imagine how the history of baseball would have been altered if Campanella, Hughes, and Barnhill (all elite Negro League players at their then peaks) had joined the Pirates that year.

Buck Leonard always regretted that Barnhill got away from the Homestead Grays: "He was one of the best we had in our leagues. He threw just as hard as anyone. He was right up there with Slim Jones and Satchel Paige, right next to them."[159]

The highlight of Barnhill's career was a head-to-head matchup against Satchel Paige in the 1943 East-West All-Star Game at Chicago's Comiskey Park before 51,000 fans, a game won by Paige 2–1. After missing the 1944 season when he was stabbed by his teammate Fred Wilson,[160] Barnhill returned to form in 1945.

Over the course of his time in the Negro Leagues, Barnhill was often matched up head to head against Satchel Paige to draw a bigger crowd. Veteran player Eduardo Valero claimed watching the pitching duels of Satchel Paige and "Impo" Barnhill was his greatest career thrill in Negro League ball.[161] At one point, Barnhill was even hired by the Kansas City Monarchs to back up Paige on a barnstorming tour. Dave Barnhill liked to recount a story about the tour. In one game, the Toledo manager asked the Monarchs to replace Paige, who was overwhelming the Toledo batters. Pointing to the diminutive guy in the bullpen (Barnhill) and asking if that would suffice, the Toledo manager agreed. After Barnhill pitched the last five innings without surrendering a hit and striking out 11 batters, the Toledo manager complained: "You said you'd take Satchel out but you didn't. You just took him over behind the dugout and cut his legs off and put him right back in."[162] Veteran shortstop "Pee Wee" Butts claimed it was Barnhill, not Paige, who was the toughest Negro League pitcher he ever faced.[163]

Between 1941 and 1948, Barnhill pitched 14 innings over five East-West All-Star Games, with an ERA of 1.29. In 1947, he played a major role in driving the Cuban Stars to the Negro League championship, winning every game he pitched, including a shutout win in the 1947 Negro World Series. He did just as well in Cuba in the winter league of 1947–48, leading the league in strikeouts and compiling a 2.26 ERA. The following winter he led the Cuban Winter League in both victories and completed games.

Barnhill and Ray Dandridge were signed by the New York Giants to their Minneapolis Millers AAA minor league club in 1950, where they led their team to the pennant as Barnhill went 11–3. That year, he finished third in the league in strikeouts, although he pitched only 140 innings. Then 36 years old, Barnhill never got called up to the Majors. He closed out his career in the Pacific Coast League and playing minor league ball in Florida, where he went 13–8 with a 1.19 ERA in 1952, his last year in baseball. According to Seamheads, among pitchers with 500 or more innings, Barnhill's strikeout percentage, and his strikeout-to-walk ratio, were sixth and fifth best, respectively, in all of Negro League history. During his prime Negro League period of 1941–45, he was third in total strikeouts behind only Satchel Paige and Bill Byrd. And he accomplished these feats although he was already 27 years old when he reached the New York Cubans in 1941.

Barnhill would doubtless have been an excellent Major Leaguer. In the final analysis, his career, in which he bounced from "clown ball" to the Negro Leagues to the Caribbean to the minor leagues, does not fit our modern conceptions and leaves gaping holes in his statistics. It is probably the correct conclusion that his early stint in "clown ball," which resulted in a blazing but relatively short stint in the Negro Leagues starting at the advanced age of 27, robbed him of any chance of a Hall of Fame career. Yet, the man was effective on the mound. His WAR per 162 games stands at an extraordinary 6.1, higher than five of the 10 Negro League pitchers admitted to the Hall of Fame. And his # 2 Major League Similarity Score match is Hall of Famer Gaylord Perry. Had Pittsburgh followed through on his tryout in 1942, when he was at the height of his powers, he is another player who might well have been America's "Jackie Robinson."

Bill "Cannonball" Jackman. Given the reality that black ball players could often make more money barnstorming than playing league ball, it is surprising that more players did not make their livelihood in that manner. Bill "Cannonball" Jackman has been referred to as the "the best pitcher whose name you have never heard."[164] He was a submarine fastball pitcher with excellent control. The tall Texan started his career in his home state in the early 1920s, a period for which records are scarce. His career bridged more than 30 years, from 1920 through 1953, as he became a true star outside of the official Negro Leagues. The anecdotal evidence on this guy is astonishing. The omnipresent John McGraw, after seeing Jackman strike out 18 men in a game, claimed he would pay "$50,000 to the man who could make Jackman white."[165] James A. Riley reports that players felt he was faster in his prime than either Satchel Paige or Bob Feller.[166] One New England newspaper referred to Jackman as "the Lefty Grove of the colored baseball realm and has been the envy of every Major League manager in the country."[167] The *Hartford Courier* wrote, "Jackman has the reputation as the black Babe Ruth of baseball."[168]

Like John Donaldson before him, Bill Jackman essentially began and ended his career as a barnstormer. He performed principally in the New England area and generally outside of the formal Negro League arena. In 1929, he could be found playing alongside a young Hank Greenberg in the Blackstone Valley League, where his season's record was 19–5.[169] His standard rate of pay during his prime was $175 a game, with a $10 bonus for each strikeout.[170] In 1930, the *Taunton Gazette Star* credited Jackman with a 48–4 record, two no-hitters, and called him the "world's greatest colored pitcher."[171]

When Jackman did join the Negro Leagues, for a short time in the 1930s, James A. Riley reports he went 52–2 one year and twice beat Satchel Paige in head-to-head competition. In 1939, he went 14–1 pitching on Sundays for the Portsmouth, New Hampshire, team, leading them to the New England semi-pro title with a 13-strikeout performance in the championship game.[172] In 1941, Jackman teamed with his favorite catcher, Burlin White, to record an 18-strikeout performance for the Boston Night Hawks. As late as 1942, his documented record was 10–1, with 16.5 average strikeouts per game.[173] He continued to pitch in the bushes and for semi-pro teams as a hugely popular gate attraction until he was past 50. In 1949, at the age of 52, he claimed to have pitched in his 1,200th game.[174]

Historian Dick Thompson reported that he had located 230 verified wins and almost 3,000 career strikeouts for Jackman, but believed the actual total to be over 300 wins and 8,000–10,000 strikeouts.[175] As of 2007, Dick Thompson had located 25 decisions that Jackman had against pitchers with Major League experience, for which he compiled a record of 22–3.[176] When Jackman's career ended, Art Ballou of the *Boston Globe* wrote: "Some experts rate Jackman with Satchel Paige, which is saying a lot, but in his heyday it was accepted by all and sundry that Jackman was far superior to his white counterparts on the sandlots. And, he was eminently successful in barnstorming games against major leaguers."[177]

Newspaper hyperbole aside, there is no way that Jackman did not have Major League level talent. Historian Robert Peterson quoted Negro League veteran Bill Yancey as believing Jackman was the "best of all."[178] That Jackman was also appreciated by his contemporaries, despite his limited Negro League tenure, is demonstrated by the fact that, despite his career outside of the regular Negro Leagues, he was still listed on the Roll of Honor (right behind Hall of Famer Leon Day) in the *Courier* Poll.

On July 14, 1971, shortly before his death, the State of Massachusetts and the Boston Red Sox honored Jackman with a Will Jackman Day. In a truly ironic gesture, the Boston Red Sox, on behalf of owner Tom Yawkey, who had done so much to enforce the color line against African Americans, presented Jackman with a lifetime pass to Fenway Park.[179] While he may not have had a Hall of Fame career, Bill Jackman may have had Hall of Fame talent he was never given a chance to demonstrate in a segregated world. If and when paramount barnstormer John Donaldson is admitted to the Hall of Fame, it will also serve as a tribute to all of the barnstormers such as Jackman who followed him.

Stuart "Slim" Jones was a fabulous pitcher whose meteoric brilliance flashed across the Negro League world, but did not last long. His overpowering fastball allowed the tall, 6 ft. 6 in. left-hander to dominate for a period in the mid–1930s. In 1933, he struck out 210 men in Puerto Rican winter ball. In 1934, James A. Riley reports, he had a 32–4 record against all competition, including going 22–3 in Negro League play.[180] That year, he was the paramount pitcher in black ball as he led the Philadelphia Stars to the NNL pennant and hurled a shutout in the deciding game of the championship against the Chicago American Giants. Selected as the starting pitcher in both the 1934 and 1935 East-West All-Star Games, he pitched six scoreless innings. Some regard his faceoff with Satchel Paige in 1934, a 10-inning 1–1 tie in which Jones pitched six perfect innings, as the best black baseball game of all time.[181] At the end of the 1934 season, he outdueled Dizzy Dean, a 30-game winner, in an exhibition against the world champion St. Louis Cardinals.[182]

Buck Leonard maintained that Jones, at his height, was faster than Lefty Grove, whom he had also faced in exhibition.[183] Leonard selected Slim Jones as his choice for the greatest Negro League left-hander of all time.[184] Seamheads, ESPN, and Bill James have all retroactively designated Slim Jones the best pitcher in black ball for 1934, a season in which he accumulated a WAR of 7.7, among the top 10 seasonal WARs accumulated by a pitcher in Negro League history. Jones was never the same after 1934, probably because of his fondness for liquor. In the winter of 1938, the legend is that he traded his coat for the money to buy whisky and died after contracting pneumonia.[185] It may well be true.

Based upon his peak ability, Slim Jones was selected to the all-time all-star teams of

Hall of Famers Monte Irvin, Cum Posey, Larry Doby, Leon Day, Buck Leonard, and Jud Wilson. He tied for sixth place among pitchers in the McNeil Players' Poll. He was also listed first among pitchers on the Roll of Honor in the 1952 *Pittsburgh Courier* Poll. His talent is reflected in the fact that his fourth closest Major League Similarity Score match is another lefty Hall of Famer, Warren Spahn. Slim Jones' seven-year run contained only two or three years of brilliance and lacks sufficient duration for Hall of Fame consideration.

Just as there are other top pitchers in the Major Leagues who will never make the Hall of Fame, there were certainly other great Negro League pitchers who, for one reason or another, are one rung below the more viable candidates. The following is a summary.

Leroy Matlock. A top left-hander during the 1930s who combined a solid fastball with excellent control and good breaking pitches; pitched for the legendary Homestead Grays in 1932 and Pittsburgh Crawfords between 1933 and 1938; key member of the championship teams in the 1936 *Denver Post* Tournament and 1937 Ciudad Trujillo (Santo Domingo); starter and winning pitcher in 1936 East-West All-Star Game; won 26 straight games in a streak ending in May 1936; 1935 and 1936 all-star selection of Cum Posey; Seamheads designee as top pitcher in black ball in 1933, 1935 and 1936; ESPN Cy Young Award winner for 1935; John B. Holway deemed him an all-star in 1933, 1935, and 1936; winner of both the George Stovey (Cy Young) Award and Fleet Walker (MVP) Award in 1935, when he compiled a record of 18–0 for Pittsburgh Crawfords; according to John B. Holway, his .757 winning percentage was the highest in Negro League history; played between 1937 and 1941 in the Dominican Republic, Venezuela, and Mexico before finishing up with the New York Cubans in 1942; Holway includes Matlock on his Hall of Fame nominee list; Roll of Honor selection of the *Courier* Poll; Hall of Famer Tom Glavine is his tenth closest Major League Similarity Score match.

Bill Holland. His 22-year career included a 29–2 record in 1929; John B. Holway's George Stovey (Cy Young) Award winner for 1930; Seamheads all-star in 1936; in a career extending from 1919 to 1941, ranks seventh in wins among all Negro League pitchers; career WAR 25.3 ranks in the all-time top 20 among Negro League pitchers; Cool Papa Bell called him one of the top four pitchers in Negro League history; listed second on the Roll of Honor in the 1952 *Pittsburgh Courier* Poll; named to Cum Posey's first all-star team in 1933 and to his second team in his 1936 rankings; Hall of Famer Jack Morris is his # 3 Major League Similarity Score match.

Ted Trent. Dominant big game curve ball wizard who sported a .661 winning percentage from 1927 to 1939; top pitcher in all of black ball in 1928; led his St. Louis Stars team to three straight pennants; a John B. Holway all-star selection in 1928, 1930, and 1931, as well as winner of Holway's George Stovey (Cy Young) Award and Fleet Walker Award (MVP) in 1928; Bill James' best pitcher award for 1928 and 1930; struck out 15 men against Joe Pirrone's All-Stars in a California Winter League game in October 1931[186]; remarkable four-time ESPN Cy Young designee between 1928 and 1937; appeared in four East-West All-Star Games from 1934 to 1937, starting two; Cool Papa Bell called him the best right-handed pitcher in Negro League history, saying "there was a stretch of about six years where no white all-star team could touch him"[187]; Hall of Famer Early Wynn is his thirteenth closest Similarity Score match; career cut short by drinking issues.[188]

Phil Cockrell. Spitball pitcher for Hilldale during their dominant years in the mid–1920s; best pitcher in the Eastern Independent Leagues in 1922; record in league competition between 1923 and 1927 was 10–6, 10–2, 12–3 and 11–4; John B. Holway all-star selection in 1924; Cum Posey all-star pick in 1925; started four games in the 1924 and 1925 World Series against the Kansas City Monarchs, compiling an overall ERA of 3.04 and winning the decisive sixth game in 1925; ranked by Seamheads as 16th all-time in lifetime wins among Negro League pitchers; Seamheads lists him as third best all-time defensive player on the mound; credited with four no-hitters during his career[189]; was never as effective after 1927 and closed out his career as a Negro League manager and umpire; listed third among pitchers on the Roll of Honor in the 1952 *Pittsburgh Courier* Poll; selected by Pop Lloyd and Chappie Johnson to their all-time teams; Hall of Famer Red Ruffing is his #3 Major League Similarity Score match; shot to death in a bar by a jealous husband who mistook him for another man.

Arthur "Rats" Henderson. Curveball specialist in the 1920s; solid career WAR of 19.9; best pitcher in the Eastern Colored League in 1926 (15–5 record), 1927 (19–7 record), and 1928 (13–2 record), leading his team to two consecutive pennants in 1926 and 1927; Cum Posey all-star selection in 1924 and a *Pittsburgh Courier* all-star pick in 1925; John B. Holway all-star selection and best pitcher in Negro League ball in 1926; ESPN best ECL pitcher award for 1926 and 1927; blew his arm out in the 1928 season and was never effective again; all-time team selection by veteran catcher Chappie Johnson; WAR per 162 games of 4.4 exceeds that of Hall of Famers Rube Foster and Andy Cooper; Hall of Famers Burleigh Grimes and Early Wynn are among his five closest Major League Similarity Scores; short eight-year total career disqualifies him from Hall of Fame consideration.

Laymon Yokely. Star hurler for the Baltimore Black Sox in the late 1920s and early 1930s; fastball pitcher credited with six no-hitters; John B. Holway George Stovey (Cy Young) Award winner and ESPN best pitcher designee for 1928; named *Pittsburgh Courier* all-star in 1929, when he won 17 games to lead the Black Sox to the pennant; Leon Day regarded him as his hero; became a popular gate attraction and was known variously as "Corner Pocket" or "The Mysterious Shadow"; declined in effectiveness in the early 1930s, probably from overwork; still had enough left in the tank to win 25 games for the Philadelphia Stars and 15 more wins with the semi-pro Bacharachs in 1939 (40 victories in one season); Roll of Honor designee in 1952 *Pittsburgh Courier* Poll; no Hall of Famers among his 100 closest Major League Similarity Scores; finished his career by relying on his reputation to operate the Yokely's All-Stars until 1959; short period of dominance not really Hall of Fame worthy.

Barney "Brinquitos" Brown. Left-handed screwball specialist of the late 1930s and 1940s; named to five East-West All-Star Classics, started two of them, with an overall all-star ERA of 0.71; Seamheads all-star in 1938; Seamheads top pitcher in all of Negro League ball in 1946; led Puerto Rico Winter League in victories two years; in 1946–47 Cuban winter ball, he won 16 games, with an ERA of 1.24; best pitcher in Mexico in 1941, with a record of 19–4; wore uniform No. 1 for the Philadelphia Stars (demonstrating his status) in 1942, for whom he went 23–8 against all competition; a really good hitter who often played the outfield and pinch hit; finished his career up in the Canadian Mandak League in the early 1950s; selected as one of the top seven pitchers in Negro League history in the McNeil Players' Poll; named by Quincy Trouppe to his # 1 all-time Negro League team; Andy Pettitte is his closest Major League Similarity Score match; picked by veteran catcher Bill Cash as one of black ball's two greatest pitchers.

Webster McDonald. Submarine pitcher who, according to sports reporter Halsey Hall, was "a cross between a bowler and a diamond heaver"[190]; nicknamed "56 Varieties" for his ability to mix pitches and keep batters off balance; pitched for 23 years from 1918 through 1940, with a .732 winning percentage against all competition; reputed for dominating Major League all-star teams in exhibition games, with a lifetime record of 15–2 (.833), including four wins over Dizzy Dean in his prime[191]; played on nine championship teams including the Chicago American Giants for whom he pitched four games (ERA of 2.07) in the 1926 and 1927 Negro League World Series; reportedly pitched three no-hitters for the Philadelphia Giants when they barnstormed in the Northeast in 1923; career WAR of 21.1 places him among the top 25 Negro League pitchers in that category; named to the all-time teams of veterans Ben Taylor and Monte Irvin and historians John B. Holway and Jay Sanford; listed fourth among pitchers on the Roll of Honor in the 1952 *Pittsburgh Courier* Poll; included on John B. Holway's proposed Hall of Fame ballot; marginal Hall of Fame selection Jesse Haines is only Hall of Famer among his closest 25 Similarity Scores; ended his career as an excellent manager who won the 1934 Negro National League title and managed in the 1935 East-West All-Star Game.

Dan McClellan. Curve baller regarded as one of the best pitchers during the first decade of the 1900s; Seamheads deemed him the best pitcher in the Cuban Winter League in the 1899–1900 season; first recorded perfect game in black ball history for Cuban X-Giants in 1903; pitched both ends of a doubleheader in the 1903 "colored championship of the world," winning the opener and losing the second game; pitched to a record of 9–2 in Cuba in winter of 1903–04; he and Rube Foster were the foremost pitchers leading the Philadelphia Giants to three straight championships from 1904 through 1906; in 1905, his record was 30–6 (five of the losses were by one run), with over 300 innings pitched, over 200 strikeouts, and only one home run allowed[192]; outdueled by Rube Waddell before "the largest crowd of the season" in an October 1906 exhibition game against the Philadelphia Athletics[193]; a good hitter who played at first base or in the outfield when not on the mound; box scores suggest he averaged one hit per game at the plate[194]; batted cleanup for the Philadelphia Giants in 1909–1910; historian Phil S. Dixon regards him as the best left-handed hitting pitcher in all of baseball; SABR author Phil Williams has concluded that McClellan probably accumulated 300 wins between barnstorming and independent black team games between 1897 and 1911[195]; ended his career as a Negro League manager; selected as a first team coach and to the Roll of Honor as a pitcher in the 1952 *Pittsburgh Courier* Poll (despite the fact that the poll was limited to the period 1910–1952); an all-time great pitching selection of Pop Lloyd; old time Hall of Famers Pud Galvin and Stan Coveleski are among his ten closest Major League Similarity Scores; included on the 94-name preliminary ballot for the 2006 Hall of Fame Negro Leagues Special Election.

George "Lefty" Wilson. Turn of the 19th century ace who first pitched for the Page Fence Giants in 1895; advertised as "The Palmyra Wonder"; grew up tossing balls for hours at circles on the family barn developing his curveball[196]; according to John B. Holway he was 29–4 when he left in 1895 to play for a mixed-race team from Adrian in the Michigan State League,[197] where he also hit .327 and played the outfield; after returning to the Page Fence Giants, his record against all competition for the three year period from 1896 through 1898 was 19–5, 15–1, and 8–1[198]; Seamheads deems him the top pitcher in all of back ball in 1899; after the Page Fence Giants folded, Wilson became the star pitcher for the Columbia Giants (which then merged with the Chicago Union Giants), where he teamed with catcher

Chappie Johnson to form the best battery of the era through around 1905; in 1905, Wilson and Chappie Johnson together helped win the state title for Renville, Minnesota; after 1905, Wilson's effectiveness seemed to dwindle and he pitched for lesser teams; Chappie Johnson included Wilson on his all-time team; he closed out his career with one undistinguished winter season in Cuba, in 1906–07; while records for him are scanty, in 1895 he struck out 280 batters in 298 innings over the course of 37 games[199]; only Hall of Famer among his closest 100 Similarity Scores is the marginal selection Bobby Wallace; Wilson was a pitcher who peaked for a few grand years, but whose longevity does not truly amount to a Hall of Fame career; an interesting footnote, and possibly final tribute, is that when Negro League pitcher Dave Brown hid from the law in the mid–1920s after killing a man, he travelled though the Midwest earning a living as a pitcher using the alias "Lefty Wilson."[200]

Frank "Rawhide" Wickware. Fastball pitcher active from 1910 to 1925, who posted an 18–1 record for Rube Foster's Leland Giants in 1910; pitched and completed both ends of a doubleheader multiple times, including two games head to head against Dick "Cannonball" Redding on August 24, 1912 (they split victories)[201]; the winner of John B. Holway's retroactive George Stovey Award for the best pitcher in his league in both 1910 and 1912; ESPN Cy Young award winner for 1910; became the star attraction for the Mohawk Giants in 1913–14; verified record for Mohawk Giants is 24–5, with nine shutouts[202]; his reputation was such that his appearances against Walter Johnson's all-stars became a major gate attraction; outpitched Walter Johnson in two out of three games in 1913 and 1914, when both pitchers were at the height of their abilities[203]; threw a no-hitter for the Chicago Giants on August 26, 1914, facing only 27 men (a walk was erased by a caught stealing)[204]; controversial player who engaged in many fights, was convicted of theft, and was known for jumping from team to team for more money; by 1917 his performance on the mound became erratic after drinking problems robbed him of his talent[205]; he was with Dave Brown when Brown killed a man in a barroom fight in 1925[206]; 1926 *Pittsburgh Courier* editorial claimed Wickware "liquored himself out of big time baseball"[207]; a Hall of Fame selection of leading historian Larry Lester; honorable mention on William F. McNeil's all-time Negro League team; no Hall of Famers among his closest 20 Major League Similarity Scores; listed as the seventh pitcher on the Roll of Honor in the 1952 *Courier* Poll.

Walter Ball. Turn of the century ace during the pre–Negro League era from 1903 to 1921, mostly for Chicago-area teams; considered one of four great Negro League pitchers of his time, together with Rube Foster, Dan McClellan, and Harry Buckner[208]; control pitcher who often used a spitter; went 12–1 in 1909 for the Leland Giants; pitched against Three-Finger Brown in a 1909 post-season game against the Chicago Cubs, losing 4–1 when his team committed six errors[209]; reportedly won 23 straight games for the St. Louis Giants in 1912[210]; pitching for the Brooklyn Royal Giants, struck out 15 members of the white Trenton club in 1913[211]; a key member of Rube Foster's mound corps, starting in 1915; defeated Stan Coveleski and Dutch Leonard in PCL exhibition game in 1915; in the mid–1920s, then over 40 years old, formed and led the "Walter Balls" on barnstorming tours scheduled by a young Abe Saperstein[212]; according to Seamheads, was the second best pitcher in the Negro League (behind José Méndez) for the period 1903–1911; Bill James calls him the best Negro League pitcher from 1907 to 1909; winner of John B. Holway's Fleet Walker Award (MVP) for 1909, a year in which he also hit .383; listed in the narrative of the *Courier* Poll as having received votes; WAR per 162 games of 3.8 denotes an elite pitcher; no Hall of Famers among his top 40 Major League Similarity Scores; on the pre-ballot in the 2006 Hall of Fame Negro Leagues election.

Dave Brown. Lefty with great all-around stuff; spectacular career WAR of 20.2 in only seven seasons; WAR per 162 games (5.2) exceeds that of three Hall of Fame Negro League pitchers; ESPN best pitcher in the Negro National League in 1920, 1921, and again in 1922, leading his Chicago American Giants to three NNL championships; picked up three victories in the 1921 playoff against the Bacharach Giants; regarded as one of the greatest left-handers in 1920s ball until he killed a man in a barroom fight over cocaine in 1925, at which point he may have concluded his career playing for Midwestern semi-pro teams such as the 1926 Pipestone, Minnesota, Black Sox, for whom he is believed to have pitched under the alias "Lefty Wilson"; nothing verifiable is known of him after 1930, although there are reports he died in Denver under mysterious circumstances[213]; an all-time all-star selection by Cum Posey, Pop Lloyd, and leading historian Dick Clark; a second team pick in the 1952 *Pittsburgh Courier* Poll; John B. Holway all-star each year from 1920 through 1922; a third team pick of preeminent historian Robert Peterson (who only picked two pitchers to each of his teams); # 1 Major League Similarity Score match is a fellow named Babe Ruth; his short career and character flaws disqualify him from Hall of Fame consideration.

Roy Welmaker. Pitched in seven Negro League World Series games in the early 1940s, including a 1942 opening game loss against Satchel Paige; winner of John B. Holway's Rube Foster Award as MVP of 1944 World Series; 12–4 in 1945 with Homestead Grays; 1945 winner of Holway's George Stovey (Cy Young) Award, Seamheads and ESPN top pitcher designations; two scoreless innings in 1945 East-West Classic; decent hitter who, according to James A. Riley, batted .321 in 1945 and often pinch hit; while stationed at Fort Benning during World War II, struck out 49 men in 23 innings over three games[214]; spent three seasons in Venezuela after World War II military service; 1949 walk-on to Cleveland Indians training camp, assigned to their minor league affiliate, where he won 22 games for Wilkes-Barre; ended his career with three seasons in the PCL; no Hall of Famers among his closest 100 Major League Similarity Score matches.

Roosevelt Davis. One of the Negro League's paramount spitball and emery-board specialists, Davis was a mainstay of three of the Negro League's greatest championship teams: the St. Louis Stars of the late 1920s and early 1930s, the Pittsburgh Crawfords of 1934–35 and the 1945 Cleveland Buckeyes; effective and well-traveled journeyman over three Negro League decades; career began with Candy Jim Taylor's 1924 St. Louis Stars and continued with at 14 different Negro League teams over a period of 22 years; record of 17–7 as a starter in 1925 (Seamheads); record of 8–0, pitching principally in relief, in 1928, and 11–3 for the champion 1934–35 Pittsburgh Crawfords; awful hitter, slow runner and only an average fielder—but effectively kept hitters off balance with a wide variety of pitches; continued long enough to pitch with the infamous white Bismarck semipro team in 1932, with the Ethiopian Clowns in 1939–41, and even as a starter for the Cleveland Buckeyes in their 1945 championship season; according to Seamheads, averaged 14 wins for each 162 games played over his career and had a lifetime winning percentage of .606; lifetime WAR of 18.9 further demonstrates his career value; designated one of the 29 all-time greatest Negro League players by the stat heads of the Hall of Miller and Eric; no Hall of Famers among Davis' top 100 Similarity Score matches; no support for the Hall of Fame among veterans; credited with having taught Bill Byrd the spitter.[215]

Sam Streeter. Left-handed spitballer during lengthy career stretching from 1921 to 1936; starting (and losing) pitcher in the first East-West All-Star game in 1932; record of 14–7 for the Birmingham Black Barons in 1924; career WAR in Negro League competition is 11th highest of all time among starting pitchers; won 14 games in 1927 to help lead Black Barons to the second-half NNL title; member of legendary Pittsburgh Crawfords teams 1931–36 (posted 11–3 record in 1932); according to Seamheads, averaged 16 wins per 162 games played; solid hitter posting averages over .300 in six seasons and lifetime batting average of .277 (Seamheads); named to the all-time Negro League teams of seven Negro League veterans in the McNeil Players' Poll; honorable mention on William F. McNeil's All-Time Negro League All-Star team; closest Similarity Score to a Major League player is Andy Pettitte; Negro League veteran and manager William "Pep" Young claimed Streeter topped Satchel Paige as the Negro League's greatest all-time pitcher, saying "I don't know of anyone [Streeter] didn't get out…. Lefty Gomez (fabled New York Yankee lefthander) was a white Sam Streeter."[216]

WAR Comparison of Negro League Hall of Famers and Candidates—Pitchers
All Leagues: Negro, Cuban, Mexican Leagues vs. Major Leaguers and High Minors

Name	Years	WAR (per 162 games)	Career WAR
Satchel Paige	1928–47	7.1	50.8
Bullet Rogan	1916–38	6.7	62.2
George Stovey*	1888–96	6.5	2.2
Smokey Joe Williams	1907–31	6.4	55.2
Leon Day	1934–46	6.2	22.5
Ray Brown	1932–45	6.1	44.5
Dave Barnhill	1941–48	6.1	16.1
Willie Foster	1923–37	6.0	47.4
Juan Padrón	1915–25	5.4	32.7
William Bell	1923–37	5.4	37.4
Hilton Smith	1937–48	5.4	26.1
Bill Byrd	1933–48	5.2	33.0
Dave Brown	1919–25	5.2	20.2
Jose Mendez	1907/08–1925	5.0	48.2
Nip Winters	1921–32	4.8	31.0
Leroy Matlock	1932–38	4.2	25.0
Rats Henderson	1923–28	4.4	19.9
Dick Redding	1911–31	4.4	38.8
Chet Brewer	1925–48	4.2	20.4
Sam Streeter	1921–36	4.1	25.0
Rube Foster	1902–17	4.0	15.2

Name	Years	WAR (per 162 games)	Career WAR
Ted Trent	1928–39	3.9	21.8
Walter Ball	1903–21	3.8	12.9
Barney Brown	1931–48	3.7	24.3
Webster McDonald	1922–40	3.7	21.1
John Donaldson	1915–24	3.6	11.8
Slim Jones	1932–38	3.6	8.2
Andy Cooper	1920–39	3.4	26.9
Danny McClellan	1899–1913	3.4	9.2
Eustaquio Pedroso	1907–26	3.3	37.6
Bill Holland	1919–41	3.2	25.3
Roy Welmaker	1936–45	2.9	11.3
Roosevelt Davis	1924–45	2.7	18.9
Phil Cockrell	1917–34	2.3	14.9
Dizzy Dismukes	1909–32	2.1	11.5
Frank Wickware	1910–21	1.7	8.8
Laymon Yokely	1926–44	1.0	4.7
Will Jackman*	1928–36	0.1	0.0
George Wilson*	1897–1907	-0.4	-0.2

Hall of Famers in bold. *24 Men Out candidates in italics*. WAR statistics courtesy of Seamheads.
*Recorded games are too few to render significant data.

WAR Summary—Pitcher: WAR validates Negro League lore that Smokey Joe Williams, Satchel Paige, Bullet Rogan, were the paramount Negro League pitchers. "Cannonball" Redding was a first ballot selection in the 1952 *Courier* Poll, on the initial 1971 Hall of Fame Negro League ballot, and a finalist in the 2006 Negro League Hall of Fame election. His career WAR exceeds that of any other Negro League pitcher not yet in the Hall of Fame. He is the next man up.

John Donaldson's candidacy requires inclusion of his barnstorming career, but even his limited Negro League stats are solid (albeit unspectacular). Bill Byrd was the last great Negro League pitcher whose career WAR of 33.0 exceeds that of four of the ten Negro League pitchers in the Hall of Fame. Byrd also was a skilled batsman, one of the best of the Negro League pitchers at the plate. Chet Brewer is another solid candidate whose résumé requires supplemental reference to his play in other venues around the hemisphere. His standing in veteran's and historian's polls is further evidence of his Hall of Fame talent.

William Bell is a strong Hall of Fame candidate, whose record is somewhat bedeviled by his missing statistics as a barnstormer and playing in the Texas League. His WAR indicates that he probably would have been a stronger selection than Andy Cooper as the Negro League's "Bert Blyleven." Nip Winters' short but spectacular career makes him an interesting candidate as well. Juan Padrón's high WAR (both career and per 162 games) suggests that he deserves the title as the Negro League's most underrated pitcher and is entitled to far more consideration than received to date. Dave Barnhill was another underappreciated pitcher, but his Hall of Fame credentials are impaired by his tenure in clown ball.

Pitchers José Méndez, Bullet Rogan, Danny McClellan, and Eustaquio Pedroso have increased career WAR ratings by reason of the fact that they regularly played in the field when they were not pitching. However, that actually increased their value to their teams and should hardly be discounted.

Turn of the century pitchers George Stovey, Dan McClellan and Walter Ball are worthy of serious scrutiny despite their fewer available statistics.

CHAPTER 16

Super Utility

Over the years, the term utility player has come to be a somewhat derogatory reference to an extra bench player who could fill in a hole when a regular starter needed a rest. In his post–money ball treatise *Power Ball* (2018), author Rob Neyer points to the more recent development of a super-utility player as one of the key components of a successful modern team. This change has been a direct result of the large number of slots taken up by relief pitchers on current-day rosters. On a modern-day roster of 25 players, at least 12 (and sometimes 13) players are pitchers. That leaves 12 or 13 players to man the other eight positions, two of whom are usually catchers. Neyer argues convincingly that players such as Ben Zobrist and Marwin Gonzalez played critical roles in winning World Championships for the Chicago Cubs and Houston Astros in the 21st century because of their ability to effectively carry out roles at multiple positions.

It was actually the Negro Leagues that contained the true forerunners of the modern super-utility player. Because of the short rosters in the Negro Leagues (often 15 players, including pitchers), a player who could readily play first base, second base, shortstop, or outfield because of his strong arm and fielding prowess, and others who could both catch and pitch, were invaluable in black ball. In many respects, such a player was one of the most important players on the team.

Among players already admitted to the Hall of Fame, Martin Dihigo is the leading exemplar of the super-utility player. James A. Riley, in his *Biographical Encyclopedia of the Negro Baseball Leagues,* lists Dihigo's primary positions as second base, outfield, pitcher, first base, and third base. His secondary positions are then added as shortstop, catcher, and manager. Dihigo played every position and he did it well. He was regarded as a leading pitcher, top hitter, and great fielder, with top speed and power at the plate. His lifetime batting average was .316 and his career ERA was 3.29. All of this was demonstrated in the 1935 East-West All-Star Classic. In that game, Dihigo started in center field, batted third in a powerful hitting lineup, and ended the game on the mound (although he did give up a game-winning home run to Mule Suttles). Other Hall of Famers and leading candidates for the Hall who might reasonably be regarded under the super-utility category were pitchers Bullet Rogan, José Méndez, Eustaquio Pedroso, and Bill Byrd, who all regularly played in the field when not on the mound. However, in this volume we will treat them as pitchers since this is how they were primarily regarded in the Negro League world.

The importance of super-utility players in the Negro League world is reflected in the fact that many of the major Negro League polls have used a separate utility category in designating their all-time teams. At the same time, it seems that these super-utility players have suffered in the Hall of Fame voting because they are not primarily associated with a single position. John Beckwith was an all-around utility player who played shortstop more than any other position. But, when you compare Beckwith with Pop Lloyd, how does one rank a player who was only a sometime shortstop? Is he a shortstop or is he something else? How about Double Duty Radcliffe who both pitched and played catcher on a regular basis? Is he a pitcher or a catcher? The answer is that they were both true super-utility players whose value exceeded their worth at any single position.

While the Negro Leagues may have been major league ball, they were not an exact parallel to the Major Leagues. In the Negro Leagues, it was probably the rule, more than the exception, that players fielded multiple positions. Yet, there were certain players who were esteemed in the Negro Leagues more for their versatility than as primary position players. These super-utility players who were so important to the Negro Leagues, but fairly unique in the Major Leagues (e.g., Babe Ruth, Shohei Ohtani), should receive their due in their correct category as the super-utility players they were. Not only were they some of the most gifted athletes of their time, but some of these players had Hall of Fame worthy careers.

John "The Black Bomber" Beckwith

Years	Games	Runs	Hits	HR	RBI	SB	BA	SLG*	WAR per 162g	WAR Career
1916–38	621	432	847	134	450	42	.358	.572	7.2	28.3

Career statistics (CNLBR), WAR (Seamheads), *Negro League games only.

There once was a player who was the most feared slugger in the Negro Leagues during the 1920s and early 1930s (with the possible exception of Oscar Charleston), who was known as the "Colored Babe Ruth" or "Big Johnny," was one of the great drawing cards of his era, and who has been called by sabermetricians a "cross between Rogers Hornsby and Lou Gehrig."[1] He was a super-utility man who played all nine positions, including pitcher and catcher. Primarily regarded as a shortstop or third baseman, his true position was hitter. Understanding why John Beckwith is not yet in the Hall of Fame requires a more multifaceted analysis than that for any other Negro League player.

From 1916 through 1935, Big John Beckwith was a power hitter who dominated the Negro League game. According to authors David A. Lawrence and Dom Denaro, "Next to [Josh] Gibson, … there was probably no one in the entire history of blackball who could swat a baseball as hard as John Beckwith."[2] At the same time, he was also regarded by many as moody, quick tempered, and ready and willing to settle problems with his fists. There is no other player about whom Negro League historians and players are more split as to whether his personality traits offset his on-field contributions. The conclusion really depends upon how one values performance versus character.

The on-field performance was amazing. Beckwith was a 6 ft. 3 in., 230 lb., power hitter who played all over the diamond. He played two seasons primarily as a catcher, five years mostly at shortstop, five years principally at third base, and two years at first base. According to Seamheads, his occasional stints on the mound resulted in a 3.22 ERA. It appears that a team would put him anywhere on the field to keep his big bat in the lineup.

A somewhat challenged defensive fielder, he was a huge right-handed pull hitter.[3] Prior to Josh Gibson, he was also the most feared slugger in Negro League history.[4] In 1921, Beckwith was the first man, white or black, to hit a home run over the left field stadium wall in

Cincinnati's Redland Field.[5] He was also the first man to hit the ball out of Schorling Park, the home field of the Chicago American Giants,[6] and allegedly hit the longest home run ever at Forbes Field, in 1928.[7] Negro League pitcher "Scrips" Lee, who saw them both play, said "Babe Ruth and Beckwith were about equal in power. Beckwith … used a 38-inch bat, but it looked like a toothpick when he swung it."[8]

Beckwith grew up playing on the sandlots of Chicago. He began his professional career at the age of 16 for the Montgomery Gray Sox. He truly arrived as a hitter in 1921, when Larry Lester and Dick Clark record him with a batting average of .378 for the Chicago Giants. Rube Foster brought Beckwith to the Chicago American Giants in 1922, where he hit .361, compiled a .603 slugging average, and contributed to winning the 1922 Negro League World Series.

JOHN BECKWITH

One of the great power hitters during the 1920s and early 1930s, John "The Black Bomber" Beckwith hit over .400 twice in his career and compiled a career batting average of .358. Known as the "Colored Babe Ruth," John Beckwith had the second highest batting average in Negro League history among hitters with more than 2,000 at bats. He was the first player to hit a ball out of the park in Cincinnati's Redland field. (Courtesy Helmar Brewing. Artist Sanjay Verma.)

His 1922 seasonal WAR of 5.0 is one of the highest ever accumulated in one year by a player manning the hot corner. He won his first batting title in 1924, with what James A. Riley reports was a batting average of .452 and 40 home runs against all competition, and a .402 batting average in official league games.[9] In 1925, Beckwith won John B. Holway's Fleet Walker Award as the league's MVP, when he averaged 48 home runs for each 550 at bats.

Because leading researchers' statistics vary for the period from 1921 to 1931, Beckwith's batting average ranges between .349 to .366 depending upon the source.[10] CNLBR lists his lifetime batting average as .358, somewhere in the middle. From 1921 through 1931, Beckwith hit below .320 only once and over .360 seven times. He hit over .400 twice, in 1925 and 1930.[11] According to Seamheads, he hit a combined .386 in 1929, playing both with the Homestead Grays and the Lincoln Giants, and bashed 14 home runs in 56 games. James A. Riley credits Beckwith with an absurdly high batting average of .546 in 1930. According to John B. Holway's research, John Beckwith has the second highest batting average in Negro League history among hitters with more than 2,000 at bats (trailing only Jud Wilson).[12]

Beckwith's high batting average was also consistent against Major League competition and was fully accompanied with power. The CNLBR reports that he hit .416 in two California Winter League seasons in 1927–28 and 1928–29. He also led the California Winter League in home runs in 1929–30. Both of his California Winter League teams won the championship. In 155 recorded plate appearances against Major League pitching, he hit .413, with 18 home runs, or one home run for each eight plate appearances.[13] He is the only reported Negro Leaguer to hit three home runs in one game off Major League pitching, when he took ace Rube Wahlberg deep three times in October 1928 in a barnstorming contest in Butler, Pennsylvania.[14]

He led his league in batting average twice, slugging percentage in four different years, and in home runs five times.[15] Unconfirmed newspaper articles credit Beckwith against all competition with 72 home runs in 1927, 64 home runs in 1928, and 60 home runs in 1929.[16] Babe Ruth, who opposed him in barnstorming games, once said that "not only can Beckwith hit harder than any Negro ball player, but any man in the world."[17] Double Duty Radcliffe claimed, "Nobody hit the ball harder than him [Beckwith]—Josh Gibson or nobody else."[18] On June 2, 1928, Beckwith hit five home runs in a doubleheader against the Havana Red Sox played in Uniontown, Pennsylvania.[19] According to Seamheads, his career .595 slugging percentage is the fifth highest in Negro League history.

Not surprisingly, John Beckwith's career WAR of 28.3 places him squarely in the Hall of Fame echelon. Only three other Negro League position players have a WAR in excess of Beckwith and are not in the Hall of Fame (Dobie Moore, Dick Lundy and Hurley McNair). His WAR per 162 games of 7.2 exceeds that of Hall of Fame left-side infielders Pop Lloyd and Jud Wilson. Were that not sufficient evidence that he was truly something special, Beckwith's three closest Major League matches pursuant to Seamheads' Similarity Scores are Rogers Hornsby, Joe DiMaggio and Alex Rodriguez. Ted Williams, Nap Lajoie, Tris Speaker, and Stan Musial are also among his 12 closest matches.

So how is a player, who could play any position and hit as well as anyone in Negro League history, not in the Hall of Fame? His character and attitude are reported by some to have been truly awful. Researcher James A. Riley is among the detractors who allege that his intangibles offset his value to his team: "Beckwith was moody, brooding, hot-tempered and quick to fight. Combined with a severe drinking problem, and an often lazy, unconcern about playing, his character deficiencies often negated his performance value. Sometimes he would play in an inebriated condition or exhibit meanness on the field. On one occasion, when Beckwith's error cost a game, pitcher Bill Holland tossed his glove in disgust and, in the clubhouse, after the game, Beckwith responded by knocking the pitcher unconscious."[20] In 1923, he led the league in home runs but was suspended for severely beating an umpire and had to leave town before a warrant could be served.[21]

Other evidence suggests that his "bad behavior" was somewhat exaggerated. John B. Holway interviewed Double Duty Radcliffe, who thought his bad attitude reputation was overdrawn and that it "was a bum rap."[22] Radcliffe roomed with Beckwith and felt: "He wasn't a rowdy guy but he didn't take any foolishness. He would fight in a minute if someone did something to him."[23] Hall of Famer Turkey Stearnes agreed: "John Beckwith was one of my favorite players … if you didn't bother him, he didn't bother you. I never had any trouble with him and I played on the club right beside him."[24] Unfortunately, all of that sounds a little as though you needed to stay out of his way not to get beaten up.

What is certainly true is that Beckwith was a tough player in a tough world. Playing in the California Winter League in 1928–29, his then wife stabbed him. Shortly after the attack, and supposedly on the brink of death, he returned to the playing field for a decisive game and hit two home runs.[25] He was then named the MVP of the league. John Beckwith has the highest career batting average (.413) and slugging percentage (.831) in California Winter League history.[26]

Beckwith regularly bounced from team to team during his career. In the 1920s alone, he played for the Chicago Giants, American Giants, Harrisburg Giants, Homestead Grays, Baltimore Black Sox, and the New York Lincoln Giants. On deeper analysis, his short stay on many teams, and much of the rancor he generated, appears to have been caused not by his behavior so much as his demanding to be paid what he believed he was worth. Beckwith's relationship with owner Cum Posey sheds light on the situation. In 1924, Cum Posey released Beckwith from the Homestead Grays at the height of Beckwith's powers after a financial dispute, telling the press because he "was unable to fit our organization and we felt we had to either let him go or ruin the morale of our organization."[27] Yet, shortly after Beckwith left Posey's team to join the Baltimore Black Sox, Posey had second thoughts and spent a week in Baltimore unsuccessfully trying to persuade Beckwith to return.[28]

John Beckwith was a star and demanded to be treated as such. In 1935, he was again recruited by Cum Posey for his Homestead Grays, where Posey planned to promote Beckwith as his "new Josh Gibson." However, when Beckwith showed up and insisted on being reimbursed for the catcher's equipment he had purchased, he and Posey got into a fight and Beckwith left the team.[29] Such were the economics in Negro League baseball. Whatever Cum Posey may have thought of John Beckwith, it did not stop him from naming Beckwith to his all-time Negro League all-star team.[30]

Beckwith also spent substantial time during his baseball career as team captain and a long-time manager—hardly the marks of a malcontent.[31] After 1935, he returned to New York with his second wife, Dorothy (not the one who stabbed him), and decided to play only with locally based teams. No longer active in the Negro National League, he played and managed for lesser New York black teams thereafter, including his own Beckwith All-Stars, through around 1949. His name still drew the fans, and he had enough left in the tank to allegedly hit .350 in 1937.[32] As a result, virtually all of the statistics are missing for the second half of the career of a player who would probably have hit over 500 homers in the Major Leagues. Beckwith, working also as a security guard, coached and managed industrial and semi-pro teams in the New York City area until his death of cancer, in 1956 at the age of 56.

Another factor that may have adversely affected the Hall of Fame voting for John Beckwith is that he is not associated with one particular position. However, we have seen that a true utility player was even more valuable in the Negro Leagues because of the small roster size. In point of fact, the 1952 *Pittsburgh Courier* Poll designated Beckwith as the second team all-time utility player. If one viewed Beckwith as a third baseman, where he often played, he might be fairly regarded as the best third baseman in Negro League history.

In the final analysis, conceding that John Beckwith was neither the most disciplined nor personable of players, his performance overshadowed his demons. Beckwith was deemed a Hall of Famer by 56 percent of historians in the McNeil Poll. The stat geeks of Baseball Think Factory agree. They elected Beckwith, and not third baseman Ray Dandridge, to their Hall of Merit. In a letter they collectively submitted to the 2006 Negro League voting committee members, they urged Beckwith's selection:

> Boom-Boom's [another of his nicknames] cause has grown with each passing year and his momentum is in large part to the hard work of several Hall of Merit [their own statistician's Hall of Fame] micro-film researchers. Beckwith had to overcome an initial electoral hesitance wrought by an influential and perhaps overly negative review of his character and fielding published in recent years. The diligence of

our independent researchers has uncovered numerous newspaper accounts and anecdotes that contra-indicate this harsh portrait and paint a more balanced picture of this admittedly complex man. However, one thing that no one doubts is that Beckwith could hit.[33]

Leading historian John B. Holway, who deemed Beckwith a first team Negro League all-time all-star at designated hitter, chastised the 2006 Special Committee for the Negro Leagues Hall of Fame for not picking Beckwith over some lesser candidates.[34] Holway regards Beckwith as the best player in the Negro League East in 1925 and a five-time all-star between 1925 and 1931. Seamheads rated him as an all-star in 1922, 1927, and 1930. Cum Posey designated him an All-Star in 1924 (as a catcher!) and the *Pittsburgh Courier* deemed him their all-star utility pick in 1929. Hall of Famer Ben Taylor designates Beckwith as his utility pick on his all-time team. Bill James calls him the MVP of the Negro Leagues in 1930. Monte Irvin includes him as one of the Negro League's five best shortstops, noting "It's tough to choose between Pop Lloyd, Willie Wells, Dick Lundy, and John Beckwith."[35] Even his principal detractor James A. Riley acknowledges that Beckwith had a Hall of Fame career[36] and designated him as the one of the two utility players (alongside Martin Dihigo) on his all-time Negro League all-star team. As CNLBR concluded, "When the facts speak for themselves, Beckwith was a great ball player whose career has been overlooked."[37]

John Beckwith was rightfully a finalist on the 39-name final ballot used in the 2006 Special Election, but he was not elected. Without mentioning names, Fay Vincent emphasized at the press conference following the 2006 Special Election that character, integrity, and contributions to the game were discussed intensely with respect to some players who were terrific on-field ballplayers.[38] One can easily surmise that he was talking about John Beckwith. The committee did, in fact, discuss Beckwith's "bad ass" personality at length, and it may therefore be regarded as a major factor in his failure to be elected.[39] Committee member Todd Bolton felt that, based upon the discussions, Beckwith may still have achieved at least a 50 percent vote.[40] While it is problematic whether 75 percent of the voters in any future forum will be able to overcome their view of his "character issues," John Beckwith had a Hall of Fame worthy career.

Bill "Money" Monroe

Years	Games	Runs	Hits	HR	RBI	SB	BA	SLG	WAR per 162g	WAR Career
1899–1914	305	193	324	6	148	45	.279	.344	5.7	10.7

Career statistics and WAR (Seamheads).

John McGraw was reported to have claimed that Bill Monroe was the single greatest ballplayer of all time and would have been a star in the Major Leagues.[41] There are reports that the light-complexioned Monroe was one of those players who was under consideration by McGraw to be signed for his Giants and passed off as a Cuban.[42] Monroe played all over the infield on a regular basis and also could be found occasionally playing in the outfield as the need arose. However, he most often manned the fielding slots at second, shortstop, or third base. When he played at third base, he was regarded as an excellent handler of bunts and a better fielder than his Major League contemporary Jimmy Collins.[43]

One of black ball's most important superstars at the turn of the century, Monroe was a multi-positional showman in the field and a solid hitter over a 19-year career. In an era when Negro League players were often expected to entertain fans as well as perform on the field, he was known for catching flies behind his back and talking to batters while he threw them out. He would playfully trash talk runners by yelling at them to run faster while he threw to first base.[44] He yelled benign jokes to the fans, heckled opposing managers, and encouraged umpires, all to the delight of the fans and exasperation of his targets. He had a well-advertised motto: "I never miss, hit it to me and you are out."[45] He became a crowd favorite who was nicknamed "Money" sometime around 1904, either as a take on his last name or his clutch performance.[46] Another trick of his was to kick ground balls into the air with his foot, catch the ball with his hand, and throw the runner out.[47]

John McGraw once claimed that Bill "Money" Monroe, a superstar shortly after the turn of the 20th century, was the greatest player, white or black, he had ever seen. (Courtesy Helmar Brewing. Artist Scott Pedley.)

James A. Riley tells a story about Monroe when he was facing Hall of Famer Joe McGinnity, who was pitching for a semi-pro team. After pointing his bat at McGinnity, who knocked Monroe down twice in response, Monroe then bet McGinnity $500 he would hit a home run on the next pitch. McGinnity fired a fastball and Monroe then hit it for a game winning home run and then continued his taunting by circling the bases backwards.[48] The legend does not report if McGinnity honored the bet.

By 1905, his foghorn chatter throughout the ballgame (which could be heard throughout the small ballparks) had made him renowned. As he approached the plate, he might yell "The ball is going out and a run is coming in." As he fielded the ball, "You're out chile." To spark a rally, "Oh Lord, have mercy on us for what we are about to do."[49]

But, much like Muhammad Ali in a later generation, Monroe's showmanship should not obscure his greatness as an athlete. His true exploits were on the field of play. He is often compared in the same era to Home Run Johnson, although he had more speed. Monroe was a key player on many championship teams, beginning with the Chicago Unions in 1899. Subsequent years found him joining some of the era's best teams, the Cuban X-Giants and Sol White's Philadelphia Giants, where he hit third in the lineup for each team. After a few injury-riddled campaigns, he won championships with the Philadelphia Giants from 1904 to 1906. Researcher Phil S. Dixon's study of the 1905 Philadelphia Giants has determined that Monroe, usually batting third or fourth in the order, accumulated 49 extra base hits (8 home runs, 15 triples, and 26 doubles) and stole 37 bases.[50] And he did all of this while missing a few weeks because of injury and in view of the fact that Dixon was unable to uncover box scores for at least 26 missing games.[51]

He became recognized as one of the game's leading players with the Brooklyn Royal Giants from 1907 to 1910 where he was instrumental in leading them to two Eastern championships in 1909 to 1910. Although statistics for this era are spotty, records from one major four-game series the Royals fought against the Negro League's Philadelphia Phillies in 1906 show Monroe with five hits, five runs, and four stolen bases.[52] Seamheads has uncovered 24 games played by Monroe in 1908. In those games, he hit .337, scored 26 runs, and had 13 RBIs and 10 extra base hits.

During the same time frame, he joined Rube Foster and Home Run Johnson in Cuban winter ball in 1906–08. In the 1906–07 Cuban Winter League, he hit .353. James A. Riley compiled a .333 batting average for Monroe in the 1907–08 Cuban winter campaign. By 1909, Monroe was well enough regarded to be named to Indianapolis sportswriter Harry Daniels' "All American Team." Daniels called Monroe: "the great, fastest man in baseball, and the most wonderful baserunner for the past 10 years; also strong at bat."[53]

Rube Foster must have liked what he saw in Cuba, because he then recruited Monroe to his famous Chicago American Giants club in 1911, where Monroe batted cleanup behind Pete Hill. He was designated an all-star by Seamheads in 1908 and again in 1911. John B. Holway deems him an All-Star in 1906, 1910, 1911, and 1913.

During four years in Chicago, Monroe played second base alongside shortstop John Henry Lloyd on the juggernaut 1914 Chicago American Giants, regarded by some as the greatest black ball team of all time. When the Giants won the Negro League World Championship in 1914 by sweeping the Brooklyn Royal Giants, Monroe hit fifth in the batting order and had four hits in the third game of the series to lead the offense. To the public, it was Monroe, not Lloyd, who earned a reputation as "the most sensational player" and "king of the second baseman."[54]

Regarded as a great fielder with good foot speed, Monroe's career batting prowess is somewhat unclear. Some sources credit him with a lifetime batting average in the dead-ball era of over .300.[55] On the other hand, the limited data collected by Seamheads reflects seven seasons in which Monroe hit over .300, but credits him with a career batting average of .279 over 14 seasons. Despite the many missing statistics from the pre–Negro League era, Monroe's WAR per 162 games of 5.7 still places him first among all-time Negro League second baseman who played ten years or more, which is the position where Seamheads lists him.

While he was still a productive player, Bill Monroe died suddenly of tuberculosis at his parents' home in the winter of 1915, bringing an end to his 19-year career. In an obituary for the 38-year-old infielder, John McGraw was reported to have said, "Monroe was the greatest player he had ever seen" but "could not use him on account of his color."[56] In a rare report on the death of a Negro League player, *The Sporting News* called him "one of the greatest ball players the game has ever known" and stated that "those who have seen him play say he was a [Nap] Lajoie and a [Honus] Wagner, combined."[57] After his death, the Chicago American Giants wore black crepe on their arms in memory of Monroe.[58]

It is interesting to note that Monroe's historical reputation over time may have been tarnished by the fact that his teammate and double-play partner John Henry Lloyd disliked the flashier and more popular Monroe. Lloyd, who was all business, denigrated Monroe in his old-timer reminiscences and even left him off his all-time team.[59] By this we learn that oral history can cut both ways.

What is remarkable is that Bill Monroe, who last played in 1914, was still listed first on the Roll of Honor for second basemen in the 1952 *Courier* Poll. Historian William F. McNeil named Monroe as the first team second baseman for the era 1900–1925, as one of four shortstops on his all-time Negro League all-star team, and as one of only three Negro League second baseman on his ultimate all-world all-star team. Despite the passage of time, Monroe was also able to secure a 24 percent vote in the 2001 McNeil Historians' Poll. Similarity Score analysis places four Hall of Famers among his top 100 Major League matches, including Nellie Fox.

Bill Monroe was designated an all-time great by historian James A. Riley and selected as a Hall of Fame caliber player by leading historians David A. Lawrence, Jerry Malloy, William F. McNeil, Robert Cottrell, and Lou Hunsinger, Jr. In 1957, Frank Forbes of *The Sporting News* rated Monroe as the all-time greatest Negro League second baseman. Historian Phil S. Dixon deemed him the greatest third baseman of his generation. The great black ball pitcher Dan McClellan, who played alongside Rube Foster, Pete Hill, and Home Run Johnson, regarded Bill Monroe as "the best ballplayer he ever played with."[60] Sol White considered Monroe one of Negro Ball's all-around great players and noted that he "courted attention from the moment he entered the ground until the close of the game."[61] Leading Negro League manager Candy Jim Taylor opined in a 1936 interview with the *Pittsburgh Courier* that Bill Monroe was the greatest showman in Negro League history.[62] In rating Monroe as the fifth greatest second baseman in Negro League history, Bill James concedes that he could rank higher. He does. Rube Foster, whose opinion counts more than many, also claimed that Monroe was the greatest ballplayer ever, white or black.[63] Such accolades from so many leading and reputable figures in the baseball world cannot be discounted. Bill Monroe belongs in the Hall of Fame.

Worthy of Further Discussion

Harry Buckner. It is hard to categorize Harry Buckner, one of the top black ballplayers at the turn of the century. He pitched, caught, and played all of the infield and outfield positions. As a pitcher, he was called a "speed marvel" and, according to James A. Riley, was considered "head and shoulders above" the other greats of his era: Dan McClellan, Rube Foster, and Walter Ball.[64] Seamheads deemed Buckner the best black ball pitcher in 1898. Over a 22-year career, Seamheads reports that he recorded a 2.88 ERA. He played for many of the great teams in the East and Midwest, including the Chicago Unions, Philadelphia Giants, Mohawk Giants, New York Lincoln Giants, and Chicago Giants. He was also one of the earliest players to venture to Cuba over the winter, where he achieved an ERA of 2.51 over four seasons. Buckner routinely played in the field when not on the mound, and he compiled a lifetime batting average in Negro League play of .318 (Seamheads). When not on the mound for the Chicago Giants in 1917, he batted third. His career WAR of 14.8, which is far lower than it should be because of all the missing statistics from his era, still places him tenth all-time among Negro League right fielders, where he spent the most time. Among his top ten closest Similarity Score matches as a pitcher are Hall of Famers Stan Coveleski and Pud Galvin. His Similarity Scores as a batter produce Enos Slaughter as his closest Hall of Fame match (at #3). Buckner is rarely touted, but a ballplayer who could pitch like Stan Coveleski and hit like Enos Slaughter should not be forgotten. He was one of the Negro League's early and great super-utility men.

Walter "Rev" Cannady. O.K., now it gets really interesting. Here is a player whose three closest Major League Similarity Score matches are (in order) Honus Wagner, Nap Lajoie, and Charlie Gehringer. The nearest modern player to whom he compares statistically is Jose Altuve. But there is more. In 1932, when the Pittsburgh Crawfords super-team included Hall of Famers Oscar Charleston, Josh Gibson, and Satchel Paige, as well as Cool Papa Bell, Jud Wilson, and Judy Johnson, there was another player the owner, Gus Greenlee, was advertising as the "best all-around player in baseball." Moreover, this player was an all-purpose super-utility performer who could play any position (including on the mound) and play it well. He had a 25-year career (1921–1945), with a lifetime batting average of .324 (Seamheads), and most people have never heard of him. His name is Walter "Rev" Cannady, and he is entitled to far more respect than he has received as a Hall of Fame candidate.

Playing all over the diamond, but mostly at second base, the well-travelled Cannady was one of the most consistent and productive hitters of his time, one who also had decent power and speed. He was also a versatile fielder who usually hit in the heart of his teams' batting order. Cannady was a notorious bad ball hitter who loved to wait for the curve and then jump all over it.[65] He began his career in 1921 as a 17-year-old outfielder with the Columbus Buckeyes. In 1922 he was pitching for the Cleveland Tate Stars, where he compiled a 3–1 record with a 2.50 ERA. By 1923, he was playing mostly at shortstop and second base for the Homestead Grays. His versatility was demonstrated by a game he pitched on July 23, 1923, when he hurled a seven-hit victory and hit two home runs in an exhibition game in Warren, Pennsylvania.[66] His breakout year occurred in 1925, when Cannady hit .399 for the Harrisburg Stars, finishing the year fifth in batting average and fourth in home runs in the Eastern Colored League (ECL). It was Cannady who batted cleanup behind Oscar Charleston for the 1926 Harrisburg Giants.[67] In 1927, he played at shortstop and third base, batted .336, and was third in the ECL in steals. Back with the Homestead Grays in 1929, he was the starting shortstop and he hit for a .367 batting average. In the winter of 1929–30, he played for Almendares, in the Cuban Winter League, and was the second baseman in an infield consisting of Pop Lloyd (1b), Judy Johnson (3b), and Dick Lundy (ss).[68] In seven seasons with the Homestead Grays, the statistics compiled on Seamheads reflect that Cannady hit .361 overall.

After stints with the New York Lincoln Giants, Hilldale Daisies, and the Pittsburgh Crawfords from 1930 to 1932, he had his longest tenure with the New York Black Yankees from 1933 through 1939. His best seasons in New York were 1933 (.364) and 1937 (.365).[69] Cum Posey named Cannady to his all-star selection teams in 1924, 1933, and 1936. He became the Black Yankees' third baseman and manager in 1938. That year, he replaced the top vote getter Ray Dandridge (who had jumped to Venezuela) as the starter at third base, his only appearance in the East-West All-Star Classic (he went 1 for 3 with an RBI).[70] He even had a few good years left in the tank, hitting .349 for the Chicago American Giants in 1942. In 1944, he had one final go-around with the champion Homestead Grays, a year in which he batted .356 at the age of 40, played in the Negro League World Series, and tied Cool Papa Bell for third place in the league in doubles.[71] The now aging Cannady continued to play through 1945.

Walter Cannady was deemed by Seamheads as an all-star at his position in 1925, 1930, 1931, and 1936. John B. Holway regards him as an all-star in 1930 and 1937. Viewed as a second baseman, where he spent the most time, his career WAR of 19.1 is the third highest of any second baseman in Negro League history.

There seem to be a number of reasons why Cannady does not receive his due. Firstly, he moved around to an inordinate extent, never allowing himself to build any hometown following. The man played for 13 different teams over 25 years. One of the reasons for his movement is that he was regarded as temperamental with a violent streak. There were multiple occasions where he physically attacked an umpire on the field.[72] After being ejected by an umpire on one occasion, he smashed the umpire's car windows with a baseball bat. He also had a reputation for often being lazy and lackadaisical in the field.[73] This reputation is somewhat confirmed by his inconsistent year-to-year performance. He seemed to follow up a stellar .300 plus batting average with a year in which he would hit in the low .200s. (He hit .305 in 1933 and .211 in 1934.)

In assessing what he acknowledged as Cannady's long and distinguished career in Negro League ball, historian James A. Riley noted that Cannady was "mean, angry and moody, not a favorite of other players."[74] Players stayed away from him because of his unpredictability. It certainly does not sound like he was a great guy to hang out with. He wore out his welcome quickly, which is why he was so well-travelled. During his career, Rev Cannady never seems to have been regarded by the fans as a true star,[75] as reflected by his single appearance in an East-West All-Star Classic. He may also be one of those players who suffers from the absurd prejudice of not being clearly associated with one position.

While Cannady was selected by Cum Posey to a number of his all-star teams, his support among players and historians in their polls for all-time greats is weak. He was named third on the Roll of Honor at the utility infielder position in the 1952 *Courier* Poll. However, his name does not appear in either the veterans or the historians voting in the McNeil Polls. Cannady was included on the 2006 Hall of Fame 94-name pre-ballot, but he did not make the final cut. Overall, his on-field performance, when measured alongside his other characteristics, do not seem to add up to a Hall of Fame career. Then again, there are those Similarity Scores!

Sam Bankhead was the Negro Leagues' ultimate utility player. One of five brothers playing in the Negro Leagues, Sam was the older brother of Dan Bankhead, Major League baseball's first black pitcher. But it was Sam who was the true standout of the brothers. His remarkable ability to play all positions well is demonstrated by the fact that he was selected to start in nine East-West All-Star Games at five different positions (2b, ss, lf, cf, rf). Think about that for a second!

According to Garnett Blair, of the Homestead Grays: "Sam Bankhead … played shortstop and he would go behind third to get it and throw you out waist high across the diamond. He could not only play short, he could play second, third, he could play outfield, he could pitch and he could catch. He was all around … [wherever he played] let it go there because if he got his glove on it, he was going to throw you out."[76] Judy Johnson called him one of the Negro League's greatest outfielders and pitcher Wilmer Fields regarded him as the Negro League's "greatest team player."[77]

In a lengthy career spanning from 1929 through 1950, Bankhead was a perpetual winner who CNLBR reports played on 25 championship teams in the United States and the Caribbean. Sam Bankhead was a standout on such legendary teams as the Homestead Grays (1943–45), Ciudad Trujillo (1937), and the Pittsburgh Crawfords (1935–36), a team that fielded five future Hall of Famers and which many regard as the greatest black team of all time. Legend claims that the Crawfords' 1935 outfield of Bankhead, Cool Papa Bell, and Jimmie Crutchfield was so fast that they could keep a field dry by catching raindrops before they hit the ground.[78] According to James A. Riley, Bankhead's batting averages for the Crawfords were .354 in 1935 and .324 in 1936. In 1937, Bankhead joined Satchel Paige and Josh Gibson on the Ciudad Trujillo team in the Dominican Republic where he hit.309, and then joined the team as they romped to the championship of the Denver Post Tournament.

Seamheads selected him as their all-star pick in 1934, 1936, and again in 1943. Cum Posey deemed him his all-star center fielder in 1936. He was chosen on the 1937–38 Cuban all-star team and the 1942 and 1945 Puerto Rico all-star units. In 1940 and 1941, Bankhead joined his buddy Josh Gibson in playing in Mexico, showing solid power and even leading the Mexican league with 32 stolen bases in 1940 at the age of 37. He and Josh Gibson returned to the Homestead Grays in 1942. Bankhead became their starting shortstop as they won four straight pennants and he made four more Negro League all-star appearances.

Sam Bankhead was a voracious fielder with a cannon arm. His teammate on the Homestead Grays Maurice Peatross said, "When he played shortstop, he just poured the ball over to first base—no wrinkle on his throws. Just like a bullet."[79] Seamheads defensive statistics rate him as the 12th best fielding shortstop in the domestic based Negro Leagues, the position where he spent most of his time. But he was also a clutch hitter and excellent baserunner. The CNLBR reports a career batting average for Bankhead of .311 for 20+ years of Negro League ball. According to CNLBR, he hit .387 in nine East-West All-Star Games, won the 1937–38 Cuban League batting title with a .366 batting average and a .457 slugging average, batted .342 in 21 career games against Major League pitchers, and compiled a .351 career average in the California Winter League. Later on, he feasted on the Mexican League—leading the league in stolen bases (32) in 1940 and twice in hitting (.351 in 1941 and .308 at age 46 in 1946).[80] In the final years of the Homestead Grays, he served as their player-manager until they disbanded as the Negro Leagues dissolved. In 1951, he was the first African American named to manage a white professional team when he was named manager of the Farnham Pirates of the Canadian Provincial League.[81]

Significantly, Sam Bankhead was selected to be the first team "utility player" in the 1952 *Courier* Poll. Bankhead is one of only three first team players from the *Courier* Poll who are not in the Hall of Fame. William F. McNeil also selected Bankhead, together with Martin Dihigo, as the first team utility players on his all-time Negro League all-star team based upon his combined poll of Negro League players and historians.[82] His 20 closest Seamheads Similarity Scores among Major League players include Hall of Famers Roberto Alomar, George Davis and Billy Herman, among others. Sam Bankhead's exceptionally high career WAR of 24.2 clearly places him line for serious Hall of Fame consideration and almost makes one work to find reasons not to elect him.[83]

In terms of his off-field qualities, pitcher Wilmer Fields called Sam Bankhead "the most respected man I met in baseball."[84] It was Sam Bankhead who took charge of Josh Gibson, Jr., following his father's death in 1947.[85] Sam Bankhead is another player who appears to have been adversely affected in the Hall of Fame voting because he is not associated with a single position. Of course, that was his strength in the black ball world. In a short-roster world, Bankhead moved team to team because they all knew they could use him to fill any slot on a solid basis and he was a .300+ hitter to boot. Perhaps his clearest tribute was Double Duty Radcliffe's response when asked on his 102nd birthday what single player he thought of as most emblematic of the Negro Leagues. His answer: Sam Bankhead.[86]

Historian John B. Holway reports that Sam Bankhead, who worked as a garbage man in Pittsburgh after his playing days were over, became the model for Troy Maxson in August Wilson's Pulitzer Prize–winning play *Fences*. Holway interviewed Bankhead and reported that, because of the racism he endured, he was one of the few players he ever talked to who looked back on his playing career with bitterness. Sam Bankhead said he never attended another game after his career was over, saying "I cannot be a fan."[87] Sam Bankhead was shot to death in a bar fight in 1976. Wouldn't it be something if the real-life inspiration for *Fences* were to be elected to the Hall of Fame? His career warrants strong consideration.

Ted "Double Duty" Radcliffe was a 20-year Negro League veteran who became a successful manager. He was nicknamed "Double Duty" by Damon Runyon, who saw him catch a shutout of Satchel Paige in the opening game of a 1932 Yankee Stadium doubleheader, hit a home run in support of Paige, and then pitch his own shutout in the night cap.[88] There were not many utility players who could switch from catcher to pitcher and produce successfully at both positions. Radcliffe could pitch, catch, and hit at a high level. He played on many of the top Negro League teams of the 1930s including the 1930 St. Louis Stars, the 1931 Homestead Grays, and the 1932 Pittsburgh Crawfords, all leading candidates in the discussion for the greatest Negro League team of all time. During that three-year period, Radcliffe hit .283, .298, and .325 while compiling a pitching record of 10–2, 9–5, and 19–8.[89] In 1931, Cum Posey designated him an all-star selection as a pitcher.

He was a smart, strong-armed catcher who used his knowledge of pitching to think along with the pitcher as he caught. As a pitcher, he utilized an effective arsenal that included some illegal pitches, such as the emery ball.[90] Historian Kyle P. McNary calculated that, as a pitcher, Radcliffe compiled a .727 winning percentage against all opposition and that, as a hitter, he had a .303 batting average, with 10 home runs for each 550 at-bats. McNary believes that, if all statistics for Radcliffe were available, he would be shown to have over 500 victories as a pitcher, and 4,000 base hits and 430 home runs as a hitter.[91] Of course, these statistics would have been against all opposition, including semi-pro teams. William F. McNeil reports that, against Major League opposition, he hit .403 in 22 games and went 3–0 as a pitcher.[92]

Like many other top players in demand, Radcliffe was a true baseball nomad, jumping from team to team chasing the highest paycheck. He played for well over a dozen leading black teams in his career. Among his career highlights were joining Satchel Paige on the Bismarck team that won the 1935 Wichita tournament, outdueling Martin Dihigo by throwing a five-hit shutout in the 1939–40 Cuban Winter League,[93] a stint in the Mexican League with Josh Gibson and Cool Papa Bell in the 1940s, and selection as the Negro American League MVP in 1943.

Once the East-West All-Star Game commenced, he appeared in six of them either as a pitcher or a catcher. He shone in all-star competition with a lifetime batting average of .385. In 1944, with his mother watching from the stands, he won his only decision as a pitcher in the East-West Classic, hit a critical home run to help win the game and was designated the game MVP. However, John B. Holway deemed him a true all-star only in 1937. He closed out his career as a manager of the Chicago American Giants in 1950.

Radcliffe was a durable player on the mound and at the plate. In his own words: "I never had a sore arm in my life…. I don't understand these ballplayers now. This finger's been broke four times. This finger was split two or three times…. And I wasn't out but a month. Nowadays it's a disgrace."[94] He was also reputed by Negro League veterans to lead the league in both talking and fibbing. Once in Mexico, he told the owner that his mother had died and he needed an advance to return home. The owner's response: "I thought you told me she died last month."[95]

William F. McNeil has named him, together with Martin Dihigo, as one of two Negro League utility players worthy of Hall of Fame consideration.[96] Radcliffe was designated both as a catcher (listed first) and as a pitcher (listed sixth) on the Roll of Honor in the *Pittsburgh*

Courier Poll. He was also a top 40 selection in the 1999 SABR Poll. Yet, Double Duty failed to achieve close to 50 percent of the vote by either the players or the historians in the Mc-Neil Polls. Whether viewed as a pitcher or a catcher, not a single one of the 80 Major League players with Similarity Scores closest matching Radcliffe's, either as a hitter or a pitcher, are in the Hall of Fame.

His reputation was clearly enhanced by his colorful personality, the fact that he had one of the best nicknames in baseball history, and that he also performed at a successful level as a pitcher, catcher, and manager over a lengthy career stretching from 1928 through 1950. Perhaps "Triple Duty" would have then become a more appropriate nickname. Despite being one of the most intriguing and well-traveled figures in Negro League history, his WAR of 2.2 (per 162 games), lifetime batting average of .269 as a hitter, and ERA of 4.24 as a pitcher (Seamheads) are those of a solid journeyman and do not scream out for Hall of Fame recognition. Nor does the fact that John B. Holway deemed him an all-star in only one season (1937) or that his career WAR of 12.4 does not even rank him within the top 125 Negro League players in that category (and that is with having received additional credit as a pitcher and catcher). According to Seamheads, neither Radcliffe's offensive nor defensive statistics pace him among the top 10 all-time catchers, and his pitching stats do not position him within the top 100 all-time pitchers. In naming his own all-time team, he selected himself neither as a catcher nor a pitcher, but as its manager.[97]

Radcliffe lived on to be 103 (he died in 2005) during which time he served as a colorful raconteur and leading spokesman for the Negro Leagues. His longevity and grace certainly enhanced his reputation. Historian James A. Riley summarized him well: "There may have been better pitchers, better catchers, and better hitters, and there may have been a more colorful player, but there has never been another single player imbued with the diverse talents he manifested during his baseball career."[98]

WAR Comparison of Negro League Hall of Famers and Candidates—Super Utility
All Leagues: Negro, Cuban, Mexican Leagues, vs. Major Leaguers and High Minors

Name	Years	WAR (per 162 games)	Career WAR
John Beckwith	1919–37	7.2	28.3
Martin Dihigo	1922/23–45	6.7	60.3
Bill Monroe	1899–1914	5.7	10.7
Sam Bankhead	1933–48	4.4	24.2
Harry Buckner	1896–1917	4.4	14.8
Walter Cannady	1921–45	3.8	19.1
Ted Radcliffe	1928–46	2.2	12.4

Hall of Famers in bold. *24 Men Out* candidates in italics. WAR statistics courtesy of Seamheads.

WAR Summary—Super Utility: John Beckwith is a rightful Hall of Famer. Bill Monroe, the great dead-ball infielder, is a solid Hall of Fame selection based upon his acclaim from veterans and the fact that his WAR per 162 games is the highest of any ten year Negro Leaguer who played primarily at second base. Sam Bankhead is also an intriguing choice based upon his extraordinary versatility and reputation among the players. Walter "Rev" Cannady's on-field performance was strong, but his attitude issues do not help his cause. Old timer Harry Buckner's worth has been underappreciated. Even though his value was enhanced because he both pitched and caught, Ted Radcliffe does not really have the WAR to support a strong Hall of Fame bid.

CHAPTER 17

Manager

With the exception of certain players and executives such as Rube Foster or Cum Posey, who served a dual role as owners and managers in the Negro Leagues (Foster was also a prominent pitcher), there is no individual admitted to the Hall of Fame principally in his role as a manager. Yet there were some great ones who deserve selection.

C.I. Taylor

Charles Isham "C.I." Taylor is generally regarded, together with Rube Foster, as one of the two greatest managers of the emerging pre–Negro Leagues. Taylor was the oldest of the four Taylor brothers, who strode across early Negro League history. His younger brother Ben Taylor was elected to the Hall of Fame in 2006, and he had another brother, "Candy Jim" Taylor, who also became a top manager in the Negro Leagues. Although a solid infielder as a collegiate player, Taylor realized early that his true calling lay in ownership and management. He became known as a tough but fair disciplinarian who required his players to dress and act as role models. When not in uniform, his players were required to wear collars, ties, and have their shoes buffed. Taylor tried to serve as a role model for black youth and was actively involved in community affairs. He also became a master recruiter and molder of young talent and one of the game's early strategists on the ballfield.[1]

Taylor began his 19-year career in 1904 when he formed and acted as a player-manager for the first black professional team in Birmingham, Alabama, the Birmingham Giants.[2] An-

C.I. Taylor, regarded as the Negro Leagues' first great strategist, had the highest winning percentage in Negro League history for managers with ten or more years of service. (Courtesy Helmar Brewing. Artist Scott Pedley.)

chored by the four Taylor brothers, including pitcher "Steel Arm" Taylor, they became one of the leading teams of the South, winning the 1907 "Colored Championship of the South" from Smokey Joe Williams' San Antonio Black Broncos. They repeated as Southern Champions again in 1908 and 1909. By 1909, they were firmly established as the best team in the South when they finished the season with a record of 79–22 (.782).[3] After five seasons, Taylor moved his team to West Baden, Indiana, where he played second base and managed the West Baden Sprudels to the Springs Valley League championship in 1910 and 1912.[4]

In 1914, Taylor merged his West Baden team into the Indianapolis ABCs, in which he became a part owner and manager. It was there that he became the architect of the great Indianapolis ABCs, which he reconstructed from a decent semi-professional team to a national power in one year. His 1914 record of 51–19 was bettered only by Rube Foster's Chicago American Giants. In 1915, C.I. Taylor's Indianapolis team defeated Rube Foster's Chicago American Giants in three of their five games, but that did not prevent Foster from claiming the "Colored Championship of the West" that year since there was no formal playoff.[5]

By 1916, Taylor was ready to firmly stake his claim at the top of the Western Negro League world. After a winter season in which his team represented Royal Poinciana in the Florida Hotel League, Taylor assembled a team in 1916 with Oscar Charleston, Dave Malarcher, Bingo DeMoss, and two of his brothers. In October 1916, they met the Chicago American Giants in a formal championship series. Led by their ace Dizzy Dismukes, C.I. Taylor's team won four of five games to defeat Rube Foster's Chicago American Giants. That series was mired in controversy, which came to a head in game 3. Ben Taylor, playing first base for the ABCs, objected to Rube Foster coaching first base while wearing a fielder's glove. When instructed to remove the glove by the umpires, Foster refused and was ejected from the game. Foster then pulled his team from the field. When Chicago declined to return to the playing field, the umpires forfeited the game to the ABCs by a 9 to 1 score.[6] It is worthy of note that the ABCs were leading the game 1–0 at that time. Stung by losing four of five games (including the forfeit), Rube Foster challenged the result of the series in the media. He claimed that the series was intended to be 12 games long and that the umpires were biased against him. The Foster claims were not sympathetically viewed by the public and resulted in an ongoing feud with C.I. Taylor.[7] Taylor's teams played only a partial season in 1918 and no season at all in 1919 after the team was decimated by the draft for World War I.[8]

In 1920, C.I. Taylor, despite their animosity, attended the meeting called by Rube Foster to form the Negro National League. Taylor took on major administrative responsibilities for the new league and was voted in as Foster's vice-president of what would become the first successful black baseball league. It is doubtful that the NNL would have existed without C.I. Taylor's assistance to Foster.[9] His ABCs participated in the new league but were never able to overcome the defections and injuries that prevented substantial success. In February 1922, while preparing for a new season, C.I. Taylor died of pneumonia at age 47, still at the helm of the Indianapolis ABCs and at a prime age for managerial prowess. Rube Foster gave one of the eulogies at his funeral.[10]

C.I. Taylor's known win-loss record for his 17-year black ball career was 639–371 (.633), the highest winning percentage in Negro League history for managers with ten or more years of service. Even with all of his missing statistics from his pre–Negro League days, he still is known to have amassed the second largest win total of any manager in Negro League history. Overall, his teams won at least 11 championships during his tenure. In interleague competition against white Major League and minor league teams, his win-loss record was 19–10 (.655).[11]

Taylor may have also been the greatest discoverer and cultivator of baseball talent in the Negro Leagues. He was particularly adept at signing and patiently developing young players. It was C.I. Taylor who uncovered and refined Oscar Charleston, Biz Mackey, Dave Malarcher, Dizzy Dismukes, Frank Warfield, Bingo DeMoss, Otto Briggs, and his brothers "Candy Jim" and Ben Taylor, every one of whom went on to become an outstanding Negro League manager in his own right.[12] After his premature death, C.I. Taylor's imprint continued to live on in black ball in the players and managers he mentored who carried on his traditions. Could there be any greater tribute to the man?

It is also worthy of note that C.I. Taylor played in the field sporadically from 1907 through 1921; however, his statistics are unremarkable (lifetime .176 batting average with no power). As a manager, he was known for his vigorous workouts and training, sometimes requiring his players to perform three hours a day of calisthenics during spring training. He preached on-field communication, emphasized constant training in the basics, focused on community relations to build a fan base, and inspired and motivated his players. He cultivated the black media and had excellent management skills. The discipline he instilled in his players often inspired them to perform at their best and was years ahead of the practices utilized by other teams. His team dressed well and travelled first-class.[13] He was the first Negro League manager known to have clubhouse meetings and hold strategy sessions discussing the attributes of opposing players.[14] The *Freeman* referred to him as the "Wizard of the Game"[15] for his on-field management skills.[16]

He was also a dignified, suave and highly respected gentleman whose integrity was never questioned. James A. Riley tells of one dispute with an umpire where he confronted the umpire's bad call with a simple "If I were a cursing man, I would curse you," and then returned to the bench.[17] Another time, when he was playing, he was called safe at third base and he stood up and addressed the crowd: "Ladies and gentlemen, I am an honest man. The umpire's decision was incorrect. I therefore declare myself out."[18]

C.I. Taylor was a finalist on the 39-name final ballot in the 2006 Negro League Special Election. He was tied for first place with Rube Foster as All-Time Negro League manager in the McNeil Players' Poll and ranked second behind Rube Foster in the McNeil Historians' Poll. Despite his having died in the early Negro League era, he was deemed the all-time best Negro League manager by Negro League veterans Cum Posey, Monte Irvin. and Quincy Trouppe. C.I. Taylor was selected to the all-time greats Negro League teams of leading historians William F. McNeil, James A. Riley, Todd Bolton, Leslie Heaphy, Sammy J. Miller, Robert Peterson, and Jay Sanford. Taylor was designated the second-team coach in the 1952 *Pittsburgh Courier* Poll. When interviewed in 1927 as to his pick for the greatest figures in modern Negro League history, Hall of Famer Sol White picked C.I. Taylor right behind Rube Foster.[19] His stellar character, and having served as the first vice-president of the Negro National League, certainly add to his résumé.

That he was not elected to the Hall of Fame is hard to fathom. Perhaps it is possible that the 2006 Negro Leagues Special Committee felt it was more important to honor the players and the game's founders. Yet C.I Taylor was one of the game's true pioneers as a founder of the Indianapolis ABCs and the Negro National League, as well as its first great manager. One 2006 voting committee member, Todd Bolton, who noted that there might have been no Negro National League had C.I. Taylor not worked side by side with Rube Foster, believed that not electing C.I. Taylor to the Hall was a huge mistake.[20] There should be room in the Hall of Fame for the man who, together with his compatriot and rival Rube Foster, was one of the Negro League's greatest figures from its early days.

"Candy Jim" Taylor

James "Candy Jim" Taylor, younger than Charles "C.I." Taylor, was another of the four Taylor brothers who were major figures in the Negro Leagues. His younger brother Ben was admitted to the Hall of Fame as a first baseman in 2006, and his older brother John "Steel Arm" Taylor was an excellent pitcher in the early 1900s. "Candy Jim" began his career as a third baseman. Born in South Carolina 1884, the 5 ft. 4 in. "Candy Jim" (nickname of unknown origin but always used by his brothers)[21] began playing with local and semi-pro teams around 1901. In 1904, he joined the Birmingham Giants, where he became known for his sure-handed glove and strong throwing arm, committing only three errors in 55 games.[22] He was also an excellent hitter. According to James A. Riley, he had batting averages between .290 and .340 over a span from 1904 to 1908.[23] As a player, he was a key member of eight championship teams, including the legendary 1909 St. Paul Gophers, the 1912 Chicago American Giants, and the 1916 Indianapolis ABCs. Over a span from 1923 to 1928 when he was 39 to 44 years old, he batted .352.[24] This period included an amazing 1923 season when, at age 39, he hit .372, with a .712 slugging average, and led the league with 20 home runs.[25] "Candy Jim" was still taking random at bats as late as 1942 when he was 58 years old. According to Seamheads, he got an RBI in his final at-bat.

Jim Taylor is credited by CNLBR with a lifetime batting average of .289 for his Negro League career and .298 against all levels of competition. He was also a solid fielder and reputed for his speed on the bases. In terms of Seamheads' defensive statistics alone, Jim Taylor ranks as the twelfth all-time best fielding third baseman in the Negro Leagues. He was good enough all-around to be deemed an all-star by Seamheads in 1914 and 1916. John

"Candy Jim" Taylor won more games as a manager than anyone else in the history of Negro League baseball. (Courtesy Helmar Brewing. Artist Scott Pedley.)

B. Holway designated him as an all-star in five separate years between 1911 and 1923. Veteran pitcher Dizzy Dismukes named him as the starting third baseman on his all-time team. According to Seamheads, Candy Jim accumulated the eighth highest career WAR (15.9) of any Negro League third baseman. In his role as a player, Taylor was a Roll of Honor designee at third base in the 1952 *Courier* Poll. Hall of Fame third baseman Brooks Robinson is among his closest 100 Major League Similarity Scores.

Yet, it was as a manager that he truly made his mark. Beginning in 1919, Candy Jim managed for 30 seasons through 1948. While he also continued to play on the field on a regular basis through 1924, and occasionally thereafter, he became one of the game's great managers. Candy Jim Taylor proceeded to win more games as a manager than anyone else in the history of Negro League baseball. According to CNLBR, he compiled a win-loss record of

907–809 in regular season league games, for a .529 winning percentage. Candy Jim actually recorded over 250 more wins against top Negro League competition than any other manager in history, despite the fact that he managed mediocre teams for much of his career.[26] During his managing career, Taylor was in high demand but ended up for many years with some of black ball's truly miserable teams, such as the 1920 Dayton Marcos (16–36) and the god-awful 1926 Cleveland Elites (5–32). If one were to include all games for which CNLBR has located records, including non-league matches, Taylor accumulated 1,094 wins.[27] No one else comes close.

During his career as manager, he won at least 11 championships. Taylor guided his teams to three Negro National League championships and led the Homestead Grays to two Negro League World Series victories (1943 and 1944). His teams also won two California Winter League championships (1935–36 and 1936–37) and the famous *Denver Post* Tournament, in 1936. That he was held in esteem by his peers is shown by the fact that he managed teams in four East-West All-Star Games and appeared as a coach in six others. As an executive, he also served as vice chairman of the Negro National League.

Moreover, "Candy Jim" was extremely well respected by his players. He was a highly regarded strategist on the field, known for his knowledge of the game, no-nonsense attitude, and integrity. His low-key approach, accompanied by discipline and an emphasis on fundamentals, also helped him become a great teacher of young players. He was a proponent of small ball, knowing how to manufacture runs and win tight ballgames. He was able to achieve the dual feat of becoming well regarded both as a player's manager and a disciplinarian who enforced rules equally against stars and scrubs. The players said of him that he would leave his mother behind if she were late for the team bus.[28] According to Hall of Famer Buck Leonard, "He was more relaxed and a better teacher than [Vic] Harris. The players responded to Candy Jim better than Vic. A lot better. Candy Jim knew what he was taking about."[29]

He was also extremely superstitious, forbidding his players from eating peanuts in the dugout, which he considered bad luck.[30] As a teacher, Taylor discovered and mentored Ray Dandridge, who credited Taylor with teaching him how to hit. Generally regarded as a good judge of talent, he was certainly not infallible. Candy Jim cut Josh Gibson from the Memphis Red Sox in 1930, believing he would never work out as a catcher.[31] During spring training in 1948, "Candy Jim" had been hired to manage the Baltimore Elite Giants. He went into the hospital for an undiagnosed ailment and never left, dying prematurely at age 64, on April 3, 1948.[32]

A finalist on the 39-name ballot considered by the 2006 Negro Leagues Special Committee, his overall accomplishments as a player and a manager merit strong Hall of Fame consideration. Many seem to have lost focus on how solid of a third baseman "Candy Jim" was during his career, a five-time John B. Holway all-star who accumulated one of the highest career WAR ratings of all time at the hot corner. He was also a master tactician, regarded by fellow manager Felton Snow, among others, as "the greatest strategist in baseball."[33] As a manager who won the most games in Negro league history, "Candy Jim" was listed as one of the two all-time greatest Negro League managers by leading veterans Monte Irvin, Buck O'Neil, Quincy Trouppe and Wild Bill Wright. Popular with the players and fans, "Candy Jim" was tied with Oscar Charleston as the player's choice for the greatest Negro League manager of all time in the McNeil Players' Poll, and he was one of two managers selected in the 1993 Negro League Baseball Museum member's poll. Historian William F. McNeil named Taylor as one of the managers on his all-time Negro League team.

His 40 plus year career spanned from the pre–Negro League days, to the advent of the Negro National League in 1920, and then to the post Jackie Robinson era. Jim Taylor was a baseball lifer who never married and dedicated his life to the game.[34] In the final analysis, it is harder to manufacture arguments against electing "Candy Jim" to the Hall of Fame than to simply accept that he belongs enshrined together with his two brothers.

Worthy of Further Discussion

Dave Malarcher. A case could be made for "Gentleman Dave" joining the Hall of Fame based solely upon his play at third base. Joining the Indianapolis ABCs in 1916, he developed into one of the finest fielding Negro League third baseman of all time. A speedy switch-hitter, he is also reputed to be one of the greatest clutch hitters in Negro League history. Seamheads lists his career WAR as 18.8, which places him fifth all-time among Negro League third basemen. Bill James also ranks Malarcher as the fifth best third basemen in Negro League history.

An expert bunter and superb base thief, Malarcher was decades ahead of his time in patiently drawing walks in order to use his speed on the basepaths in order to generate runs. Malarcher's batting philosophy sounds like it came right out of *Moneyball*: "When I came up to the plate I only swung at strike three. I would wear pitchers down. If I came up to the plate and the bases were empty, I would try to walk—the easiest way to getting on base."[35]

While CNLBR's statistics show that Malarcher compiled only a .278 career batting average, there were at least four seasons between 1916 and 1922 when he hit over .300. By 1917, he was regarded as the Negro League's best third baseman.[36] He was a John B. Holway all-star at his position in 1917 and a Seamheads all-star position in 1918. Cum Posey selected him as his all-star third baseman in 1924. He played 19 years in the Negro Leagues, winning five league championships as a starting third baseman with the Chicago American Giants in the 1920s. His philosophy was a perfect match for the small ball era. He got on base and used his speed to cause chaos and score runs, often batting from the first two spots on Rube Foster's 1920s Chicago American Giants teams.[37] His WAR per 162 games of 3.8 is higher than that of Negro League Hall of Fame third baseman Judy Johnson.

Malarcher's recorded WAR may not be sufficiently amplified by the fact that defensive data are so lacking for the Negro Leagues. Yet he is reputed to have had great range and a strong throwing arm. The CNLBR reports that many regarded him as the best all-around third baseman of his era. Bill James calls him as the greatest fielding third baseman in Negro League history. The Seamheads partial fielding data does not quite agree with these assessments, ranking his fielding prowess at the hot corner as only fifth best in domestic Negro League history, trailing that of Hall of Fame third basemen Judy Johnson, but higher than that of Hall of Famer Jud Wilson. There are no Hall of Famers among Malarcher's closest 100 Major League Similarity Scores.

Dave Malarcher's leadership skills on the field or in the dugout were exemplary and unchallenged. Malarcher had a strong work ethic, which he picked up from his youth toiling in the cotton fields of Louisiana and from having put himself through college. He was a hardworking player who believed in conditioning. He was always in great shape and encouraged his teammates to do the same. Malarcher was considered one of the finest quality individuals in the Negro Leagues. He was college educated, served in the European theater during World War I, was a lifetime reader, a regular churchgoer, and he never joined his teammates in drinking, swearing, or carousing. His calm temperament and intellectual bent caused other players to nickname him "Gentleman Dave." Legend claims he was never ejected from a game for arguing with an umpire.[38]

All of these qualities served Malarcher well when he moved on to become one of the best managers in Negro League history. It was to Dave Malarcher that Rube Foster turned over the reins of the Chicago American Giants when Foster's health broke down in 1926. Having learned from Rube Foster and earlier from C.I. Taylor, when Malarcher had been a member of the Indianapolis ABCs, Malarcher was ready for his new role. Veteran third baseman Alec Radcliffe called him the best manager he ever saw: "If you made a great catch or a great hit, he would come up and shake your hand, congratulate you, make you feel good. He was in the ball players corner."[39]

Becoming player-manager of the Chicago American Giants, the 1926 and 1927 Negro League World Series more than demonstrated Malarcher's continuing value to the team on the field. Malarcher led the Giants to two World Series victories, in 1926 and 1927, becoming the only manager who will ever win a World Series in two consecutive years while simultaneously leading both World Series in stolen bases. Over the course of those two World Series, Malarcher also led his team in runs by scoring 16 runs while only getting 15 hits.[40] In 1933, he also led his Cole's American Giants to a "Black World Series" victory over the Negro Southern League champions, after Gus Greenlee arbitrarily awarded the Negro National League championship to his own Pittsburgh Crawfords (passing over Malarcher's team, which had a better record).[41]

Mentored by Rube Foster and C.I. Taylor, Malarcher, in his role as manager, developed into one of the game's leading strategists. According to CNLBR, Malarcher has the highest winning percentage (.665) of any of the top 10 winning managers in Negro League history. Managing only seven seasons before he retired, Malarcher won three pennants and two Negro League World Series titles. He never had a losing season as a manager, finishing first or second every season (except for third once) before retiring in 1934. Malarcher also managed the West in the 1934 East-West All-Star Game and went 5–0 when managing in exhibition games against Major League All-Star teams.

Dave Malarcher was named as both a second team coach and listed third on the Roll of Honor among third baseman in the 1952 *Courier* Poll. William F. McNeil named Malarcher as a third baseman on his all-time team. Hall of Famers Willie Foster and Monte Irvin both included Dave Malarcher among their top picks for all-time manager.

Dave Malarcher was one of the most well-respected and classiest individuals in Negro League ball; he was one of the better fielding third baseman in Negro League history; he was a scrappy sparkplug of a hitter who knew how to get on base and use his speed to create runs; he was a winner who consistently seemed to end up on and play a key role on multiple championship teams; he can also lay claim to having been the most successful manager in Negro League history. As a third baseman alone, he was not of Hall of Fame caliber. Combined with his role as a manager, he deserves strong Hall of Fame consideration.

Elander "Vic" Harris is yet another individual who had a superb career as a player but went on to become an even better manager. Harris was a player, coach, and manager in the Negro Leagues from 1923 through 1952. He was unusual for the Negro Leagues in that he spent virtually his entire career with one team, the Homestead Grays. The only two exceptions were half a season spent with the Detroit Wolves, in 1932, and one season with the

Pittsburgh Crawfords, in 1934. He also spent winter stints in the Florida Hotel League, the California Winter League, and the Cuban and Puerto Rican winter leagues. Harris was on the field for 12 months a year for much of his career.

As a player from 1923 to 1945, he was a line-drive hitter with decent power, and slightly above average in the field. According to Seamheads, he was a .307 lifetime hitter. He was also consistent. Harris hit exactly .300 in his first full season in the Negro Leagues in 1923 and hit exactly .300 again in 1943, his last full season as a player (CNLBR). His best years came in the early 1930s. In 1930, he hit .362, with a slugging percentage of .572, for the Homestead Grays, batted .429, with a .514 slugging percentage, in the 1931–32 California Winter League, and hit .366 for the 1934 Pittsburgh Crawfords.[42] Historian Phil S. Dixon states that Harris collected 52 hits over a 35 game period in 1931.[43] According to John B. Holway, he batted .432 for the 1932 Detroit Wolves.[44]

Harris was a solid defensive player known for his hustle and was regarded one of the best players in the game during his prime. Seamheads fielding statistics rank him as the Negro League's fourth best defensive left fielder. He had average speed at best but was feared as "Vicious Vic" on the basepaths. Historian James A. Riley calls him as one of the "four big bad men" of Negro League ball, who were known for playing hard with their fists and spikes.[45] (Two of the other "bad men," Oscar Charleston and Jud Wilson, are in the Hall of Fame.) According to veteran second baseman Dick Seay, "He would cut you in a minute. Cut you and laugh."[46] As a player, Vic Harris accumulated a career WAR of 16.6, ranking him fourth all-time among Negro League left fielders.

Harris was also a winner and was actually revered for his fierce play. Research by CNLBR has determined that, in 29 seasons, Vic Harris was on 25 championship teams,[47] including perhaps the two greatest teams of all time: the 1930–1931 Homestead Grays and the 1934 Pittsburgh Crawfords. Harris was also selected to seven East-West Classic All-Star Games as a player between 1933 and 1947. He was a Seamheads all-star selection in both 1927 and 1932. John B. Holway regards him as an all-star in 1931, 1932 and 1938. Rollo Wilson of the *Pittsburgh Courier* picked him as an all-star in 1929. Cum Posey named him to his all-star unit in 1933, 1935, and 1938. John B. Holway deemed him an All-Star in 1931, 1932, and 1938. In 1927, he was named captain of the Homestead Grays and held that position until he became the team's manager, in 1937. Negro League veterans Larry Doby and Double Duty Radcliffe are among many who have opined that Harris should be in the Hall of Fame based solely on his accomplishments as an outfielder.[48] Leading historians John B. Holway, Larry Lester, Phil S. Dixon and Jay Sanford have similarly concluded that Harris is Hall of Fame qualified as a left fielder alone.[49]

Hall of Famer Willie Foster said the following about Harris: "The most underrated ball player I've known was Vic Harris. Every time I saw him, he played a heck of a game, offensively and defensively. Left-handed hitter, he'd spray the ball, hit it over here, hit it over there. Day in and day out, year in and year out. I don't know why I haven't seen much written about Vic, but he's always been … in my book."[50]

Yet it was as a manager that Harris truly made history. As player-manager in 1938, Harris led his team by hitting .380, with 10 home runs and 17 stolen bases, to capture both halves of the season and obviate the need for a playoff. In 12 years of managing from 1936 to 1948 (he took off two years as manager in 1943 and 1944 to work in a defense plant),[51] Harris managed the Homestead Grays to eight Negro National League (NNL) pennants and two Negro League series wins. It was Harris who managed the Homestead Grays when they were the most dominant team in Negro League ball from 1937 until 1948, right up to the time Negro League began its fade after the entry of African Americans into Major League ball.

Harris accumulated a solid win-loss percentage of .630 in official Negro League games over the course of his career as a manager. The CNLBR credits Harris with a winning percentage of .682 and 754 wins in games against all opposition. His 400 wins accumulated in official "league" games places him fourth all-time among Negro League managers. According to pitcher Wilmer Fields, the vicious player became a quiet manager who got along well with his players.[52] That he was well regarded is also demonstrated by the fact that he was selected as a manager for the East in eight East-West All-Star Games, from 1941 to 1948, and as a coach in one other game. No other manager was selected to more than four East-West All-Star Games.

Altogether, Harris was a perennial all-star player and manager, a lifetime .300 hitter, a key member of 25 championship teams, and one of the Negro League's all-time greats. Leading historians Jim Overmyer, James A. Riley, Brent Kelley, John B. Holway, and Hall of Famer Buck Leonard have all designated him as a manager on their all-time teams. He was deemed Hall of Fame qualified by 39 percent of the voters in the McNeil Players' Poll. Monte Irvin named him as the fourth best manager in Negro League history. The 1952 *Pittsburgh Courier* Poll listed him as a Roll of Honor designee both as a coach and a player. There are 11 Hall of Famers among Vic Harris' 100 closest major League Similarity Scores, including Paul Monitor and Lou Brock. Assessing his overall career as a player and manager, there are no real holes in Vic Harris's résumé for the Hall of Fame.

Buck O'Neil: See Overall Contribution (Chapter 19).

All-Time Negro League Managers:
Official Negro League Games

	Manager	*Number of Seasons*	*Won-Loss Record*	*Pct.*	*Pennants*	*World Series Wins*
1	*Candy Jim Taylor*	30	907–809	.529	3	2
2	C.I. Taylor***	17	639–371	.633	—	—
3	Oscar Charleston*	24	529–446	.543	4	0
4	Vic Harris	12	400–231	.630	7	1
5	Dave Malarcher	7	321–162	.665	3	2
6	John "Buck" O'Neil**	8	311–210	.597	3	0
7	Dick Lundy	10	293–185	.613	3	1
8	Buster Haywood	7	288–261	.525	3	0
9	Rube Foster*	7	283–168	.627	3	0
10	José Méndez*	5	275–107	.647	3	1
11	Frank Warfield	9	264–171	.607	3	1
12	Bullet Rogan*	5	262–124	.679	1	0
13	Jose Maria Fernandez	11	210–210	.500	1	1
14	Winfield Welch	6	203–135	.601	3	0
15	Frank Duncan, Jr.	6	200–152	.568	2	1

	Manager	Number of Seasons	Won-Loss Record	Pct.	Pennants	World Series Wins
16	Dizzy Dismukes	7	175–149	.540	2	0
17	Pop Lloyd*	7	166–136	.550	2	0
18	Quincy Trouppe	4	165–118	.583	2	1
19	Biz Mackey*	4	127–86	.596	1	1
20	John Reese	2	111–33	.762	2	0
21	Andy Cooper*	4	108–50	.684	4	0

Statistics courtesy of CNLRB. *24 Men Out* candidates in italics.

*Admitted to Hall of Fame as a player.

** Proposed for Hall of Fame based upon Overall Contribution.

*** C.I. Taylor's record is missing a majority of his games, which took place too early in pre–Negro League history to be recorded.

CHAPTER 18

Executive

Long overdue was the 2006 admission of five executives of the pre–Negro Leagues and Negro Leagues by the Historian's Panel. Three of those chosen were towering figures of African American baseball history (Sol White, Cum Posey, and J.L. Wilkinson). More intriguing were the selection of two other team owners: Alex Pompez, a Cuban-born promoter who ran the Latino-dominated New York Cubans, and Effa Manley, the first woman elected to the Hall of Fame, who operated the Newark Eagles. Pompez was also a member of Dutch Schultz's mob and a policy racketeer, whose team suspended operations for the 1937 season after he was indicted and fled to Mexico.[1] While Pompez, through his Cuban Stars franchise, should be credited with bringing major Cuban players to the domestic Negro Leagues, it was hardly the juggernaut that some other teams represented. Manley was the public face of the Newark Eagles franchise and garnered great publicity and future acclaim for her anti-lynching campaigns. Yet the other reality was that she ran her team as partners with her racketeer husband Abe.[2]

Neil Lanctot has demonstrated in *Negro League Baseball: The Rise and Ruin of a Black Institution*,[3] his excellent study of the business of Negro League baseball, that those running a numbers racket were among the wealthiest African Americans in the 1930s and that backing a local baseball team was a natural outgrowth of their success. Operating a baseball team gave these numbers barons acclaim in their communities as well as a good way to launder their earnings. Based upon the discrimination they faced, there was probably no better way for African Americans to earn substantial monies in the black world, and the teams with the best funding attracted the top players. Accordingly, one can make a strong case that Alex Pompez and Effa Manley both ran successful franchises and participated in important Negro League activities, regardless of their sources of funding. Pompez also stands as an important symbol of Latin American influence in the Negro Leagues, and Effa Manley was the most important female figure in baseball prior to 1947.

In the post-election press conference held the for the 2006 Negro Leagues Special Election, reporters were quick to single out Effa Manley and Alex Pompez for scrutiny. Committee member Leslie Heaphy noted that Effa Manley was a pioneer in integrating the community and pushing forward a civil rights agenda. Latin American expert Adrian Burgos talked about Alex Pompez's long Negro League tenure and his role in integrating the New York Giants at the end of the Negro League era.[4] Both of those points are unarguably true. But the suspicion lingers that Pompez and Manley may have had some support from the Hall of Fame voters for who (a Latino and a woman) and what they represented as well as what they contributed to baseball. For there are certainly other executives who made particularly strong contributions to the game:

Gus Greenlee

A numbers king and bootlegger, Gus Greenlee was also one of the most dynamic figures in the Negro Leagues. Raised in a professional family (his brothers all earned law or medical degrees), Greenlee chose a separate path. He dropped out of college and moved to Pittsburgh at the age of 19. He bought a taxi and began using it to run bootleg liquor for the mobster Joe Tito. There are two versions of how Greenlee became involved in the illegal numbers game. One version, cited by Greenlee's brother Charles, has Greenlee and Alex Pompez observing the game in operation in Cuba in the 1920s and bringing it back to the States, Pompez in New York and Greenlee in Pittsburgh.[5] Another version, told by one of Greenlee's operators, Ralph Kroger, is that Effa Manley (not her husband, Abe) picked up the idea while touring the islands and alerting the others.[6] In either event, Greenlee seems no more culpable as a numbers operator than Hall of Fame entrants Manley or Pompez. The numbers game was a poor man's lottery that paid off either 500-to-1 or 600-to-1 on any three-digit combination of numbers. Bets could be as low as a penny and were seen by many in the community as the best way to secure a quick stake. It is important to note that the numbers games, when run properly, were devoid of violence and, with payoffs to the police and politicians, generally ignored by the community.[7]

GREENLEE, CRAWFORDS

Gus Greenlee founded the Negro National League in the 1930s, was the impetus behind the East-West All-Star Classic, and owned and operated the Pittsburgh Crawfords during the 1930s, perhaps the greatest Negro League team of all time. (Courtesy Helmar Brewing. Artist Sanjay Verma.)

In or about 1926, Greenlee, his partner Woogie Harris, and Tito began an illegal numbers operation in Pittsburgh, which propelled Greenlee in short order into a powerful community and political figure.[8] Legend has it that, after Greenlee paid off on a particularly large numbers "hit" at a great loss to him, he developed a reputation for honesty that led to his assuming control of the North Side numbers game.[9] The take soon grew to at least $20,000 to $25,0000 a day.[10] The large profits he made in turn led Greenlee to invest in businesses and real estate, including a popular club named the Crawford Grille.

By the 1930s, looking to further launder his earnings and become a more powerful and respected community leader, Greenlee entered the sports business. In

1930, Greenlee purchased the semi-pro Pittsburgh Crawfords.[11] When Cum Posey's powerful crosstown Homestead Grays, the strongest team in baseball, ran into financial trouble in 1931 as the Great Depression deepened, Greenlee pounced upon and signed most of their stars to salaries with his Crawfords. The 1932 Pittsburgh Crawfords team he assembled was a powerhouse featuring Josh Gibson, Satchel Paige, Cool Papa Bell, Oscar Charleston, Judy Johnson, Rap Dixon, Ted Radcliffe, Jud Wilson, and other top players. Greenlee spent freely on his players, and even drove the bus when he took them to spring training, in Hot Springs, Arkansas. Viewed as a dangerous cross-town rival by Cum Posey and his Homestead Grays, Posey had Greenlee's Crawfords excluded from the East-West League in 1932. The Crawfords, playing as an independent, proceeded to barnstorm to a record of 99 wins and 36 losses in 1932.[12] The Depression was then at its low point and the Crawfords were the only team still paying salaries. As a result of all these factors, Posey eventually relented and scheduled a few games with the Crawfords as the 1932 season progressed.

Greenlee was just getting started. In 1932, he located a plot of land and built a stadium for his team, called Greenlee Field. The concrete and steel structure seated 7,500 and cost $100,000,[13] and it was regarded as the first black-owned stadium for the Negro Leagues. In truth, he was in partnership on the stadium with the original land owner Dr. Joseph F. Toms, and some of the investment money came from the mobster Joe Tito.[14] Greenlee ran the baseball operations at his new field, but his silent lender insisted on hiring white ushers, which lost Greenlee some goodwill in the black community.[15] By adding floodlights to the field in August, Greenlee Field also became the first stadium in the country to feature night baseball.[16] In its first year of operations, Greenlee Field had paid attendance of $119,000 for all events, with baseball accounting for 60 percent.[17]

With a new park under his control, he was the impetus in resurrecting the Negro National League (NNL) in 1933 after the East-West League folded the previous year. Greenlee initiated the meetings forming the new league and served as president for its first five years. With the new NNL foundering in 1933, it was Greenlee who seized the helm and saved the league. Despite his own team losing money, he reportedly lent money to other owners to keep the league going, which allowed it to survive that season.[18] In 1933, the Crawfords lost the first half of the season by one game. When the standings for the second half became confused, Greenlee, as league president, unilaterally declared the Crawfords the 1933 champions, although it was disputed.[19] The Negro National League, starting with six teams, would survive until the effective death of Negro League ball in 1948.

Greenlee's greatest contribution to the Negro Leagues may have occurred when he organized, with Robert Cole of the Chicago American Giants, the first East-West All-Star Game, in 1933, to be played in Chicago's Comiskey Park shortly after the Major Leagues played their first all-star game in the same venue.[20] While the concept for such a game seems to have emanated from the African American press, it was Greenlee who seized the initiative, organized the successful plan for the event, and paid the $2,500 rental to Comiskey Park to make it all happen.[21]

The East-West All-Star Game developed into the leading attraction in all of Negro League ball, attracting crowds of African Americans from all over the country each year for a weekend celebration. Attendance was often in the 30,000 to 50,000 range and sometimes outdrew that of the Major League All-Star Game in the same year. Over a period of 20 years, it developed into a superior money-making operation for the Negro Leagues.

The annual showcase provided by the East-West All-Star Game gave sportswriters the chance to observe and write about the black players in action. As a result, many believe it caused the Major League owners to realize the substantial revenue that could be brought in through the African American fans. Greenlee himself noted that the East-West Classic's "profit angle ... was secondary" and "had the effect of arousing interest among colored players and made a decided hit among sports writers."[22] As such, the annual all-star game was doubtless a major factor in the eventual decision to integrate the Major Leagues.[23] While the Negro Leagues lumbered on after 1949 as a shell of its former self, the East-West Classic event continued as its last defining feature, with the final game of this annual event played on August 26, 1962, in Kansas City.

As he showed by bringing the East-West Classic to Chicago's big league Comiskey Park, Gus Greenlee was also instrumental in pushing forward the agenda on integration by opening up first class venues to Negro League ball. It was also Greenlee who initially conceived of four-team doubleheaders as a way to secure Yankee Stadium,[24] a popular event which propelled the black game further in baseball's other great setting.

Greenlee's 1935 Pittsburgh Crawfords club, with Josh Gibson, Oscar Charleston, Judy Johnson, Cool Papa Bell, Sam Bankhead, Leroy Matlock, and Jimmie Crutchfield, may have been the greatest team in all of baseball history.[25] They won the NNL championship by taking 39 of 54 games, for a .722 winning percentage, and then won a third NNL championship in 1936. In 1933 and 1936, the only two seasons for which attendance is known, the Crawfords played for over 200,000 paying fans, a significant number for the Negro Leagues.[26] Unfortunately, whether because their payroll was so high, or because of Greenlee's bookkeeping (numbers game operators were not known for keeping orderly records), Greenlee lost money on the Crawfords. Cum Posey claimed Greenlee lost $16,000 in 1932 and $6,000 in 1933.[27]

It all completely fell apart for Greenlee in 1937 when Dominican dictator Trujillo's representatives raided his team by signing eight of his stars, including Satchel Paige and Josh Gibson. It was the same tactic Greenlee had used against Cum Posey to build his franchise. Unable to make payroll or pay the expenses on Greenlee Field, Greenlee folded his team and sold Greenlee Field. The premises were eventually seized by the city under eminent domain for use as a housing project.[28] Having lost his clout with the other NNL owners, Greenlee was forced to resign as president in 1939.

What is fascinating about Greenlee is that he did not seem to use any mob tactics with his players, who loved him. John B. Holway interviewed players who knew Greenlee. Ted Page who recalled Gus Greenlee as "a great big man and a fine guy.... And his heart was as big as an automobile. He'd give you money in the middle of winter. When a player requested money, no problem." According to Jesse Hubbard, "Greenlee was the swellest fellow you ever met in your life ... he'd do you a favor—any favor you asked.... And ballplayers—he'd give them his heart."[29] Monte Irvin was effusive about Greenlee:

> I liked him very much. He was the nicest guy in the world. I know he took from the community with his numbers racket, but he gave back to the community too. He never reneged on a pay-off ... always willing to help out and support members of the community who had a valid need or a worthwhile endeavor.... Not only did Gus pay his players top dollar, but he also treated them well. His team travelled first class ... and he handed out bonuses at the end of the season for outstanding play.[30]

The record supports the fact that Greenlee treated his players well and that he financed many charitable and worthwhile causes, such as a soup line and benefit games for the NAACP and charitable causes.[31] When a black family needed help with a medical bill, the rent or groceries, Greenlee freely gave money. He handed out hundreds of turkeys at

Thanksgiving. He paid for a number of young African Americans to attend college. In other words, he used his wealth to effectively operate as a ward chairman.[32]

After 1939, Greenlee unsuccessfully tried to re-enter black ball a number of times and was not averse to causing trouble when he did not get a receptive hand from Negro League ball. In 1944, he interfered with the East-West All-Star Game by riling up the players to demand more pay for participation.[33] His final foray into black ball was as a member of Branch Rickey's short lived all-black United States League (USL) in 1945. Probably unbeknown to Greenlee, the USL was a cover created by Rickey to scout black talent, and it lost its purpose when Jackie Robinson joined the Dodgers.[34] Never successful in his attempt to revive his past, Greenlee spent the last years of his life fighting off tax fraud claims by the Internal Revenue Service, defending indictments for election fraud and numbers racketeering, dealing with the loss of the Crawford Grille to fire, and fending off creditors and other racketeers who poached on his numbers business. He died of a stroke in 1952 at the age of 50 and was buried in the same cemetery as Josh Gibson.[35]

There are some good reasons why Gus Greenlee has not been elected to the Hall of Fame to date. He was a complicated individual. He could be pushy and overbearing. Greenlee was a numbers king, a team owner who blatantly raided other teams' players, and was not above using his role as NNL president to dictate to other teams. He even went so far as to arbitrarily award the 1931 pennant to his own team in a blatant conflict of interest. He bounced checks to creditors and was even accused (unproven) of a game-fixing scheme involving the Brooklyn Bushwicks, in 1936.[36] Later on, he stirred up trouble for the NNL when he was unable to secure readmission. His productive tenure in black ball was also short, lasting only from 1931 through 1938.

It is also true that, when he had it, he used his money to recruit the best black players from other teams. But, by doing so, was he any more than the George Steinbrenner of his time? It is also a given that he used illegal money to finance his baseball ventures. But so did many of the other Negro League teams, such as those led by Abe and Effa Manley and Alex Pompez, two of whom are in the Hall of Fame. The dichotomy is that he was also treated his players fairly and paid them well. He was well respected in the community and supported many worthy causes. There are all levels of racketeers. The numbers game he ran seems to have been done honestly and was no more than a precursor to the modern lottery. It was one of the few avenues available at the time to achieving real wealth in the African American community.

Greenlee's concrete contributions to the Negro Leagues were second to no one. Greenlee created and ran the Pittsburgh Crawfords in the 1930s. His Crawfords won three league titles and are one of the leading candidates for the greatest team in baseball history. He built Greenlee Field for his team in 1932, the first black-owned and operated baseball stadium. In 1933, he was the visionary and motivating force behind creating the East-West All-Star Game, the most popular creation of the Negro Leagues. If that were not enough, he personally resurrected the Negro National League in 1933 and led it through its formative years, creating the longest-lasting and most successful Negro League in history.

Monte Irvin ranked Greenlee, whom he respected, as the second most important organizer in Negro League history. He noted that "Rube Foster was 'father of Negro Leagues baseball,' but in his own way, Gus Greenlee was as much a patriarch as Foster."[37] Monte Irvin, who knew them all, expressly deemed Greenlee a more significant owner than either Effa Manley or Alex Pompez.[38] Leading historian Larry Lester calls Greenlee the "Guiding Light of Modern Negro Baseball" and also believes that Greenlee could stake an equal claim to that of Rube Foster as the Father of Black Baseball.[39] Gus Greenlee made the pre-ballot, but not the final ballot, in the 2006 Hall of Fame Negro League voting. Yet, the concept that Effa Manley or Alex Pompez, the Negro League owners admitted to the Hall of Fame in 2006, were more important to the Negro Leagues than Gus Greenlee is illogical. The Negro League game would not have been recognizable as it was without one of its seminal characters. It's time to honor Gus Greenlee's contributions with a Hall of Fame plaque.

Ed "Chief" Bolden

A Philadelphia postal worker, Ed Bolden was one of the most influential and important executives in Negro League history. The diminutive and bespectacled Bolden stood only 5 ft. 7 in. and weighed less than 150 lbs., a physical stature which belied his forceful nature. In a career spanning 40 years, Bolden co-founded the Eastern Colored League (ECL) in 1922. He served as chairman of the ECL from 1923 through 1926 and as its president in 1928. Bolden was also intimately involved in the formation of the American National League (ANL) in 1929 and was its president during its short, one-year existence. Later on, Bolden became president of the Negro National League in 1936 and its vice president from 1939 through 1944.

In addition to his administrative duties, he also founded, owned, and operated the legendary Hilldale Daisies in the 1920s and the Philadelphia Stars from 1933 through 1950. While he performed all of the above functions, Ed Bolden held down a full-time job at the Philadelphia Post Office.

Bolden's career in black ball started back in 1910, after he umpired a game for the Hilldale A.C.[40] When the players sought the more mature Bolden to manage their team, Bolden accepted and over a period of years developed Hilldale into one of the great Negro League teams in the country. Bolden was the foremost proponent to that time of marketing and strong community relations for the black ball game. Despite his shy and modest demeanor, he bombarded the newspapers with press releases and placed ads in those papers to secure publicity for his team. He also aggressively signed top black talent from other teams and gave his players a monthly salary (as opposed to being paid by the game)[41] and profit-sharing plan. Bolden implemented mandatory practice schedules and pre-game workouts, which were hardly the norm.[42] By 1917, his Hilldale club had managed to sign Spottswood Poles, Bill Pettus, Otto Briggs, and other leading players. At the end of the 1917 season, he added Dick Lundy and Smokey Joe Williams to Hilldale in order to take on a Major League All-Star unit, known as the "All Americans." His team won but one of the three games (the one pitched by Smokey Joe Williams) against the All Americans, but the series generated a solid profit and great publicity for his club.[43]

In 1918, he added Louis Santop and Phil Cockrell to the club and sometimes assumed the role as manager on the field. Bolden was savvy enough to have secured the rights for Hilldale to play their games at Hilldale Park, starting in 1914, allowing him to create a recognizable home venue in which to oppose top quality white and black teams and rent out the venue to secure supplementary profits.[44] Bolden worked out a deal with the trolley service to route their trolleys to Hilldale Park on game day. A proponent of clean ball on the field and good behavior in the stands, Bolden once brought suit against his own patrons for their rowdy behavior.[45] To enforce these standards, Bolden hired private security guards to police the stands during home games.[46]

Bolden had created the top black ball team in the East by 1920, a team which defeated the Brooklyn Royal Giants, led by Pop Lloyd, to become crowned as the Colored Champion of the East. That October, Bolden's team barnstormed against Major League All-Star teams, including splitting two games against the Babe Ruth All-Stars. At the end of the 1920 season, Bolden's Hilldale Daisies joined the Negro National League as an associate member, and in 1921 they again won the Colored Championship of the East.

But Bolden was just getting rolling. Responding to a threat that Rube Foster's new Negro National League (founded in 1920) might move East, Bolden withdrew from the NNL and joined with booking agent Nat Strong to form the Eastern Colored League, in December of 1922. As founder of the ECL in the 1920s, it was Bolden who had led raids to secure players on the more established NNL in violation of their existing NNL contracts, creating the significant enmity of Rube Foster and the other NNL owners. Signing Pop Lloyd, Tank Carr, Biz Mackey, Nip Winters, Frank "Weasel" Warfield, and

Ed "Chief" Bolden, who worked in the Philadelphia Post Office full time, was the founder of the Eastern Colored League in the 1920s and the owner-operator of the Hilldale Daisies, its most successful franchise. His 40 year career spanned from pre–Negro League ball through the signing of Jackie Robinson. (Courtesy Helmar Brewing. Artist Scott Pedley.)

others that offseason, his Hilldale franchise dominated the new ECL. The Hilldale team won the first three Eastern Colored League championships from 1923 through 1925.

The bad relations between Foster and Bolden led to a peace conference between the two men in New York in December 1924. There, they agreed to the first official Negro League World Series between the two leagues and adopted both a reserve clause and standard form of player contract.[47] Hilldale lost to the Kansas City Monarchs in the initial 1924 Negro World Series, and then came back and defeated the Monarchs by winning five of six games in the 1925 Negro World Series. In 1926, Hilldale joined the integrated Interstate League, in addition to the ECL, and won the Interstate League Title. Playing a six-game series against the Major League All-Stars after the 1926 season, Hilldale won five.[48]

The ECL ultimately proved hard to govern, as it was ruled by a commission with each team having a vote, thwarting any effective chance for one authority to enforce discipline. Teams readily abandoned league games when more lucrative exhibitions came along.[49] In 1927, Bolden was removed as president of the ECL because the other teams alleged a conflict in his being both a team owner and president of the league.[50] That same year, Bolden, worn down by his work schedule, suffered a nervous breakdown and resigned from all of his administrative roles. (It may be more than a coincidence that his rival Rube Foster, who also managed both a league and a team, collapsed from a nervous breakdown in 1926, a breakdown from which Foster would never recover.)

In 1928, Bolden's health had improved and he reassumed his role as a team owner and officer of the ECL, just in time to view its dissolution because of a lack of cooperation from team owners in honoring league schedules.[51] Bolden then joined Cum Posey in 1929 to form a new American Negro League, in which Bolden entered his Hilldale team. Bolden's 1929 Hilldale team included four future Hall of Famers: Oscar Charleston, Martin Dihigo, Judy Johnston, and Biz Mackey. Bolden also assumed the role of president of the new league, but both the league and the Hilldale franchise folded after one season. In 1930, under pressure from the post office to increase his efficiency because of his time spent on baseball endeavors, Bolden took two years off from the game.[52]

Bolden returned to black ball in 1933 with a new partner and a new team. He joined with a white booking agent, Eddie Gottlieb, to form the Philadelphia Stars, which operated initially as a barnstorming team. In doing so, he was criticized for having surrendered a black-owned franchise to a white man, but he had determined that he simply could not find the money in the black community to carry on any other way.[53] Bolden, unlike many other owners such as Abe Manley and Gus Greenlee, was a postal employee and did not have access to the profits available to a numbers kingpin. Bolden and Gottlieb created a 50–50 ownership interest in the Stars, but Bolden remained the public face of the franchise and handled the day-to-day operations,[54] while Gottlieb acted as a booker. This arrangement remained in place until the Stars folded. Proving that longevity can be as important in life as any other factor, Ed Gottlieb, an enemy to many in the black ball world because of what they regarded as his exorbitant booking fees, would emerge again in 1971 as a member of the first Negro Leagues Special Committee, which elected the first Negro Leaguers to the Hall of Fame.

In 1934, the Stars joined the Negro National League as the economy improved. Ed Bolden's 1934 Philadelphia Stars team was the best Negro League team on the East Coast, a juggernaut led by ace pitcher Slim Jones, and hitters Jud Wilson, Rap Dixon, Dick Lundy, and Biz Mackey. It won the pennant and the 1934 NNL championship playoff. Bolden would remain at the helm of the Philadelphia Stars for 18 years through 1950, but they were never more than mediocre after 1934. This was attributed to the fact that Bolden, unlike the numbers kings who ran other ball clubs, simply did not have his own source of funding. It appears that his booking agent partner Gottlieb was hesitant to advance monies for new players as he was far more interested in generating booking fees, often against white teams, rather than fielding a winning team in the Negro National League.[55]

In 1936, Bolden was elected president of the NNL when Gus Greenlee resigned. He valiantly tried to enforce adherence to league scheduling, but failed when the other teams continued to follow their short-term financial interest by giving a priority to barnstorming.[56] After one year, he was forced out of his role as league president but would return as its vice president from 1939 to 1944. Bolden, however, remained in charge of the Stars until he died of a stroke in September 1950 at the age of 68. His funeral attracted civil rights leaders, important community officials, and many Negro League luminaries.[57]

Ed Bolden was not without his detractors. He endured some criticism from his fan base and the media because, during the Depression when his funding was unavailable from any other source, he forged a partnership with a white booking agent after almost two decades of going it on his own.[58] He also offended others in the black community by hiring a white umpire supervisor for the ECL in 1925 when he felt the quality of black umpiring was not sufficient.[59] While he was generally regarded as a gentleman, he was also resented by others by acting in his self-interest by aggressively raiding talent from other teams. Yet he accomplished his successful recruitment simply by paying the players more money than they were making elsewhere and by adopting profit sharing for his team.

It is, however, an indisputable fact that Ed Bolden was instrumental in founding two Negro Leagues, including the truly significant Eastern Colored League in the 1920s. Without the ECL, the great Negro League World Series of the 1920s would not have occurred and there would have been no counterbalance to Rube Foster's Western circuit. Bolden was also an officer (often president or chairman) of the Eastern Colored League, the American Negro League, and the Negro National League most years from 1923 through 1944. Bolden's contributions were well recognized in his time. He is the first name listed as a manager on the Roll of Honor in *Courier* Poll. In a 1927 interview, Hall of Famer Sol White designated Ed Bolden as one of the five greatest figures in modern Negro League history.[60]

One of the black executives central to the history of Negro League ball, and one of the first to successfully embrace the media, the bottom line is that Bolden became a hugely successful as a club owner, and sometimes manager, without substantial money of his own. His teams used top level talent to win four Eastern Colored League championships, one Negro League World Series title, one Negro National League title, one Interstate League title, and three unofficial "championship" series in the pre–ECL era. He ran his teams on the principle that an African American owned business could both make a profit and benefit the community. And he accomplished all of this while he was working full time in the United States Post Office for over 40 years. His lengthy career spanned from the pre–Negro League era to the signing of Jackie Robinson by the Brooklyn Dodgers. Bolden was named to the preliminary ballot in the 2006 Negro League election to the Hall of Fame but did not make the final ballot. A man who made a successful career in black ball with the tools available to him in a segregated world, Ed Bolden is one of black baseball's pivotal executives, and *the* major figure in the history of Philadelphia Negro League ball.

Worthy of Further Discussion

Frank C. Leland is generally regarded as the premier organizer, owner, and manager during the first decade of black ball in the early 1900s.[61] Born in 1869, Leland began his baseball career as an outfielder with the Unions in 1887. Realizing his strength lay in management and not on the field, he joined with a group of Chicago businessmen to form the Chicago Unions in 1888. The college-educated Leland was a multifaceted entrepreneur who held various full-time private and government jobs in the Chicago area until 1896, when he also assumed the position of the Chicago Unions' traveling manager. By 1900, the Unions had developed into the best black baseball team in Chicago, dominating the opposition. According to Sol White, they had a won-loss record of 613–118–2 between 1898 and 1900.[62]

In 1901, after the Chicago Unions lost their lease on their home field, Leland struck out on his own by combining the Unions and the Columbia Giants to form the Chicago Union Giants.[63] Acting as both owner and manager, he strengthened the new team in 1902 by adding a young Texas pitcher named Andrew "Rube" Foster, creating the best black ball team in the West. After losing the "Colored Championship of the West" to the Algona Brownies in 1903, Leland changed the name of his team to the Leland Giants in 1905. With Leland acting as manager, the 1905 Leland Giants reportedly played to a win-loss record of 112–10 (.918), including a 48-game winning streak.[64]

Following a disappointing 1906 season, Leland raised $100,000 in a stock offering for his baseball and other ventures.[65] He then lured Rube Foster (who had jumped to the Cuban X-Giants) back to the Leland Giants as a player-manager in 1907. The 1907 Leland Giants were again a powerhouse, a team that also included Pete Hill, Jap Payne, and Walter Ball. At the close of the 1907 season, the Leland Giants won the Chicago City League title, beat the Milwaukee Brewers of the American Association, and swept all four games against the Chicago League All-Stars.[66] It is important to understand that Leland accomplished all of this while holding other full-time jobs. In 1907 alone, in addition to being general manager of the Giants, he served as Cook County Commissioner and ran a skating rink.[67]

But Leland's most intriguing contribution may have been his prescient recognition of the need for a strong league of black baseball teams and his actions to implement the same. In the winter of 1907–08, he worked extensively to develop a plan to create a "National Colored League of Professional Baseball Clubs." Following a successful organizational meeting with other teams, the election of officers, and the adoption of guidelines, the league received favorable press in the newspapers but never got off the ground. One of the key reasons the league failed was that overwork (those numerous full-time jobs) caused Leland himself to become ill with heart failure.[68]

Nonetheless, the Leland Giants remained the dominant team in black baseball. The 1909 *Spalding Guide* reported that, led by pitcher Rube Foster, they were in a "class by themselves" and "as good as the major leagues."[69] When Rube Foster and Frank Leland had a falling out in 1909, Leland sold his shares and left the club. Leland then started a new ballclub named the "Leland's Chicago Giants Baseball Club" as opposed to Rube Foster's "Leland Giants." After a court battle, Leland lost the right to use his name on his new ballclub. The feud between Leland and Foster became bitter and continued for years. An example of their enmity is a hyperbolic column Rube Foster wrote in the *Chicago Defender*: "The downfall of colored baseball in Chicago … lies at the feet of Frank C. Leland who is a mere accident in baseball…. I [Rube Foster] accomplished more in one season than he did in a lifetime."[70]

Leland's new team played well in 1910 and received an invitation (instead of Rube Foster's team) to participate in the Chicago City League, in which they finished in second place. Frank Leland's team then travelled to the West Coast during the winter of 1910–11, competing against white teams. While records are incomplete, that team played above .500 ball. In 1911, CNLBR reports that Leland's Giants achieved a .900 winning percentage and won 20 straight games. At the end of that season, Leland's Giants and Foster's Giants collided in a "Battle of the Giants," which was won by Rube Foster's Giants. This result must have really stung because it also caused Leland to lose a $500 side bet to Foster.[71] Leland decided at that point to leave baseball and run for Cook County Commissioner. His heart problems, and probably overwork, caused his early demise in 1914 at age 45.

An early pioneer in the pre–Negro Leagues, Leland discovered much top talent and led some of the era's best teams. Among the players he signed and nurtured were Rube Foster, Pete Hill, Home Run Johnson, Bill Monroe, Walter Ball, and Harry Buckner. Between 1900 and 1909, teams he ran or managed claimed eight championship titles, ranging from that of the Chicago area to that of the World.[72] His 1907–08 plan to create the "National Colored League of Professional Baseball," the first true Negro League, was visionary but never implemented because of his failing health. Ultimately, those medical issues and his feud with Rube Foster seem to have aborted any real shot at the Hall of Fame. Frank Leland was on the 2006 Negro Leagues Preliminary list for the Hall of Fame vote, but he did not make the final ballot. That seems about right.

CHAPTER 19

Pioneer/Overall Contribution

A number of individuals have been admitted to the Hall of Fame over the years who were not honored in their capacity as either a player, manager, or executive. Alexander Cartwright was chosen for being a pivotal figure in spreading the game of baseball across the country. Henry Chadwick was admitted to the Hall of Fame as an inventor of scorekeeping and as an editor/writer of early baseball journals, a role that led to the popularization of the game. In fact, there are 30 members of the Hall of Fame who have been inducted for their role as pioneers, executives, or organizers. There are two other figures whose overall lifetime contributions to the Negro League baseball game warrant their inclusion in the Hall of Fame:

Bud Fowler

There once was a player who grew up playing ball on the playgrounds of Cooperstown in the 19th century, spent much of his lifetime promoting and organizing the game of baseball throughout the country, and who became regarded as the "sage of baseball." And it was not Abner Doubleday. His name was Bud Fowler.

Born John W. Jackson in 1858,[1] Jackson for some unknown reason adopted the name Fowler and picked up his nickname for his tendency to call everyone "Bud." Little is known about his early years until he turned up in Chelsea, Massachusetts, during the 1878 season playing for the otherwise all-white Lynn Live Oaks.[2] The Lynn Live Oaks were a member of the International Association, a minor league operated in cooperation with the National League. In that manner, Fowler became the first openly African American player in organized minor league history and is generally regarded as baseball's first pro black player.[3] Beginning his career primarily as a pitcher and sometimes catcher, Fowler is known to have hurled a 2–1 victory over the Boston Nationals in an exhibition game in April of 1878.[4]

For the next five years, Fowler wandered the world of amateur, black, and semi-professional ball from Ontario to New Orleans.[5] Typical of Fowler's experience during this period was when he moved north of the border to play for an otherwise all-white Ontario team in 1881, until he was dropped after a revolt by his teammates objecting to his presence.[6] In the early 1880s, he joined the New Orleans Pickwicks and then assumed the role of player-manager for the all-black Richmond Black Swans, in 1882. With the color line not yet firmly drawn, 1884 found Fowler playing for Stillwell, Minnesota, where he pitched and hit .302 for the season. Arm troubles, or perhaps the growing trend towards overhand pitching, resulted in his switch to second base around that time.[7]

In 1885 and 1886, Fowler played for teams in Iowa, Colorado and Kansas. In a full season in Topeka in 1886, Fowler batted .309 and led the league with 12 triples.[8] It is important to recognize that Fowler was not just another infielder who happened to be a "first." Researcher Brian McKenna notes Fowler was a "stellar player" for numerous minor league clubs over two decades starting in the late 1870s. Historian Robert Peterson regarded Fowler as a major-league star caliber player. Fowler was also reputed for his flashy fielding and a no-holds-barred aggressiveness on the base paths. Playing with numerous clubs each year until he was driven out of each by overt racism, he is credited with popularizing wooden slats to protect his shins from sliding runners.[9]

That he was deemed something special by the public is proven by his entry into the popular lexicon. Marilynne Robinson, in her Pulitzer Prize novel *Gilead* writes: "Once my grandfather took me to Des Moines on the train to see Bud Fowler play. He was with Keokuk [Iowa] for a season or two. The old man fixed me with that eye of his and told me that there was not a man on this round earth who could out-run or out-throw Bud Fowler. I was pretty excited."[10] In his 1954 autobiography, Carl Sandburg reminisced about his youth when he watched a "second baseman, professional name Bud Fowler, a left-handed[11] Negro, fast and pretty in his work."[12] And this in 1885 from *Sporting Life,* hardly a supporter of black ball: "He [Fowler] is one of the best general players in the country, and if he had a white face would be playing with the best of them."[13]

In 1887, after a return organized white ball with the Binghamton Bingos, Fowler was second in batting average in the International Association, hitting .350. However, when his white teammates threatened to strike over his presence on the roster,[14] the International Association formally banned black ballplayers. On the exact date (July 14, 1887) that the ban was adopted by the International League, Major Leaguer Cap Anson led a walkout in an exhibition game against Newark of the International League, a team that contained two black players, George Stovey and Fleet Walker.[15] The ban (in the form of an unwritten gentlemen's agreement) was subsequently adopted by the two Major Leagues, at that time known as the American Association and the National League.

Forced out of the highest levels of white ball, Fowler continued to play for the next 12 years, through 1899, with integrated teams in leagues that did not adhere to the ban. In one four season span, he played with 10 different teams.[16] He played in the Western League, the Colorado League, the New England League, the Central Interstate League, the New Mexico League, the Michigan State League, the Illinois-Iowa League, and the Nebraska

Bud Fowler, the first recognized professional African American player, spent his life promoting and organizing the game after being driven out of organized white baseball. He is reputed to have played for more clubs and in more games in the minors than any other black player before integration in 1947, hitting .308 in more than 2,000 at bats. (Courtesy Helmar Brewing. Artist Scott Pedley.)

State League. In other words, he played with whoever would sign him. In most instances, he appeared only for short stints or never even got to play on ballclubs before he was again dismissed for racial reasons. As but one example, in 1888, his contract was annulled by the Lafayette, Indiana, club when Fowler showed up to pitch and it was "discovered that he was a genuine darkey."[17]

In 1887, he organized the New York Gorhams, an all-black team recognized by historian Robert Peterson as the first barnstorming club.[18] Fowler was especially noted for his stay in New Mexico in the late 1880s, when he introduced the sport in a professional manner to a fairly raw territory.[19] While statistics are few for this time, Bud Fowler's 1889 season with Greenville, Michigan, saw him hit .302, with 46 stolen bases, in 92 games played.[20] In 1899 he was with an independent team in Findlay, Ohio, where he also worked as a barber in the off-season. He continued to play with Findlay until July of 1899, when the players on his team threatened to quit rather than play further with an African American.[21]

Not content with his treatment during this period, Fowler tried to help establish the first national black league. In 1886, Fowler, representing Cincinnati, was among the contingent that met and formed the League of Colored Baseball Players. Remarkably, the League of Colored Baseball Players was permitted to sign the National Agreement granting it formal membership in Organized Baseball. The new league actually fielded teams and began play in 1887. Unfortunately, the League of Colored Baseball Players folded after only 10 days, when two teams dropped out.[22]

In 1895, Fowler was the driving force, together with Home Run Johnson, when he co-founded the infamous all-black Page Fence Giants in Michigan. The Page Fence Giants featured such leading players as Home Run Johnson, Billy Holland, George Wilson, and Sol White, with Fowler acting as the playing manager. One of the earliest successful barnstorming teams, the Page Fence Giants set the pattern for the era, which would be followed during the next 50 years. They traveled in parlor cars and paraded on bicycles (Monarch Bicycle was a minority sponsor of the team) to each ballpark to stir up interest.[23] The team developed routines for entertaining during games that became a prototype for many black barnstormers. But they were not just showmen; they were a superb ball club. Playing independent teams, in 1895 the Page Fence Giants compiled a .766 winning percentage, with Fowler batting .357.[24] Fowler left the Page Fence Giants in mid–July, however, drawn by an offer to play for Adrian, Michigan, in a rejuvenated Michigan State League. After that year, Fowler, now 37 years old, never played again for an integrated team, which was more a result of the growing color ban than his talent.[25]

In 1897, Fowler travelled to Texas and tried again to form a new league: The Lone Star Colored Baseball League of Texas. The plan was to secure eight franchises and Fowler served as proxy for many of them in an effort to drum up support. Eventually six cities submitted application fees, club uniforms were selected, players signed, workouts begun, and Fowler spearheaded arrangements for the coming season. Fowler even told one reporter that was "an assured fact" that the league would be a success. For some reason, the league never happened.[26]

The year 1898 found Fowler at the age of 40 playing on with the Cuban Giants. Unfortunately, that year Fowler was savagely beaten unconscious by a gang of tramps when he hopped a freight train in Harlem on route to visit his sister.[27] With the color line firmly established by 1900, Fowler spent the balance of his life promoting black baseball as an organizer, scout, and promoter. He formed, managed and often played for black barnstorming teams in the American West, where racism was not as firmly entrenched. Serving as his own publicist, his endeavors helped popularize the sport of baseball throughout the entire country. Teams with which he was associated during this period included the Smoky City Giants in 1901, the Kansas City Stars in 1904, and the All-American Black Tourists for various seasons between 1900 and 1909. Fowler also served as an advisor to various fledgling Negro League clubs, and he may have accompanied the Philadelphia Giants to Cuba in 1907.[28]

In 1910, Fowler announced an ambitious 11,000-mile continental tour of great African American players, including Home Run Johnson and Bill Monroe. However, that tour, like many of his planned barnstorming tours, never materialized, presumably because of lack of funding.[29] In 1913, Fowler died in poverty at age 54 from pernicious anemia and was buried in an unmarked grave in Frankfort, New York. The Society for American Baseball Research purchased a headstone for his grave in 1987, acknowledging Fowler as a "Black Baseball Pioneer." In 2013, Cooperstown, New York, honored Fowler with a street named Bud Fowler Way.

An 1896 *Sporting News* article comes close to encapsulating his extraordinary career as black ball's "Forrest Gump":

> But for Fowler's black skin he would have helped make the history of the National League. He was a crack second baseman when second basemen were few and far between. As old as he is he can still play the bag now [he was 50] as well as the average second baseman. There are not many ball players in the big League to-day, who haven't at one time or another played ball either with or against Bud Fowler. The veteran ballplayer has played with ball teams not only in every state from Maine to California, and from the South end of Texas to the lakes, but in some states he has played in nearly every country [sic]. Fowler played with a team in Hudson, N.Y. thirty years ago. He has played in match games in mining camps of the far West, in which gold dust has been wagered on the result. He has played for skins and furs of the trappers and in games with cow-punchers where a small herd of cattle was wagered on the result. He has played with teams second only to big league teams.[30]

First and foremost, Bud Fowler was of major league star caliber. According to SABR author Brian McKenna, "He played for more clubs and in more games in the minors than any other black player before the 1950s, hitting .308 in more than 2,000 at bats in organized baseball."[31] He was also the first openly acknowledged black baseball player to play professionally for an integrated team, one of the first African American promoters of black league ball, and the first black captain of an integrated team. Later on, Fowler developed into a true pioneer of black ball by dedicating his life to African American ownership and management of the sport he played and loved. According to Hall of Famer Sol White, Bud Fowler came to be recognized as the "Sage of Baseball."[32]

In many respects, Bud Fowler can be viewed as the doppelgänger of Jackie Robinson. It was Fowler, also a standout second baseman, who was one of the leading players whose performance was directly responsible for the creation of the wall against African American players that Robinson shattered. Like Robinson, Fowler encountered and fought racial prejudice his entire life. Unlike Robinson, racial prejudice prevailed and forced him out of the highest levels of the game as a full-time player. Yet he persevered, and by the end of his career, he was proud to tell people that he had played on teams in 22 states and Canada.[33]

In his full-length biography *Bud Fowler: Baseball's First Black Professional*, Jeffrey Michael Lang concludes:

> Perhaps Bud Fowler's greatest contribution to the sport was sheer longevity and perseverance in light of the many contributing factors that forced nineteenth-century African American ballplayers to be constantly on the move "lack of money, heckling and antagonism from teammates, managements" fears of losing games by forfeit if they kept their black players, and white teams' often letting black players go after a season regardless of their performance.[34] Such doggedness in pursuit of a professional

career in baseball led this African American pioneer to a truncated ten-year career in organized baseball, a 20-plus career of playing the sport at the highest levels in which he was allowed to participate, and 30 years of trying to use his entrepreneurial skills to carve out a place for all-black baseball within the national pastime.[35]

Ultimately, it is true that Bud Fowler failed in his efforts to create the first black ball league or to establish the long-term barnstorming team that he envisioned. It is also a given that many of the plans that he announced to the public and issued in the press never materialized. Yet, it is also a fact that Bud Fowler's path to self-determination in creating the first African American owned touring teams and the 1895 Page Fence Giants set the foundation for the Negro Leagues to come. His overall contribution to American baseball as a player, organizer, pioneer, and symbol of dignified resistance to the racism of his day more than warrants a Hall of Fame plaque. Maybe Bud Fowler's plaque should be placed next to that of Cap Anson.

John "Buck" O'Neil

So much has been written about the controversy surrounding Buck O'Neil's failure to be elected to the Hall of Fame in the 2006 Special Negro Leagues election that the facts seem to have been lost in the emotion. The facts deserve mention.

The Player. The 6 ft. 2 in., 190 lb. right-hander began his career with the semi-pro Sarasota Tigers in 1924. After attending college for four years in Jacksonville, Florida, where he played baseball and football, he joined the barnstorming Tampa Black Smokers in 1933 and then the Miami Giants in 1934. Miami's best player then was Oliver Marcelle, who recruited O'Neil to play in the 1935 Denver Post tournament. O'Neil had to "ride the rails" to get to Denver and talked in later years about riding in freight trains, eating in hobo camps and being shot at by railroad cops.[36] Unfortunately, his team finished in 13th place once he arrived in Denver.

O'Neil's barnstorming career ended when he caught the eye of future Hall of Fame team owner J.L. Wilkinson, who bought his contract in 1937 as the first baseman joined the Kansas City Monarchs of the brand-new Negro American League (NAL). With a starting role blocked by a veteran first baseman, O'Neil then jumped to Abe Saperstein's Zulu Cannibal Giants, a dispiriting experience in which he wore warpaint and a grass skirt, and generally acted like a fool to entertain the fans.[37] Quickly feeling that he had made a mistake, O'Neil signed with the Memphis Red Sox of the NAL before rejoining the Monarchs in 1938. O'Neil became the starting first baseman for the Kansas City Monarchs in 1938, a role he would occupy for the next 18 years. The Monarchs, with O'Neil as an anchor at first base, and then later as their manager, would go on to win 12 Negro American League championships, including four in a row from 1939 to 1942.

By 1940, O'Neil had developed into one of the better hitters in the league, with a .344 batting average. The ESPN has designated him as NAL's MVP for 1940. He was an opposite-field-type punch hitter, who hit for high average but with little power. His fellow first baseman Buck Leonard commented: "He would find the gap in the outfield and hit it there. He was one of the best ballplayers I have ever seen."[38] After a hiatus for many years during which a Negro League World Series was not played, Buck O'Neil played in the 1942 Negro League World Series as the Monarchs swept the Homestead Grays, going 6 for 17 over four games, with one stolen base. He believed that the 1942 Monarchs (with Hall of

Famers Satchel Paige, Hilton Smith, and Willard Brown) were the best team he ever played on and could have taken on the New York Yankees that year.[39]

O'Neil was hitting .351 in 1943 when he was called up for military service.[40] Buck served as part of the Navy's construction battalion through 1945.[41] Having lost some prime baseball years to the war, O'Neil returned to the Monarchs after three years of service, in 1946, and won the Negro American League batting championship by hitting .350.[42] (Since he hit .351 and .350 in the years before and after he was in the Navy, it is easy to imagine the quality years he lost.) The 1946 Monarchs won the Negro American League title in 1946 but lost the Negro League World Series to the Newark Eagles. O'Neil went 9 for 27, with two home runs and a triple (.333 average), in the 1946 Negro League World Series.

Throughout his career, O'Neil also played in winter leagues in Cuba and Mexico and was a member of the Satchel Paige All-Stars who toured with the Bob Feller All-Stars after the 1946 season. In 12 games for which box scores have been located for the Bob Feller tour, O'Neil went 6 for 18 against top Major League pitching (.333 batting average).[43] That winter he was a member of the 1946–47 Almendares Alacranes team, which won the Cuban Winter League title. After hitting .308 for the Monarchs in 1947, O'Neil became their player-manager in 1948. He would continue to serve in that dual role through 1955.

John "Buck" O'Neil was an All-Star first baseman, a successful manager, a Hall of Fame scout, and the voice of Negro League baseball after the demise of the Negro Leagues. When Buck O'Neil was himself passed over for election to the Hall of Fame in 2006, he volunteered and acted as the acceptance spokesman at the Hall of Fame induction ceremony for the 17 members selected, none of whom were still alive. (Courtesy Helmar Brewing. Artist Scott Pedley.)

Although sources differ as to his lifetime batting average, CNLBR has calculated O'Neil's to be .303 in the NAL and .305 against all levels of competition.[44]

But it was as a fielder that O'Neil built his reputation. Buck O'Neil is generally regarded as the greatest defensive first baseman in Negro League history.[45] His reputation on defense is supported by some, but not all, accumulated data. Although defensive statistics are scanty throughout Negro League history, CNLBR has located defensive statistics for three years between 1948 and 1951. In each of those years, O'Neil led all first baseman in the league in fielding percentage.[46] Yet, truth be told, the limited career fielding statistics accumulated by Seamheads for O'Neil would rank behind those of Hall of Fame first basemen Ben Taylor, Buck Leonard, and Mule Suttles.

He was valued as an overall player, however, as demonstrated by the fact he was named to play in four East-West All-Star Games between 1942 and 1949, which is quite a streak considering he lost three years to the war. His worth is also demonstrated by the fact that so many Negro League veterans have deemed Buck O'Neil the player to be Hall of Fame worthy. Among those naming him as their Hall of Fame choice at first base are Dave Barnhill, Ross Davis, Bernard Fernandez, Rudy Fernandez, James "Red" Moore, Ulysses A. Redd, Tommy Sampson, Harold Tinker, Tweed Webb, and Jim LaMarque. Sabermetrician Bill James regards O'Neil as the fourth best first baseman in Negro League history. Leading historian William F. McNeil has included O'Neil as an honorable mention as a player on his all-time Negro League all-star team. The 1999 SABR Poll listed O'Neil as tied for 23rd among the greatest Negro League players of all time. Historians Luis Alvelo, Jan Finkel, Ted Knorr, Ryan Christoff, and Lyle K. Wilson have also opined that O'Neil is a Hall of Fame worthy first baseman.

The Manager. Buck O'Neil served as player-manager of the Monarchs from 1948 until 1955, winning or sharing in six NAL titles and managing his team to four wins in five East-West All-Star Games (he was named to manage a sixth game but took ill).[47] In only eight seasons at the helm, he accumulated a record of 311–210, placing him sixth in all-time wins as a manager in Negro League history. In his role as field general, he was regarded by his players as a smart, intelligent field leader.[48] As the color line eroded in the Major Leagues, Buck O'Neil managed 15 players who would eventually make it to the "white" Major Leagues, more than any other manager.[49] Buck was also active as a manager in the off-season, leading the Major League All-Stars on their 1955 post-season tour and the Willie Mays All-Stars on their 1962 barnstorming tour.

The Scout & Coach. Beginning with a part-time assignment with the Chicago Cubs in 1953, Buck O'Neil became a Major League scout for the Cubs in 1955. His role was substantive. O'Neil played a key role in finding and developing such players as Lou Brock, Ernie Banks, Billy Williams, Lee Smith, Joe Carter, and Oscar Gamble for the Cubs. It was he who directed Elston Howard to the attention of the Yankees.[50] One of the most interesting stories is how Buck O'Neil pursued a young Billy Williams to rejoin the Cubs after he fled back home with homesickness. It took Buck many family meals and much coaxing to convince the future Hall of Famer to return to the Cubs.[51] The Chicago Cubs may have been an awful team in those days, but imagine what they would have been like without the players he helped recruit. Buck O'Neil was elected to the Baseball Scouts Hall of Fame in St. Louis, in 2002. In 1962, O'Neil became the first African American coach in the Major Leagues, with the Chicago Cubs. Largely unknown to history is that after five years with the Cubs, Buck O'Neil was one of two finalists under serious consideration by Cubs owner William Wrigley, Jr., as the next Cubs' general manager; however, he did not get the job.[52] Buck O'Neil's greatest role was yet to come.

The Negro League Ambassador. Whether through intent or happenstance, Buck O'Neil morphed into the leading spokesman for the Negro Leagues in a time when they were virtually unknown to the general baseball public. He travelled the country giving talks and interviews extolling the great African American players of the Negro Leagues. In that role, he served as an ingratiating and charismatic spokesman whose stories and reminiscences became legendary in themselves. O'Neil rose to national prominence with the American public in the 1990s as the face and voice of the Negro League *Shadow Ball* segment of Ken Burns' 1994 PBS baseball documentary. Either as a guest on David Letterman's late-night television show, or as an invited guest at baseball functions throughout the nation, he communicated, with eloquence, love and vigor, the hardships and the grandeur of black ball. His well-read autobiography, *I Was Right on Time,* was cited by Bill James as the Negro League book that "you absolutely can't beat."[53] Joe Posnanski's book detailing his travels around the country with Buck O'Neil was so intriguing that it was the winner of the prestigious Casey Award as the best baseball book of 2007, a tribute to both its composition and the subject matter.

On a practical level, the charismatic O'Neil always seemed to be at the forefront of any major Negro League development in the post–Negro League era and evolved into a living icon for the Negro Leagues. As a member of the 18-person Hall of Fame Veterans Committee, it was O'Neil who became the go-to person to whom the other members turned in their selection of Negro League entrants to the Hall of Fame. Seven Negro Leaguers over those years owe their entrance to the Hall of Fame to Buck O'Neil's efforts on the Veterans Committee. In 1990, O'Neil led the successful effort to establish the Negro Leagues Baseball Museum, in Kansas City, and served as its chairman of the board until his death. (When the museum opened in a small one-room office in 1990, O'Neil and former Kansas City Royal Frank White took turns paying the rent.)[54]

When Buck O'Neil was himself passed over for election to the Hall of Fame in 2006 (he was a finalist on the 2006 ballot), he immediately volunteered and acted as the acceptance spokesman at the Hall of Fame induction ceremony for the 17 members selected, none of whom were still alive.[55] In his induction speech for them, he told stories of the Negro Leagues and succinctly summed up their importance: "I'd rather be right here, representing these people who helped build the bridge across the chasm of prejudice…. I am proud to have been a Negro League ballplayer…. This is quite an honor for me."[56] It was the last public speech he would ever make.

The public's outrage at Buck O'Neil's failure to be elected to the Hall of Fame led the Hall to commission a statue in his honor and to announce that its Hall of Fame Lifetime Achievement Award would thereafter be known as the Buck O'Neil Award. On December 7, 2006, Buck O'Neil was posthumously awarded the Presidential Medal of Freedom by President George W. Bush.

As a player, Buck O'Neil was a lifetime .300 hitter, a batting champion, and a top defensive first baseman. He was an exemplary manager who was one of the most successful pilots in the annals of the Negro League. He was also a winner who, despite losing three playing years to World War II, participated as a player or manager on 13 championship teams in the Negro Leagues and in Cuba. The CNLBR has determined that Buck was on the best team in the Negro American League over 70 percent of the time.

It was doubtless true that some 2006 electors did not really know how to define Buck's contribution and overly focused on his role as a first baseman. It is also possible that there was some political backlash by a few electors against Buck's role with the Negro League Baseball Museum, which had engaged in litigation with some historians (see Chapter 4). Other than this, Buck's failure to win 75 percent of the vote that year is inexplicable. Two of the 12 voters and non-voting member Fay Vincent had loudly announced their support of Buck prior to the vote.[57]

Buck O'Neil's accomplishments as a ballplayer and manager alone do not seem to warrant Hall of Fame admission. But, in fairness, Buck O'Neil's post–Negro League career must also be considered. He was an extremely successful scout and the man who broke the color line for coaches in the Major Leagues. It is doubtful that anyone did more than Buck O'Neil to bring the Negro Leagues to the public's attention. He served as a vigorous member of the Hall of Fame Veterans Committee and was a founder and chairman of the board of the Negro Leagues Baseball Museum, in Kansas City. He dedicated the last decades of his life as a tireless spokesman for the grandeur and quality of the Negro League game and its players.

Award winning author Jules Tygiel declares he "reigned as a symbol of baseball's past and the game's greatest good-will ambassador."[58]

It is understandable that the 2006 Historian's Panel, formed to review underappreciated Negro Leaguers based upon newly created statistical data they themselves compiled, did not select Buck O'Neil as a player. However, some on the 2006 panel argued that O'Neil's role in keeping the Negro Leagues alive in the public eye after they faded out made him as much of a pioneer as Sol White at the inception.[59] In the final analysis, his overall role as the soul of Negro League history must be properly recognized. For the Hall of Fame to have named its lifetime achievement award in his honor is warranted, but it is not sufficient. In his lifetime, Buck O'Neil may have contributed as much to the spirit of American baseball as any other person who ever lived. It is appropriate that Buck O'Neil now be admitted posthumously to the Hall of Fame, achieving a victory in the same fight he led for so many of the Negro League veterans. This conclusion is warranted even if no contemporary of Buck is left to give his speech at the induction ceremony.

PART FOUR

A Path Forward

Chapter 20

Conclusions

Remarkably, the overall voting for the Negro Leagues by the Hall of Fame has achieved a solid result to date. The 35 individuals selected so far are all well qualified to enter the Hall of Fame. Despite the haphazard and ad hoc manner of the early phases of the voting processes, many of the leading lights of the Negro Leagues are now enshrined in Cooperstown. It does not appear that any of the selectees do not warrant their selection.

To the extent that there is a parallel between the Hall of Fame voting results to date and the statistical data, the strongest correlation can be found with the career WAR accumulated by players in the domestic-based Negro Leagues alone (see Appendix G). On this basis, the 15 players who established the highest career WAR in the Negro League play in the United States are all in the Hall of Fame. Therefore, it is fair to conclude that the voters have correctly chosen the best of the elite.

After that, the consistency between career WAR in domestic Negro League play and the actual voting results breaks down a bit. Let's use Hall of Famer Louis Santop as an example. With a solid career WAR of 16.2, Santop ranks 26th among the Negro Leaguers admitted to the Hall of Fame. Yet there are 66 Negro League players with a higher career WAR in the American Negro Leagues than Santop who are not in the Hall of Fame. Dick Redding, Bill Byrd, Dick Lundy, Dobie Moore, and John Beckwith, all Negro League stars in their day, each had a higher career WAR (often significantly higher) than 11 of the Negro League Hall of Fame players admitted to date. It is therefore fair to conclude that the current 35 Negro Leaguers in the Hall of Fame are not the 35 best players and are not all who should be enshrined.

What happened? What happened is that the Hall of Fame voting was conducted for many years without the benefit of solid statistics, was overly political at the player level, ridiculously unfair at the veterans' level, and even subject to inherent bias at the historians' level. This ad hoc system has resulted in the passing over of well-qualified players, managers, and executives. As a result, the 35 Negro League inductees to date are not the 35 most qualified candidates, nor are the well-qualified individuals limited to the chosen 35. That the Hall of Fame voting process to date has achieved a far-from-perfect result is well demonstrated by the fact that Dick "Cannonball" Redding and Dick Lundy, two obviously qualified figures from the pantheon of Negro League ball, have not yet been elected to the Hall.

Part of this outcome has arisen from the fact that the Hall of Fame process has always been overly focused on statistical data when the truth is that because statistics were never fully or accurately compiled for the Negro Leagues, the data will never be close to complete. Certainly, the 2001–2005 Hall of Fame project seeking to compile a comprehensive database of Negro League statistics, led by Larry Lester, Dick Clark and Dr. Larry Hogan, as well as the extraordinary analytical work of John B. Holway, James A. Riley and other historians, is laudable. Ongoing compilation of statistics, which includes much new data discovered since the 2006 Negro Leagues Special Election, has now given a sufficient base to judge the players from at least the more formal Negro Leagues era from 1920 to 1948. This work has led to the discovery and renewed appreciation of some Negro Leaguers (e.g., Andy Cooper's extraordinary winning percentage, Chino Smith's almost absurdly high batting average) who may have been overlooked based upon their recorded performances. Yet it will always remain a hard, historical truth that the Negro Leagues never kept statistics consistently. They were at best a loose working confederation of barnstorming teams that played mostly non-league games even during the Negro League season. In that way, the Negro Leagues kept the game alive and vibrant in towns, villages, and in the African American communities of cities as they played day after day against each other and local and independent teams. As a result of all the missing statistics from the non-league world in which the Negro Leaguers played most of their games, it would be a mistake for the Hall of Fame voting process for the Negro Leagues to be solely dependent upon data.

Other Negro Leaguers played in the early dark ages of their sport and virtually all of their statistics will forever be lost to time. Nonetheless, the pre–Negro Leagues contained many of the finest players ever to walk onto a ballfield, and their legends survive largely in anecdotal evidence. It was John Donaldson's pitching talent that gave him the opportunity to jump from semi-pro team to team in search of the best payday (a custom emulated by Satchel Paige) rather than relying on the lower salary provided in Negro League baseball. Spot Poles may or may not have been a superior base runner than his contemporary Ty Cobb, but the answer does not lie in statistics. Only if Donaldson and Poles had been eligible to play in the Major Leagues would they have had the opportunity to achieve the verifiable records against consistent opposition that fans and the Hall of Fame voters value. That Negro Leaguers were not given this opportunity does not diminish their greatness or accomplishment. Nor should it prevent their selection to Cooperstown.

One particular anomaly of the Hall of Fame voting results for the Negro Leagues is that they have passed over many of the greatest infielders who ever played the game in order to admit power hitters and pitchers of greater renown. Particularly ignored are second and third basemen, whose batting statistics do not leap off the page but who were the glue of many championship teams. After all, how much easier is it to accept the consensus on Josh Gibson than do the homework necessary to appreciate "Home Run" Johnson? Extraordinarily qualified middle-infielders such as Sammy T. Hughes and Newt Allen are badly underrepresented while the work of the electors with respect to catchers and first basemen seems to be more complete.

There were so many great outfielders and pitchers in the Negro Leagues that any fair assessment would conclude that there remain Hall of Fame qualified candidates in these categories. Men such as Cannonball Dick Redding and Charlie Smith should clearly be in the National Hall of Fame. When Satchel Paige referred in his induction speech to the many other "Satchels and Joshs" of the Negro Leagues, it was to this type of player that he was referring.

Old-time African American players (pre–Negro Leaguers), executives, and managers have also had no natural constituency until the advent of the 2006 Historian's panel, and the full and fair assessment of these individuals is also not finished. The 2006 panel was clearly correct to elect Cum Posey, but what about his contemporary and rival Gus Greenlee? These titans of black ball went head to head in life and their plaques should do so as well in the Hall.

Other Negro Leaguers, such as Buck O'Neil, appear to have been considered in the wrong category. Specifically, it appears that the 2006 Historian's panel may have been overly focused on O'Neil as a player while he needs to be more properly assessed for his overall contribution to the Negro Leagues and baseball as a whole. O'Neil was the first to admit he was not a Hall of Fame first baseman. In his autobiography, he says, with only slight inaccuracy, that he would have been lucky to make the 12th team.[1] While he was a solid first baseman, top manager, and successful scout, it was really as a spokesman and advocate of the Negro Leagues that he made his true contribution to baseball.

Other players have been adversely affected by a strange sort of positional prejudice. There were a fairly large number of super utility players in the Negro Leagues who played multiple positions on a regular basis and played them well. Men such as John Beckwith and Sam Bankhead have not really received the attention they deserve because, unlike MLB players, they are not clearly associated with one position. Major League baseball reveres Babe Ruth and Shohei Ohtani for the unique ability of being able to both pitch and play field positions in order to keep their elite bat in the lineup. The Negro Leagues had multiple Ruths and Ohtanis. Some of the more notables were Martin Dihigo, José Méndez, Bill Byrd, Bullet Rogan, Double Duty Radcliffe, John Donaldson, and Eustaquio Pedroso. Any fair-minded analysis would determine that these players were more valuable, not less, than single-position players. Other top players such as Dave Malarcher, Vic Harris and "Candy Jim" Taylor segued into great managers. They also should have their entire careers considered.

Pre–Negro League players have still not received their due. While we will never locate most of their statistics from their prime playing days, Home Run Johnson and Bud Fowler are the most outstanding figures from this era not currently in the Hall of Fame. They have particularly strong résumés. "Home Run" Johnson may well have been the single best African American player of his time.

Similarly, there has been a lack of voting support for Hall of Fame caliber Latinos (e.g., Juan Vargas, Pancho Coimbre, Alejandro Oms) who were stars in their home countries, played only a portion of their careers in the United States, and are already members of the Halls of Fame of their homelands. In most of these cases, however, this result seems justified because these players' limited performances in the United States do not necessarily warrant their inclusion in the American Hall.

At first glance, it might appear that players who began their careers in the Negro Leagues, but also spent time in the Major Leagues, have received adequate attention. In fact, numerous players who fall into this category, such as Willie Mays, Hank Aaron, Ernie Banks, Larry Doby, Roy Campanella, and Monte Irvin, have been duly selected either by the Negro League or the Major League electors. Of course, there were many other Negro Leaguers, such as Sam Jethroe, Luke Easter, Joe Black, Elston Howard, Connie Johnson, and Bob Boyd, who enjoyed a substantial Major League career after their start in the Negro Leagues. However, the only player in this latter category who may truly warrant Hall of Fame selection is Minnie Minoso, who spent the largest portion of his career in the Major Leagues and clearly belongs in the Major League category. Despite a strong showing in the Major League voting, Minoso, rightly or wrongly, has failed to make it to the Hall of Fame to date. But the point is that he has been considered by the correct grouping of electors and may (and should) one day be elected by them.

Of broader significance is the fact that there has been an inherent tendency for the Hall of Fame voters to ignore American players who became stars in the Negro Leagues but were compelled by the racial circumstances of their times to play a significant portion of their careers as barnstormers or in overseas leagues. Obviously, players in this category will be lacking all of the statistics of those who stayed in the United States. It is also understandable that the voters in the 2006 Hall of Fame election would have focused upon the statistics from only the official Negro League games in the United States, since they themselves had compiled that database for the Hall of Fame. However, the lack of support afforded by the Hall of Fame voters to players who were forced abroad is not warranted. These players, providing they met the 10-year minimum requirement in the United States, should be given further consideration based upon their full careers throughout the hemisphere. They were driven abroad both by racism and the fairer pay available to black ball superstars in other venues. They should not be penalized for taking the best opportunities available to them. Men such as "Wild Bill" Wright, John Donaldson, Quincy Trouppe, and Chet Brewer were among the greatest figures in Negro League history and require fuller and fairer scrutiny.

In assessing the overall voting results to date, it also seems that Hall of Fame voting for the Negro Leagues has been too focused on the absolute requirement of 10 years of service in the Negro Leagues. The 10-year standard is an excellent guiding rule but has been already been waived in the Major League voting. Chino Smith, who died prematurely but whose accomplishments were brilliant over a consistent period of time, must receive more serious consideration. The Hall of Fame made an exception for Addie Joss who died early and was admitted with less than 10 years of play in the Major Leagues. The Hall should not hesitate to do so again where warranted. Dobie Moore is another player whose accomplishments in fewer than 10 years of official Negro League play merit further study because he spent a substantial part of his career playing top-level military ball in the United States before the Negro Leagues even existed.

It is likewise interesting that only the initial 1971 ballot created for the Negro League elections (see Appendix B) was prepared by Negro League veterans and historians, although they did have input in creating the final 39-name ballot in the 2006 election. The Hall of Fame, which may not be the best judge of the candidates, has often controlled the preparation of the initial ballots. In fact, the 2005 Negro Leagues Screening Committee, which was composed of researchers and historians, was specifically instructed that they were not permitted to consider any names not on the pre-ballot they were given. This anomaly may have (and I believe *has*) resulted in qualified candidates being entirely excluded from the process. Hopefully, any future elections will allow the most knowledgeable groups more input into the creation of the list of nominees.

It is hard not to conclude that the voting panel in the 2006 Hall of Fame Special Election for the Negro Leagues overly eschewed controversy by focusing their picks on players who would show the Negro Leagues in their best light. While character counts, no player who had any raps at all on his reputation was selected. John Beckwith, Dobie Moore, Oliver Marcelle, and George Scales were all passed over even though some of their rougher traits seem overblown. To paraphrase one 2006 voting committee member who spoke with this author: "How would you like to explain to the press that Dobie Moore's career ended with a whorehouse shooting?"

It is clear as well that the Hall of Fame voting at each phase has had the effect of either expressly or implicitly limiting the number of Negro Leaguers afforded entry to the Hall of Fame. In the first phase, the players were initially limited to one or two candidates per year. Monte Irvin acknowledged that the initial Committee on Negro Baseball Leagues (1971–1977) felt pressure not to overstay their welcome and "voluntarily" disbanded after admitting a token nine-man all-star team. In the second phase, the Veterans' Committee had little interest in or knowledge of Negro Leaguers and limited itself to the approval of only two players over 16 years. In the third phase, a requirement and cap of one player per year for seven years was simply a quota system, albeit one in which well-qualified players gained admission.

In the fourth phase, the historians were presented with a final ballot of 39 names which had been greatly reduced from the original list of 94 names: many of those not making the final ballot were well qualified for Hall of Fame consideration. Presented with a ballot of only 39 names, one can surmise that the Historians' Panel, as two members of that panel have indicated, also felt inherent pressure to limit their admissions to a reasonable percentage of their overall ballot.[2] Quotas can be implied as well as expressed. Under these circumstances, it is impressive that the Historian's Panel admitted as many as 17 members (about 44 percent) from the final ballot to the Hall of Fame. Think of who the electors might have chosen if presented with the full 94 name ballot, or if they had multiple opportunities over a reasonable period of years to assess and admit candidates.

At each of the four distinct phases of Hall of Fame voting for the Negro Leagues, those charged with the voting always faced the possibility that no more Negro Leaguers would be admitted to the Hall of Fame in the future. Committee members Todd Bolton and James Overmyer have stated that this very thought weighed heavily on the voters' minds in the 2006 Special Election.[3] This may have also created a psychological rush to judgment, leading the voters to admit their favorites instead of being able to build a consensus for the most deserving players over a reasonable period of time, as the Baseball Writers' Association of America (BBWAA) is permitted to do. Imagine how BBWAA voting would be different if its Hall of Fame decisions were required to be made only in the initial year of eligibility.

The Hall of Fame voting for the Major Leagues has continuously provided multiple levels of consideration. After being reviewed by the BBWAA writers for many years, there was always a veterans committee (in various formats) available to catch and correct mistakes. In 2018, the Modern Era Committee voted Harold Baines into the Hall of Fame, a player whose vote total had never exceeded 7 percent in the many years he was considered by the BBWAA writers. To the contrary, the voting for the Negro Leagues has always been subject to a limited window of opportunity and often accompanied by a strict or implied quota. With the exception of the 2006 Historian's Committee—and even that was limited to a one-time opportunity to review a 39-name ballot covering over 50 years of play—there has never been an unrushed, full and fair open assessment of the entire black ball world.

The Hall of Fame voting process for the admission of Negro Leaguers is getting close to a fair conclusion but is not yet complete. While there will always be valid debates as to who should be in the Hall of Fame, there are still at least 24 Negro Leaguers who appear to be entitled to Hall of Fame admission based upon fair criteria. Whether these 24 individuals are the best remaining candidates for admission to the Hall of Fame, or how many more admissions are truly warranted, should be left to the discretion of Hall of Fame voters. In fact, it may be that some of the individuals listed in the Worthy of Further Discussion sections of this volume are also entitled to admission.

The admission of 24 more Negro Leaguers would bring the total number of Negro League inductees to 59, approximately the same number of years that the Negro Leagues existed. One player for each year of the Negro League's existence is modest compared to the number of Hall of Fame admissions for the pre-integration Major Leagues. In fact, it has often been cited as a truism that the Hall of Fame should be reserved for only the top 1 percent of all ballplayers. The 2005 Hall of Fame database compiled for the Negro League vote uncovered more than 6,000 Negro League players during the period 1920–1948: 1 percent of 6,000 is 60—suggesting that a total of 59 Negro Leaguers in the Hall of Fame is not out of line. As but one example that this number may even be low, the 10-name pre-ballot released by the Hall of Fame for its Modern Era Committee election in 2018 contained the names of four African Americans.

In compiling his own list of the top 100 baseball players of all time, Bill James included 12 Negro League players. He also observed that the Negro Leagues produced five of the top 100 players of all time during the seven years the league petered out. James concluded, "If those leagues could produce five players like that in seven years, what about the previous forty?"[4]

Even as strong an advocate as author Joe Posnanski, who has argued forcefully for the admission of additional Negro Leaguers to the Hall of Fame, has stated "that the very best Negro Leagues players are [already] in the Hall."[5] With all due respect, he is incorrect except as it may relate to the top few. One merely need peruse Appendix F, which sets forth WAR per 162 games in official American Negro League games. Grant "Home Run" Johnson, Dobie Moore, and Charlie "Chino" Smith each have WARs per 162 games in excess of every one of the 35 Negro League Hall of Famers. Dick "Cannonball" Redding, Dick Lundy, and Bill Byrd all have career WARs in excess of 15 of the Negro League players admitted to the Hall of Fame. The WARs of the *24 Men Out* are fully comparable to the current Negro League Hall of Famers. There may not be any more Oscar Charlestons out there, but Charleston was arguably the greatest player in baseball history. No, the Hall of Fame voting process to date has left clear gaps.

The argument that Negro Leaguers were not as great as their white counterparts has been revealed to be a great lie. It was not a fluke that John B. Holway's research revealed that Negro Leaguers won the majority of games against white Major Leaguers, causing Commissioner Judge Kenesaw Mountain Landis to attempt to thwart such games.[6] In the California Winter League, an integrated league where Negro League teams often competed as one unit against white teams comprised of Major League and Minor League players, Negro League teams won over 60 percent of their games.[7] Negro League teams captured 13 of the 16 California Winter League pennants between 1924 and 1939, playing against teams including Major League stars such as Bob Feller, Tony Lazzeri and Babe Herman. Catcher Joe Greene argued that "the colored leagues were the real major leagues."[8]

Buck O'Neil's principal argument in support of the Negro Leagues was neither based upon sentiment, nor an appeal to undo the racism of the past, but rather founded upon his deep conviction that the Negro League players and their game were as good as that of their white Major League counterparts. African American athletes who entered the white Major Leagues after the eclipse of the Negro Leagues, men such as Willie Mays, Jackie Robinson, Ernie Banks, Roberto Clemente, and Hank Aaron, revolutionized Major League Baseball in the 1950s and 1960s. Other Negro Leaguers would doubtless have done the same earlier if given the opportunity. Imagine the National Basketball Association (NBA) or the National Football League (NFL) today without African Americans and you will have a snapshot of the white Major Leagues prior to integration. (Between 1989 and 2017, African Americans comprised 12.7 percent of the population in the United States but comprised 66.5 percent of the players in the NFL and 76.5 percent of the players in the NBA.)[9] The Negro Leagues were not minor league baseball. They were segregated major league baseball. It is time to treat all historical components of major league baseball as one integral whole.

CHAPTER 21

Reopening the Door

Following the work of the 2006 Special Committee of the Negro Leagues, the Hall of Fame took the position that its job in relation to the Negro Leagues was finished. Brad Horn, spokesman for the Hall of Fame, stated that the 2006 Special Committee was "intended to review those [Negro League] candidacies on a one-time consideration. It doesn't mean there's not another opportunity in the future, if and when more research emerges. But this was a project to evaluate those individuals who really stood out. It's not intended to be a yearly event."[1] Horn has also been quoted as saying on behalf of the Hall of Fame that "the board is always willing to consider candidates in the regular course of business … [but] at this point the board feels there is not the need for an election process that considers new [Negro League] candidates."[2]

The Hall of Fame then further shut the door on the Negro Leagues when it abolished its Veterans Committee in two stages. In 2010, it implemented in its place a three-tier Era Committee system. There were committees for the Pre-Integration Era (1871–1946), the Golden Era (1947–1972), and the Expansion Era (1973–Present), each of which would meet every three years. Hall of Fame President Jeff Idelson acknowledged in an interview with the *Sporting News* that Negro Leaguers would not be eligible for the Era Committee ballots because their Special Election in 2006 had closed the process "unless new research came out that would warrant another look."[3]

Leading baseball author Joe Posnanski responded by pointing out that refusing to allow further Negro Leaguers to be eligible for consideration in the Pre-Integration Era, alongside the already picked-over Major Leaguers who remained eligible, was tone deaf: "I think the Hall of Fame made a mistake by simply closing the book on the Negro Leagues. That said, if they were going to do that, it would look a lot better if they would also close the book entirely on pre–1947 baseball."[4]

In practice, the Pre-Integration Era Committee system was a mess. In its first election, in 2012, with no Negro League candidates permitted, the Pre-Integration Era Committee elected umpire Hank O'Day, owner Jacob Ruppert, and the ancient Deacon White. Hank O'Day!? The ballot used by the Pre-Integration Committee in its subsequent 2015 election featured such lesser figures as former Cardinals owner Sam Breadon and shortstop Marty Marion (career batting average .263, with 36 home runs; won 1944 NL MVP award during the height of World War II). Not surprisingly, the Pre-Integration Era Committee elected no one that year.

Not only was the Pre-Integration Era Committee ineffective because so few qualified Major League figures from the pre–1947 era were left, it was criticized for its Pre-Integration name. Some critics euphemistically renamed it as the "Segregation Era" or "Jim Crow Era" Committee.[5] The criticisms were buttressed by the fact that non-white Negro Leaguers, who had been barred from Major League baseball before 1947, were once again excluded from consideration by the Era Committees.

In 2016, Hall of Fame board retooled the Committee structure and replaced it with four separate Eras Committees: Today's Game (1988 to present); Modern Baseball (1970–1987); Golden Days (1950–1969) and Early Baseball (1871–1949). The Today's Game and Modern Baseball Committees were scheduled to meet twice every five years; the Golden Days Committee to meet once every five years; and the Early Baseball Committee to meet once every 10 years. Chairman of the Board of Directors Jane Forbes Clark indicated that the reason that the Early Baseball Committee would meet only once every 10 years, and have its selectees limited to only four at most during any election, is that "those who served the game long ago and have been evaluated many times on past ballots will now be reviewed less frequently."[6]

The Early Baseball Committee (previously known as the Pre-Integration Committee) was now restricted to meeting only once a decade. This committee was the only one of the four Era Committees which, because of its given time span of inquiry, could have addressed the Negro Leaguers. However, the Hall of Fame again precluded even this possibility by limiting its purview to "Major League" players, managers, and umpires with at least 10 Major League seasons and executives who are at least 70 years old or who have been retired for at least five years. All of these criteria would have applied equally to Negro Leaguers except for the restriction to "Major League" baseball. In response to strong criticism, the Hall of Fame backtracked and announced on July 23, 2016, that Negro Leaguers would be eligible for consideration by the Early Baseball Committee.[7]

So now the door to the Negro Leagues was open again. However, in practice, the door had only been only slightly ajar for Negro Leaguers because they were now lumped together with the overrepresented pre-1950 Major League players who were up for consideration only once every 10 years. And while the pre–1950 white Major Leaguers were already well represented because they had been continuously picked over by the Veteran's Committees for decades, the same was not true for the Negro Leaguers.

Through the elections of January 2020, there have been a total of 333 members elected to the Hall of Fame, of whom 35 are Negro Leaguers. That means Negro Leaguers now constitute slightly over 10 percent of the Hall's membership. As the pre–Negro League and Negro League era existed for approximately 60 years (1890–1950), there is far less than one Negro Leaguer admitted to the Hall for each year of the Negro League's existence. Major league baseball has close to three members in the Hall for each year of the Major League's existence.

But it should never just be a numbers game. Quotas are rarely justified where merit is being valued. As Frank Robinson argued to the 2006 Historians' panel, the proper test should be performance rather than symbolically correcting social wrongs. It should always be about facts and performance. Here is one fact: After the National League integrated in 1947, former Negro League players won the National League MVP award nine times in the 11-year period from 1948 through 1959. And that was with an informal quota system still in effect limiting the African American players to only a few per team. Is that more than 10 percent?

It should also be kept in mind that, with the exception of an aging Satchel Paige, the greatest stars of the Negro Leagues never made it to the majors. Players such as Willie Mays and Hank Aaron represented just a smattering of the Negro League's unproven youngsters—yet they came to dominate the game.[8] This Era Committee process was enacted to correct the fact that the board believed there were too many Hall of Fame members from early baseball and that there was a need to reassess more modern players to balance this inequity. Again, this was hardly true with respect to the Negro Leagues, which have always been subject to an express or implied quota system.

While the Pre-Integration Committee has now been renamed the Early Baseball Committee, the composition of the voters on the Early Baseball Committees is also problematic. The mix of BBWAA members, together with Major League veterans and historians, constitute neither an educated nor a proper nominating group or electorate for the Negro Leagues. This makes it even less likely that the Negro Leaguers will receive a full and fair hearing. With the passing of the Negro Leaguers themselves, there is no natural constituency for Negro League election other than Negro League historians. Therefore, the board should, at a minimum, add at least some Negro League historians to both the screening group and the voting pool for the Early Baseball Committee to make it even remotely equitable. A few Negro League historians will hardly control the committee, but at least they will have a chance to make a case to the other voters.

Upon examination, the current era committee system comes awfully close to mirroring the rules of the exclusionary pre-integration era. Since the voters on the Early Baseball Committee are limited to voting for four candidates off a 10-person ballot once every 10 years, it is unlikely that more than one or two Negro League players would ever get elected in any 10-year voting cycle, if that many. The Hall of Fame has claimed that it is not closing the door to future Hall of Fame admission by Negro Leaguers, but then it has adopted a process that effectively limits their admission. So, while Negro Leaguers will now be technically eligible to gain admittance to the Hall through the Early Baseball Committee, the Hall has effectively carried forward the tradition of lack of diversity featured by the prior Veterans Committee.

Aside from restructuring the screening and voting pools for the Early Baseball Committee, another possibility to fairly consider the Negro Leagues is reconvening the Negro Leagues Special Committee, which last met in 2006. The ballots and procedures are already in place, although I would believe a nominating subcommittee should have the right to expand the 2005 preliminary ballot to contain new names, in their reasonable discretion. I would also advocate changing some of the members of the committees to reflect a greater variety of opinion.

But there exists a clearer and fairer path for allowing future consideration for Negro Leaguers. It would be completely consistent with the process developed by the Hall of Fame for its Era Committees. It would also retain an extremely high bar for Negro Leaguers to secure admission to the Hall of Fame—but provide a road forward that would at least be equivalent to that of their Major League counterparts.

To suggest a better remedy, it is first necessary to fully understand the existing process. The Early Baseball Era Committee (1871–1949) works as follows. Meeting every 10 years starting in 2020, the Baseball Writers' Association of America is charged with appointing a screening committee of 10–12 representatives who are charged with identifying a total of 10 candidates for consideration by all four era committees. The Hall of Fame's Board of Directors then appoints 16 Early Baseball Committee electors, whose vote requires a 75 percent majority for Hall of Fame Admission. No voting member of the Early Baseball Committee can vote for more than four persons at any time.[9]

The best and most equitable approach would involve appointing a fifth era committee—one that is limited to the Negro Leagues. Even accepting the Hall of Fame's criteria that the door would not be reopened for future Negro League consideration until new re-search evolved after 2006, we have seen that that this standard has been met. Significant new research has been developed since 2006 and is readily available on Seamheads and elsewhere. There now needs to be a full and fair process for its consideration. The Screening Committee and the Voting Committee for the Negro Leagues Era Committee could both be composed of Negro League historians since they are the most knowledgeable about Negro League ball. Other than this change, the rules applicable to the Negro Leagues Era Commit-tee would be the same as those applied to the other Era Committees. One minor distinction to accommodate the reality of the Negro League world might be issuing a guideline that, once a player has established all or part of 10 years in American Negro Leagues, his perfor-mance either in any other league that did not impose the color line should be fully consid-ered. In this way, American players who became stars in the Negro Leagues, but were driven by racism to spend a large portion of their careers as barnstormers or overseas, would still receive fair evaluation. Of course, the Era Committee should also be authorized to apply the Addie Joss exception for players who died before 10 years of service could be established.

Like the Golden Days Era Committee, a Negro Leagues Era Committee would meet once every five years, be subject to a 75 percent majority vote, work off a 10-name ballot, and be limited to four maximum votes per elector. In determining the 10-name ballot, the Screening Panel could start with the original 94-name 2005 pre–Negro Leagues ballot, not the 39-name final ballot used in the 2006 Special Election for the Negro Leagues, which omitted many qualified names. (That the names of all of the 24 individuals listed in this book as qualified for the Hall of Fame appear on the 94-name pre-ballot suggests that the pre-ballot is the correct starting point for consideration.) This will result in a remaining pre-ballot of 77 names (94 names less the 17 individuals elected to the Hall of Fame in 2006). The historians on the screening panel should have the right to add names to the bal-lot as they see fit, as there are some other viable candidates who seem to have been passed over altogether on the 94-name ballot. Quincy Trouppe is a particularly strong candidate not on the initial ballot. To achieve a broadened base of opinion and increase its overall expertise, leading historians who were not on the initial panel, such as James A. Riley, John B. Holway, William F. McNeil, and Phil S. Dixon, might be invited to participate.

A new Negro Leagues Era Committee would also have the significant advantage of being able, with recent analytical breakthroughs, to compare the Negro Leaguers to their peers and even to Major Leaguers. It is all very well and good to call Newt Allen the best Negro League second baseman of the 1920s and early 1930s, or to refer to Clint Thomas as the "Black DiMaggio." But the real issue is where they stood in comparison to the players of their times, which is exactly what WAR and Similarity Scores determine. The WAR measure objectively establishes that Newt Allen accumulated the best career WAR of any second baseman of all time and that he belongs in the Hall of Fame. Similarity Scores show Chino Smith's three closest Major League statistical matches are Babe Ruth, Ted Williams and Rogers Hornsby. The objective evidence is there.

Since this volume set forth the cases for at least 24 Negro Leaguers who may have been unfairly passed over by the Hall of Fame as a result of the ad hoc voting processes to date, a Negro Leagues Era Committee seems to be the proper approach. Hall of Fame President Jeff Idelson, now retired, who furnished a strong guiding hand in implementing the 2006 Special Election for the Negro Leagues, is already on record that the Hall of Fame would be receptive to reopening the door fully to the Negro Leagues. Idelson acknowledged in 2016 that "if new research came out that shed light and called for another Negro Leagues election—you wouldn't do it for one person, but for the Negro Leagues—I'm sure he [talking about Buck O'Neil] would be considered again."[10]

It has now been more than a decade since the last election for the Pre-Negro and Negro Leagues, and the threshold standard set by Idelson has been met. Perhaps the new leadership of the Hall of Fame, after Jeff Idelson's retirement, is prepared to pick up the mantle. The new statistics and data gathered by the Seamheads Negro Leagues Database, CNLBR, and others since that time makes the adoption of a new Era Committee a reasonable step for the Hall of Fame to take. The concept of WAR is now readily ascertainable thanks to the extraordinary work of Gary Ashwill and other contributors to Seamheads, information that was not even available at the time of the 2006 Special Election for the Negro Leagues.

This revision of the Era Rules to provide for a Negro Leagues Era Committee will also take the Hall of Fame at its word that it will never be truly closed to future Negro Leaguers. A five-year time period between each election is also fairer than the 10-year period provided for the over-represented pre–1947 white Major Leaguers. Adding a fifth Era Committee focused on the Negro Leagues is the only effective way of considering the extensive research and knowledge on the Negro Leagues that has been developed since the 2006 Negro Leagues Special Election. Considering that the original 1971 Committee and the Veterans Committee worked in the past with no real statistical basis, this path seems appropriate to fairly continue the process. Both 2006 Committee members interviewed by this author strongly advocated for reopening the process because they believe, despite their participation in the 2006 election process, that Hall of Fame qualified Negro Leaguers are still out there.[11]

A Negro Leagues Era Committee would retain an extremely high bar for future Negro League admission to the Hall of Fame. A candidate would need to be one of no more than 10 candidates selected for consideration and would be eligible for election only once every five years. Of this group, since no elector can vote for more than four candidates, it effectively creates a cap of only a few candidates who could be elected in any election cycle. Finally, a candidate would need to achieve a 75 percent vote of the designated committee. This would establish a high aggregate barrier for any Negro Leaguer to achieve, and only the elite will ever do so. This is as it should be.

A hypothetical 10-name initial ballot for the first Negro Leagues Era Committee might look as follows:

- Dick Lundy
- Grant "Home Run" Johnson
- John Donaldson
- Dick "Cannonball" Redding
- John Beckwith
- C.I. Taylor
- Spottswood Poles
- Gus Greenlee
- Buck O'Neil
- Charlie Smith

No other Hall of Fame Era Committee will ever have a stronger ballot. (Appendix E sets forth three separate hypothetical 10-name Hall of Fame ballots, which could be used for consideration by the Hall of Fame voters. Each contains strong candidates.)

It is doubtful that all, or even most, of the Negro League players I have postulated have Hall of Fame credentials will ever get into the Hall of Fame even under these proposed modifications. It is readily open to debate whether the *24 Men Out* are the correct candidates, or even all of the proper candidates. I would argue that at least some of those players listed as Worthy of Future Discussion should also receive plaques in Cooperstown. William Bell, Heavy Johnson and Sam Bankhead are extremely strong candidates who were not even included in my list of *24 Men Out*. But these modest changes to the structure of the Era Committees would finally create an equitable and inclusive framework for consideration of Negro Leaguers, one which would be on a comparable basis and subject to the same procedures as that for the Major Leaguers. Right now, the addition of Negro Leaguers for possible consideration by the Early Baseball Committee feels like an ad hoc reaction to public outcry, which is exactly what it is. When 17 Negro Leaguers were enshrined en masse in 2006, there was no public outcry—only praise. There will be no uproar if more worthy Negro League veterans join them in the Hall in the future. Moreover, the Negro Leagues Era Committee solution would solve the criticism leveled at the 2006 mass induction by permitting an individual focus on the fewer players who might be selected every five years.

If one considers for a moment why the year 1949 was chosen by the Hall of Fame as the dividing line between the Early Baseball Committee and the Modern Baseball Committee, it is apparent that "1949" is code for pre-integration. (Did anything important happen in baseball history in the late 1940s that was more significant than the integration that occurred with Jackie Robinson joining the Dodgers?) In this manner, African Americans playing baseball before 1950, the very year that the Negro Leagues began their death spin, are being excluded from full and fair consideration by being lumped together with those pre–1950 Major Leaguers already overrepresented in the Hall of Fame.

In the rush to judgment resulting from the first four phases of the Hall of Fame voting for the Negro Leagues, it is apparent that some amazing players were overlooked. Josh Gibson and Satchel Paige may have been the most famous black ball stars, but "Cannonball" Redding, Dick Lundy, Charlie "Chino" Smith, and "Home Run" Johnson were extraordinary as well. It is well past time to honor all of those who truly deserve it. Many of the Negro League stars lie today in unmarked graves, but their greatness and contributions to the game live on. They paved the way for the modern game of baseball, and they need to be fully acknowledged so that their names are never forgotten.

The Hall of Fame plays a special and exalted role in honoring all of American Baseball. The Hall is an American institution—not, despite its close association, a Major League Baseball organization. The Negro League constituency is growing as new research and statistics emerge. The Negro Leaguers should always have a fair hearing open to them since they hardly secured one during their careers. Are the Negro Leaguers entitled to anything less? Is the Hall of Fame entitled to less?

When Satchel Paige gave his induction speech in 1971, he was gracious but wary of anything less than full and equal status. Subtly placed in his speech was the following line: "Today baseball has turned Paige from a second-class citizen into a second-class immortal."[12] The 2006 Negro Leagues special election was an extraordinary and warranted process that was well conceived and thoughtfully carried out by the Hall of Fame. A Negro Leagues Era Committee, composed of Negro League researchers and historians, is the best forum for carrying the mission forward. Until the Hall of Fame includes all deserving members, it will always be a partial Hall of Fame, falling short of its true mission. It will never be time to treat the great Negro League stars as anything less than first-class baseball immortals. It will never be time to close the door.

Acknowledgments

This book is based on a foundation of research and analysis by all of those historians and researchers who followed in the footsteps of Robert Peterson's 1970 *Only the Ball Was White*, the original work which tweaked my interest in the world of the Negro Leagues. I have particularly relied on the groundwork laid by John B. Holway, William F. McNeil, James A. Riley, Larry Lester, Neil Lanctot, Bill James, Phil S. Dixon, Dick Clark, Scott Simkus, Eric Chalek, Robert Charles Cottrell, and Bob Luke. I especially appreciate Gary Ashwill of Seamheads and Dr. Layton Revel of the Center for Negro League Baseball Research, who generously allowed me to cite from their remarkable statistical compilations. I readily acknowledge that the heavy lifting was done by them and their brethren.

Historians Todd Bolton and James E. Overmyer were generous with their time in allowing me to interview them and sharing their thoughts concerning their work on the 2006 Hall of Fame Special Committee for the Negro Leagues. Leslie Heaphy's comments on an earlier draft of this work were appreciated. Ted Knoor's comments and expertise on Rap Dixon were useful. The work of the Society for American Baseball Research and the Negro League Baseball Museum in compiling online biographies of many Negro Leaguers were particularly useful. The librarians at the National Hall of Fame were helpful in assisting me in exploring their archives. While the many African American newspapers of the day left a record of the Negro Leagues, it was the efforts of all of those associated with the *Pittsburgh Courier* that proved the most insightful to me.

I particularly appreciate the assistance of Charles Helmar of Helmar Brewing, which has produced wonderful sets of contemporary Negro League baseball cards. Helmar artists Scott Pedley and Sanjay Verma produced the extraordinary artwork included herein. The cards can be further explored at helmarbrewing.com.

Appreciation is also due to the editorial staff at McFarland & Company and my word processing guru Rachel Mei who helped me shape the manuscript. Authors Susan Shapiro and Rebecca Gearhart helped guide me in the right direction. Thanks to my son Max for his editorial suggestions and to my wife Jeanne for her patience and support.

I also need to recognize all of those Negro League veterans who took the time and effort to document their rankings and leave their thoughts concerning their fellow players. Particularly insightful were the labors of Cum Posey, Monte Irvin, Buck O'Neil, Buck Leonard, and Quincy Trouppe. Without their contributions, it would not have been possible to fully honor their compatriots.

Appendix A: Current Negro League Hall of Famers

	Name	Year Admitted	Admitted By	Principal Positions
1	Satchel Paige	1971	1971–77 Negro Leagues Committee	P
2	Josh Gibson	1972	1971–77 Negro Leagues Committee	C
3	Buck Leonard	1972	1971–77 Negro League Committee	1B
4	Monte Irvin	1973	1971–77 Negro Leagues Committee	OF
5	Cool Papa Bell	1974	1971–77 Negro Leagues Committee	OF
6	Judy Johnson	1975	1971–77 Negro Leagues Committee	SS/3B
7	Oscar Charleston	1976	1971–77 Negro Leagues Committee	OF
8	Martin Dihigo	1977	1971–77 Negro Leagues Committee	OF/2B/P
9	Pop Lloyd	1977	1971–77 Negro Leagues Committee	SS
10	Rube Foster	1981	Veterans Committee	P/ Pioneer/Owner
11	Ray Dandridge	1987	Veterans Committee	3B
12	Leon Day	1995	Veterans Committee	P
13	Willie Foster	1996	Veterans Committee	P
14	Willie Wells	1997	Veterans Committee	SS
15	Bullet Joe Rogan	1998	Veterans Committee	P/OF
16	Smokey Joe Williams	1999	Veterans Committee	P
17	Turkey Stearnes	2000	Veterans Committee	OF
18	Hilton Smith	2001	Veterans Committee	P
19	Raymond Brown	2006	2006 Historian's C.	P
20	Willard Brown	2006	2006 Historian's C.	OF
21	Andy Cooper	2006	2006 Historian's C.	P

	Name	Year Admitted	Admitted By	Principal Positions
22	Frank Grant	2006	2006 Historian's C.	2B
23	Pete Hill	2006	2006 Historian's C.	OF
24	Biz Mackey	2006	2006 Historian's C.	C
25	Effa Manley	2006	2006 Historian's C.	Owner
26	José Méndez	2006	2006 Historian's C.	P/OF
27	Alex Pompez	2006	2006 Historian's C.	Owner
28	Cum Posey	2006	2006 Historian's C.	Owner
29	Louis Santop	2006	2006 Historian's C.	C
30	Mule Suttles	2006	2006 Historian's C.	1B
31	Ben Taylor	2006	2006 Historian's C.	1B
32	Cristóbal Torriente	2006	2006 Historian's C.	OF
33	Sol White	2006	2006 Historian's C.	Pioneer/2B
34	J.L. Wilkinson	2006	2006 Historian's C.	Owner
35	Jud Wilson	2006	2006 Historian's C.	1B

Appendix B: Negro League Hall of Fame Ballots

Names in bold have been elected to the Hall of Fame off of the indicated ballot.
*Selected by Veterans Committee (1981–1987).

1971 Ballot of the Special Committee on the Negro Leagues			
James "Cool Papa" Bell	Chet Brewer	Ray Brown	Oscar Charleston
Leon Day	Ray Dandridge*	Martin Dihigo	Rube Foster*
Willie Foster	Josh Gibson	Sammy T. Hughes	Monte Irvin
Judy Johnson	Buck Leonard	John Henry Lloyd	Dick Lundy
Biz Mackey	Satchel Paige	Dick "Cannonball" Redding	Wilber "Bullet" Rogan
Louis Santop	"Turkey" Stearnes	George "Mule" Suttles	Willie Wells
"Smokey Joe" Williams			

1995 Ballot Submitted to Veterans Committee			
Willard Brown	Leon Day	Willie Foster	Bullet Joe Rogan
Hilton Smith	Turkey Stearnes	Willie Wells	Joe Williams

2006 Preliminary Ballot of Negro Leagues Special Committee (Names Not Selected for Final Ballot)			
Walter Ball	Sam Bankhead	Bernardo Baro	Ed Bolden
Chester Brooks	Dave Brown	Larry Brown	Rev Cannady
Bill Cash	Phil Cockrell	Pancho Coimbre	Bingo DeMoss
Frank Duncan	Jose Fernandez	Bud Fowler	Jelly Gardner
Charlie Grant	Gus Greenlee	Vic Harris	Bill Holland
Sam Jethroe	Heavy Johnson	Henry Kimbro	Frank Leland
Jimmie Lyons	Dave Malarcher	Abe Manley	Max Manning
J.B. Martin	Horacio Martinez	Verdell Mathis	Dan McClellan
Hurley McNair	Bill Monroe	John Patterson	Jap Payne
Bruce Petway	Alex Radcliffe	Ted Radcliffe	Neal Robinson

Nat Rogers	Chino Smith	Clarence Smith	George Stovey
Juan Vargas	Moses Walker	Frank Warfield	Chaney White
Frank Wickware	Wabishaw "Doc" Wiley	Clarence Williams	George Williams
George Wilson	Nip Winters	"Wild Bill" Wright	

2006 Final Ballot of Negro Leagues Special Committee

Newt Allen	John Beckwith	William Bell	Chet Brewer
Ray Brown	**Willard Brown**	Bill Byrd	**Andy Cooper**
Rap Dixon	John Donaldson	**Frank Grant**	**Pete Hill**
Sammy T. Hughes	Fats Jenkins	Home Run Johnson	Dick Lundy
Biz Mackey	**Effa Manley**	Oliver Marcelle	**José Méndez**
Minnie Minoso	Dobie Moore	Buck O'Neil	Alejandro Oms
Red Parnell	Spottswood Poles	**Alex Pompez**	**Cum Posey**
Dick Redding	**Louis Santop**	George Scales	**Mule Suttles**
Ben Taylor	C.I. Taylor	"Candy Jim" Taylor	**Cristóbal Torriente**
Sol White	**J.L. Wilkinson**	**Jud Wilson**	

Appendix C: 1952 Pittsburgh Courier Experts' Poll

Position	First Team	Second Team
1B	Buck Leonard	Ben Taylor
2B	Jackie Robinson	Bingo DeMoss
SS	John Henry Lloyd	Willie Wells
3B	Oliver Marcelle	Judy Johnson
LF	Monte Irvin	Pete Hill
CF	Oscar Charleston	Cool Papa Bell
RF	Cristóbal Torriente	Chino Smith
C	Josh Gibson / Biz Mackey	Roy Campanella / Bruce Petway
P	Smokey Joe Williams	Dave Brown
P	Satchel Paige	Dick "Cannonball" Redding
P	Bullet Joe Rogan	Nip Winters
P	John Donaldson	Dizzy Dismukes
P	Willie Foster	Don Newcombe
Utility OF	Martin Dihigo	John Beckwith
Utility IF	Martin Dihigo	Newt Allen
Utility IF	Sam Bankhead	Clint Thomas
Coaches	Dizzy Dismukes	C.I. Taylor
Coaches	Danny McClelland	Dave Malarcher
Manager	Rube Foster	Cum Posey

Roll of Honor in Order Listed (Others Receiving Substantial Support):

(1B) Jud Wilson, Eddie Douglas, George Carr, Leroy Grant, "Mule" Suttles.

(2B) Bill Monroe, George Scales, Bunny Downs, Nate Harris, Sam Hughes, Frank Warfield, Ray Dandridge, Willie Wells, George Wright, Harry Williams.

(SS) Richard (Dick) Lundy, Doby Moore, Pelayo Chacon, Gerard Williams, Bobby Williams, Martin (Specs) Clark.

(3B) Jud Wilson, Ray Dandridge, Dave Malarcher, Bill Francis, Jim Taylor.

(OF) Rap Dixon, Larry Doby, "Fats" Jenkins, Jimmy Lyons, Mule Suttles, Spot Poles, Frank Duncan, Turkey Stearnes, Jelly Gardner, Orestes Minoso, Andrew (Jap) Payne, Blaine Hall, Ted Strong, Bullet Rogan, Ted Page, Vic Harris.

(C) Ted Ratcliffe, Louis Santop, Frank Duncan, Bill Pierce, Bill Wiley, Specks Webster.

(P) "Slim" Jones, Bill Holland, Phil Cockrell, Webster McDonald, Bill Byrd, "Double Duty" Radcliffe, Frank

Wickware, Dan McClellan, Leon Day, Bill Jackman, "String Bean" Williams, Ray Brown, Arthur Henderson, Lefty Tiant, Leroy Matlock, José Méndez, Laymon Yokely
   (Utility IF) Emmett Bowman, Dick Wallace, Walter Cannady, José Méndez
   (M) Ed Bolden, Oscar Charleston, Vic Harris.

Appendix D: 1952 Pittsburgh Courier "Fan Poll"

The listings consist of the Experts' Poll with additional third through fifth teams based upon the order of names listed on the experts' roll of honor

First Team: (1B) Buck Leonard, (2B) Jackie Robinson, (SS) Pop Lloyd, (3B) Oliver Marcelle, (OF) Monte Irvin, (OF) Oscar Charleston, (OF) Cristóbal Torriente, (C) Josh Gibson, (C) Biz Mackey, (P) Joe Williams, (P) Satchel Paige, (P) Bullet Joe Rogan, (P) John Donaldson, (P) Bill Foster, (Utility) Martin Dihigo, (Utility) Sam Bankhead, (Mgr) Rube Foster, (Coach) Dizzy Dismukes, (Coach) Danny McClellan.

Second Team: (1B) Ben Taylor, (2B) Bingo DeMoss, (SS) Willie Wells, (3B) Judy Johnson, (OF) Pete Hill, (OF) Cool Papa Bell, (OF) Chino Smith, (C) Roy Campanella, (C) Bruce Petway, (P) Dave Brown, (P) Dick Redding, (P) Nip Winters, (P) Dizzy Dismukes, (P) Don Newcombe, (Utility) John Beckwith, (Utility) Newt Allen, (Mgr) Cum Posey, (Coach) C.I. Taylor, (Coach) Dave Malarcher.

Third Team: (1B) Jud Wilson, (2B) Bill Monroe, (SS) Dick Lundy, (3B) Jud Wilson, (OF) Rap Dixon, (OF) Larry Doby, (OF) Fats Jenkins, (C) Double Duty Radcliffe, (C) Louis Santop, (P) Slim Jones, (P) Bill Holland, (P) Phil Cockrell, (P) Webster McDonald, (P) Bill Byrd, (Utility) Emmett Bowman, (Utility) Dick Wallace, (Mgr) Ed Bolden.

Fourth Team: (1B) Ed Douglas, (2B) George Scales, (SS) Doby Moore, (3B) Ray Dandridge, (OF) Jimmy Lyons, (OF) Mule Suttles, (OF) Spottswood Poles, (C) Frank Duncan, (C) Bill Perkins, (P) Double Duty Radcliffe, (P) Frank Wickware, (P) Danny McClellan, (P) Leon Day, (P) Bill Jackman, (Utility) Rev Cannady, (Utility) José Méndez, (Mgr) Vic Harris.

Fifth Team: (1B) George Carr, (2B) Bunny Downs, (SS) Pelayo Chacon, (3B) Dave Malarcher, (OF) Frank Duncan, (OF) Turkey Stearnes, (OF) Jelly Gardner, (C) Doc Wiley, (C) Speck Webster, (P) String Bean Williams, (P) Ray Brown, (P) Rats Henderson, (P) Luis Tiant, (P) Leroy Matlock.

Others receiving votes: (1B) Leroy Grant, Mule Suttles; (2B) Nate Harris, Sammy T. Hughes, Frank Warfield, Ray Dandridge, George Wright, Harry Williams; (SS) Gerard Williams, Bobby Williams, Morton Clark; (3B) Bill Francis, Jim Taylor; (OF) Minnie Minoso, Jap Payne, Blaine Hall, Ted Strong, Ted Page, Vic Harris; (P) José Méndez, Laymon Yokely.

Appendix E: Three Hypothetical Ballots for Consideration by a Proposed Negro Leagues Era Committee

First Tier Ballot

Dick Lundy
Grant "Home Run" Johnson
John Donaldson
Dick "Cannonball" Redding
John Beckwith

C.I. Taylor
Spottswood Poles
Gus Greenlee
Buck O'Neil
Charlie "Chino" Smith

Second Tier Ballot

Rap Dixon
Newt Allen
"Wild Bill" Wright
Bud Fowler
Oliver Marcelle

Ed Bolden
Bill Byrd
"Candy Jim" Taylor
Chet Brewer
Walter "Dobie" Moore

Third Tier Ballot (with a few alternates)

George Scales
Sammy T. Hughes
Bill Monroe
Bingo DeMoss
Dave Malarcher or Vic Harris

William Bell or Nip Winters
Sam Bankhead or Artie Wilson
Fats Jenkins or Hurley McNair
Heavy Johnson or George Stovey
Quincy Trouppe or Alec Radcliffe

Appendix F: Comparative WAR Per 162 Games (1887–1948)

Hall of Famers vs. *24 Men Out* player candidates (non–Hall of Famers) limited to performance: Negro League/Pre–Negro League Games (USA only). *Elected as an executive/pioneer. **Proposed as a manager. *** Proposed for overall contributions.

Negro League Players Elected to the National Baseball Hall of Fame		*24 Men Out:* HOF Player Candidates	
Josh Gibson	9.8	Grant "Home Run" Johnson	11.0
Willard Brown	9.1	Dobie Moore	10.5
Turkey Stearnes	8.0	Charlie "Chino" Smith	9.4
Buck Leonard	7.8	John Beckwith	7.1
Willie Wells	7.6	Dick Lundy	6.4
Pete Hill	7.6	Rap Dixon	5.7
Oscar Charleston	7.5	Bill Byrd	5.2
Cristóbal Torriente	7.2	Dick "Cannonball" Redding	5.1
Satchel Paige	7.1	George Scales	4.9
Pop Lloyd	6.9	Bill Monroe	4.6
Martin Dihigo	6.8	Spottswood Poles	4.4
Bullet Rogan	6.7	"Wild Bill" Wright	4.3
Smokey Joe Williams	6.6	Chet Brewer	4.2
Jud Wilson	6.5	Newt Allen	4.1
Frank Grant	6.5	Oliver Marcelle	3.9
Monte Irvin	6.4	Sammy T. Hughes	3.8
Mule Suttles	6.3	John Donaldson	3.6
Ray Brown	6.1	Bingo DeMoss	3.5
Leon Day	6.1	"Candy Jim" Taylor**	2.9
Willie Foster	5.9	Buck O'Neil***	1.3
Hilton Smith	5.8	**And a Few Others of Note:**	
Louis Santop	5.8	Artie Wilson	9.6

Negro League Players Elected to the National Baseball Hall of Fame		24 Men Out: HOF Player Candidates	
Ben Taylor	5.0	Sam Jethroe	7.8
Biz Mackey	4.5	Bill Pettus	7.4
Cool Papa Bell	4.3	Bus Clarkson	6.1
Rube Foster	4.1	Minnie Minoso	6.0
Jose Mendez	3.9	Alejandro Oms	5.7
Sol White*	3.5	William Bell	5.4
Andy Cooper	3.4	Edgar Wesley	5.1
Judy Johnson	3.3	Nip Winters	5.1
Ray Dandridge	3.0	Sam Bankhead	3.7

All WAR values courtesy of Seamheads Negro Leagues Database.

Appendix G: Comparative Career WAR (1887–1948)

Hall of Famers vs. *24 Men Out* player candidates (non–Hall of Famers) limited to performance: Negro League/Pre–Negro League Games (USA only). * Elected as a player and as an executive/pioneer. ** Proposed as a manager. *** Proposed for overall contributions.

Negro League Players Elected to the National Baseball Hall of Fame		24 Men Out: HOF Player Candidates	
Oscar Charleston	68.0	Dick Lundy	34.0
Bullet Rogan	59.3	Bill Byrd	33.1
Turkey Stearnes	52.0	Dick Redding	32.3
Willie Wells	51.6	Dobie Moore	30.7
Cristóbal Torriente	49.9	John Beckwith	27.0
Satchel Paige	47.9	Newt Allen	26.8
Josh Gibson	47.9	George Scales	25.8
Smokey Joe Williams	45.0	Rap Dixon	21.6
Ray Brown	44.5	Chet Brewer	20.4
Willie Foster	44.3	Bingo DeMoss	19.0
Jud Wilson	43.8	"Candy Jim" Taylor**	15.5
Pop Lloyd	43.2	Grant "Home Run" Johnson	13.1
Mule Suttles	39.4	Charlie "Chino" Smith	13.0
Cool Papa Bell	37.8	Oliver Marcelle	12.9
Ben Taylor	34.2	John Donaldson	12.0
Pete Hill	33.4	"Wild Bill" Wright	10.2
Buck Leonard	31.1	Sammy T. Hughes	10.2
Biz Mackey	30.9	Spottswood Poles	8.2
Martin Dihigo	29.6	Bill Monroe	7.3
Andy Cooper	27.1	Buck O'Neil***	2.8
Hilton Smith	24.0	**And a Few Others of Note:**	
Willard Brown	23.7	William Bell	35.7

Negro League Players Elected to the National Baseball Hall of Fame		24 Men Out: HOF Player Candidates	
Judy Johnson	20.6	Juan Padrón	31.7
Leon Day	20.6	Hurley McNair	30.3
Jose Mendez	17.8	Nip Winters	29.8
Louis Santop	16.2	Sam Streeter	24.8
Monte Irvin	11.3	Bill Holland	23.4
Rube Foster*	11.2	Rats Henderson	19.9
Ray Dandridge	4.6	Walter Cannady	18.3
Sol White*	1.5	Sam Bankhead	16.0
Frank Grant	1.4	Alejandro Oms	13.8

All WAR values courtesy of Seamheads Negro Leagues Database

Appendix H: John McGraw's Negro League Dream Team

Blackball players publicly coveted by John McGraw.

Player	Reported substance of quote or action
Bruce Petway	Finest catcher in baseball, black or white
Bill Monroe	Single greatest ballplayer of all time
Charlie Grant	Tried to pass him off as "Chief Tokahoma"
Dick Lundy	Greatest shortstop who ever lived, save Honus Wagner
Spottswood Poles	One of blackball's four top talents
Pop Lloyd	One of blackball's four top talents
Dick Redding	One of blackball's four top talents
Smokey Joe Williams	One of blackball's four top talents
John Donaldson	Greatest pitcher I have ever seen, worth $50,000 if permitted in Major Leagues
Bill "Cannonball" Jackman	$50,000 to the man who could make Jackman white; flirted with the idea of sending Jackman to Cuba and importing him as a Cuban
Walter Ball	Too bad that he is black
Rube Foster	Would give anything in the world if he were white

McGraw commenting to Rube Foster on the 1910 Leland Giants, a team that included Pop Lloyd, Pete Hill, Frank Wickware, Bruce Petway, Rube Foster, and Home Run Johnson: "If I had a bucket of whitewash that wouldn't wash off, you wouldn't have five players left tomorrow." (*Indianapolis Freeman*, February 8, 1915, 7)

"Not long after his [McGraw's] death, his wife found among his effects a list of all the great black players he had secretly wished he could hire over the decades." (Geoffrey C. Ward and Ken Burns, *Baseball: An Illustrated History*, New York: Alfred A. Knopf, 1994, 209) To my knowledge, that list has never been published.

Chapter Notes

Introduction

1. Todd Peterson, "The Case for the Negro Leagues," in *The Negro Leagues Were Major Leagues* (Jefferson, NC: McFarland, 2020), 38.
2. Todd Peterson, "May the Best Man Win, The Black Ball Championships 1866–1923," *The Baseball Research Journal* 42, no. 1 (Spring 2013): 7–24.
3. Peterson, "The Case for the Negro Leagues," 38.

Chapter 1

1. Ted Williams, with John Underwood, *My Turn at Bat: The Story of My Life* (New York: Simon and Schuster, 1969), 249.
2. John B. Holway, *Black Giants* (Bloomington, IN: Xlibris, 2009), ix–x.
3. Bob Luke, *Willie Wells: "El Diablo" of the Negro Leagues* (Austin: University of Texas Press, 2007), 104–107.
4. Bowie Kuhn, *Hardball: The Education of a Baseball Commissioner* (New York: Times Books, 1987), 109.
5. Luke, *Willie Wells*, 107.
6. Monte Irvin with James A. Riley, *Nice Guys Finish First: The Autobiography of Monte Irvin* (New York: Carroll & Graf, 1996), 194.
7. Luke, *Willie Wells*, 111.
8. Kuhn, *Hardball*, 109–110.
9. Luke, *Willie Wells*, 108.
10. Kevin Johnson, "The 'technically … not' Hall of Fame," Seamheads, February 14, 2019, http://seamheads.com/blog/2019/02/14/the-technically-not-hall-of-fame.
11. Luke, *Willie Wells*, 110.
12. According to Robert W. Peterson, Bill Yancey was also one of Judy Johnson's best friends. See "How *Only the Ball Was White* Came to Be Written," *Black Ball* 1, No. 1 (2008), 11.
13. Luke, *Willie Wells*, 112.
14. Duke Goldman, "The Business Meetings of Negro League Baseball: 1933–1962," in *Baseball's Business: The Winter Meetings Volume 2: 1958–2016* (Phoenix, AZ: Society for American Baseball Research, 2017), 440.
15. Holway, *Black Giants*, x–xi.
16. Negro League Selection Committee Minutes, January 15, 1991, BL-175.2003, National Baseball Hall of Fame Library.
17. Negro League Selection Committee Minutes, January 15, 1991, BL-175.2003, National Baseball Hall of Fame Library.
18. Negro League Selection Committee Minutes, January 15, 1991, BL-175.2003, National Baseball Hall of Fame Library.
19. Office of The Commissioner Press Release, February 3, 1971, BL-175.2003, National Baseball Hall of Fame Library.
20. Paul Kerr Memo to Veteran's Committee, February 4, 1971, BL-175.2003, National Baseball Hall of Fame Library.
21. Joseph Durso, "A New Hall of Fame Committee Tackles an Old Problem," *The New York Times*, January 29, 1978, S1.
22. Press release from Office of the Commissioner, February 9, 1971 (HOF file).
23. Luke, *Willie Wells*, 114.
24. Luke, *Willie Wells*, 115.
25. Luke, *Willie Wells*, 116.
26. Luke, *Willie Wells*, 116.
27. Wells Trombly, "Crumbs for the Outcast," *The Sporting News*, February 20, 1971, 41.
28. Doc Young letter to Monte Irvin, February 9, 1971, BL-175.2003, National Baseball Hall of Fame Library.
29. A summary of the public debate leading to the reversal by the Hall of Fame can be found at Luke, *Willie Wells*, 112–117.
30. James, *Whatever Happened to the Hall of Fame*, 188.
31. Luke, *Willie Wells*, 117.
32. Holway, *Black Giants*, xi.
33. Kuhn claims that this result was always part of his plan. Kuhn, *Hardball*, 110.
34. Office of the Commissioner Press Release, February 8, 1972, BL-175.2003, National Baseball Hall of Fame Library.
35. Office of the Commissioner Press Release, February 8, 1972, BL-175.2003, National Baseball Hall of Fame Library.
36. Joe Reichler Letter to Effa Manley, August 14, 1972, BL-175.2003, National Baseball Hall of Fame Library, 1.
37. Effa Manley Letter to Joe Reichler, August 9, 1972, BL-175.2003, National Baseball Hall of Fame Library, 1.
38. Roberta J. Newman and Joel Nathan Rosen,

Black Baseball, Black Business: Race Enterprise and the Fate of the Segregated Dollar (Jackson: University Press of Mississippi, 2014), 96.

39. Luke, *Willie Wells*, 119.

40. Luke, *Willie Wells*, 118–119.

41. Luke, *Willie Wells*, 118.

42. John B. Holway, "Shutting the Door on Negro League Stars," *The New York Times*, July 31, 1977, S2.

43. Joseph Durso, "A New Hall of Fame Committee Tackles an Old Problem."

44. Joe Reichler Letter to Effa Manley, August 14, 1972, BL-175.2003, National Baseball Hall of Fame Library, 1.

45. Holway, *Black Giants*, xi.

Chapter 2

1. "Too Few Black Baseball Greats in Hall: Powell," *Chicago Daily Defender*, August 12, 1972.

2. Luke, *Willie Wells*, 120.

3. John M. Coates II, "Ex-umpire Tabs Blacks for Hall of Fame," *Chicago Daily Defender*, September 29, 1973 (in HOF file).

4. Holway, *Black Giants*, xii.

5. Luke, *Willie Wells*, 122–123.

6. Holway, *Complete Book*, 464.

7. "Chandler in Plea for Black Stars," *The New York Times*, July 31, 1982, 16.

8. Red Smith, "From Jim Crow to Cooperstown," *New York Times*, February 14, 1978.

9. Interestingly, Peterson chose to conclude his seminal work with a prescient epilogue in which he argues that the Negro League stars should be admitted to the Hall of Fame as the best method of recognizing their accomplishments and according them equality.

10. Luke, *Willie Wells*, 126–127.

11. Kuhn, *Hardball*, 109.

Chapter 3

1. Luke, *Willie Wells*, 130.

2. Buck O'Neil with Steve Wulf and David Conrads, *I Was Right on Time* (New York: Simon & Schuster, 1996), 6.

3. Luke, *Willie Wells*, 130.

4. O'Neil, *I Was Right*, 6.

5. Luke, *Willie Wells*, 130.

Chapter 4

1. Luke, *Willie Wells*, 130–131.

2. Wikipedia, s.v. "Baseball Hall of Fame balloting, 2006 / The Committee on African-American Baseball," accessed November 8, 2018, https://en.wikipedia.org/wiki/Baseball_Hall_of_Fame_balloting,_2006#The_Committee_on_African-American_Baseball/.

3. John B. Holway, "What If Effa Manley Had Been an Ugly Man?," Baseball Guru, http://baseballguru.com/jholway/analysisjholway61.htm.

4. Jim Overmyer, interview with author, January 17, 2019.

5. "Seventeen from Negro Leagues, Pre–Negro Leagues Eras Elected to the Hall of Fame by Special Committee," Negro League Baseball Players Association, February 27, 2006, http://www.nlbpa.com/news/febuary-27-2006-2.

6. Jim Overmyer, interview with author, January 17, 2019.

7. Jim Overmyer, interview with author, January 17, 2019.

8. Todd Bolton, interview with author, January 19, 2019.

9. "Transcript of Negro Leagues, Pre-Negro Leagues Special Election Results Announcement," Negro League Baseball Players Association, February 27, 2006, http://www.nlbpa.com/news/febuary-27-2006.

10. Jim Overmyer, interview with author, January 17, 2019.

11. Todd Bolton, interview with author, January 19, 2019.

12. Todd Bolton, interview with author, January 19, 2019.

13. Jim Overmyer, interview with author, January 17, 2019.

14. Jim Overmyer, interview with author, January 17, 2019.

15. Jim Overmyer, interview with author, January 17, 2019.

16. Todd Bolton, interview with author, January 19, 2019.

17. "Transcript of Negro Leagues."

18. "Transcript of Negro Leagues."

19. "Transcript of Negro Leagues."

20. Jim Overmyer, interview with author, January 17, 2019.

21. Vahe Gregorian, "Buck O'Neil Was Left Out of the Hall of Fame 10 Years Ago, but His Response Still Inspires Today," *Kansas City Star*, February 26, 2016, https://www.kansascity.com/sports/spt-columns-blogs/vahe-gregorian/article62807672.html.

22. Randy Covitz, "Did Feud Sabotage Buck O'Neil's Bid for Hall?," Kansas City Star, October 9, 2006, https://www.kansascity.com/sports/article295469.html.

23. Covitz, "Did Feud Sabotage."

24. Gregorian, "Buck O'Neil Was Left Out."

25. Covitz, "Did Feud Sabotage."

26. Covitz, "Did Feud Sabotage."

27. Gregorian, "Buck O'Neil Was Left Out."

28. Jim Overmyer, interview with author, January 17, 2019.

29. "Transcript of Negro Leagues."

30. Todd Bolton, interview with author, January 19, 2019.

31. Leslie Heaphy, letter to author, August 2009.

32. The Baseball Guru—John B. Holway's Baseball Page, http://baseballguru.com/jholway.

33. Holway, *Black Giants*, xvi.

34. Todd Bolton, interview with author, January 19, 2019.

35. Jim Overmyer, interview with author, January 17, 2019.

36. Jim Overmyer, interview with author, January 17, 2019.

37. Todd Bolton, interview with author, January 19, 2019.

38. Bill James email to Bill Francis March 8, 2006, Hall of Fame archives file "2006 Hall of Fame Day."

39. Rob Centorani, "Negro leaguers deserved more time," *Oneonta Daily Star*, July 31, 2006, Hall of Fame archives file "2006 Hall of Fame Day."

40. Jim Overmyer, interview with author, January 17, 2019; Todd Bolton, interview with author, January 19, 2019

41. "Seventeen from Negro Leagues, Pre-Negro leagues Eras Elected to the Hall of Fame by Special Committee," Negro League Baseball Players Association, February 27, 2006, http://www.nlbpa.com/news/febuary-27-2006-2.

Chapter 5

1. James E. Overmyer, interview with the author, January 17, 2019.

2. The Negro American League ceased operations after the East-West All-Star game in 1962.

3. In 1940, one third of all players in the Mexican League were Negro Leaguers. By 1942, the percentage of Negro Leaguers in the Mexican League was up to 40%. Kevin Johnson, "The Mexican Leagues Are Here!," Seamheads.com, October 11, 2019 and November 17, 2019, https://seamheads.com/blog/2019/10/11/the-mexican-leagues-are-here/.

4. William F. McNeil, *Cool Papas and Double Duties: The All-Time Greats of the Negro Leagues* (Jefferson, NC: McFarland, 2000), 87.

5. Adrian Burgos, Jr., "Minnie Minoso was victim of unfair Hall of Fame election rules," Sporting News, http://www.sportingnews.com/us/mlb/news/minnie-minoso-dead-dies-hall-of-fame-obituary-white-sox-indians-election/6k7o72rs966f1utvju92wsadk.

6. Dr. Layton Revel and Luis Munoz, *Forgotten Heroes: Francisco "Pancho" Coimbre* (Carrollton, TX: Center for Negro League Baseball Research, 2009), 25.

7. James A. Riley, *The Biographical Encyclopedia of the Negro Baseball Leagues* (New York: Carroll & Graf, 1994), 184.

8. Revel and Munoz, *Coimbre*, 21.

9. William F. McNeil, *Baseball's Other All-Stars* (Jefferson, NC: McFarland, 2000), 189.

10. Todd Peterson, "The Case for the Negro Leagues," in *The Negro Leagues Were Major Leagues*, ed. Todd Peterson (Jefferson, NC: McFarland, 2020), 19.

11. Peterson, "The Case for the Negro Leagues," 21.

12. Ted Knorr, "The Top Ten Reasons Why the Negro Leagues Should Be Declared a Major League," in *The Negro Leagues Were Major Leagues*, ed. Todd Peterson (Jefferson, NC: McFarland, 2020), 106.

13. Scott Simkus, "Gray Area: Homestead vs. the Minor Leagues," in *The Negro Leagues Were Major Leagues*, ed. Todd Peterson (Jefferson, NC: McFarland, 2020), 54.

14. William F. McNeil, *Black Baseball Out of Season* (Jefferson, NC: McFarland, 2007), 109.

15. Phil S. Dixon, *The Dizzy and Daffy Dean Barnstorming Tour* (Lanham, VA: Rowman & Littlefield, 2019), p.90–91.

16. Peterson, "The Case for the Negro Leagues," 28.

17. Peterson, "The Case for the Negro Leagues," 31.

18. See Bill James, *Whatever Happened to the Hall of Fame: Baseball, Cooperstown, and the Politics of Glory* (New York: Simon & Schuster, 1995), 67.

19. Dr. Layton Revel and Luis Munoz, *Forgotten Heroes: Newton "Newt" Allen* (Carrollton, TX: Center for Negro League Baseball Research, 2011), 37.

20. Dr. Layton Revel and Luis Munoz, Forgotten Heroes: *Grant "Home Run" Johnson* (Carrollton, TX: Center for Negro League Baseball Research, 2016), 45.

21. See Averell Smith, *The Pitcher and the Dictator: Satchel Paige's Unlikely Season in the Dominican Republic* (Lincoln: University of Nebraska Press, 2018).

22. Rules for Selection of Great Stars of Negro Baseball for Recognition in Cooperstown (1971), BL-175.2003, National Baseball Hall of Fame Library, 4.

23. Robert Peterson, *Only the Ball was White: A History of Legendary Black Ball Players and All Black Professional Teams* (Englewood Cliffs, NJ: Prentice-Hall, 1970), 254.

24. John B. Holway, *The Complete Book of Baseball's Negro Leagues: The Other Half of Baseball History* (Fern Park, FL: Hastings House, 2001), 465.

25. Eric Chalek, "Fixing the Hall (or not?): Negro Leagues Representation by the Numbers," Hall of Miller and Eric, https://homemlb.wordpress.com/2019/03/08/fixing-the-hall-or-not-negro-leagues-representation-by-the-numbers.

Chapter 6

1. Bill James Online, www.billjamesonline.com.

2. See James A. Riley, *The Biographical Encyclopedia of the Negro League Baseball Leagues*; John B. Holway, *The Complete Book of Baseball's Negro Leagues*; Jorge Figueredo, *Cuban Baseball: A Statistical History, 1878–1961* (2003); Dick Clark and Larry Lester, eds., *The Negro Leagues Book* (1994); and many books by Phil Dixon and John B. Holway.

3. "Courier 'Experts' Name All-Time, All-American Baseball Team!," *Pittsburgh Courier*, April 19, 1952, 14.

4. See, for example, John Holway, *Blackball Stars* (Westport, CT: Meckler Books, 1988), 384; and www.baseball-fever.com/forum/general-baseball/the-negro-leagues.

5. John Holway, *Blackball Stars* (Westport, CT: Meckler Books, 1988), 384.

6. J. Fred Brillhart, "An Analysis of the 1952

Pittsburgh Courier Negro League Baseball Poll by Fredrico," The Donaldson Network, 9, http://john-donaldson.bravehost.com/pdf/00237.pdf.

7. McNeil, *Cool Papas.*

8. William F. McNeil, *Baseball's Other All-Stars: The Greatest Players from the Negro Leagues, the Japanese Leagues, the Mexican League, and the Pre-1960 Winter Leagues in Cuba, Puerto Rico and the Dominican Republic* (Jefferson, NC: McFarland, 2000).

9. *The 2006 ESPN Baseball Encyclopedia*, ed. Gary Gillette and Pete Palmer (New York: Sterling Publishing, 2006), 1641–1646.

10. James A. Riley, *The All-Time All-Stars of Black Baseball* (Cocoa, FL: TK Publishers, 1983).

11. Cum Posey promulgated multiple lists of All-Time All-Stars during his lifetime, many of which are gathered in Larry Lester, *Black Baseball's National Showcase: The East-West All-Star Game, 1933–1953* (Lincoln & London: University of Nebraska Press, 2001), 479–480.

12. Holway, *Complete Book*, 463–481.

13. See list compiled at McNeil, *Cool Papas*, 196.

14. See full list compiled at http://www.baseball-almanac.com/legendary/lisabr40.sht.

15. Bill James, *The New Bill James Historical Baseball Abstract* (New York: Free Press, 2001), 166–196.

16. Many of these lists are gathered at Lester, *Black Baseball's National Showcase*, 479–482; John B. Holway, *Blackball Stars* (Westport, CT: Meckler Books, 1988), 381–286; Robert Charles Cottrell, *The Best Pitcher in Baseball: The Life of Rube Foster, Negro League Giant* (New York: NYU Press, 2001), 174–176; and McNeil, *Cool Papas*, 193–196.

17. Lester, *Black Baseball's National Showcase*, 479–482, and Kevin Keating and Mike Kolleth, *The Negro Leagues Autograph Guide* (Dubuque, IA: Tuff Stuff Books, 1999), 33.

18. See Holway, *Complete Book.*

Chapter 7

1. See *The Bill James Handbook 2019* by Baseball Info Solutions (Chicago: ACTA Sports, 2018), 26.

2. See John B. Holway, "What If Effa Manley Had Been an Ugly Man?," Baseball Guru, http://baseball-guru.com/jholway/analysisjholway61.htm.

3. Bill James, *The 1986 Bill James Baseball Abstract* (New York: Ballantine Books 1986), 24–29.

Chapter 9

1. Bill James, *The New Bill James Historical Baseball Abstract*, rev. ed. (2003; New York: Free Press, 2001), 194.

2. Holway, *Complete Book*, 483.

3. Riley, *Biographical Encyclopedia*, 624.

4. Riley, *Biographical Encyclopedia*, 624.

5. *Seattle Star*, April 5, 1913.

6. *Pittsburgh Courier*, March 1, 1930.

7. Riley, *Biographical Encyclopedia*, 624.

8. Stephen V. Rice, "Bruce Petway," SABR Biography Project, https://sabr.org/bioproj/person/9a57c095.

9. Chris Jensen, "Negro Players Who May Have Been Overlooked by the Hall of Fame," Seamheads.com, August 29, 2013, http://seamheads.com/blog/2013/08/29/negro-leagues-players-who-have-been-overlooked-by-the-hall-of-fame/.

10. *Oakland Tribune*, December 29, 1914.

11. Riley, *Biographical Encyclopedia*, 624.

12. Riley, *Biographical Encyclopedia*, 624.

13. Eric Chalek, "Evaluating More Negro Leagues Catchers," The Hall of Miller and Eric, January 31, 2018, https://homemlb.wordpress.com/2018/01/31/evaluating-more-negro-leagues-catchers/.

14. McNeil, *Cool Papas*, 160.

15. Riley, *Biographical Encyclopedia*, 254.

16. Riley, *Biographical Encyclopedia*, 254.

17. Riley, *Biographical Encyclopedia*, 256.

18. Todd Peterson, *Early Black Baseball in Minnesota* (Jefferson, NC: McFarland, 2010), 64.

19. Riley, *Biographical Encyclopedia*, 432.

20. Peterson, *Early Black Baseball*, 64.

21. Peterson, *Early Black Baseball*, 28; Holway, *Complete Book* 47.

22. Peterson, *Early Black Baseball*, 64.

23. Riley, *Biographical Encyclopedia*, 433.

24. Peterson, *Early Black Baseball*, 64.

25. Peterson, *Early Black Baseball*, 210.

26. Robert Charles Cottrell, *The Best Pitcher in Baseball: The Life of Rube Foster* (New York: NYU Press, 2001), 174–175.

27. Peterson, *Early Black Baseball*, 211–212.

28. Riley, *Biographical Encyclopedia*, 841.

29. Holway, *Complete Book*, 95.

30. Riley, *Biographical Encyclopedia*, 841.

31. Chalek, "Evaluating More Negro Leagues Catchers."

32. John Holway, *Voices from the Great Black Baseball Leagues* (Mineola, NY: Dover, 2010), 213.

33. Holway, *Voices, 207–209.*

34. Holway, *Voices*, 209.

35. Holway, *Complete Book*, 282.

36. Riley, *Biographical Encyclopedia*, 122.

37. Riley, *Biographical Encyclopedia*, 123.

38. Holway, *Voices*, 206.

39. James, *New Historical Baseball Abstract*, 181.

40. Riley, *Biographical Encyclopedia*, 337.

41. Holway, *Voices*, 300.

42. Holway, *Voices*, 301.

43. Holway, *Voices*, 300.

44. Riley, *Biographical Encyclopedia*, 337.

45. Holway, *Complete Book*, 401.

46. Riley, *Biographical Encyclopedia*, 337.

47. Holway, *Complete Book*, 452.

48. Holway, *Voices*, 300.

49. Riley, *Biographical Encyclopedia*, 338.

50. Riley, *Biographical Encyclopedia*, 791.

51. Quincy Trouppe, *Twenty Years Too Soon: Prelude to Major League Integrated Baseball* (St. Louis: Missouri Historical Society Press, 1995), 5.

52. Jay Hurd, "Quincy Trouppe," SABR Biography Project, https://sabr.org/bioproj/person/0d89ee6b.

53. Trouppe, *Twenty Years*, 37.

54. "Strat-O Fan Just E-mailed Me," Baseball Think Factory Hall of Merit (Quincy Trouppe note

54), January 29, 2007, http://www.baseballthinkfactory.org/hall_of_merit/discussion/quincy_trouppe.

55. Strat-O Fan, "I'm doing some research on Bismarck right now," Baseball Think Factory Hall of Merit (Quincy Trouppe note 53), January 23, 2007, http://www.baseballthinkfactory.org/hall_of_merit/discussion/quincy_trouppe.

56. Trouppe, *Twenty Years*, 66.

57. Riley, *Biographical Encyclopedia*, 791–792.

58. Trouppe, *Twenty Years*, 82.

59. Riley, *Biographical Encyclopedia*, 792.

60. Trouppe, *Twenty Years*, 104–105.

61. Jay Hurd, "Quincy Trouppe," SABR Biography Project, https://sabr.org/bioproj/person/0d89ee6b.

62. Jay Hurd, "Quincy Trouppe."

63. Larry Lester, introduction to Trouppe, *Twenty Years*, 6.

64. Riley, *Biographical Encyclopedia*, 792.

65. Riley, *Biographical Encyclopedia*, 792.

66. Lester, introduction to Trouppe, *Twenty Years*, 4.

67. "Trouppe vs Campanella," Baseball Think Factory Hall of Merit (Quincy Trouppe note 36), October 24, 2005, http://www.baseballthinkfactory.org/hall_of_merit/discussion/quincy_trouppe.

Chapter 10

1. Riley, *Biographical Encyclopedia*, 830.

2. Richard Bak, "Stearnes and Wesley: The Bash Brothers of Mack Park," Detroit Athletic Co., September 5, 2015, https://www.detroitathletic.com/blog/2015/09/05/stearnes-and-wesley-the-bash-brothers-of-mack-park/.

3. Holway, *Complete Book*, 182.

4. Bak, "Stearnes and Wesley."

5. Bak, "Stearnes and Wesley."

6. Bak, "Stearnes and Wesley."

7. McNeil, *Baseball's Other All Stars*, 52.

8. Richard Bak, *Turkey Stearnes and the Detroit Stars* (Detroit, MI: Wayne State Univ. Press, 1995), 265.

9. Holway, *Complete Book*, 475.

10. Dr. Layton Revel and Luis Munoz, *Forgotten Heroes: George "Tank" Carr* (Carrollton, TX: Center for Negro League Baseball Research, 2015), 1.

11. Revel and Munoz, *Carr*, 49.

12. Revel and Munoz, *Carr*, 3.

13. Revel and Munoz, *Carr*, 4.

14. David Lawrence and Dom Denaro, *Eastern Colored League* (San Francisco, CA: AJ Publishing, 2003), 55.

15. Revel and Munoz, *Carr*, 49.

16. Revel and Munoz, *Carr*, 49.

17. Revel and Munoz, *Carr*, 49.

18. Revel and Munoz, *Carr*, 29.

19. Revel and Munoz, *Carr*, 41.

20. Riley, *Biographical Encyclopedia*, 154.

21. Revel and Munoz, *Carr*, 32.

22. Revel and Munoz, *Carr*, 49.

23. Revel and Munoz, *Carr*, 49.

24. James, *New Historical Baseball Abstract*, 181.

25. Justin Murphy, "Luke Easter," SABR Biography Project, https://sabr.org/bioproj/person/f29a4070.

26. Murphy, "Luke Easter."

27. O'Neil, *I Was Right*, 151.

28. Murphy, "Luke Easter."

29. Murphy, "Luke Easter."

30. Easter shaved years off his age during his playing days but was actually born on August 4, 1915. Justin Murphy, "Luke Easter."

31. Riley, *Biographical Encyclopedia*, 261.

32. Holway, *Complete Book*, 460.

33. Monte Irvin, *Few and Chosen: Defining Negro Leagues Greatness* (Chicago, IL: Triumph Books, 2007), 28.

34. Eric Chalek, "Evaluating More Negro Leagues First Basemen, Part 1," Hall of Miller and Eric, February 14, 2018, https://homemlb.wordpress.com/2018/02/14/evaluating-more-negro-leagues-first-basemen-part-1/.

35. Murphy, "Luke Easter."

36. Riley, *Biographical Encyclopedia*, 262.

37. Irvin, *Few and Chosen*, 19.

38. James Goodrich, "Luke Easter, King of Swat?" *Negro Digest*, August 1950.

39. Chalek, "Evaluating More Negro Leagues First Basemen, Part 1."

40. Sunnyday2, "James ranks Easter as the #2 NeL 1B," Baseball Think Factory Hall of Merit (Luke Easter note 3), August 17, 2005, http://www.baseballthinkfactory.org/hall_of_merit/discussion/luke_easter.

41. Riley, *Biographical Encyclopedia*, 622.

42. "Pettus Caught for Babe Adams," *Albuquerque Morning Journal*, October 20, 1909, 3.

43. Riley, *Biographical Encyclopedia*, 623.

44. Eric Chalek, "Evaluating More Negro Leagues First Basemen, Part 2," Hall of Miller and Eric, February 21, 2018, https://homemlb.wordpress.com/2018/02/21/evaluating-more-negro-leagues-first-basemen-part-2/.

45. Riley, *Biographical Encyclopedia*, 623.

46. Riley, *Biographical Encyclopedia*, 623.

47. Riley, Biographical Encyclopedia, 623.

Chapter 11

1. Riley, *Biographical Encyclopedia*, 228.

2. Riley, *Biographical Encyclopedia*, 228.

3. Riley, *Biographical Encyclopedia*, 228.

4. Riley, *Biographical Encyclopedia*, 228.

5. Riley, *Biographical Encyclopedia*, 228–229.

6. Gary A, "Bingo DeMoss played much of his career in the dead-ball era," Baseball Think Factory Hall of Merit (Newt Allen note 9), February 22, 2005, http://www.baseballthinkfactory.org/hall_of_merit/discussion/newt_allen.

7. McNeil, *Baseball's Other All-Stars*, 53.

8. "Bingo DeMoss," Baseball Think Factory Hall of Merit, September 14, 2004, http://www.baseballthinkfactory.org/hall_of_merit/discussion/bingo_demoss.

9. Riley, *Biographical Encyclopedia*, 31.

10. Dixon, *Dizzy and Daffy Barnstorming Tour*, 103.

11. Dr. Layton Revel and Luis Munoz, *Forgotten Heroes: Newton "Newt" Allen* (Carrollton, TX: Center for Negro League Baseball Research, 2011), 2.

12. Revel and Munoz, *Allen*, 1.

13. McNeil, *Cool Papas*, 123.

14. Holway, *Voices*, 94–95.

15. Riley, *Biographical Encyclopedia*, 32.

16. Revel and Munoz, *Allen*, 1.

17. Revel and Munoz, *Allen*, 37.

18. Revel and Munoz, *Allen*, 37.

19. Revel and Munoz, *Allen*, 37.

20. Revel and Munoz, *Allen*, 25.

21. Revel and Munoz, *Allen*, 37

22. Revel and Munoz, *Allen*, 27.

23. Peterson, *Only The Ball*, 230.

24. Dr. Layton Revel and Luis Munoz, *Forgotten Heroes: Sammy T. Hughes* (Carrollton, TX: Center for Negro League Baseball Research, 2012), 1.

25. Riley, *Biographical Encyclopedia*, 400–401.

26. Revel and Munoz, *Hughes,* 1.

27. Revel and Munoz, *Hughes,* 1.

28. Revel and Munoz, *Hughes,* 1.

29. "Sammy Hughes," Baseball Reference, https://www.baseball-reference.com/register/player. fcgi?id=hughes000sam.

30. Riley, *Biographical Encyclopedia*, 401.

31. Revel and Munoz, *Hughes,* 19.

32. Holway, *Complete Book*, 333–334.

33. Revel and Munoz, *Hughes,* 12.

34. Revel and Munoz, *Hughes,* 12.

35. Riley, *Biographical Encyclopedia*, 401.

36. McNeil, *Cool Papas*, 195.

37. McNeil, *Baseball's Other All-Stars*, 182.

38. Holway, *Black Giants*, 141.

39. James, *New Historical Baseball Abstract*, 103.

40. Dr. Layton Revel and Luis Munoz, *Forgotten Heroes: Frank Warfield* (Carrollton, TX: Center for Negro League Baseball Research, 2014), 1.

41. James, *Historical Baseball Abstract*, 183.

42. Revel and Munoz, *Warfield*, 1.

43. Revel and Munoz, *Warfield*, 38.

44. Revel and Munoz, *Warfield*, 49.

45. Revel and Munoz, *Warfield*, 2.

46. Riley, *Biographical Encyclopedia*, 815.

47. Revel and Munoz, *Warfield*, 40.

48. Revel and Munoz, *Warfield*, 41.

49. Revel and Munoz, *Warfield*, 38.

50. Brian McKenna, "Charlie Grant," SABR Biography Project, https://sabr.org/bioproj/person/ bd564010.

51. Riley, *Biographical Encyclopedia*, 151.

52. McKenna, "Charlie Grant."

53. McKenna, "Charlie Grant."

54. James, *Historical Baseball Abstract*, 183.

55. Dr. Layton Revel and Luis Munoz, *Forgotten Heroes: Lorenzo "Piper" Davis* (Carrollton, TX: Center for Negro League Baseball Research, 2010), 5.

56. Jeb Stewart, "Lorenzo 'Piper' Davis," in *Bittersweet Goodbye: The Black Barons, the Grays, and the 1948 Negro League World Series* (Phoenix, AZ: Society for American Baseball Research, 2017), 30.

57. Holway, *Complete Book*, 452–453.

58. Stewart, "Lorenzo 'Piper' Davis," 31.

59. James A. Riley, *Of Monarchs and Black Barons* (Jefferson, N.C.: McFarland, 2012), 197–198.

60. Riley, *Of Monarchs*, 197.

61. Holway, *Complete Book*, 478.

62. Revel and Munoz, *Davis*, 25.

63. Revel and Munoz, *Davis*, 15.

64. Revel and Munoz, *Davis*, 25.

65. Eric Enders, "This was already posted in the Artie Wilson thread," Baseball Think Factory Hall of Merit (Piper Davis note 6), October 5, 2005, http://www.baseballthinkfactory.org/hall_of_merit/discussion/piper_davis.

66. Revel and Munoz, *Davis*, 37.

67. Stewart, "Lorenzo 'Piper' Davis," 33.

68. Revel and Munoz, *Davis*, 35.

69. Allan Barra, "What Really Happened to Ben Chapman, the Racist Baseball Player in *42*?," *The Atlantic*, April 15, 2013, https://www.theatlantic.com/entertainment/archive/2013/04/what-really-happened-to-ben-chapman-the-racist-baseball-player-in-i-42-i/274995/.

70. Riley, *Biographical Encyclopedia*, 709.

71. Riley, *Biographical Encyclopedia*, 709.

72. Riley, *Biographical Encyclopedia*, 858.

73. Dr. Layton Revel and Luis Munoz, *Forgotten Heroes: Marvin Williams* (Carrollton, TX: Center for Negro League Baseball Research, 2018), 48

74. Revel and Munoz, *Marvin Williams*, Introduction.

75. Riley, *Biographical Encyclopedia*, 858–9.

76. Revel and Munoz, *Marvin Williams*, 49.

77. Revel and Munoz, *Marvin Williams*, 47.

Chapter 12

1. Riley, *Biographical Encyclopedia*, 498.

2. Riley, *Biographical Encyclopedia*, 497.

3. Revel and Munoz, *Lundy*, 28.

4. Revel and Munoz, *Lundy*, 28.

5. Stephen V. Rice, "Dick Lundy," SABR Biography Project, https://sabr.org/node/43819.

6. Revel and Munoz, *Lundy*, 24.

7. Revel and Munoz, *Lundy*, 37.

8. Revel and Munoz, *Lundy*, 36.

9. Revel and Munoz, *Lundy*, 36.

10. Revel and Munoz, *Lundy*, 32.

11. Revel and Munoz, *Lundy*, 29.

12. *Afro American*, August 17, 1940.

13. Holway, *Blackball Stars*, 140.

14. Revel and Munoz, *Lundy*, 34.

15. Jim Overmyer, interview with author, January 17, 2019.

16. Todd Bolton, interview with author, January 19, 2019.

17. James, *New Historical Baseball Abstract*, 186.

18. Joe Posnanski, *The Soul of Baseball: A Road Trip Through Buck O'Neil's America* (New York: William Morrow, 2007), 165.

19. See Revel and Munoz, *Lundy*, 27.

20. Dr. Layton Revel and Luis Munoz, *Forgotten*

Heroes: Grant Johnson (Carrollton, TX: Center for Negro League Baseball Research, 2016), 1.

21. *Schenectady Gazette*, March 4, 1913, p.11.

22. Revel and Munoz, *Grant Johnson*, 2.

23. Riley, *Biographical Encyclopedia*, 435.

24. Revel and Munoz, *Grant Johnson*, 5.

25. Mitch Lutzke, *The Page Fence Giants* (Jefferson, NC: McFarland, 2018), 238.

26. Mitch Lutzke, *Page Fence Giants*, 240.

27. Chris Cobb, "Here's a summary of the published data available on Grant Johnson," Baseball Think Factory Hall of Merit (Grant Johnson note 19), June 27, 2008, http://www.baseballthinkfactory.org/hall_of_merit/discussion/grant_johnson.

28. Revel and Munoz, *Grant Johnson*, 30.

29. Revel and Munoz, *Grant Johnson*, 37.

30. Riley, *Biographical Encyclopedia*, 435.

31. Revel and Munoz, *Grant Johnson*, 43.

32. Revel and Munoz, *Grant Johnson*, 45.

33. Sol White, *Sol White's Official Baseball Guide*, reprint (Columbia, SC: Camden House, 1984), 109.

34. Revel and Munoz, *Grant Johnson*, 38.

35. Todd Bolton, interview with author, January 19, 2019.

36. Eric Chalek, "Evaluating Negro Leagues Short-stops Part 1," The Hall of Miller and Eric, November 29, 2017, https://homemlb.wordpress.com/2017/11/29/evaluating-negro-leagues-shortstops-part-1/.

37. Revel and Munoz, *Grant Johnson*, 45.

38. Dr. Chaleeko, "Lastly, the player synopsis, heavily revised," Baseball Think Factory Hall of Merit (Hall of Fame's 2006 Negro League Election, post 50), July 28, 2005, http://www.baseballthinkfactory.org/hall_of_merit/discussion/hall_of_fames_2006_negro_league_election.

39. Joe Dimino, "The Hall of Merit," in *The Hardball Times Baseball Annual 2006* (Skokie, IL: ACTA Sports, 2005), 123.

40. Jim Overmyer, interview with the author, January 17, 2019.

41. Dr. Layton Revel and Luis Munoz, *Forgotten Heroes: Walter "Dobie" Moore* (Carrollton, TX: Center for Negro League Baseball Research, 2009), 1–2.

42. Revel and Munoz, *Moore*, 1–2.

43. Revel and Munoz, *Moore*, 2.

44. John B. Holway, "Dobie Moore," *Baseball Research Journal* 1982, 170.

45. John B. Holway, "Dobie Moore," *Baseball Research Journal* 1982, 169.

46. Marty Appel, *Casey Stengel: Baseball's Greatest Character* (New York: Doubleday, 2017), 62.

47. Revel and Munoz, *Moore*, 2.

48. Revel and Munoz, *Moore*, 17.

49. Revel and Munoz, *Moore*, 15.

50. Revel and Munoz, *Moore*, 15.

51. Revel and Munoz, *Moore*, 17.

52. Revel and Munoz, *Moore*, 17.

53. Revel and Munoz, *Moore*, 16.

54. Riley, *Biographical Encyclopedia*, 566.

55. John B. Holway, "Dobie Moore," *Baseball Research Journal* 1982, 169–170.

56. John B. Holway, "Dobie Moore," *Baseball Research Journal* 1982, 169.

57. Revel and Munoz, *Moore,* 15.

58. John B. Holway, "Dobie Moore," *Baseball Research Journal* 1982, 171.

59. Revel and Munoz, *Moore*, 11.

60. Revel and Munoz, *Moore*, 11.

61. McNeil, *Cool Papas*, 106.

62. Koufax, "I am the author of several Negro league books," Baseball Think Factory Hall of Merit (Dobie Moore note 70), May 29, 2005, http://www.baseballthinkfactory.org/hall_of_merit/discussion/dobie_moore.

63. Todd Bolton, interview with the author, January 19, 2019.

64. Dr. Layton Revel and Luis Munoz, *Forgotten Heroes: Artie Wilson* (Carrollton, TX: Center for Negro League Baseball Research, 2010), 29.

65. Rob Neyer, "Artie Wilson," SABR Biography Project, https://sabr.org/bioproj/person/38b3a4b8.

66. Revel and Munoz, *Artie Wilson*, 29.

67. Revel and Munoz, *Artie Wilson*, 26, 29.

68. Riley, *Biographical Encyclopedia*, 866.

69. Revel and Munoz, *Artie Wilson*, 29.

70. Revel and Munoz, *Artie Wilson*, 29.

71. Revel and Munoz, *Wilson*, 29.

72. Revel and Munoz, *Wilson*, 19.

73. Neyer, "Artie Wilson."

74. Neyer, "Artie Wilson."

75. Gaylon H. White, *Singles and Smiles: How Artie Wilson Broke Baseball's Color Barrier* (Lanham, MD: Rowman & Littlefield, 2018), 96.

76. Neyer, "Artie Wilson."

77. Revel and Munoz, *Wilson*, 29.

78. Gaylon H. White, *Singles and Smiles*, 59.

79. Eric Enders, "The Last .400 Hitter," 2000. (Reprinted at Baseball Think Factory [Artie Wilson post 15], http://www.baseballthinkfactory.org/hall_of_merit/discussion/artie_wilson/.)

80. Revel and Munoz, *Wilson*, 19.

81. McNeil, *Cool Papas*, 81.

82. McNeil, *Cool Papas*, 196.

83. Holway, "What if Effa Manley Had Been an Ugly Man?"

84. Riley, *Biographical Encyclopedia*, 176.

85. Riley, *Biographical Encyclopedia*, 176.

86. Riley, *Biographical Encyclopedia*, 176.

87. Riley, *Biographical Encyclopedia*, 176.

88. McNeil, *Baseball's Other All-Stars*, 145.

89. Riley, *Biographical Encyclopedia*, 176.

90. Eric Chalek, "Evaluating More Negro Leagues Shortstops Part 2," Hall of Miller and Eric, May 2, 2018, https://homemlb.wordpress.com/2018/05/02/evaluating-more-negro-leagues-shortstops-part-2/.

91. "Bus Clarkson," Baseball Think Factory Hall of Merit, September 21, 2005, http://www.baseballthinkfactory.org/hall_of_merit/discussion/bus_clarkson.

Chapter 13

1. Riley, *Biographical Encyclopedia*, 511.

2. O'Neil, *Right on Time*, 45.

3. Dr. Layton Revel and Luis Munoz, *Forgotten Heroes: Oliver "The Ghost" Marcelle* (Carrollton, TX: Center for Negro League Baseball Research, 2012), 1.

4. Riley, *Biographical Encyclopedia*, 511.

5. Revel and Munoz, *Marcelle*, 24.

6. Revel and Munoz, *Marcelle*, 24.

7. Revel and Munoz, *Marcelle*, 25.

8. Revel and Munoz, *Marcelle*, 25.

9. Revel and Munoz, *Marcelle*, 26.

10. Revel and Munoz, *Marcelle*, 26.

11. John B. Holway, *Blackball Stars: Negro League Pioneers* (Westport, CT: Mecklermedia, 1988), 143–147.

12. Revel and Munoz, *Marcelle*, 22.

13. Revel and Munoz, *Marcelle*, 22.

14. Trouppe, *20 Years*, 151.

15. Holway, *Black Giants*, 56.

16. Holway, *Black Giants*, 56.

17. Dr. Layton Revel and Luis Munoz, *Forgotten Heroes: George "Tubby" Scales* (Carrollton, TX: Center for Negro League Baseball Research, 2015), 1.

18. Riley, *Biographical Encyclopedia*, 699.

19. Revel, *Scales*, 1.

20. Revel, *Scales*, 22.

21. Sammy Miller, "Pre-Negro Leagues Candidate Profile: George Walter 'Tubby' Scales," National Baseball Hall of Fame, http://web.archive.org/web/20070608102049/http://www.baseballhalloffame.org/hofers_and_honorees/scales_tubby.htm.

22. Phil S. Dixon, *Phil S. Dixon's American Baseball Chronicles Volume 1: Great Teams: The 1931 Homestead Grays* (Xlibris, 2009), 290.

23. Dixon, *Phil S. Dixon's American Baseball Chronicles*, 290.

24. Revel, *Scales*, 23.

25. Revel, *Scales*, 15.

26. Holway, *Black Giants*, 56.

27. Holway, *Black Giants*, 59–60.

28. Revel and Munoz, Scales, 27.

29. Revel and Munoz, *Scales*, 1.

30. Holway, *Black Giants*, 61–62.

31. Holway, *Black Giants*, 62.

32. Riley, *Biographical Encyclopedia*, 647.

33. Kyle McNary, "Alec Radcliffe," Baseball History Comes Alive, March 10, 2016, https://www.baseballhistorycomesalive.com/negro-league-featured-piece-by-kyle-mcnary-alec-radcliffe/.

34. Holway, *Black Giants*, 123.

35. Riley, *Biographical Encyclopedia*, 647.

36. Riley, *Biographical Encyclopedia*, 648.

37. Riley, *Biographical Encyclopedia*, 648.

38. Lester, *Black Baseball's National Showcase*, 481–482.

39. Dr. Layton Revel and Luis Munoz, *Forgotten Heroes: Orestes "Minnie" Minoso* (Carrollton, TX: Center for Negro League Baseball Research, 2014), 1.

40. Revel and Munoz, *Minoso*, 24.

41. Revel and Munoz, *Minoso*, 4.

42. Revel and Munoz, Minoso, 31.

43. Todd Bolton, interview with the author, January 19, 2019.

Chapter 14

1. Holway, *Blackball Stars*, 293.

2. John Holway, "Charlie 'Chino' Smith," Baseball Research Journal (1978), 67.

3. Dr. Layton Revel and Luis Munoz, *Forgotten Heroes: Charles "Chino" Smith* (Carrollton, TX: Center for Negro League Baseball Research, 2011), 1.

4. Revel and Munoz, *Smith*, 3.

5. Revel and Munoz, *Smith*, 3.

6. Revel and Munoz, *Smith*, 5.

7. Revel and Munoz, *Smith*, 6.

8. Holway, Charlie 'Chino' Smith,' BRJ, 66.

9. Revel and Munoz, *Smith*, 9.

10. Revel and Munoz, *Smith*, 11.

11. Koufax, "Answer to Sunnyday2," Baseball Think Factory Hall of Merit (Chino Smith post 20), May 30, 2005, http://www.baseballthinkfactory.org/hall_of_merit/discussion/chino_smith.

12. John Holway, "Charlie 'Chino' Smith," *Baseball Research Journal* (1978), 63–67.

13. Holway, Charlie 'Chino' Smith,' BRJ, 65.

14. Holway, Charlie 'Chino' Smith,' BRJ, 64.

15. Revel and Munoz, *Smith*, 1.

16. Holway, Charlie 'Chino' Smith,' BRJ, 67.

17. John Thorn et al., eds., *Total Baseball: The Official Encyclopedia of Major League Baseball*, 6th ed. (New York: Total Sports, 1999), 165.

18. Revel and Munoz, *Smith*, 17.

19. Irvin, *Few and Chosen*, 115.

20. Dr. Layton Revel and Luis Munoz, *Forgotten Heroes: Burnis "Wild Bill" Wright* (Carrollton, TX: Center for Negro League Baseball Research, 2008), 1.

21. Riley, *Biographical Encyclopedia*, 881.

22. Holway, *Black Giants*, 149.

23. Revel and Munoz, *Wright*, 1.

24. Holway, *Black Giants*, 148.

25. Revel and Munoz, *Wright*, 1.

26. Revel and Munoz, *Wright*, 13–15.

27. Revel and Munoz, *Wright*, 3.

28. Revel and Munoz, *Wright*, 3.

29. Riley, *Of Monarchs*, 184.

30. Revel and Munoz, *Wright*, 5.

31. Revel and Munoz, *Wright*, 4–5.

32. Revel and Munoz, *Wright*, 13–15.

33. Holway, *Black Giants*, 148.

34. Revel and Munoz, *Wright*, 7.

35. Holway, *Black Giants*, 148.

36. Holway, *Black Giants*, 154.

37. Holway, *Black Giants*, 155.

38. Revel and Munoz, *Wright*, 14.

39. Revel and Munoz, *Wright*, 11.

40. Holway, *Black Giants*, 148.

41. Dr. Layton Revel and Luis Munoz, *Forgotten Heroes: Spottswood Poles* (Carrollton, TX: Center for Negro League Research, 2013), 1.

42. Revel and Munoz, *Poles*, 1.

43. Revel and Munoz, *Poles*, 22.

44. Revel and Munoz, *Poles*, 2.

45. Revel and Munoz, *Poles*, 21.

46. Revel and Munoz, *Poles*, 25.

47. Revel and Munoz, *Poles*, 28.

48. Revel and Munoz, *Poles*, 29.

49. Riley, *Biographical Encyclopedia*, 632.
50. Revel and Munoz, *Poles*, 21.
51. Revel and Munoz, *Poles,* 19.
52. McNeil, *Baseball's Other All-Stars*, 56.
53. Revel and Munoz, *Poles*, 28.
54. Revel and Munoz, *Poles*, 1.
55. John Holway, "Spottswood Poles," *Baseball Research Journal* 4 (1975), 68.
56. Revel and Munoz, *Poles*, 21.
57. Riley, *Biographical Encyclopedia*, 632.
58. Revel and Munoz, *Poles*, 22.
59. Holway, "Spottswood Poles," 66.
60. James, *Historical Abstract*, 359.
61. Revel and Munoz, *Poles*, 1.
62. Kazuo Sayama and Bill Staple, Jr., *Gentle Black Giants: A History of Negro Leaguers in Japan* (Fresno, CA: Nisei Baseball Research Project Press, 2019), 344.
63. Chester Washington, Rap's Homer Beats Grays, *The Pittsburgh Courier*, 3 August 1935, 14. Historian James A. Riley claims his nickname derived from the fact that he grew up along the Rappahannock River. See Riley, *Biographical Encyclopedia*, 239.
64. Riley, *Biographical Encyclopedia*, 239.
65. See Ted Knorr, "The Greatest Outfield in Baseball History," *2018 The National Pastime*, SABR.
66. Dr. Layton Revel and Luis Munoz, *Forgotten Heroes: Herbert "Rap" Dixon* (Carrollton, TX: Center for Negro League Baseball Research, 2012), 1.
67. Revel and Munoz, *Dixon*, 1.
68. Riley, *Biographical Encyclopedia*, 239.
69. "Pre-Negro Leagues Candidate Profile: Herbert Allen 'Rap' Dixon," National Baseball Hall of Fame, http://web.archive.org/web/20070608095746/http://baseballhalloffame.org/hofers_and_honorees/dixon_rap.htm.
70. Revel and Munoz, *Dixon*, 25.
71. Revel and Munoz, *Dixon*, 25
72. Revel and Munoz, *Dixon,* 25.
73. "Pre-Negro Leagues Candidate Profile: Herbert Allen 'Rap' Dixon," National Baseball Hall of Fame, http://web.archive.org/web/20070608095746/http://www.baseballhalloffame.org/hofers_and_honorees/dixon_rap.htm.
74. Revel and Munoz, *Dixon*, 24.
75. Sayama and Staple, *Gentle Black Giants*, 344.
76. Ted Knorr, "The Greatest Outfield in Baseball History," *2018 The National Pastime*, SABR.
77. Revel and Munoz, *Dixon*, 18.
78. Riley, *Biographical Encyclopedia*, 239–240.
79. Revel and Munoz, *Dixon*, 18.
80. Revel and Munoz, *Dixon*, 25.
81. Dr. Layton Revel and Luis Munoz, *Forgotten Heroes: Oscar "Heavy" Johnson* (Carrollton, TX: Center for Negro League Baseball Research, 2010), 1.
82. Revel and Munoz, *Oscar "Heavy" Johnson*, 3.
83. Revel and Munoz, *Oscar "Heavy" Johnson*, 19.
84. Revel and Munoz, *Oscar "Heavy" Johnson*, 9.
85. Holway, *Complete Book*, 165.
86. Revel and Munoz, *Oscar "Heavy" Johnson*, 21.
87. Riley, *Biographical Encyclopedia*, 441.
88. Riley, *Biographical Encyclopedia*, 441.
89. Riley, *Biographical Encyclopedia*, 441.
90. Revel and Munoz, *Oscar "Heavy" Johnson*, 20.
91. Revel and Munoz, *Oscar "Heavy" Johnson*, 21.
92. Revel and Munoz, *Oscar "Heavy" Johnson*, 17.
93. McNeil, *Cool Papas*, 130.
94. Dr. Layton Revel and Luis Munoz, *Forgotten Heroes: Hurley McNair* (Carrollton, TX: Center for Negro League Baseball Research, 2016), 1.
95. Riley, *Biographical Encyclopedia*, 541.
96. Holway, *Voices*, 222.
97. Riley, *Biographical Encyclopedia*, 541.
98. Revel and Munoz, McNair, 34.
99. Revel and Munoz, *McNair*, 41.
100. Revel and Munoz, *McNair*, 41.
101. Revel and Munoz, *McNair*, 34.
102. Revel and Munoz, *McNair*, 38.
103. Revel and Munoz, *McNair*, 41.
104. Revel and Munoz, *McNair*, 33.
105. Riley, *Biographical Encyclopedia*, 541.
106. Dr. Layton Revel and Luis Munoz, *Forgotten Heroes: Clarence "Fats" Jenkins* (Carrollton, TX: Center for Negro League Baseball Research, 2011), 1.
107. Holway, *Complete Book*, 472.
108. Riley, *Biographical Encyclopedia*, 423.
109. Revel and Munoz, *Jenkins*, 23.
110. Revel and Munoz, *Jenkins*, 19.
111. Revel and Munoz, *Jenkins*, 19.
112. Revel and Munoz, *Jenkins*, 20.
113. John Struth, "Alejandro Oms," SABR Biography Project, https://sabr.org/node/28415.
114. Riley, *Biographical Encyclopedia*, 588.
115. Riley, *Biographical Encyclopedia*, 588.
116. Struth, "Alejandro Oms."
117. James, *New Historical Baseball Abstract*, 191.
118. Riley, *Biographical Encyclopedia*, 588.
119. Struth, "Alejandro Oms."
120. Struth, "Alejandro Oms."
121. Revel and Munoz, *Oms,* 9.
122. Revel and Munoz, *Oms,* 9.
123. Revel and Munoz, *Oms*, 11.
124. Holway, *Black Giants*, xvi.
125. James, *New Historical Baseball Abstract*, 191.
126. Todd Bolton, interview with the author, January 19, 2019.
127. Riley, *Biographical Encyclopedia*, 249.
128. Riley, *Biographical Encyclopedia*, 249.
129. Riley, *Biographical Encyclopedia*, 249.
130. McNeil, *Baseball's Other All-Stars*, 107.
131. Riley, *Biographical Encyclopedia*, 833–834.
132. Riley, *Biographical Encyclopedia*, 834.
133. David M. Jordan, "Another Quaker City Champion: The 1934 Philadelphia Stars," *Black Ball* 5, no. 1 (Spring 2012), 27.
134. Riley, *Biographical Encyclopedia*, 834.
135. Riley, *Biographical Encyclopedia*, 774.
136. Riley, *Biographical Encyclopedia*, 774.
137. Riley, *Biographical Encyclopedia*, 426.
138. Riley, *Biographical Encyclopedia*, 500.
139. Dr. Layton Revel and Luis Munoz, *Forgotten Heroes: James "Jimmie Lyons"* (Carrollton, TX: Center for Negro League, Baseball Research, 2017), 43.
140. James, *New Historical Baseball Abstract*, 190.
141. Riley, *Biographical Encyclopedia*, 88.
142. Riley, *Biographical Encyclopedia*, 751.

143. Riley, *Biographical Encyclopedia,* 750.

144. Riley, *Biographical Encyclopedia,* 63–64.

145. William J. Plott, *The Negro Southern League: A Baseball History, 1920–1951* (Jefferson, NC: McFarland, 2015), 55.

146. Dr. Layton Revel and Luis Munoz, *Forgotten Heroes: Roy "Red" Parnell"* (Carrollton, TX: Center for Negro League, Baseball Research, 2018), 45.

147. Revel and Munoz, *Parnell,* 44.

148. Revel and Munoz, *Parnell,* 44.

149. Revel and Munoz, *Parnell,* 43–44.

150. Riley, *Biographical Encyclopedia,* 712.

Chapter 15

1. Riley, *Biographical Encyclopedia,* 654

2. Riley, *Biographical Encyclopedia,* 654.

3. Dirk Lammers, "Ahead of Their Time: Negro Leagues No-Hitters," Society for American Baseball Research, https://sabr.org/bioproj/topic/ahead-their-time-negro-leagues-no-hitters.

4. Holway, *Blackball Stars,* 80.

5. Dr. Layton Revel and Luis Munoz, *Forgotten Heroes: Dick "Cannonball" Redding* (Carrollton, TX: Center for Negro League Baseball Research, 2013), 2.

6. Revel and Munoz, *Redding,* 6.

7. Revel and Munoz, *Redding,* 6–7.

8. Riley, *Biographical Encyclopedia,* 654.

9. Revel and Munoz, *Redding,* 38.

10. John Holway, "The Cannonball," *Baseball Research Journal* 9 (1980), http://research.sabr.org/journals/cannonball.

11. Holway, "The Cannonball."

12. Revel and Munoz, *Redding,* 38, 40.

13. Riley, *Biographical Encyclopedia,* 654.

14. Revel and Munoz, *Redding,* 49

15. Revel and Munoz, *Redding,* 39.

16. Revel and Munoz, *Redding,* 48.

17. Gary Ashwill, "Cobb & Redding, 1916," Agate Type, April 5, 2019, https://agatetype.typepad.com/agate_type/2019/04/cobb-redding-1916.html.

18. Holway, *Blackball Stars,* 82.

19. Revel and Munoz, *Redding,* 19.

20. Revel and Munoz, *Redding,* 49.

21. Revel and Munoz, *Redding,* 27.

22. Revel and Munoz, *Redding,* 38–39.

23. Revel and Munoz, *Redding,* 40.

24. Revel and Munoz, *Redding,* 40.

25. Revel and Munoz, *Redding,* 40.

26. Holway, "The Cannonball."

27. Revel and Munoz, *Redding,* 41.

28. Holway, *Blackball Stars,* 87.

29. Revel and Munoz, *Redding,* 40.

30. McNeil, *Baseball's Other All-Stars,* 50.

31. Eric Chalek, "Evaluating More Negro Leagues Pitchers, Part 7," Hall of Miller and Eric, June 20, 2018, https://homemlb.wordpress.com/2018/06/20/evaluating-more-negro-leagues-pitchers-part-7.

32. Jim Overmyer, interview with the author, January 17, 2019.

33. Todd Bolton, interview with the author, January 19, 2019.

34. Brian Flaspohler, "John Donaldson," SABR Biography Project, https://sabr.org/node/51038.

35. Riley, *Biographical Encyclopedia,* 242.

36. Flaspohler, "John Donaldson."

37. Flaspohler, "John Donaldson."

38. Jacob Bielecki, "John Donaldson: The Unknown Ace, the Greatest Pitcher to Never Play in MLB," Bleacher Report, July 11, 2011, https://bleacherreport.com/articles/761791-john-donaldson-the-unknown-ace-the-greatest-pitcher-to-never-play-in-the-mlb.

39. Riley, *Biographical Encyclopedia,* 242.

40. Riley, *Biographical Encyclopedia,* 242.

41. Flaspohler, "John Donaldson."

42. Flaspohler, "John Donaldson."

43. John Klima, "John Donaldson: The Greatest Pitcher You've Never Heard Of," ThePostGame, March 27, 2011, http://www.thepostgame.com/features/201103/greatest-pitcher-youve-never-heard.

44. Flaspohler, "John Donaldson," note 15.

45. Flaspohler, "John Donaldson."

46. Flaspohler, "John Donaldson."

47. Flaspohler, "John Donaldson."

48. Flaspohler, "John Donaldson."

49. The John Donaldson Network Research Website, http://johndonaldson.bravehost.com/.

50. Flaspohler, "John Donaldson."

51. Flaspohler, "John Donaldson."

52. Holway, "What if Effa Manley Had Been an Ugly Man?"

53. Murray Chass, "A Special Election for Rediscovered Players," *New York Times,* February 26, 2006.

54. Irvin, *Few and Chosen,* 150.

55. Scott Simkus, "The Jimmy-John Situation," Outsider Baseball Bulletin 4, no. 1, January 2, 2013.

56. Riley, *Biographical Encyclopedia,* 242.

57. Simkus, "The Jimmy-John Situation."

58. O'Neil, *I Was Right,* 78.

59. Simkus, "The Jimmy-John Situation."

60. Jim Overmyer, interview with the author, January 17, 2019.

61. Steve Hoffbeck and Pete Gorton, "John Donaldson and Black Baseball in Minnesota," *The National Pastime* (2012), 117–122.

62. The John Donaldson Network Research Website.

63. "Courier 'Experts,'" *Pittsburgh Courier,* 14.

64. J. Fred Brillhart, "An Analysis of the 1952 Pittsburgh Courier Negro League Baseball Poll by Fredrico," The Donaldson Network, 9, http://johndonaldson.bravehost.com/pdf/00237.pdf.

65. Chass, "A Special Election."

66. John Holway, "The Original Baltimore Byrd," *Baseball Research Journal* 19 (1990), 26.

67. Riley, *Biographical Encyclopedia,* 140.

68. Holway, *Black Giants,* 160.

69. Holway, "The Original Baltimore Byrd," 23.

70. Holway, "The Original Baltimore Byrd," 23.

71. Holway, *Black Giants,* 161.

72. Riley, *Of Monarchs,* 168.

73. Holway, *Black Giants,* 165.

74. Holway, "The Original Baltimore Byrd," 26.

75. Holway, *Black Giants,* 164, 171.

76. Holway, "The Original Baltimore Byrd," 27.

77. Holway, "The Original Baltimore Byrd," 24.

78. Holway, *Black Giants*, 172.

79. Holway, *Black Giants*, 164.

80. Riley, *Of Monarchs*, 167.

81. Holway, "The Original Baltimore Byrd, "23.

82. John Holway once quipped that Byrd would probably be in the Hall of Fame if he had uttered Satchel Paige's "Don't look back. Something may be gaining on you." Holway, "The Original Baltimore Byrd," 23.

83. No mischief or malfeasance is ascribed to Monte Irvin. It appears that, in an era before statistics and solid history existed, Monte Irvin simply voted for the players he knew best, his teammates.

84. Holway, *Black Giants*, 161.

85. Riley, *Of Monarchs*, 165.

86. Phil Dixon, *The Dizzy and Daffy Dean Barnstorming Tour: Race, Media, and America's National Pastime* (Lanham, MD: Rowman & Littlefield, 2019), 84–85.

87. See Dr. Layton Revel and Luis Munoz, *Forgotten Heroes: Chet Brewer* (Carrollton, TX: Center for Negro League Baseball Research, 2014), 53–55.

88. Revel and Munoz, *Chet Brewer*, 51.

89. John B. Holway, *Black Diamonds: Life in the Negro Leagues from the Men Who Lived It* (Westport, CT: Meckler Books, 1989), 20.

90. Sayama and Staple, *Gentle Black Giants*, 346.

91. Riley, *Biographical Encyclopedia*, 105.

92. Holway, *Black Diamonds*, 18.

93. Revel and Munoz, *Chet Brewer*, 63.

94. Revel and Munoz, *Chet Brewer*, 51.

95. Revel and Munoz, *Chet Brewer*, 65.

96. Revel and Munoz, *Chet Brewer*, 9.

97. Revel and Munoz, *Chet Brewer*, 10.

98. Holway, *Black Diamonds*, 19.

99. Dixon, *Dizzy and Daffy Dean Barnstorming Tour*, 86.

100. Revel and Munoz, *Chet Brewer*, 50.

101. Revel and Munoz, *Chet Brewer*, 22.

102. Revel and Munoz, Chet Brewer, 57.

103. Holway, *Black Diamonds*, 19.

104. Revel and Munoz, *Chet Brewer*, 50.

105. Revel and Munoz, *Chet Brewer*, 51.

106. Holway, *Black Diamonds*, 19.

107. Revel and Munoz, *Chet Brewer*, 65.

108. Although not listed on the 1948 roster, Revel has uncovered a photo showing him in his team uniform in the team photo. See Revel and Munoz, *Brewer*, 56.

109. Sayama and Staple, *Gentle Black Giants*, 346.

110. Sayama and Staple, *Gentle Black Giants*, 346.

111. Sayama and Staple, *Gentle Black Giants*, 346.

112. Dr. Layton Revel and Luis Munoz, *Forgotten Heroes: William Bell* (Carrollton, TX: Center for Negro League Baseball Research, 2014), 26.

113. Revel and Munoz, William Bell, 1.

114. Riley, *Biographical Encyclopedia*, 75

115. Revel and Munoz, *William Bell*, 3.

116. Revel and Munoz, *William Bell*, 1.

117. Revel and Munoz, *William Bell*, 15.

118. Revel and Munoz, *William Bell*, 15.

119. Revel and Munoz, *William Bell*, 30.

120. Todd Bolton, interview with the author, January 19, 2019.

121. Brian McKenna, "George Stovey," SABR Biography Project, https://sabr.org/bioproj/person/8ff10f5c.

122. McKenna, "George Stovey."

123. McKenna, "George Stovey."

124. Lou Hunsinger, Jr., "George W. Stovey," *The National Pastime* 14 (1994), 81.

125. McKenna, "George Stovey."

126. McKenna, "George Stovey."

127. McKenna, "George Stovey."

128. Hunsinger, *Stovey*, 81.

129. Hunsinger, *Stovey*, 81.

130. Riley, *Biographical Encyclopedia*, 747.

131. Hunsinger, *Stovey*, 81–82.

132. McNeil, *Baseball's Other All-Stars*, 11.

133. Dr. Layton Revel and Luis Munoz, *Forgotten Heroes: Jesse "Nip" Winters* (Carrollton, TX: Center for Negro League Baseball Research, 2014), 28.

134. Revel and Munoz, *Nip Winters*, 37.

135. Riley, *Biographical Encyclopedia*, 877.

136. Riley, *Biographical Encyclopedia*, 877.

137. Revel and Munoz, *Nip Winters*, 25.

138. Revel and Munoz, *Nip Winters*, 29.

139. Revel and Munoz, *Nip Winters*, 25.

140. McNeil, *Cool Papas*, 82.

141. Riley, *Biographical Encyclopedia*, 236.

142. Holway, *Complete Book*, 103.

143. Riley, *Biographical Encyclopedia*, 237.

144. O'Neil, *Right on Time*, 188–189.

145. Eric Chalek, "Evaluating More Negro Leagues Pitchers, Part 6," The Hall of Miller and Eric, May 23, 2018, https://homemlb.wordpress.com/2018/05/23/evaluating-more-negro-leagues-pitchers-part-6/.

146. See Riley, *Biographical Encyclopedia*, 594–595.

147. Kevin Johnson, "The Greatest Pre-1920's Blackball Players," *Outsider Bulletin* 3, no. 42 (October 2012).

148. Chalek, "Evaluating More Negro Leagues Pitchers, Part 6."

149. *Pittsburgh Courier*, April 3, 1943, 18.

150. Riley, *Biographical Encyclopedia*, 614

151. Riley, *Biographical Encyclopedia*, 614.

152. "CUBANS IN SPORTS: 'Papá Montero,' 'The Black Diamond' and the Forgotten 'Bombín' Pedroso," TheCubanHistory.com, April 30, 2018, http://www.thecubanhistory.com/2018/04/cubans-in-sports-papa-montero-the-black-diamond-and-the-forgotten-bombin-pedroso-cubanos-en-deportes-papa-montero-el-diamante-negro-y-el-olvidado-bombin-pedroso/.

153. Riley, *Biographical Encyclopedia*, 614.

154. Riley, *Biographical Encyclopedia*, 61.

155. Holway, *Black Diamonds*, 139.

156. Riley, *Biographical Encyclopedia*, 61.

157. Holway, *Black Diamonds*, 131.

158. James A. Riley, "Dave Barnhill," *Baseball Research Journal* 10 (1981), http://research.sabr.org/journals/dave-barnhill.

159. Riley, "Dave Barnhill."

160. Riley, *Biographical Encyclopedia*, 62.
161. McNeil, *Cool Papas*, 191.
162. Riley, "Dave Barnhill."
163. Holway, *Voices,* 324.
164. Mike Schell, "The Legend of Cannonball Jackman," The Cannonball Foundation, http://thecannonballfoundation.org/legend-cannonball-jackman.
165. Dick Thompson, "Cannonball Bill Jackman: Baseball's Great Unknown," *The National Pastime* 27 (2007), 43.
166. Riley, *Biographical Encyclopedia*, 411.
167. *Lowell Sun*, July 22, 1932.
168. Thompson, "Cannonball Bill Jackman," 44.
169. Thompson, "Cannonball Bill Jackman," 43.
170. Riley, *Biographical Encyclopedia*, 411.
171. Schell, "The Legend of Cannonball Jackman."
172. Thompson, "Cannonball Bill Jackman," 48–49.
173. Thompson, "Cannonball Bill Jackman," 50.
174. Kevin Larkin, "The Cream of the Crop: Negro Leagues 100 Best Players (#30–21)," January 4, 2018, http://legendsondeck.com/cream-crop-negro-leagues-100-best-players-30-21/.
175. Gary Ashwill, "R.I.P. Dick Thompson," Agate Type, January 11, 2008, https://agatetype.typepad.com/agate_type/2008/01/rip-dick-thomps.html.
176. Thompson, "Cannonball Bill Jackman," 45.
177. *Boston Globe*, July 13, 1971.
178. Peterson, *Only the Ball Was White*, 218–219.
179. Thompson, "Cannonball Bill Jackman," 52–53.
180. Riley, *Biographical Encyclopedia*, 451.
181. Riley, *Biographical Encyclopedia*, 451.
182. Riley, *Biographical Encyclopedia*, 451.
183. Riley, *Of Monarchs*, 116.
184. Nicholas Acocella and Donald Dewey, *The Greatest Team of All Time: As Selected by Baseball's Immortals* (Holbrook, Mass: Bob Adams, Inc., 1994), 66.
185. Riley, *Biographical Encyclopedia*, 451.
186. Phil Dixon, *The Dizzy and Daffy Dean Barnstorming Tour: Race, Media, and America's National Pastime* (Lanham, MD: Rowman & Littlefield, 2019), 42.
187. Acocella and Dewey, *Greatest Team*, 11.
188. Riley, *Biographical Encyclopedia*, 790.
189. Riley, *Biographical Encyclopedia*, 182.
190. Dr. Layton Revel and Luis Munoz, *Forgotten Heroes: Webster McDonald* (Carrollton, TX: Center for Negro League Baseball Research, 2014), 1.
191. Riley, *Biographical Encyclopedia*, 534.
192. Phil Dixon, *Phil Dixon's American Baseball Chronicles: The 1905 Philadelphia Giants* (Charleston, SC: BookSurge, 2006), 152, 159–160.
193. *Philadelphia Item*, October 14, 1906.
194. Phil Williams, "Dan McClellan," SABR Biography Project, https://sabr.org/node/49150.
195. Williams, "Dan McClellan."
196. Mitch Lutzke, *The Page Fence Giants: A History of Black Baseball's Pioneering Champions* (Jefferson, NC: McFarland, 2018), 9.
197. Holway, *Complete Book*, 32.
198. Lutzke, *Page Fence Giants*, 239–40.
199. Lutzke, *Page Fence Giants*, 238.
200. Riley, *Biographical Encyclopedia*, 118.
201. Stephen V. Rice, "Frank Wickware," SABR Biography Project, https://sabr.org/bioproj/person/200cf3c2.
202. Frank M. Keetz, The Mohawk Colored Giants of Schenectady (Schenectady, NY: self-published, 1999), 7.
203. Riley, *Biographical Encyclopedia*, 839.
204. Rice, "Frank Wickware."
205. Riley, Biographical Encyclopedia, 839–840.
206. Riley, *Biographical Encyclopedia*, 839.
207. *Pittsburgh Courier*, April 3, 1926.
208. Riley, *Biographical Encyclopedia*, 47.
209. Terry Bohn, "Walter Ball," SABR Biography Project, https://sabr.org/node/29370.
210. Bohn, "Walter Ball."
211. Bohn, "Walter Ball."
212. Bohn, "Walter Ball."
213. Riley, *Biographical Encyclopedia*, 118.
214. Riley, *Biographical Encyclopedia*, 829.
215. Riley, *Biographical Encyclopedia*, 220.
216. Lee D. Jenkins, "Late Sam Streator [*sic*] tops Young's list…Unknown Rated Over Paige." *Daily Defender*. johndonaldson.bravehost.com/bv.html.

Chapter 16

1. Gadfly, "You asked me to weigh in on Bullet Rogan," Baseball Think Factory Hall of Merit (John Beckwith, post 28), November 27, 2004, http://www.baseballthinkfactory.org/hall_of_merit/discussion/john_beckwith.
2. Lawrence and Denaro, *ECL*, 54.
3. Buck O'Neil on John Beckwith: "Never heard of him, have you? He was another great slugger like Mule Suttles. He was mean as a snake too, but that don't mean nothing. Some of the greatest sluggers ever were mean." Posnanski, *The Soul of Baseball*, 165.
4. Dr. Layton Revel and Luis Munoz, *Forgotten Heroes: John Beckwith* (Carrollton, TX: Center for Negro League Baseball Research, 2014), 1.
5. John B. Holway, "More Negro Leaguers for the Hall," *The National Pastime* 15 (1995), 94.
6. Revel and Munoz, *Beckwith*, 21.
7. Revel and Munoz, *Beckwith*, 21.
8. John Holway, "The Black Bomber Named Beckwith," *Baseball Research Journal* 5 (1976), 100.
9. Riley, *Biographical Encyclopedia*, 69.
10. Revel and Munoz, *Beckwith*, 19.
11. Revel and Munoz, *Beckwith*, 16.
12. Holway, *Complete Book*, 472.
13. Revel and Munoz, *Beckwith*, 33.
14. *Indiana Evening Gazette*, October 12, 1928.
15. Revel and Munoz, *Beckwith*, 31.
16. Revel and Munoz, *Beckwith*, 21.
17. James, *New Historical Baseball Abstract*, 185.
18. Revel and Munoz, *Beckwith*, 19.
19. Revel and Munoz, *Beckwith*, 21.
20. Riley, *Biographical Encyclopedia*, 70.
21. Riley, *Biographical Encyclopedia*, 70.

22. Revel and Munoz, *Beckwith*, 25.

23. John Holway, "The Black Bomber Named Beckwith," *Baseball Research Journal* 5 (1976), 100.

24. Revel and Munoz, *Beckwith*, 1.

25. Gadfly, "Notes on John Beckwith," Baseball Think Factory Hall of Merit (John Beckwith, post 20), November 25, 2004, http://www.baseballthinkfactory.org/hall_of_merit/discussion/john_beckwith.

26. Revel and Munoz, *Beckwith*, 33.

27. *Pittsburgh Courier*, June 21, 1924.

28. Revel and Munoz, *Beckwith*, 6.

29. Gadfly, "Notes on John Beckwith."

30. See Lester, *Black Baseball's National Showcase*, 479.

31. Revel and Munoz, *Beckwith*, 25.

32. Revel and Munoz, *Beckwith*, 23.

33. Dr. Chaleeko, "Lastly, the Player Synopses, Heavily Revised."

34. Holway, *Black Giants*, xvii.

35. Monte Irvin, *Few and Chosen: Defining Negro Leagues Greatness* (Chicago: Triumph Books, 2007), 60.

36. Gary Gillette and Pete Palmer, eds., *The 2006 ESPN Baseball Encyclopedia* (New York: Sterling, 2006), 1642.

37. Revel and Munoz, *Beckwith*, 25.

38. "Transcript of Negro Leagues."

39. Jim Overmyer, interview with the author, January 17, 2019.

40. Todd Bolton, interview with the author, January 19, 2019.

41. Riley, *Biographical Encyclopedia*, 561.

42. Riley, *Biographical Encyclopedia*, 561.

43. Riley, *Biographical Encyclopedia*, 560..

44. Holway, *Complete Book*, 36.

45. "Bill Monroe," Baseball Reference, https://www.baseball-reference.com/register/player.fcgi?id=monroe000bil.

46. Phil Williams, "Bill Monroe," SABR Biography Project, https://sabr.org/node/50855.

47. Riley, *Biographical Encyclopedia*, 560.

48. Riley, *Biographical Encyclopedia*, 560–1.

49. Williams, "Bill Monroe."

50. Phil S. Dixon, *Phil Dixon's American Baseball Chronicles: Great Teams: The 1905 Philadelphia Giants Volume Three* (Charleston, SC: BookSurge, 2006), 2.

51. Williams, "Bill Monroe."

52. Williams, "Bill Monroe."

53. "The Base Ball Spirit in the East," *Indianapolis Freeman*, December 25, 1909, 7, http://negroleagues.bravehost.com/pdf/001968.pdf.

54. Riley, *Biographical Encyclopedia*, 561.

55. McNeil, *Baseball's Other All-Stars*, 53.

56. "Will S. Monroe Famous Ball Player Dies at Chattanooga," *Chicago Defender*, March 20, 1915, https://agatetype.typepad.com/agate_type/2007/05/bill_monroe.html.

57. "Caught on the Fly," *The Sporting News*, April 8, 1915, 4.

58. "Recruit Pitchers Beat Black Team," *The Morning Oregonian*, March 22, 1915, 10.

59. Burniswright, "No one has, thus far, mentioned the following anecdotal component of the argument for Monroe," Baseball Think Factory Hall of Merit (Bill Monroe post 49), December 7, 2007, http://www.baseballthinkfactory.org/hall_of_merit/discussion/bill_monroe.

60. W. Rollo Wilson, "Sports Shots," *Pittsburgh Courier*, April 11, 1931.

61. Sol White, "Sol White's Column of Baseball Dope," *Cleveland Advocate*, March 22, 1919.

62. "Candy Jim Taylor Reminisces," Baseball History Daily, January 24, 2019, https://baseballhistorydaily.com/2019/01/24/candy-jim-taylor-reminisces/?fbclid=IwAR0owLzt7pyyOfXZV_GR9lWvcSZAOFpxLpBaXDeUo-DCWlzX4Iu2kPeXUGQ.

63. McNeil, *Baseball's Other All-Stars*, 53.

64. Riley, *Biographical Encyclopedia*, 131.

65. Riley, *Biographical Encyclopedia*, 151.

66. Dixon, *Dizzy and Daffy Dean*, 134.

67. Riley, *Biographical Encyclopedia*, 151.

68. "Rev Cannady," Baseball Reference, http://www.baseball-reference.com/bullpen/Rev_Cannady.

69. "Rev Cannady," Baseball Reference, http://www.baseball-reference.com/bullpen/Rev_Cannady.

70. Riley, *Biographical Encyclopedia*, 151.

71. "Rev Cannady," Baseball Reference, http://www.baseball-reference.com/bullpen/Rev_Cannady.

72. Michael E. Lomax, *Black Baseball Entrepreneurs: 1902–1931* (Syracuse, NY: Syracuse University Press, 2014), 352.

73. Riley, *Biographical Encyclopedia*, 151.

74. Riley, *Biographical Encyclopedia*, 151.

75. "Rev Cannady," Baseball Reference, http://www.baseball-reference.com/bullpen/Rev_Cannady.

76. Dr. Layton Revel and Luis Munoz, *Forgotten Heroes: Samuel "Sam" Bankhead* (Carrollton, TX: Center for Negro League Baseball Research, 2011), 1.

77. Dave Wilkie, "Sam Bankhead," SABR Biography Project, https://sabr.org/node/38084.

78. Larry Lester, *Black Baseball's National Showcase* (Lincoln, University of Nebraska Press, 2001), 88.

79. Revel and Munoz, *Bankhead*, 11.

80. Revel and Munoz, *Bankhead*, 30.

81. Revel and Munoz, *Bankhead*, 41.

82. McNeil, *Cool Papas*, 199.

83. See, Richard "Pete" Peterson, Why Isn't Sam Bankhead in the Baseball Hall of Fame, 2018 *The National Pastime*, SABR.

84. James, *New Historical Baseball Abstract*, 187.

85. Richard "Pete" Peterson, Why Isn't Sam Bankhead in the Baseball Hall of Fame, 2018 *The National Pastime*, SABR.

86. Dave Wilkie, "Sam Bankhead."

87. Holway, *Black Giants*, 96–97.

88. McNeil, *Cool Papas,132.*

89. Riley, *Biographical Encyclopedia*, 649.

90. John Holway, *Voices from the Great Black Baseball Leagues* (Mineola, NY: Dover Publications, 2010), 172.

91. Kyle McNary, *Ted "Double Duty" Radcliffe: 36 Years of Pitching & Catching in the Negro Leagues* (Minneapolis: McNary Pub., 1994).

92. McNeil, *Cool Papas*, 133.
93. Riley, *Biographical Encyclopedia*, 649.
94. Holway, *Voices*, 185.
95. Holway, *Voices,* 169–70.
96. McNeil, *Baseball's Other All Stars*, 90.
97. McNeil, *Cool Papas*, 162.
98. Riley, *Biographical Encyclopedia*, 650.

Chapter 17

1. Dr. Layton Revel and Luis Munoz, *Forgotten Heroes: Charles Isham "C.I." Taylor* (Carrollton, TX: Center for Negro League Baseball Research, 2016), 1.
2. Revel and Munoz, *"C.I." Taylor*, 3.
3. Revel and Munoz, *"C.I." Taylor*, 5.
4. Revel and Munoz, *"C.I." Taylor*, 5.
5. Revel and Munoz, *"C.I." Taylor*, 12.
6. Revel and Munoz, *"C.I." Taylor*, 17–18.
7. Revel and Munoz, *"C.I." Taylor*, 19.
8. Revel and Munoz, *"C.I." Taylor*, 22.
9. Revel and Munoz, *"C.I." Taylor*, 23–24.
10. Revel and Munoz, *"C.I." Taylor*, 27.
11. Revel and Munoz, *"C.I." Taylor*, 32.
12. Revel and Munoz, *"C.I." Taylor*, 33.
13. Revel and Munoz, *"C.I." Taylor*, 33.
14. Irvin, *Few and Chosen*, 155.
15. Revel and Munoz, *"C.I." Taylor*, 33.
16. Revel and Munoz, *"C.I." Taylor*, 33.
17. Riley, *Biographical Encyclopedia*, 763.
18. Irvin, *Few and Chosen*, 157.
19. *The Pittsburgh Courier*, 3/12/1927.
20. Todd Bolton, interview with the author, January 19, 2019.
21. Bill Johnson, "Jim Taylor," SABR Biography Project, https://sabr.org/bioproj/person/2415ff22.
22. Dr. Layton Revel and Luis Munoz, *Forgotten Heroes: James Allen "Candy Jim" Taylor* (Carrollton, TX: Center for Negro League Baseball Research, 2013), 1.
23. Riley, *Biographical Encyclopedia*, 765.
24. Revel and Munoz, *"Candy Jim" Taylor*, 52.
25. Revel and Munoz, *"Candy Jim" Taylor*, 52.
26. Revel and Munoz, *"Candy Jim" Taylor*, 40.
27. Revel and Munoz, *"Candy Jim" Taylor*, 51.
28. Revel and Munoz, *"Candy Jim" Taylor*, 43.
29. Revel and Munoz, *"Candy Jim" Taylor*, 42.
30. Irvin, *Few and Chosen*, 158.
31. Riley, *Biographical Encyclopedia*, 766.
32. Revel and Munoz, *"Candy Jim" Taylor*, 37.
33. Revel and Munoz, *"Candy Jim" Taylor*, 37.
34. Johnson, "Jim Taylor."
35. Dr. Layton Revel and Luis Munoz, *Forgotten Heroes: David "Gentleman Dave" Malarcher* (Carrollton, TX: Center for Negro League Baseball Research, 2014), 1.
36. Holway, *Voices*, 47.
37. Revel and Munoz, *Malarcher*, 1.
38. Revel and Munoz, *Malarcher*, 2.
39. Revel and Munoz, *Malarcher*, 2.
40. Revel and Munoz, *Malarcher*, 34.
41. Revel and Munoz, *Malarcher,* 30–31.
42. Dr. Layton Revel and Luis Munoz, Forgotten Heroes: Elander Victor "Vic" Harris (Carrollton, TX: Center for Negro League Baseball Research, 2011), 33.
43. Dixon Dizzy p. 202.
44. Revel and Munoz, *"Vic Harris,* 19.
45. Riley, *Biographical Encyclopedia*, 360.
46. Charlie Fouche, "Vic Harris," SABR Biography Project, https://sabr.org/node/38098.
47. Revel and Munoz, *Vic Harris*, 1.
48. McNeil, *Cool Papas*.
49. McNeil, *Cool Papas*.
50. Holway, *Black Giants*, 102.
51. Revel and Munoz, *Vic Harris*, 11.
52. Holway, *Black Giants*, 106.

Chapter 18

1. Riley, *Biographical Encyclopedia*, 634.
2. Riley, *Biographical Encyclopedia*, 509.
3. See Neil Lanctot, *Negro League Baseball: The Rise and Ruin of a Black Institution* (Philadelphia: University of Pennsylvania Press, 2004).
4. "Transcript of Negro Leagues."
5. Rob Ruck, *Sandlot Seasons* (Chicago: University of Illinois Press, 1987),142.
6. Ruck, *Sandlot*, 142.
7. Ruck, *Sandlot*, 144.
8. Brian McKenna, "Gus Greenlee," SABR Biography Project, https://sabr.org/bioproj/person/fabd8400.
9. Holway, *Blackball Stars*, 308.
10. Ruck, *Sandlot*, 145.
11. Ruck, *Sandlot*, 152–53.
12. Ruck, *Sandlot*, 157.
13. McKenna, "Gus Greenlee."
14. Roberta J. Newman and Joel Nathan Rosen, *Black Baseball, Black Business: Race Enterprise and the Fate of the Segregated Dollar* (Jackson: University Press of Mississippi, 2014), 68.
15. Newman and Rosen, *Black Baseball*, 68.
16. Lester, *Black Baseball's National Showcase*, 14.
17. Ruck, Sandlot, 157.
18. Ruck, *Sandlot*, 145.
19. Holway, *Blackball Stars*, 312.
20. Holway, *Blackball Stars*, 312.
21. Goldman, "Business Meetings," 395.
22. Ruck, *Sandlo*t, 23.
23. Lester, *Black Baseball's National Showcase*,155.
24. Dixon, *Dizzy and Daffy Dean*, 174.
25. See Rob Neyer and Eddie Epstein, *Baseball Dynasties: The Greatest Teams of All Time* (New York: Norton, 2000), 227–228; Kevin Johnson, *Bakers's Dozen: The Greatest Negro League Teams of All-Time, Outsider's Baseball Bulletin* Vol. 3, Issue 37 (#119) 9/12/12.
26. Ruck, *Sandlot*, 157.
27. Ruck, *Sandlot*, 158.
28. Ruck, *Sandlot,* 164.
29. Holway, *Blackball Stars*, 308–309.
30. Irvin, *Few and Chosen*, 174.
31. Lester, *Black Baseball's National Showcase*, 12–13.

32. Ruck, Sandlot, 150.
33. McKenna, "Gus Greenlee."
34. McKenna, "Gus Greenlee."
35. McKenna, "Gus Greenlee."
36. McKenna, "Gus Greenlee."
37. Irvin, *Few and Chosen*, 174.
38. Irvin, *Few and Chosen*, 169.
39. Lester, *Black Baseball's National Showcase*, 9.
40. Dr. Layton Revel and Luis Munoz, *Forgotten Heroes: Ed Bolden* (Carrollton, TX: Center for Negro League Baseball Research, 2015), 1.
41. Michael J. Haupert, "Ed Bolden: Black Baseball's Great Modernist," *Black Ball* 5, no. 2 (Fall 2012), 64.
42. Haupert, "Ed Bolden: Black Baseball's Great Modernist," 63–64.
43. Revel and Munoz, Bolden, 35–6.
44. Revel and Munoz, *Bolden*, 3.
45. Haupert, "Ed Bolden: Black Baseball's Great Modernist," 62.
46. Revel and Munoz, *Bolden*, 5.
47. Revel and Munoz, *Bolden*, 18.
48. Revel and Munoz, *Bolden*, 21.
49. Michael Haupert, "Ed Bolden," SABR Biography Project, https://sabr.org/bioproj/person/84ab-3bca.
50. Revel and Munoz, *Bolden*, 21.
51. Haupert, "Ed Bolden."
52. Haupert, "Ed Bolden."
53. Revel and Munoz, *Bolden*, 27.
54. Courtney Michelle Smith, *Ed Bolden and Black Baseball in Philadelphia* (Jefferson, NC: McFarland, 2017), 81.
55. Revel and Munoz, *Bolden*, 40.
56. Haupert, "Ed Bolden."
57. Smith, *Ed Bolden*, p. 153.
58. Lanctot, *Negro League Baseball*, 31.
59. Haupert, "Ed Bolden."
60. *The Pittsburgh Courier*, 3/12/1927.
61. Dr. Layton Revel and Luis Munoz, *Early Pioneers of the Negro Leagues: Frank C. Leland* (Carrollton, TX: Center for Negro League Baseball Research, 2016), 1.
62. Revel and Munoz, *Leland*, 3.
63. Revel and Munoz, *Leland*, 3.
64. Revel and Munoz, *Leland*, 7.
65. Revel and Munoz, *Leland*, 9.
66. Revel and Munoz, *Leland*, 11.
67. Revel and Munoz, *Leland*, 29
68. Revel and Munoz, *Leland*, 13–14.
69. Revel and Munoz, *Leland*, 17.
70. Revel and Munoz, *Leland*, 26.
71. Revel and Munoz, *Leland*, 26.
72. Revel and Munoz, *Leland*, 29.

Chapter 19

1. Peter Morris, "Bud Fowler's Lost Years," *Black Ball* 2, no. 2 (2009), 12–13.
2. Jeff Laing, "Bud Fowler's Coming of Age," *Black Ball* 4 (Fall 2011), 5.
3. The first black player may actually have been Williams Edward White, a mixed-race player who passed as white on his birth certificate and in life. He played one game for Providence Grays of the National League in in 1879. See Peter Morris and Stefan Fatsis, *Baseball's Secret Pioneer, Slate* 2/4/2014.
4. L. Robert Davids, "Bud Fowler, Black Baseball Star," *Road Trips* (Cleveland, OH: Society for American Baseball Research, 2004), 23.
5. Jeffrey Michael Laing, *Bud Fowler: Baseball's First Black Professional* (Jefferson, NC: McFarland, 2013), 69.
6. Davids, "Bud Fowler, Black Baseball Star," 23.
7. Brian McKenna, "Bud Fowler," SABR Biography Project, https://sabr.org/bioproj/person/200e2bbd.
8. Laing, *Bud Fowler*, 87.
9. McKenna, "Bud Fowler."
10. Marilynne Robinson, *Gilead* (New York: Farrar, Strauss & Giroux, 2004), 46.
11. Fowler was probably right-handed. See Riley, *Biographical Encyclopedia*, 294.
12. Davids, Road Trips p. 23.
13. Laing, *Bud Fowler*, 87.
14. Laing, "Bud Fowler's Coming of Age," 8–9.
15. McKenna, "Bud Fowler."
16. Davids, "Bud Fowler, Black Baseball Star," 24.
17. Laing, "Bud Fowler's Coming of Age," 9.
18. McKenna, "Bud Fowler."
19. See Laing, *Bud Fowler*, 101–116.
20. Laing, *Bud Fowler*, 117.
21. Davids, "Bud Fowler, Black Baseball Star," 24.
22. McKenna, "Bud Fowler."
23. McKenna, "Bud Fowler."
24. Lutzke, *Page Fence Giants*, 239.
25. Laing, *Bud Fowler*, 134.
26. Morris, "Bud Fowler's Lost Years," 14.
27. Morris, "Bud Fowler's Lost Years," 15.
28. Morris, "Bud Fowler's Lost Years," 20.
29. Laing book p. 181.
30. *Sporting News*, October 31, 1896, 4. Cited in Morris, "Bud Fowler's Lost Years," 12.
31. Brian McKenna, "Bud Fowler," SABR Biography Project, https://sabr.org/bioproj/person/200e2bbd.
32. Sol White, *Sol White's History of Colored Baseball with Other Documents on the Early Black Game, 1886–1936*, introduction by Jerry Malloy, reprint (Lincoln: University of Nebraska Press, 1995), 74.
33. Riley, *Biographical Encyclopedia*, 295.
34. Citing Leslie A. Heaphy, *The Negro Leagues: 1869–1960* (Jefferson, NC: McFarland, 2003), 18.
35. Jeffrey Michael Laing, *Bud Fowler: Baseball's First Black Professional* (Jefferson, NC: McFarland, 2013), 195.
36. O'Neil, *I Was Right*, 54–59.
37. O'Neil, *I Was Right*, 70–71.
38. Dr. Layton Revel and Luis Munoz, introduction to *Forgotten Heroes: John "Buck" O'Neil* (Carrollton, TX: Center for Negro League Baseball Research, 2013).
39. O'Neil, *I Was Right*, 119.
40. Revel and Munoz, *O'Neil*, 11.
41. Revel and Munoz, *O'Neil*, 12.
42. Revel and Munoz, *O'Neil*, 12.

43. Revel and Munoz, *O'Neil*, 14.
44. Revel and Munoz, *O'Neil,* 37.
45. James, *Historical Baseball Abstract*, 178.
46. Revel and Munoz, *O'Neil*, 27.
47. Revel and Munoz, *O'Neil,* 37.
48. Revel and Munoz, introduction to *O'Neil*.
49. Revel and Munoz, *O'Neil*, 20.
50. Revel and Munoz, *O'Neil*, 20.
51. Revel and Munoz, *O'Neil*, 20.
52. Tyler W. Evans, "Buck O'Neil: Kansas City's Best Friend," *Black Ball 9: New Research in African American Baseball History* (2017), 122.
53. James, *Historical Baseball Abstract*, 177.
54. Bob LeMoine, "Buck O'Neil," SABR Biography Project, https://sabr.org/bioproj/person/da2d63d5.
55. Evans, *"Buck O'Neil,"* 125.
56. Buck O'Neil, "Buck O'Neil—Baseball Hall of Fame Induction Ceremony Speech," 2006, https://www.youtube.com/watch?v=LtE2I6jsung.
57. Evans, *"Buck O'Neil,"* 124.
58. Lawrence D. Hogan, *Shades of Glory: The Negro Leagues and the Story of African-American Baseball* (Wash, D.C.: National Geographic, 2006), xxii.
59. Jim Overmyer, interview with the author, January 17, 2019.

Chapter 20

1. O'Neil, *I Was Right*, 151.
2. Jim Overmyer, interview with the author, January 17, 2019; Todd Bolton interview with the author January 19, 2019.
3. Jim Overmyer, interview with the author, January 17, 2019; Todd Bolton interview with the author January 19, 2019.
4. James, *Historical Abstract*, 359.
5. "Posnanski: Hall of Fame Is 'Tone Deaf,'" The Negro Leagues Up Close, June 20, 2018, https://homeplatedontmove.wordpress.com/2016/02/03/posnanski-hall-of-fame-is-tone-deaf/.
6. See David Pietrusza, *Judge and Jury: The Life and Times of Judge Kenesaw Mountain Landis* (South Bend, Ind: Diamond Communications, 1998), 412–415 and Monte Irvin with James A. Riley, *Nice Guys Finish First: The Autobiography of Monte Irvin* (New York: Carroll & Graf, 1996), 215–216.
7. William F. McNeil, *The California Winter League* (Jefferson, NC: McFarland, 2001), 237.
8. Holway, *Voices*, 310.
9. Peterson, "The Case for the Negro Leagues," 32.

Chapter 21

1. Covitz, "Did Feud Sabotage."
2. Ryan Whirty, "HOF: No More Negro Leaguers, and No Changes to Policy," The Negro Leagues Up Close, January 14, 2006, https://homeplatedontmove.wordpress.com/2016/01/14/hof-no-more-negro-leaguers-and-no-changes-to-policy/.
3. *The Sporting News*, January 26, 2016.
4. "Posnanski: Hall of Fame is 'tone deaf,'" The Negro Leagues Up Close, June 20, 2018, https://homeplatedontmove.wordpress.com/2016/02/03/posnanski-hall-of-fame-is-tone-deaf/.
5. John Tuberty, "Seven Changes That Would Improve the Era Committee Hall of Fame Election Process," Tubbs Baseball Blog, July 6, 2016, http://tubbsbaseballblog.blogspot.com/2016/07/seven-changes-that-would-improve-era_6.html.
6. "Hall of Fame Makes Series of Announcements," National Baseball Hall of Fame, July 23, 2016, https://baseballhall.org/discover-more/news/hall-of-fame-announcements.
7. "Hall of Fame Makes Series of Announcements."
8. "Hall of Fame Makes Series of Announcements."
9. "Eras Committees," National Baseball Hall of Fame, https://baseballhall.org/hall-of-famers/rules/eras-committees.
10. Graham Womack, "Hall of Fame president Jeff Idelson: 'We're very comfortable with the process of election,'" *Sporting News*, January 26, 2016, http://www.sportingnews.com/us/mlb/news/baseball-hall-of-fame-president-jeff-idelson-election-process-pete-rose-buck-oneil/ljnb9g3yv6g11o85iu26nj75.
11. Jim Overmyer, interview with the author, January 17, 2019; Todd Bolton interview with the author January 19, 2019.
12. Mark Ribowsky, *A Complete History of the Negro Leagues: 1884 to 1955* (New York, NY: Birch Lane Press, 1995), 319.

Bibliography

Acocella, Nicholas, and Donald Dewey. *The Greatest Team of All Time: As Selected by Baseball's Immortals.* Holbrook, Mass: Bob Adams, 1994.

Aiello, Thomas. *The Kings of Casino Park: Black Baseball in the Lost Season of 1932.* Tuscaloosa: University of Alabama Press, 2011.

Aleshire, William A. *Sandlot: Soul of Baseball."* Westminster, MD: Heritage, 2005.

Bak, Richard. *Turkey Stearnes and the Detroit Stars.* Detroit: Wayne State University Press, 1994.

Bankes, James. *The Pittsburgh Crawfords: The Lives and Times of Black Baseball's Most Exciting Team!* Dubuque, IL: William Brown Publishers, 1991.

Beer, Jeremy. *Oscar Charleston: The Life and Legend of Baseball's Greatest Forgotten Player.* Lincoln: University of Nebraska Press, 2019.

Bjarkman, Peter C. *A History of Cuban Baseball, 1864–2006.* Jefferson, NC: McFarland, 2007.

Black, Joe. *Ain't Nobody Better Than You.* Scottsdale, AZ: Ironwood Lithographers, 1983.

Bruce, Janet. *The Kansas City Monarchs: Champions of Black Baseball.* Lawrence: University Press of Kansas, 1985.

Burgos, Adrian, Jr. *Playing America's Game: Baseball, Latinos, and the Color Line.* Los Angeles: University of California Press, 2007.

Carroll, Brian. *When to Stop the Cheering? The Black Press, the Black Community, and the Integration of Professional Baseball.* New York: Routledge, 2007.

Chadwick, Bruce. *When the Game Was Black and White: The Illustrated History of Baseball's Negro Leagues.* New York: Abbeville, 1992.

Chiarello, Mark, and Morelli, Jack. *Heroes of the Negro Leagues.* New York, Abrams, 2007.

Clark, Dick, and Larry Lester, eds. *The Negro Leagues Book.* Cleveland: Society for American Baseball Research, 1994.

Cottrell, Robert. *The Best Pitcher in Baseball: The Life of Rube Foster, Negro League Giant.* New York, NYU Press, 2001.

Debono, Paul. *The Chicago American Giants.* Jefferson, NC: McFarland, 2007.

_____. *The Indianapolis ABCs.* Jefferson, NC: McFarland, 1997.

Dixon, Phil S. *The Dizzy and Daffy Dean Barnstorming Tour: Race, Media, and America's National Pastime.* Lanham, MD: Rowman & Littlefield, 2019.

_____. *John "Buck" O'Neil: The Rookie, the Man, the Legacy 1938.* Bloomington, IN: Author House, 2009.

_____. *The Monarchs, 1920–1938: Featuring Wilber "Bullet" Rogan.* Sioux Falls, SD: Mariah, 2002.

_____. *Phil Dixon's American Baseball Chronicles, Volume 1: Great Teams, the 1931 Homestead Grays.* Xlibris, 2009.

_____. *Wilber "Bullet" Rogan and the Kansas City Monarchs.* Jefferson, NC: McFarland, 2010.

Dixon, Phil S., with Patrick J Hannigan. *The Negro Baseball Leagues: A Photographic History.* Mattituck, NY: Amereon, 1992.

Echevarria, Roberto Gonzalez. *The Pride of Havana: A History of Cuban Baseball.* New York: Oxford University Press, 1999.

Essington, Amy. *The Integration of the Pacific Coast League: Race and Baseball on the West Coast.* Lincoln: University of Nebraska Press, 2018.

Etkin, Jack. *Innings Ago (Recollections by Kansas City Ballplayers).* Kansas City, MO: Normandy Square Publications, 1987.

Figueredo, Jorge S. *Cuban Baseball: A Statistical History, 1878–1961.* Jefferson, NC: McFarland, 2003.

_____. *Who's Who in Cuban Baseball, 1878–1961.* Jefferson, NC: McFarland, 2003.

Fullerton, Christopher D. *Every Other Sunday.* Birmingham, AL: R. Boozer, 1999.

Garry, Philip, III. *Negro League Baseball Collectibles Guide.* Self-Published, 2013.

Gillette, Gary, and Palmer, Pete, ed. *The 2006 ESPN Baseball Encyclopedia.* New York: Sterling, 2006.

Goldman, Duke. "The Business Meetings of Negro League Baseball: 1933–1962." In *Baseball's Business: The Winter Meetings Volume 2: 1958–2016.* Steve Weingarden and Bill Nowlin, eds.

Phoenix: Society for American Baseball Research, 2017.

Hardwick, Leon Herbert. *Blacks in Baseball*. Los Angeles: Pilot Press, 1980.

Hauser, Christopher. *The Negro Leagues Chronology: Events in Organized Black Baseball, 1920–1948*. Jefferson, NC: McFarland, 2006.

Heaphy, Leslie A., ed. *Black Baseball and Chicago: Essays on the Players, Teams and Games of the Negro Leagues' Most Important City*. Jefferson, NC: McFarland, 2006.

_____. *The Negro Leagues, 1869–1960*. Jefferson, NC: McFarland, 2003.

_____, ed. *Satchel Paige and Company: Essays on the Kansas City Monarchs, Their Greatest Stars and Negro Leagues*. Jefferson, NC: McFarland, 2007.

Hogan, Lawrence D. *The Forgotten History of African American Baseball*. Santa Barbara, CA: Praeger, 2014.

_____ *Shades of Glory: The Negro Leagues and the Story of African-American Baseball*. Washington, D.C.: National Geographic Society, 2006.

Holway, John B. *Black Ball Tales*. Portland: Scorpio, 2008.

_____. *Black Diamonds: Life in the Negro Leagues from the Men Who Lived It*. Westport, CT: Mecklermedia, 1989.

_____. *Black Giants*. Bloomington, IN: Xlibris, 2009.

_____. *Blackball Stars: Negro League Pioneers*. Westport, CT: Mecklermedia, 1988.

_____. *The Complete Book of Baseball's Negro Leagues: The Other Half of Baseball History*. Fern Park, FL: Hastings House, 2001.

_____. *Smokey Joe and the Cannonball*. Washington, D.C.: Capitol Press, 1983.

_____. *Voices from the Great Black Baseball Leagues*. Revised edition. New York: Da Capo, 1992.

Irvin, Monte, with James A. Riley. *Nice Guys Finish First: The Autobiography of Monte Irvin*. New York: Carroll & Graf, 1996.

Irvin, Monte, with Phil Pepe. *Few and Chosen: Defining Negro Leagues Greatness*. Chicago: Triumph, 2007.

Jaffe, Jay. *The Cooperstown Casebook*. New York: St Martin's, 2017.

James, Bill. *The New Bill James Historical Baseball Abstract*. New York: Free Press, 2001.

_____. *The Politics of Glory: How Baseball's Hall of Fame Really Works*. New York: Macmillan, 1994.

Keating, Kevin, and Mike Kolleth. *The Negro Leagues Autograph Guide*. Dubuque, IA: Tuff Stuff, 1999.

Keetz, Frank M. *The Mohawk Colored Giants of Schenectady*. Schenectady, NY: Self Published 1998.

Kelley, Brent P. *"I Will Never Forget": Interviews with 39 Former Negro League Players*. Jefferson, NC: McFarland, 2003.

_____. *The Negro Leagues Revisited: Conversation with 66 More Baseball Heroes*. Jefferson, NC: McFarland, 2000.

_____. *Voices from the Negro Leagues: Conversation with 52 Baseball Standouts of the Period 1924–1960*. Jefferson, NC: McFarland, 1998.

Kirwin, Bill. *Out of the Shadows: African American Baseball from the Cuban Giants to Jackie Robinson*. Lincoln: University of Nebraska Press, 2005.

Lacy, Sam, with Moses J. Newton. *Fighting for Fairness: The Life Story of Hall of Fame Sportswriter Sam Lacy*. Centreville, MD: Tidewater Publishers, 1999.

Laing, Jeffrey Michael. *Bud Fowler: Baseball's First Black Professional*. Jefferson, NC: McFarland, 2013.

Lanctot, Neil. *Fair Dealing and Clean Playing: The Hilldale Club and the Development of Black Professional Baseball, 1910–1932*. Jefferson, NC: McFarland, 1994.

_____. *Negro League Baseball: The Rise and Ruin of a Black Institution*. Philadelphia: University of Pennsylvania Press, 2008.

Lawrence, David, and Dom Denaro. *The Eastern Colored League*. South San Francisco: A J Publishing, 2003.

Leonard, Buck, with James A. Riley. *Buck Leonard, the Black Lou Gehrig: An Autobiography*. New York: Carroll & Graf, 1995.

Lester, Larry. *Baseball's First Colored World Series: The 1924 Meeting of the Hilldale Giants and Kansas City Monarchs*. Jefferson, NC: McFarland, 2006.

_____. *Black Baseball in New York City: An Illustrated History, 1885–1959*. Jefferson, NC: McFarland, 2017.

_____. *Black Baseball's National Showcase: The East-West All-Star Game, 1933–1953*. Lincoln: University of Nebraska Press, 2001.

Lomax, Michael E. *Black Baseball Entrepreneurs, 1860–1901: Operating by Any Means Necessary*. Syracuse, NY: Syracuse University Press, 2003.

Loverro, Thom. *The Encyclopedia of Negro League Baseball*. New York: Checkmark, 2003.

Luke, Bob. *Willie Wells: "El Diablo" of the Negro Leagues*. Austin: University of Texas Press, 2007.

Lutzke, Mitch. *The Page Fence Giants*. Jefferson, NC: McFarland, 2018.

Manley, Effa, and Leon Herbert Hardwick. *Negro Baseball … Before Integration*. Chicago: Adams Press, 1976.

McDonald, Thomas. *An Irishman's Tribute to the Negro Leagues*, 2nd ed. Bloomington, Ind.: Author House, 2018.

McNary, Kyle. *Black Baseball: A History of African*

Americans and the National Game. New York: Sterling Pub, 2003.

_____. *Ted "Double Duty" Radcliffe: Years of Pitching & Catching in Baseball's Negro Leagues.* St. Louis Park, MN: McNary, 1994.

McNeil, William F. *Baseball's Other All-Stars: The Greatest Players from the Negro Leagues, the Japanese Leagues, the Mexican League, and the Pre-1960 Winter Leagues in Cuba, Puerto Rico, and the Dominican Republic.* Jefferson, NC: McFarland, 2000.

_____. *Black Baseball Out of Season: Pay for Play Outside of the Negro Leagues.* Jefferson, NC: McFarland, 2007.

_____. *The California Winter League: America's First Integrated Professional Baseball League.* Jefferson, NC: McFarland, 2002.

_____. *Cool Papas and Double Duties: The All-Time Greats of the Negro Leagues.* Jefferson, NC: McFarland, 2000.

_____. *The King of Swat: An Analysis of Baseball's Home Run Hitters from the Major, Minor, Negro and Japanese Leagues.* Jefferson, NC: McFarland, 1997.

Minoso, Orestes 'Minnie.' *Extra Innings: My Life in Baseball.* Chicago, Ill: Regnery Gateway, 1983.

Moore, Joseph. *Pride Against Prejudice: The Biography of Larry Doby.* New York: Praeger, 1988.

Newman, Roberta J., and Rosen, Joel Nathan. *Black Baseball Black Business.* Jackson: University Press of Mississippi, 2014.

O'Neil, Buck, with Steve Wulf and David Conrads. *I Was Right on Time.* New York: Simon & Schuster, 1996.

Overmyer, James E. *Black Ball and the Boardwalk: The Bacharach Giants of Atlantic City, 1916–1929.* Jefferson, NC: McFarland, 2014.

Paige, Satchel, as told to David Lipman. *Maybe I'll Pitch Forever.* Garden City, NY: Doubleday, 1961. Reprint by University of Nebraska, 1993.

Paige, Satchel, as told to Hal Lebowitz. *Pitchin' Man: Satchel Paige's Own Story.* Cleveland: Cleveland News, 1948.

Peterson, Robert. *Only the Ball Was White: A History of Legendary Black Players and All-Black Professional Teams.* Englewood Cliffs, NJ: Prentice-Hall, 1970.

Peterson, Todd. *Early Black Ball in Minnesota.* Jefferson, NC: McFarland, 2010.

_____. "May the Best Man Win: The Black Ball Championships 1866–1923." *The Baseball Research Journal* 42, no. 1 (Spring 2013): 7–24.

_____, ed. *The Negro Leagues Were Major Leagues: Historians Reappraise Black Baseball.* Jefferson, NC: McFarland, 2020.

Pietrusza, David. *Judge and Jury: The Life and Times of Judge Kenesaw Mountain Landis.* South Bend, Ind.: Diamond Communications, 1998).

Plott, William J. *Black Baseball's Last Team Standing: The Birmingham Black Barons, 1919–1962.* Jefferson, NC: McFarland, 2019.

_____. *The Negro Southern League: A Baseball History, 1920–1951.* Jefferson, NC: McFarland, 2015.

Pollock, Alan J., with James A. Riley, ed. *Barnstorming to Heaven: Syd Pollock and His Great Teams.* Tuscaloosa: University of Alabama Press, 2006.

Posnanski, Joe. *The Soul of Baseball: A Road Trip Through Buck O'Neil's America.* New York: William Morrow, 2007.

Powell, Larry. *Black Barons of Birmingham: The South's Greatest Negro League Team and Its Players.* Jefferson, NC: McFarland, 2009.

Reisler, Jim. *Black Writers / Black Baseball: An Anthology of Articles from Black Sportswriters Who Covered the Negro Leagues.* Jefferson, NC: McFarland, 1994.

Revel, Layton, and Luis Munoz. *Forgotten Heroes of the Negro Leagues and Latin Baseball.* Carrollton, TX: Center for Negro League Baseball Research, 2009.

_____, and _____. *Forgotten Heroes: Alejandro "El Caballero" Oms.* Carrollton, TX: Center for Negro League Baseball Research, 2008.

_____, and _____. *Forgotten Heroes: Alonzo Perry.* Carrollton, TX: Center for Negro League Baseball Research, 2009.

_____, and _____. *Forgotten Heroes: Artie Wilson.* Carrollton, TX: Center for Negro League Baseball Research, 2010.

_____, and _____. *Forgotten Heroes: Burnis "Wild Bill" Wright.* Carrollton, TX: Center for Negro League Baseball Research, 2008.

_____, and _____. *Forgotten Heroes: Charles "Chino" Smith.* Carrollton, TX: Center for Negro League Baseball Research, 2011.

_____, and _____. *Forgotten Heroes: Chet Brewer.* Carrollton, TX: Center for Negro League Baseball Research, 2014.

_____, and _____. *Forgotten Heroes: Clarence "Fats" Jenkins.* Carrollton, TX: Center for Negro League Baseball Research, 2011.

_____, and _____. *Forgotten Heroes: David "Gentleman Dave" Malarcher.* Carrollton, TX: Center for Negro League Baseball Research, 2014.

_____, and _____. *Forgotten Heroes: Ed Bolden.* Carrollton, TX: Center for Negro League Baseball Research, 2015.

_____, and _____. *Forgotten Heroes: Elander Victor "Vic" Harris.* Carrollton, TX: Center for Negro League Baseball Research, 2011.

_____, and _____. *Forgotten Heroes: Francisco "Pancho" Coimbre.* Carrollton, TX: Center for Negro League Baseball Research, 2009.

_____, and _____. *Forgotten Heroes: George "Tank" Carr.* Carrollton, TX: Center for Negro League Baseball Research, 2015.

_____, and _____. *Forgotten Heroes: Grant "Home*

Run" Johnson. Carrollton, TX: Center for Negro League Baseball Research, 2016.

_____, and _____. *Forgotten Heroes: Herbert "Rap" Dixon.* Carrollton, TX: Center for Negro League Baseball Research, 2012.

_____, and _____. *Forgotten Heroes: Hurley McNair.* Carrollton, TX: Center for Negro League Baseball Research, 2016.

_____, and _____. *Forgotten Heroes: John Beckwith.* Carrollton, TX: Center for Negro League Baseball Research, 2010.

_____, and _____. *Forgotten Heroes: John "Buck" O'Neil.* Carrollton, TX: Center for Negro League Baseball Research, 2013.

_____, and _____. *Forgotten Heroes: Lorenzo "Piper" Davis.* Carrollton, TX: Center for Negro League Baseball Research, 2010.

_____, and _____. *Forgotten Heroes: Newton "Newt" Allen.* Carrollton, TX: Center for Negro League Baseball Research, 2011.

_____, and _____. *Forgotten Heroes: Oliver "The Ghost" Marcelle.* Carrollton, TX: Center for Negro League Baseball Research, 2012.

_____, and _____. *Forgotten Heroes: Orestes Minoso.* Carrollton, TX: Center for Negro League Baseball Research, 2014.

_____, and _____. *Forgotten Heroes: Oscar "Heavy" Johnson.* Carrollton, TX: Center for Negro League Baseball Research, 2010.

_____, and _____. *Forgotten Heroes: Richard "Dick" Lundy.* Carrollton, TX: Center for Negro League Baseball Research, 2012.

_____, and _____. *Forgotten Heroes: Sammy T. Hughes.* Carrollton, TX: Center for Negro League Baseball Research, 2012.

_____, and _____. *Forgotten Heroes: Samuel "Sam" Bankhead.* Carrollton, TX: Center for Negro League Baseball Research, 2011.

_____, and _____. *Forgotten Heroes: Walter "Dobie" Moore.* Carrollton, TX: Center for Negro League Baseball Research, 2009.

_____, and _____. *Forgotten Heroes: Webster McDonald.* Carrollton, TX: Center for Negro League Baseball Research, 2014.

_____, and _____. *Forgotten Heroes: William Bell.* Carrollton, TX: Center for Negro League Baseball Research, 2014.

Ribowsky, Mark. *A Complete History of the Negro Leagues, 1884 to 1955.* New York: Birch Lane, 1995.

Riley, James A. *The All-Time All-Stars of Black Baseball.* Cocoa Beach, FL: TK Publishers, 1986.

_____. *The Biographical Encyclopedia of the Negro Baseball Leagues.* New York: Carroll & Graf, 1994.

_____. *Of Monarchs and Black Barons.* Jefferson, NC: McFarland, 2012.

Rogosin, Donn. *Invisible Men: Life in Baseball's Negro Leagues.* New York: Atheneum, 1983.

Ruck, Rob. *Sandlot Seasons: Sport in Black Pittsburgh.* Urbana: University of Illinois Press, 1987.

Sanford, Jay. *The Denver Post Tournament: A Chronicle of America's First Integrated Professional Baseball Event.* Cleveland: Society of American Baseball Research, 2003.

Sayama, Kazuo, and Bill Staples, Jr. *Gentle Black Giants: A History of Negro Leaguers in Japan.* Fresno, CA: Nisei Baseball Research Project Press, 2019.

Singletary, Wes. *The Right Time: John Henry "Pop" Lloyd and Black Baseball.* Jefferson, NC: McFarland, 2011.

Smith, Averell "Ace." *The Pitcher and the Dictator: Satchel Paige's Unlikely Season in the Dominican Republic.* Lincoln: University of Nebraska Press, 2018.

Smith, Courtney Michelle. *Ed Bolden and Black Baseball in Philadelphia.* Jefferson, NC: McFarland, 2017.

Snyder, Brad. *Beyond the Shadow of the Senators: The Untold Story of the Homestead Grays and the Integration of Baseball.* New York: McGraw-Hill, 2003.

Trouppe, Quincy. *20 Years Too Soon: Prelude to Major-League Integrated Baseball.* Los Angeles: Sands Enterprises, 1977. Reprint, St. Louis: Missouri Historical Society Press, 1995.

Tye, Larry. *Satchel: The Life and Times of an American Legend.* New York: Random House, 2009.

Tygiel, Jules. *Baseball's Great Experiment: Jackie Robinson and His Legacy.* New York: Oxford University Press, 1983.

Van Hyning, Thomas E. *Puerto Rico's Winter Leagues: A History of Major League Baseball's Launching Pad.* Jefferson, NC: McFarland, 1995.

_____. *The Santurce Crabbers: Sixty Seasons of Puerto Rican Winter League Baseball.* Jefferson, NC: McFarland, 1999.

Ward, Geoffrey C., and Ken Burns. *Baseball: An Illustrated History.* New York: Alfred A. Knopf, 1994.

Ward, Geoffrey C., and Ken Burns with Jim O'Connor. *Shadow Ball: The History of the Negro Leagues.* New York: Alfred A. Knopf, 1994.

Warneke, Kevin, and Ogden, David. *The Call to the Hall.* Jefferson, NC: McFarland, 2018.

Westcott, Rich. *The Mogul: Eddie Gottlieb, Philadelphia Sports Legend and Pro Basketball Pioneer.* Philadelphia: Temple University Press, 2008.

Wheelock, Sean D. *Buck O'Neil: A Baseball Legend.* Mattituck, NY: Amereon, 1994.

White, Gaylon H. *Singles and Smiles: How Artie Wilson Broke Baseball's Color Barrier.* Lanham, MD: Rowman & Littlefield, 2018.

White, Sol. *Sol White's History of Colored Baseball with Other Documents on the Early Black Game, 1886–1936,* with introduction by Jerry Malloy.

Reprint, Lincoln: University of Nebraska Press, 1995.

Withers, Ernest C. *Negro League Baseball: Photographs by Ernest C. Withers.* New York: Harry N. Abrams, 2004.

Young, A.S. "Doc." *Great Negro Baseball Stars and How They Made the Major Leagues.* New York: A.S. Barnes, 1953.

Zang, David W. *Fleet Walker's Divided Heart: The Life of Baseball's First Black Major Leaguer.* Lincoln: University of Nebraska Press, 1995.

Index

Numbers in *bold italics* indicate pages with illustrations